Learn SpriteBuilder for iOS Game Development

Steffen Itterheim

Apress®

Learn SpriteBuilder for iOS Game Development

Copyright © 2014 by Steffen Itterheim

ISBN-13 (pbk): 978-1-4842-0263-0

ISBN-13 (electronic): 978-1-4842-0262-3

Managing Director: Welmoed Spahr
Lead Editor: Michelle Lowman
Development Editor: Douglas Pundick
Technical Reviewers: Leland Long and Martin Walsh
Editorial Board: Steve Anglin, Mark Beckner, Gary Cornell, Louise Corrigan, Jim DeWolf, Jonathan Gennick, Robert Hutchinson, Michelle Lowman, James Markham, Matthew Moodie, Jeff Olson, Jeffrey Pepper, Douglas Pundick, Ben Renow-Clarke, Gwenan Spearing, Matt Wade, Steve Weiss
Coordinating Editor: Kevin Walter
Copy Editor: Roger LeBlanc
Compositor: SPi Global
Indexer: SPi Global
Artist: SPi Global
Cover Designer: Anna Ishchenko

Distributed to the book trade worldwide by Springer Science+Business Media New York, 233 Spring Street, 6th Floor, New York, NY 10013. Phone 1-800-SPRINGER, fax (201) 348-4505, e-mail orders-ny@springer-sbm.com, or visit www.springeronline.com. Apress Media, LLC is a California LLC and the sole member (owner) is Springer Science + Business Media Finance Inc (SSBM Finance Inc). SSBM Finance Inc is a Delaware corporation.

For information on translations, please e-mail rights@apress.com, or visit www.apress.com.

Apress and friends of ED books may be purchased in bulk for academic, corporate, or promotional use. eBook versions and licenses are also available for most titles. For more information, reference our Special Bulk Sales–eBook Licensing web page at www.apress.com/bulk-sales.

Any source code or other supplementary material referenced by the author in this text is available to readers at www.apress.com. For detailed information about how to locate your book's source code, go to www.apress.com/source-code/.

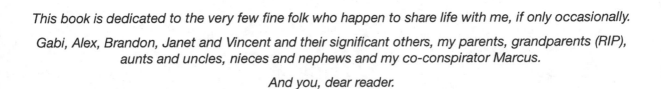

This book is dedicated to the very few fine folk who happen to share life with me, if only occasionally.

Gabi, Alex, Brandon, Janet and Vincent and their significant others, my parents, grandparents (RIP), aunts and uncles, nieces and nephews and my co-conspirator Marcus.

And you, dear reader.

Contents at a Glance

Contents

Table of Contents

About the Author

Steffen Itterheim has been working in the game industry since 1999. After a 7-year tenure as a software engineer with the Electronic Arts Phenomic studio, he became a self-employed Cocos2D developer, book author and blogger. Since 2014 he has been working for Apportable on SpriteBuilder while dabbling with Unity in his free time for a change of perspective. Quite literally.

Steffen is an active StackOverflow.com participant when he's not playing games—most recently, Grimrock 2 and Sniper Elite III. He also has a thing for model railroads.

About the Technical Reviewers

Leland Long's programming career began on a VIC-20 computer. He moved up to the Apple IIe and then on to the Mac 512, where he began using Lightspeed Pascal to write fancier and more complex games.

As a hobbyist, Leland has written a few programs over the years in BASIC and Pascal, but he never pursued learning the more common languages (like C) or learning object-oriented concepts. The release of the iPhone SDK changed that! Based on that event, Leland dove headfirst into learning all that he could about Objective-C and iOS programming. He is currently an IT Director for a flooring-installation company in South Carolina, where he lives with his youngest daughter. His other two daughters and six grandchildren live close enough to keep life entertaining.

Martin Walsh is an indie game developer and co-founder of the startup game studio Pedro. He is also a regular contributor to the popular open source gaming framework Cocos2D and the SpriteBuilder development suite. When not coding he is usually dabbling in VR with the Oculus Rift, soldering old, retro arcade PCBs or reading about Synthetic biology. Martin is also a serial Kickstarter backer.

You can find him most days in the SpriteBuilder forum helping fellow devs and sharing resources at `twitter.com/martin64k`.

Acknowledgments

This book would not have been possible without the Cocos2D community. Kudos to you; keep making crazy stuff!

The book wouldn't be possible either, and certainly not at this level of quality, without the hardworking people at Apportable, including those who, like me, are scattered around the world. Specifically, I'd like to thank (in no particular order) Viktor Lidholt, Collin Jackson, Christina Kelly, Nicky Weber, Scott Lembcke, Martin Walsh, Benjamin Encz, Lars Birkemose, and Thayer Andrews for their cooperation and support and for enduring me getting hopelessly lost in translation.

Of course, I shall not forget those who worked directly with me on this book. Many thanks go to Kevin Walter and Mark Powers for keeping me both up to date and busy, Peter Alau and Michelle Lowman for signing me on, and Leland Long and Martin Walsh for providing technical feedback.

Then there's Marcus, who I collaborate with in the same office: thanks for providing me with much needed changes in perspective, a surprisingly well-engineered, armchair-fitting gambling table for keyboard and mouse and steering-wheel controlled games, a virtual reality helmet (Self-made? We wish!), and the occasional coop game and movie.

I wish to thank everyone else who I might have forgotten to mention here. Rest assured, it was merely my lack of long-term memory that you aren't mentioned here by name. By now I probably regret not having expressed my thanks to you specifically.

Introduction

After I updated my previous book, *Learn cocos2d 2* to its 3rd edition (published late 2012), I had absolutely no intention of writing another technical book. Certainly not one about Cocos2D.

For one, writing a book is a lot of work and that makes it even more painful to see it go out of date even before it is published. This fate is shared by many technical books.

On the other hand, Cocos2D in its 2.x version was fairly stable. It also didn't seem to have gone anywhere. It was merely being maintained at the time, with new features being developed not in the best interest of the community, but instead in the best interest of the company that had, at the time, internalized the development of the open source project Cocos2D.

In fall 2013, Apple released iOS 7. With it came Sprite Kit, a 2D rendering engine very similar to Cocos2D at the time. Interest in Cocos2D waned rapidly.

It was at that time that Apportable took to Cocos2D. It hired developers from the community to work on Cocos2D to improve it and, ultimately, to make it better than Sprite Kit in every regard. And so work on the 3.x branch began.

At the same time, SpriteBuilder was to become not just one of many but *the* visual editor for Cocos2D. It was well integrated, without quirky setup steps, and there was no having to wait for it to catch up to support newer Cocos2D versions.

Over the course of 2014, SpriteBuilder and Cocos2D became one. And exciting new features were added: a fully integrated Objective-C version of the Chipmunk physics engine, a new renderer API that transparently supports both OpenGL and Metal, and built-in shader effects without having to write any shader code.

Cocos2D is now more alive and vibrant like never before.

When Apportable came to me with the idea for a book on SpriteBuilder and Cocos2D, it didn't take long for me to accept the challenge. Too much had changed that I didn't want to leave undocumented, and I was excited that SpriteBuilder and Cocos2D might become what I always hoped they would become.

Knowing what goes out of date most quickly, I was confident that I could avoid most of the pitfalls of technology becoming outdated in order to keep the book valid and applicable for a longer time. The fact that the book revolves mostly around SpriteBuilder will certainly help in that regard, as did writing the book against the very latest development branches. As I write these lines, it's early November 2014 and SpriteBuilder v1.3, which this book covers, has just been submitted to the Mac App Store for review.

My next project will have me updating the SpriteBuilder and Cocos2D online documentation. It is intended to be a reference manual that goes well with this book. I will do my best to point out anything that may have changed significantly since the book was published.

You will find this documentation online at `http://www.cocos2d-swift.org/docs`. The first version will cover SpriteBuilder v1.3 and Cocos2D v3.3. I recommend that you keep this link open in a browser tab while reading through this book.

Personally, I'm glad that I can recover from writing now by...writing more documentation. Online documentation is a different format with different requirements and possibilities, and I look forward to updating and improving that side of things, too.

I also very much look forward to getting your feedback on the SpriteBuilder (`http://forum.spritebuilder.com`) and Cocos2D (`http://forum.cocos2d-swift.org`) forums so that I can integrate that feedback in the online documentation.

And who knows, perhaps after another period of never wanting to write another book again I'll get back to making revisions to this book. I'm starting to think that technical writing is, in fact, dangerously addictive.

In any case, I hope you will enjoy reading this book as much as I enjoyed getting high on writing it.

Introducing SpriteBuilder and Cocos2D-iphone version 3

Introduction

Welcome to *Learn SpriteBuilder for iOS Game Development*. This chapter serves as an introduction. It explains what you will get out of this book, the program versions used by the book, and where to get the resource files, just to name a few items.

What's in This Book?

In this book, you will learn SpriteBuilder by example. The book will guide you through the creation of a physics-driven, parallax-scrolling game with the help of SpriteBuilder and Cocos2D (Cocos2d-Swift to be precise). The main influence in the design of the example game have been top-selling apps Badland and Leo's Fortune. The level-based structure will enable you to add more content to the game, even without writing additional code.

As your guide, I will walk you through the individual steps necessary to create the game project. Along the way, I'll explain the SpriteBuilder features, caveats, workarounds, and helpful tips and tricks as you are most likely to come across or need them.

The book's projects and resources are available for download on http://www.apress.com and http://www.spritebuilder.com. It is recommended to use the provided resources, but of course you are free to use your own images, audio, and font files. The example projects allow you to start or continue with any chapter.

> **Caution** The book projects are in folders numbered from 00 to 16. The project numbers do not correlate with chapter numbers. You will find the corresponding projects mentioned in each chapter, usually near the end of a chapter.

Whenever there's an easy way and a more efficient way, I'll be sure to teach you the efficient way. In most cases, it doesn't even amount to notably more work in any stage of the process. If I had to pick one such efficiency-boosting feature, it would be prefabs accessible through the *Tileless Editor View* and the Sub File node. It is very important to create as many reusable CCB files for individual parts of your game as is feasible. It's the object-oriented approach to designing scenes.

This book is not a complete reference to SpriteBuilder, although it covers almost all that is nontrivial. You are welcome and encouraged to explore the SpriteBuilder menus, dialogs, preferences, and even its codebase on your own to learn more. However, this is not a requirement to be able to successfully and efficiently use SpriteBuilder.

If at any point you need to look something up that's not explained in this book, you can refer to SpriteBuilder's online guide maintained by the folks at MakeGamesWith.Us at `https://www.makegameswith.us/docs` or ask a question in the SpriteBuilder forum at `http://www.spritebuilder.com`.

Who Is This Book for?

You've already picked up this book and are reading this paragraph to see if it would be a good fit for you. That tells me you have an interest in developing games or graphical apps for iOS, you tend to prefer working visually rather than program everything, or at least you find the concept intriguing. And perhaps you're already familiar with Cocos2D and want to learn how SpriteBuilder because a visual design tool could change your workflow. If so, this is the right book for you.

You certainly want to know whether this book fits your experience level, your programming and technology knowledge, and perhaps even your exact requirements for the app you have in mind. This will be more difficult to assess because I don't know you, nor your goals. I do know that if you have an interest in SpriteBuilder, Cocos2D, and game development in general you'll definitely get something out of this book.

I'll try by making some assumptions.

These are the three archetype developers I have in mind for whom this book would be a good fit. Beginning developers and those without prior SpriteBuilder experience will get the most of the step-by-step development of a game with SpriteBuilder while learning the SpriteBuilder user interface and basics of Cocos2D.

Experienced developers will pleasantly acknowledge the benefits of using a graphical design tool like SpriteBuilder. The workflow tips that I'll showcase in this book will improve your efficiency. Plus you'll get some candy on top—tricks and topics you'll hardly find covered online, such as creating soft-body physics, cool visual effects, and porting your SpriteBuilder game to Android.

The Absolute Beginner

First, assuming you've never ever programmed a mobile app before, if you have no experience with Xcode and Cocoa touch whatsoever, and you don't know any Objective-C either, I would strongly recommend picking up an introductory book that goes along with this book. Any recent book or tutorial that teaches iOS app development with Objective-C and Xcode from the ground up will be helpful. This book assumes you have a working knowledge of Objective-C and Xcode, so a guide or reference on Objective-C and Xcode would come in handy. Fortunately, there are plenty of tutorials and books to choose from. But start by consulting the Apple Developer Library first.

As a beginner, you can do a lot within SpriteBuilder and reduce the amount of code quite significantly. You may even be able to create simple games with very little programming. However, I'm cautious about spelling this out because it may create false expectations. You may need to tone down your initial expectations for your first SpriteBuilder game, especially considering that at this point it may be almost impossible for you to judge what is and is not possible with SpriteBuilder in the first place.

But if you go ahead with a motivation to learn, and perhaps do not try to implement your grandest design as your first game, I'm sure you'll get along just fine. Expect to invest a lot of time into any and all technology, since this isn't just a single program you set out to learn—it's a whole, seemingly overwhelming conglomerate of terms and technologies when you venture into game app development. As long as you stay patient and eager to learn, it won't be unpleasant. Plus there's a friendly and helpful community that embraces newcomers like you.

The Experienced App Developer

My second assumption is that you may be a seasoned iOS app developer but haven't tried making games yet, perhaps because you would not want to miss out on graphical design tools like Interface Builder. For you, it should be fairly simple to pick up how the Cocos2D framework works, after all there's plenty of documentation available. You may want to learn specifically how games are designed and how this is different from using Interface Builder. You'll be able to pick up a lot of these concepts by reading the book.

You may need to change some habits and expectations, but besides that I do not see any reason why you wouldn't benefit from reading this book if your goal is to make games with SpriteBuilder. I suppose the same could be said if you have prior mobile game development experience, just not with Cocos2D or SpriteBuilder.

The Experienced Cocos2D Game Developer

Finally, I can imagine you may be an experienced Cocos2D developer. Perhaps you haven't been using the latest Cocos2D version, or perhaps you just want to learn whether you should really give up some coding and do some designs in SpriteBuilder instead, and how that might work out.

You'll find the programming aspects a walk in the park, and you'll enjoy the workflow benefits of using SpriteBuilder that I'll present to you throughout the book. You may even be astonished about how much fun it is *not* to write program code, and you'll appreciate being able to free your mind from tedious, repetitive programming tasks while being able to do more of the cool programming tricks you haven't had time to explore yet.

Requirements

In order to learn from this book, you obviously need to download SpriteBuilder for free from the Mac App Store. To run SpriteBuilder, you need a Mac running OS X 10.8 Mountain Lion or newer.

Cocos2D comes bundled with SpriteBuilder—you do not have to download it separately. There's still a benefit in doing so, however. If you get the installer version from `http://www.cocos2d-swift.org/download` and install it, you will have the Cocos2D API reference documentation available in Xcode. But you can also access it online: `http://www.cocos2d-swift.org/docs/api`.

> **Note**   SpriteBuilder can automatically update the Cocos2D version used by your SpriteBuilder projects. If there's a new version available, you will be asked to update, and if you allow it, SpriteBuilder will create a backup copy of Cocos2D before installing the new version to that project specifically. However, this will not update your downloaded copy of Cocos2D nor the Cocos2D Xcode documentation files. If you want to keep the Cocos2D Xcode documentation up to date, you will have to manually download and install each new Cocos2D version.

Speaking of Xcode: in order to develop apps for iOS, you need to install Xcode, which is also available for free from the Mac App Store or Apple's Developer Center: `https://developer.apple.com/devcenter/ios`.

The iOS SDK, the iOS Simulator, and the Cocoa touch frameworks come bundled with Xcode. You do not need to download anything else to develop iOS or OS X apps. But you may want to open Xcode ➤ Preferences and navigate to the Downloads pane to download the offline documentation for faster access or offline access to the iOS SDK documentation. The documentation is also available online: `https://developer.apple.com/library/ios/navigation`.

It is not necessary to register as an iOS Developer with Apple to learn from this book. Still I recommend it, even though it costs a fee of currently $99 per year. Being a registered Apple developer has many benefits, most importantly the ability to deploy and test your app on an iOS device. If you plan on releasing your app to the App Store, you should register now rather than later.

The iOS Simulator can be used to verify that your code functions, but it cannot measure how well your app performs—questions regarding slow Simulator performance are aplenty on the web. In short, iOS Simulator rendering performance is abysmal even on the fastest Macs. Yet the Simulator will gladly use your Mac's multiple gigabytes of memory and plenty of CPU time—much more than iOS devices provide. Plus your app can feel very different when controlled by imprecise fingers covering parts of the screen, and you can't simulate the accelerometer or multitouch gestures with the iOS Simulator.

In short, you cannot reliably test your game for being fun, easy to handle, precise to control, and having good performance without testing on an actual device. So while it's not strictly necessary, it's highly recommended to sign up for the developer membership.

About SpriteBuilder

SpriteBuilder is a free, open-source visual design tool for OS X, created specifically to work in combination with Cocos2d-Swift. Originally, it was conceived as CocosBuilder by Viktor Lidholt and released in 2011. Viktor works for Apportable as the lead developer on SpriteBuilder, and he is joined with an entire team working on both SpriteBuilder and Cocos2D.

Many SpriteBuilder and Cocos2D developers actually work for Apportable, a company that specializes in cross-compiling Objective-C code and, specifically, SpriteBuilder apps for the Android platform. In the ideal case, you just take your iOS app and build it for Android and it'll work, just like that. You'll find an introduction to the Android porting process in Chapter 13.

SpriteBuilder integrates nicely with Cocos2D. Releases for both projects are now on the same schedule to ensure both tools work together in harmony. Gone are the days of incompatible file versions and unwitting changes to Cocos2D that break editor compatibility.

SpriteBuilder can also be used to create OS X apps. As I'm writing this, the developers are working on adding OS X support. So I'm confident that by the time you are reading this, you will be able to start OS X projects with SpriteBuilder. Most of what you'll learn in this book can be applied to OS X apps as well, some exceptions notwithstanding.

> **Tip**   In case SpriteBuilder doesn't yet support creating OS X apps by the time you read this, you can find a tutorial on how to enable OS X support here: `http://jademind.com/blog/posts/porting-cocos2d-game-to-osx-using-spritebuilder/`.

Why Use SpriteBuilder?

SpriteBuilder's major benefit is seeing what you're doing when you're doing it (WYSIWYG). If you've been doing any game or graphical programming without a design tool, you'll know the typical development cycle: Change a few lines of code or perhaps just a value, build the code, deploy the app onto the Device or Simulator, launch your app, navigate to where you made the change in your app, look at the change, and behold—it's not quite right. Start over. Rinse, and repeat. Tedious, tiresome, time-consuming, and error-prone.

With SpriteBuilder, you can do a lot of things visually and see exactly how they'll look in your app. You can even switch between simulated device resolutions to test your change for all supported resolutions with a mouse click. Even more astonishing is the way you create timeline animations, and the fact that you can preview them live in SpriteBuilder. You see exactly how the layer moves into view and scales up to fill the screen over time. Or how your menu buttons roll in one by one in quick succession before coming to rest at their designated positions.

Moreover, SpriteBuilder manages the app's resource file versions, scaling them automatically for different device resolutions as needed. This frees you from performing many tedious, error-prone chores when developing for multiple screen resolutions and aspect ratios. It also means you don't have to use one or several external tools, each performing only a small aspect of the development cycle.

So, in summary, you could say that learning SpriteBuilder is a worthy endeavor not only because it can significantly reduce development time, but also because it's fun to play with and experiment with. At the end of the day, you don't just get results faster, you also get better results. What's more, you can still write code for whatever you feel would still be faster to code rather than design visually. Once a node designed in SpriteBuilder has been loaded, you are free to write code that modifies, replaces, or discards the node as you see fit.

About Cocos2D

Cocos2D in this book refers specifically to Cocos2d-Swift. It's actually just Cocos2d-iPhone rebranded under the Cocos2d-Swift name because it now officially supports making games using Apple's Swift programming language.

Of course, you can still use Cocos2d-Swift to write apps with 100% Objective-C code, and the engine behind Cocos2d-Swift is still essentially Cocos2d-iPhone, written entirely in Objective-C and plain C. But now you can also write your program code in Swift, either by optionally adding Swift code mixed with Objective-C or by creating apps entirely with Swift code.

> **Note**   This book will make no use and little mention of Swift. As I started writing this book, Swift wasn't even available to developers.

Cocos2d-Swift is a popular, free, and open-source 2D rendering engine with a physics framework. It was originally created as Cocos2d-iPhone by Ricardo Quesada in 2008 and became probably the most popular 2D game engine for iOS. It was so popular that by 2013 Apple released its own 2D rendering framework with iOS 7, named *Sprite Kit*. Much of Sprite Kit's design and terminology is borrowed from Cocos2d-iPhone at that time.

Sprite Kit's release was an unexpected and long overdue catalyst for creating the third major iteration of the Cocos2d-iPhone engine, which also got a new name along the way: Cocos2d-Swift. Now an entire team of developers have essentially touched and improved every aspect of the engine to make it better than Sprite Kit in every aspect.

Cocos2D includes the tightly integrated Chipmunk(2D) physics engine and plenty of cool new features to boot. For example, the renderer is now equal to, if not faster than, Sprite Kit's and optionally uses Apple's new Metal rendering framework. There is a *CCEffectNode* that enables developers to create stunning visual shader effects without having to write actual shader code. Customizing and debugging Cocos2D apps is generally easier than doing the same with Sprite Kit because you can step into, analyze and, if need be, modify the underlying engine source code.

About Apportable

You may be wondering: who is Apportable and what exactly are they doing?

Their mission statement is simple: to enable developers to write apps in Objective-C and port them to Android through cross-compilation with native performance. You can learn more about Apportable on its website: http://www.apportable.com.

In the ideal case, no code changes are necessary to port an existing iOS app written in Objective-C to Android with Apportable. In reality, you may need to do a little more if you haven't been testing your project on Android from the start. Specifically, because there's so many different Android devices with wildly varying features and specifications.

If you look at Apportable's impressive list of customers, you'll notice they are all game developers. Apportable paid respect to that, having hired many developers who now work on Cocos2D and SpriteBuilder. All of these technologies are free and open source, and they will remain free and open source. Only if you want to use Apportable to port to Android and you need more than the basic features, you may need to dole out some cash. The terms of service and prices have not been determined at the time of this writing.

The value in having an option like Apportable is to be able to focus on the platform, tools, and technologies you are familiar with, while still being able to make the app work on Android devices when the time comes. And you can do so without having to rewrite large parts of your codebase and without having to compromise by either using more archaic or less performant programming languages.

About Program Versions

Matching and advances in technology are issues we need to discuss before you set out to read the rest of this book.

This book was written for and tested with Xcode 6, iOS 8 as well as SpriteBuilder v1.3 and Cocos2d-Swift v3.3. As I'm writing these lines, it's October 9, 2014. But by the time you read this book, some or several of these technologies may have advanced to the next minor or major release version.

I did my best to avoid using any (potentially) version-specific code or features. However, my abilities to predict future changes are somewhat limited, judging by my failure to win the lottery thus far.

In my experience from writing three "Learn Cocos2D" editions, these differences are usually marginal. So don't put the book away just because there might be, say, Xcode 6.2 or SpriteBuilder v1.5 available now.

I wish to apologize in advance for any inconveniences caused by updated versions that slightly alter the way things work, but there's nothing I can do to prevent that. I can, however, provide you with ways to help you work around such issues.

As far as SpriteBuilder and Cocos2D are concerned, you can visit `http://www.spritebuilder.com`, `http://www.cocos2d-swift.org`, or `http://www.learn-cocos2d.com` to learn of the major changes affecting the book with instructions on how to work around the issues or how exactly to change the code to make it fit the new versions.

Regarding Xcode and iOS, if an Xcode 7 or iOS 9 is available by the time you're reading this book, you can always grab Xcode 6 (and thus the iOS 8 SDK) to compile the book's code if you want to completely avoid any potential issues.

Specifically for Xcode updates, it's not so much about instructions that will no longer apply, but additional compiler warnings and errors that Apple continues to introduce with every new Xcode version. These improvements can seemingly turn once perfectly acceptable code into a series of "oh no you can't do that anymore, are you insane?!?" statements. For experienced developers, it's highly welcome that the compiler catches ever more potential issues; however, for developers trying to learn by example with code not tested with the latest Xcode, it can be a sobering, if not frustrating, experience.

Therefore, if you don't feel up to the task of working around the occasional nitpicking by updated compiler versions, I recommend using Xcode 6. You can find older Xcode versions at `https://developer.apple.com/downloads/index.action?name=Xcode%206`. Note that you need to be a registered Apple iOS or OS X developer in order to access this link.

About Xcode Versions

Some screenshots were taken with Xcode 5.1. In some cases, this was intentional; other times, it was simply because Xcode 6 wasn't available at the time. It wasn't always possible or feasible to update screenshots with the latest Xcode 6 version.

I verified that the functionality is identical. Any difference between Xcode 5.1 and Xcode 6.0 as far as the screenshots are concerned is purely visual.

About the Example Projects

This book comes with a downloadable archive that you can download from the book's website: `http://www.apress.com/9781484202630`. In the archive, you will find resource files and complete SpriteBuilder projects. Each contains a snapshot of the Bouncy Beast project at various stages.

Tip   I recommend that you keep the archive after unpacking it. If you make a breaking change to one of the projects, you can restore the original state from the archive.

When you open one of these example SpriteBuilder projects, SpriteBuilder will most likely offer to update Cocos2D to the latest version for you. I recommend that you not update Cocos2D, but rather continue using the Cocos2D version the project was tested with. A new Cocos2D version may require you to make changes to your code, or it may break existing code in other ways. I assume that when you open one of the example projects, you'd rather see it working rather than having to go in, debug, and fix any breaking changes.

Tip   You can always update a SpriteBuilder project's Cocos2D version at a later time by choosing File ➤ Update Cocos2D from SpriteBuilder's menu.

SpriteBuilder may also ask you to convert the project format to the new Packages format. This is typically safe to do, but there's no harm done by not doing it. Packages essentially only change the location of resource files within the SpriteBuilder project. Packages were introduced sometime near the end of the book, so most example projects will ask you to switch over to using Packages.

Once you have an example project opened in SpriteBuilder, you have to publish it. The published resource files have been stripped from the Xcode project to reduce the archive size.

When you open the SpriteBuilder project's Xcode project and build it, you may get warnings or even errors. The projects were all tested with Xcode 6.0. If you're using Xcode 6.1 or later, there's a chance that Apple made changes and improvements to the build settings and compiler. For instance, you may be asked to update the project's Build Settings or format. This is usually safe to do.

> **Note** The first time you run the Xcode project, it may appear to hang or take a very long time to complete. This may happen in particular when you haven't previously opened the SpriteBuilder project and published it. In that case, Xcode will launch the publish process for the SpriteBuilder project, but it won't give you any progress indication. Therefore, it's recommended that you open and publish the SpriteBuilder project first— that way, at least you get a progress indicator.

You may get some compiler warnings or errors pointing out potential problems in the code. If there are warnings originating from one of the library targets (Cocos2D, ObjectAL, or Chipmunk), you can ignore those. They are typically uncritical and may even persist for several releases. The Cocos2D developers clean up warnings from time to time. New errors in previously perfectly acceptable code can occur, too. Usually this happens with newer Xcode versions, where the compiler now treats certain cases of warnings as errors, or it simply finds new potential issues in general. As long as they're only warnings, ignore them. They are most likely artifacts caused by advancements in Xcode.

However, if you get compiler errors in the libraries, you may want to try updating Cocos2D to see if the warnings/errors go away. If there's an error in the project's code itself (the code in the Source group) and you can't fix it by yourself, please check the SpriteBuilder forum at `http://forum.spritebuilder.com` for errata and fixes.

Of the 17 SpriteBuilder projects, the majority were originally created with SpriteBuilder versions prior to v1.3. Therefore, the projects numbered 00 to 13 do not contain the necessary code to compile them for the Android platform. The projects numbered 14 through 16 do have Android support. Accordingly, the projects 00 to 13 will have different items in the schemes and platform lists than projects 14 through 16.

> **Tip** You can convert a SpriteBuilder project that doesn't have Android support to one that does by following the instructions here: `http://android.spritebuilder.com/#dealing-with-spritebuilder-projects-from-spritebuilder-1-2-and-earlier`.

Example Projects Mapped to Chapters

As I said earlier, the example project numbers do not match the chapter numbers. Table 1-1 contains a list of chapter numbers and names and what chapter particular projects belong to.

Table 1-1. Mapping Chapters to Example Projects

Chapter	Project Folder	Project Notes
02 - Laying the Groundwork	00 - Starting Point	Same as creating a new SpriteBuilder project.
02 - Laying the Groundwork	01 - Change Scenes with Buttons	Represents the stage of the project midway through Chapter 2.
02 - Laying the Groundwork	02 - Level with Player Prefab	Represents the stage of the project at the end of Chapter 2.
03 - Controlling and Scrolling	03 - Parallax Scrolling	Represents the stage of the project at the end of Chapter 3.
04 - Physics and Collisions	04 - Physics Movement and Level Borders	Represents the stage of the project at the end of Chapter 4.
05 - Timelines and Triggers	05 - Timeline Animations	Represents the stage of the project midway through Chapter 5.
05 - Timelines and Triggers	06 - Triggered Animations	Represents the stage of the project at the end of Chapter 5.
06 - Menus and Popovers	07 - Popover Menus	Represents the stage of the project at the end of Chapter 6.
07 - Main Scene and GameState	08 - Main Menu and Settings	Represents the stage of the project at the end of Chapter 7.
08 - Selecting and Unlocking Levels	09 - Level Selection Scroll View	Represents the stage of the project at the end of Chapter 8.
09 - Physics Joints	10 - Chains Ropes and Springs	Represents the stage of the project at the end of Chapter 9.
10 - Soft-Body Physics	11 - Soft-Body Player	Represents the stage of the project at the end of Chapter 10.
11 - Audio and Labels	12 - Audio Labels and Localization	Represents the stage of the project at the end of Chapter 11.
12 - Visual Effects and Animations	13 - Animations and Effects	Represents the stage of the project at the end of Chapter 12.
13 - Porting to Android	14 - HelloSpriteBuilder Android	Test project created early in Chapter 13.
13 - Porting to Android	15 - Prior to making Android-specific fixes	Starting point for an Android port midway through Chapter 13.
13 - Porting to Android	16 - Bouncy Beast for Android	Represents the stage of the project at the end of Chapter 13.

About Deployment Targets

Eventually, you'll have to make a decision on which devices your app should run on, and which iOS versions you are going to support.

In theory, Cocos2D apps can run on any device with support for OpenGL ES 2.0 running at least iOS 5. That makes the iPhone 3GS and the first iPad the oldest iOS devices you can run your app on. In theory.

However, there's a huge difference in terms of performance between the iPhone 3GS and the latest iPhone, and the first iPad compared to the latest iPad. Mobile technology is advancing fast, definitely faster than desktop computer technology.

Furthermore, market penetration of each newer iOS device is significantly higher than its predecessors. Therefore, supporting older devices like the iPhone 3GS, perhaps even the non-widescreen phones iPhone 4 and 4S, may not always be the financially sound decision that it seems to be. Historically, and in stark contrast to the Android market, you're more likely to generate a larger number of sales by specifically supporting the latest iOS version, the latest models, and their exclusive features rather than trying to reach as far back as you can.

My personal recommendation is to follow Apple as it introduces new models and discontinues old models. If you are unsure which of them to support, support those that are capable of running the latest iOS version when starting a new project. For a list of iOS devices and their newest supported operating system, refer to this list on Wikipedia: http://en.wikipedia.org/wiki/List_of_iOS_ devices.

For iOS 8, the oldest targetable devices are iPhone 4S and iPad 2. Discontinued iOS models very quickly fall by the wayside in terms of app sales. Almost the same goes for iOS versions. You can certainly require the second-to-latest major iOS version as your minimum deployment target when starting a new app project. For example, at this point in time, iOS 8 is the latest iOS version. By supporting devices running iOS 7.0 and up, your app has a potential addressable market that amounts to 94% of App Store usage as of October 5, 2014.

Apple periodically updates a chart that tells you what iOS versions users are using when they visit the App Store: https://developer.apple.com/support/appstore/. This chart reflects your addressable market, not the potential millions of devices still running iOS 6 and earlier. Most of those older devices that have been sold are either broken, stolen, or forgotten—or for the most part, their users hardly get any new apps. Maybe those users are perfectly happy with the device as is, or maybe they know that new apps are unlikely to run on their device.

But it's even more important to ensure your published app keeps running on the lowest supported device and iOS version as long as possible to keep your existing customers happy. That alone speaks against trying to support iOS versions as far back as theoretically possible, and this is particularly true for games that are more demanding on device resources than most other types of apps.

Consider that the performance span between an iPhone 6 and an iPhone 3GS is tremendous. In the GeekBench benchmark, the iPhone 6 (Plus) is more than 10 times faster than the iPhone 3GS. Compared to the iPhone 4S, the iPhone 6 (Plus) is still over 7 times faster in the same benchmark. You'll find an up-to-date performance comparison of all iOS devices here: http://browser. primatelabs.com/ios-benchmarks.

Based on this benchmark, it's not hard to predict that developers of graphically intense games will stop offering their games or reduce quality on iPhone 4S and earlier, iPad (third generation) and earlier, and the original iPad mini (non-Retina). Too far ahead are the iPhone 5 generation and newer devices in terms of performance.

Table of Contents

Following is a list of chapters in this book with short summaries.

Chapter 1—Introduction

You are currently reading this chapter.

Chapter 2—Laying the Groundwork

An introduction to SpriteBuilder and its user interface. The most commonly needed tasks are explained here. Also, the chapter contains a quick introduction to programming with Cocos2D. You end up with a project that allows you to transition between scenes by the press of a button.

Chapter 3—Controlling and Scrolling

You'll add touch input and parallax scrolling of multiple background layers in this chapter. You'll learn to use Sprite Sheets and prefabs. A player prefab is introduced, and its simplistic movement is performed by move actions.

Chapter 4—Physics and Collisions

You learn how to add physics to a game, specifically immovable, impenetrable walls as well as dynamic bodies. Player movement is replaced by actual physics. Collision callback methods are used to trigger the level exit. How to enable physics debug drawing is also explained.

Chapter 5—Timelines and Triggers

Timelines are explained in depth, and then used to animate rotating physics objects. You'll learn how to create trigger areas that run code when the player enters them. The resulting project now makes simple physics interactions possible.

Chapter 6—Menus and Popovers

A powerful, yet easy way to create popover menus, such as the pause and game over menus, is explained. The same concept can be used to create full-screen menus without interrupting the running scene. The menus are animated with the Timeline, using Timeline delegate methods to receive notifications when a Timeline has ended.

Chapter 7—MainScene and GameState

The main menu is designed with an animated background and a settings menu with audio volume sliders. A *GameState* class is introduced, which stores global, user-specific game data via *NSUserDefaults*.

Chapter 8—Selecting and Unlocking Levels

A level selection screen is added with the help of the Scroll View node. How *CCScrollView* works, how it can be programmed, and how you can respond to its delegate methods is carefully explained. The level selection pages are divided into multiple worlds, with each level unlocked by completing the previous level.

Chapter 9—Physics Joints

This entire chapter is dedicated to creating physics objects out of joints, specifically chains, ropes, and springs. How joints work and what you can and probably shouldn't do with them is explained in detail.

Chapter 10—Soft-Body Physics

The player prefab is replaced by a soft-body player. A soft-body object is a deformable physics object held together by joints, with its collision shape divided into multiple smaller bodies. This chapter also introduces custom rendering with Cocos2D because the player's texture needs to be drawn to match its deformed shape at any time.

Chapter 11—Audio and Labels

You'll learn how to play short sound effects with the Timeline and how to play them programmatically with ObjectAL, and you'll learn how to play background music. The other half of the chapter deals with Label TTF properties like shadows and outline, but it also explains how to create, import, and use bitmap fonts in SpriteBuilder.

Chapter 12—Visual Effects and Animations

You'll be creating a sprite frame animation for the first time, and you'll make it work with the player's custom rendering class. An introduction to Particle Effect nodes is mandatory in a chapter on visual effects. This culminates in the use of the Effect nodes, which are essentially shader programs that you can add and design in SpriteBuilder. At the end of this chapter, you'll hardly recognize the main menu scene.

Chapter 13—Porting to Android

At first, you'll see what is necessary to develop for Android. Then you'll create a new project with which you'll test deployment to an Android device. Finally, you'll convert the Bouncy Beast project and fix any compilation, launch, and layout issues that occur. You'll get advice on how to best approach cross-platform development with SpriteBuilder.

Chapter 14—Debugging and Best Practices

This chapter is an introduction to debugging with Xcode and Cocos2D. You'll learn about techniques to catch or prevent programming bugs. Basically, it's a self-help guide that'll quickly prove invaluable. There's also a section on troubleshooting some of the most common SpriteBuilder and Cocos2D issues.

Before You Get Started

If you have any questions regarding SpriteBuilder, Cocos2D, or related technologies and processes, please visit the SpriteBuilder forum (http://www.spritebuilder.com) and the Cocos2D forum (http://www.cocos2d-swift.org).

I'm also frequently answering programming questions on StackOverflow (http://www.stackoverflow.com) when they are tagged with Cocos2D.

With that said, have fun, enjoy the ride, and make some great games!

Chapter 2

Laying the Groundwork

In this chapter, you will learn the basics of working with SpriteBuilder, including its user interface and the first programming steps with Cocos2d-Swift using Objective-C and Xcode. You will learn how to create the most important elements in SpriteBuilder and how SpriteBuilder, Xcode, and Cocos2D are connected. At the end of this chapter, you will have a skeleton framework that you'll continue to expand on.

I assume you have downloaded and installed both SpriteBuilder and Xcode from the Mac App Store:

- SpriteBuilder: https://itunes.apple.com/app/spritebuilder/id784912885
- Xcode: https://itunes.apple.com/app/xcode/id497799835

Creating a SpriteBuilder Project

After launching SpriteBuilder, go straight to File ➤ New ➤ Cocos2D Project to start a new blank project. Save it anywhere where you'll be able to locate it again—for instance, in the Documents or Desktop folder—and preferably use a name you'll recognize again. The main example project in this book is named LearnSpriteBuilder.spritebuilder.

If you haven't used SpriteBuilder before, you should familiarize yourself with its user interface and the terminologies used throughout the book to describe specific areas and views in SpriteBuilder. The user interface is split into four main areas as shown in Figure 2-1.

Figure 2-1. SpriteBuilder user interface

1. **Resource Navigator** (on the left). This is a tab bar view where you'll find the following: from the leftmost tab to the rightmost tab: your project files in the *File View* (depicted) with a resource preview area and a list of files below the preview; a visual overview of resources in the *Tileless Editor View*; a list of available nodes in the *Node Library View*; and any warnings or errors (hopefully, none ever) in the *Warnings View*.

2. **Stage View** (at the top center). This is where the contents of a stage (which can be a scene, layer, node, particle emitter, or sprite) are displayed. You can select nodes in this view and use selection handles to move, resize, or rotate selected nodes.

3. **Timeline View** (bottom center). This is where nodes and joints in the stage are listed on the left side in hierarchical order, defining node draw order and parent-child relationships. The right side is the actual timeline, with its keyframe editor used to create animations (*animations* here being changes to a node's properties over time).

4. **Details Inspector** (on the right), also known as **Detail View**. This is also a tab bar view with four panes. From left to right they are *Item Properties*, where you'll find the selection's editable settings and properties; *Item Code Connections*, where you can assign custom classes, variables, and selectors; *Item Physics*, where you can enable physics and edit physics body and shape properties; and finally, the *Item Templates* tab, which is used to create named templates from selected nodes and their properties but is currently used only by particle effects.

The newly created project is actually a functional, runnable SpriteBuilder project. You can try this now by choosing File ➤ Publish or by clicking the corresponding Publish button on the toolbar.

The publishing process copies, converts, and caches the resources in the Xcode project associated with the SpriteBuilder project.

The SpriteBuilder Project's Xcode Project

An Xcode project is located within every *<projectname>*.spritebuilder folder with a corresponding name *<projectname>*.xcodeproj. See Figure 2-2 for an example. The topmost folder with the yellow icon named LearnSpriteBuilder.spritebuilder is the project's folder. Inside it is the project's LearnSpriteBuilder.xcodeproj file, and the source code and published resource files for the app are found inside the Source folder. The SpriteBuilder Resources folder contains the resource and CCB files that SpriteBuilder lists in its File View.

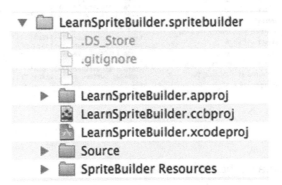

Figure 2-2. SpriteBuilder project structure as seen in Finder

Note   SpriteBuilder projects are folders with the extension *.spritebuilder*. SpriteBuilder will recognize projects only if the folder has the .spritebuilder suffix. If SpriteBuilder isn't running you can manually copy, move, or rename a SpriteBuilder project folder using Finder, provided that you keep the .spritebuilder suffix.

Double-click the project's .xcodeproj file, or open it via the File ➤ Open command in Xcode. Xcode will greet you with a user interface similar to the one shown in Figure 2-3.

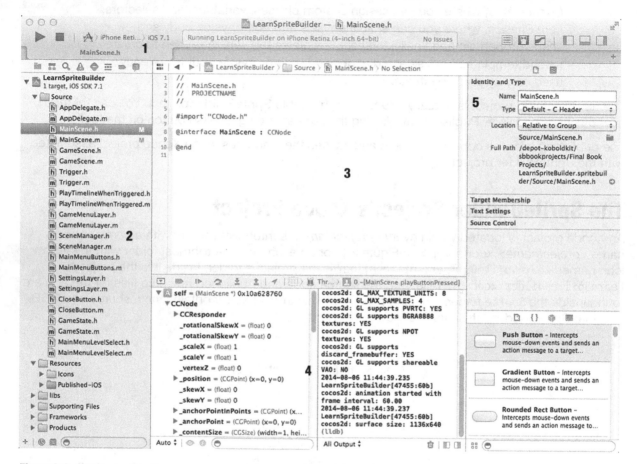

Figure 2-3. Xcode user interface

The Xcode user interface contains the following areas:

1. **Toolbar**, with scheme and device selection drop-down menu. Use the scheme drop-down menu to change which device or simulator the app should run on.

2. **Navigator area**, which contains multiple tabs. The default, leftmost tab (depicted) shows the files in the project. Other tabs allow you to search the project's files, see build warnings and errors, manage breakpoints, and perform other tasks.

3. **Editor area**, where you type in source code.

4. **Debug area**, which displays debugging information. The left side displays values of variables at runtime, while the right side is the Console, where log statements are printed.

5. **Utility area**, which contains information about selected items. In this case, it shows detailed information about the selected MainScene.m file.

You can build and run this minimal SpriteBuilder Xcode project by clicking the Play button, which is the leftmost icon on the toolbar. The project will build and launch either on a connected device or the iOS Simulator, depending on which run target is selected in the toolbar. You should see the exact same scene you saw in SpriteBuilder seconds before on your device or the iOS Simulator.

Tip If you haven't used Xcode before and need more instructions on how to use it, you should consult the Xcode Guide available via Help ➤ Xcode Overview or online at `https://developer.apple.com/library/ios/documentation/ToolsLanguages/Conceptual/Xcode_Overview`.

First Scene, First Code

The first goal is to create a second scene and then connecting buttons so you can switch back and forth between the two scenes. This second scene is going to be the game scene, while the existing MainScene will become the menu screen. This is a commonplace, rudimentary separation between game and menu scenes.

A scene contains all the content (nodes) that the game currently renders. Other scenes can replace the currently visible scene using transitions, just like Cocoa touch views can transition from one view to another with or without animations.

Note A common misconception is that scenes and nodes can be used interchangeably with views. This is not so. Cocos2D has its own UIView class named CCGLView that renders all the scenes and nodes using OpenGL instructions. Therefore, other UIView instances can be either entirely on top of or behind the Cocos2D view and the scene it currently displays.

Creating the GameScene

Go to File ➤ New ➤ File, or right-click the Project Navigator pane below the preview area and choose New File from the context menu to create a new SpriteBuilder document file, also known as a *CCB file*. Select the *Scene* type, and enter *GameScene.ccb* as the file name (as shown in Figure 2-4) and click the **Create** button.

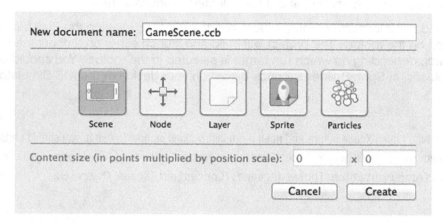

Figure 2-4. Creating the GameScene.ccb

To be precise, creating a new CCB file lets you choose one of five different types. Here's a quick rundown of their purpose and major differences:

- **Scene:** A presentable scene. Contrary to what you might expect, its root node is a CCNode, not a CCScene. It's main difference from the Node type is that it defaults to display a nice device frame around it in SpriteBuilder.

- **Node:** Essentially, the same as Scene, but it has no device frame, and it has a root node of class CCNode.

- **Layer:** The only CCB file type whose content size can be set. This makes it ideal for any fixed-size layer. Again, the root node is of class CCNode.

- **Sprite:** Because sprites are so commonplace in games, this CCB has a CCSprite as its root node. Other than that, though, it's the same as the Node type.

- **Particles:** Same as for Sprite type, except here the root node is using the CCParticleSystem class.

Note   Technically, all CCB file types can be used interchangeably. The main difference between Scene, Node, and Layer is one of terminology and how it's displayed in SpriteBuilder. The Layer type is the only one that allows for a user-definable content size. Layer need only be used over Node or Scene whenever the contents need a fixed, custom size—for instance, for game levels or fixed-size overlay menus.

The GameScene.ccb will be presented as an iPhone device frame with no contents (black screen). Time to fill it with some content.

Reviewing the Node Library

On the Resource Navigator pane (left side), click on the Node Library View tab. This brings up a list of items that can be dragged and dropped onto the stage. Most of these items are nodes, inheriting from Cocos2d's base class CCNode. The only other types of items are joints used by the physics engine. In Figure 2-5, you'll find the full list of nodes available at the time of this writing.

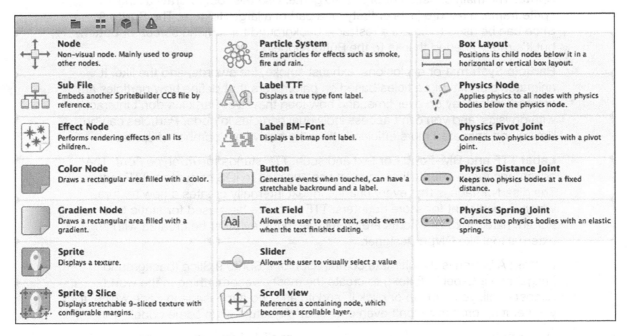

Figure 2-5. *List of available nodes in SpriteBuilder*

I'll quickly go over the various node types and their purpose

- **Node:** An invisible node that is used to group (or "layer") other nodes. Imagine them being folders that contain related items. This affects draw order, and it can be useful to access related items easier in code, or just to sort, move, or collapse nodes in the SpriteBuilder timeline.

- **Sub File:** A placeholder for embedding another CCB file. This is a very powerful node because it allows you to use other CCB files like templates and to create and edit a single CCB that is used (instantiated) multiple times. Dragging a CCB file onto a stage will automatically create a Sub File node.

- **Physics Node:** This represents the physics world. Any node with physics enabled has to be a child or grandchild of a Physics Node, or it won't have physics enabled after all. Generally, only one Physics Node should be used per scene. Multiple worlds are possible, but their children will not be able to interact with each other.

- **Color and Gradient Node:** Look at these colors, wow! Essentially, these are just sprites without images. They're great for quick-and-dirty backgrounds or for use as placeholders for as-of-yet missing graphics.

- **Sprite:** The main constituent of any 2D game. Use this tool to draw a single sprite frame, a texture in its entirety, or a part of a larger texture. The **Sprite 9 Slice** can be used to create a resizable background for a menu screen or button, but it's rarely needed thanks to the Button node.

- **Particle System:** For explosions, exhaust smoke, fire swords, and the like. It animates a bunch of particles based on parameters that define how particles are created, what they do over time, and how long they live. Particles don't interact with physics, and you can't access individual particles in code. Particles can be drawn and animated more efficiently than the equivalent number of sprites.

- **Label TTF and BM-Font:** For text and such. *TTF* stands for *Truetype Font*. The advantage these offer is that you can use any built-in iOS or custom TTF font. The disadvantage is that every change in text internally creates a new texture, which is inefficient for score counters. TTF fonts are best used for static text. For animated text, BM-Fonts are preferable, but they must be created with an external tool like Glyph Designer.

- **Button:** A button is the ultimate combination of a Sprite 9 Slice (background image) and a Label TTF (text) to create the most awesome thing in the world. Almost. Well, you can tap or click it, and it can send a message in code which, if you set it up properly, won't even crash but will actually run some code!

- **Text Field:** An editable label. A user can tap or click it and type some text, and your code receives a message either when text editing ends or even every time the text changes.

- **Slider:** A user can move the slider handle left or right. Your code receives a message while the slider is dragged. Technically, it always operates with values in the range 0.0 to 1.0.

- **Scroll View:** Despite its name, this is not meant to create scrolling game worlds. It's intended to be dragged and moved by the user and to create a scrolling and snapping effect similar to the one used for browsing photos in the Photo library. You'll later use a Scroll View to create a level selection screen.

- **Box Layout:** Makes the tedious task of evenly spacing nodes a snap. You can align its child nodes horizontally or vertically, but alas, despite its name you cannot align them on a grid with multiple rows and columns by itself. However, you can use a horizontal Box Layout that contains multiple vertical Box Layout nodes as children, each of which contains the nodes in each column—or vice versa, with the horizontal and vertical alignment Box Layout nodes swapped.

You have two ways of adding items from the Node Library onto the stage. Both involve dragging the desired item from the Node Library and dropping it either directly onto the Stage or dropping them on the left side of the Timeline View on another node. The latter approach gives you the option to determine where in the hierarchy the node should be added—in other words, what that node's parent should be.

If you drop the new node directly onto the stage, it will be added as a sibling of the currently selected node, or as a child of the root node for cases when the root node is selected or when no node is selected.

Tip Selection can be performed by clicking on a node in the stage—or more accurately, by selecting the desired node in the hierarchical Timeline View. Multiple selections are possible by holding down the Shift or Cmd key while selecting. You can delete selected nodes by pressing the Backspace key. You can Edit ➤ Undo most operations, including deletions, until you save the document.

Creating a Button

Now drag and drop a button onto the stage or timeline. Position it anywhere on the stage—that's fine for now. The new button will be selected and labeled "Title".

On the Item Properties pane (to the right), you will see a large collection of values, buttons, check boxes, and text fields. The Button node is probably the most complex node of them all. An example of its properties is shown in Figure 2-6. Feel free to play with its settings and values at this point; there's little you can do wrong. And if you do the wrong thing, you can Undo or simply delete the button and drag a new one onto the stage to start over.

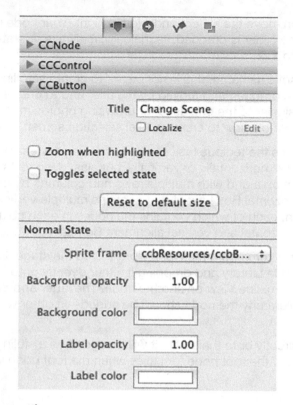

Figure 2-6. *Excerpt of CCButton properties*

For now, the only thing you probably should change is the button's text, editable under the **CCButton** section in the **Title** text box. Enter "Change Scene" or something similar as the title.

Assigning a Button Selector

The really important part is the **Code Connections** tab in the Details Inspector on the right side. Click on this tab now. See Figure 2-7 for reference.

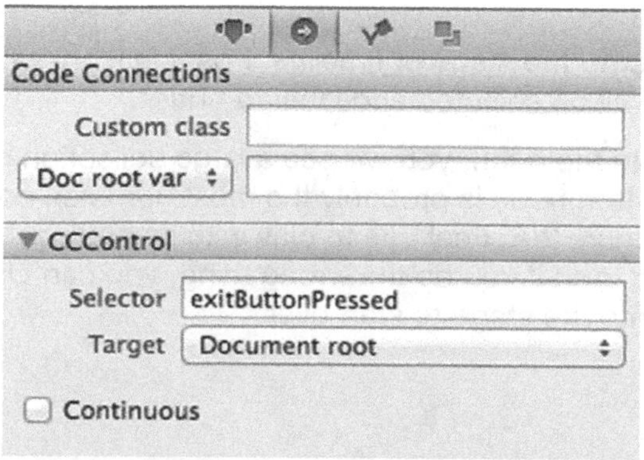

Figure 2-7. *The button's Code Connections tab*

You'll see a section labeled **CCControl** that you'll only see on user-interface nodes, namely Button, Text Field, and Slider nodes. This is where you can specify a selector, also known as "the name of a method" for those not afraid to put it in layman's terms. That's the message being sent (or simply "the method being called") when the button is pressed.

Enter *exitButtonPressed* in the **Selector** text field. As for **Target**, leave it on *Document root*. Be sure to leave the **Continuous** check box unchecked, or else the method would run every frame while the user keeps the button tapped or pressed.

What happens now if you publish and run the code, and then press the button? Darn! It's still showing the original MainScene.

Changing the Launch Scene

To change the scene with which a SpriteBuilder project launches, open the AppDelegate.m file in Xcode. Locate the `startScene` method, and modify it so it loads the GameScene file:

```
- (CCScene*) startScene
{
    return [CCBReader loadAsScene:@"GameScene"];
}
```

CCBReader is the class bundled with Cocos2d-Swift that is responsible for loading CCB files.

The `CCBReader` methods you are likely to use are `loadAsScene` and `load`, which both load the specified CCB file and return a `CCScene` and `CCNode` instance, respectively. For now, it's only noteworthy that `loadAsScene:` returns a plain `CCScene` instance with the GameScene.ccb root node as its only child. I'll explain this in more detail soon.

Publish again, and run the app. It'll bring up the GameScene with the button, but tapping the button doesn't do anything useful yet.

Creating a Custom Class for the GameScene

For code connections to work, both when specifying a selector and when assigning a node as an *ivar* (short for "instance variable of a class"), you will have to specify a custom class in SpriteBuilder. Then create the class of the same name containing the corresponding selector/ivar in Xcode. Or vice versa; the order is not important.

Both for selectors and ivars, you can specify a target, which defaults to *Document root* and *Doc root var*, respectively. This so-called "document root" refers to the root node of the CCB file which contains the currently edited node. The root node is the topmost node in the hierarchy—the one that's already there when you create a CCB file. (See Figure 2-8.) Therefore, the custom class property must be edited on the root node.

Default Timeline	↕≡	👁 🔒
Callbacks		
Sound effects		▼
▼ CCNode		👁 ·
CCButton		👁 · ▼
Joints		👁 ·

Figure 2-8. The root node is selected

> **Note** Using the *Owner* setting as the target for selectors and ivars is done only in cases where you load
> the contents of a CCB at runtime with an already existing scene. You can specify a custom object (owner) as
> the receiver of selectors and ivars. One use for this is to map an overlay-menu CCB's button selectors to the
> scene's original custom class. A common misconception is that the *Owner* setting refers to the custom class
> of the selected node—that is not the case.

Select the root node in the GameScene.ccb, and switch to the Code Connections tab on the Detail
View. The root node is always the first node in the node hierarchy. You can most easily select it in the
Timeline View, as seen in Figure 2-8.

With the root node selected, enter *GameScene* in the **Custom class** field like in Figure 2-9. Be sure
the case matches, too. If you enter "gamescene" in the custom class text field but name your class
"GameScene," the code connection is not going to work. You also have to use a valid Objective-C
class name. If in doubt, just stick to letters and numbers and don't start the class name with a
number, and you'll be fine.

Figure 2-9. GameScene.ccb root node with custom class assigned

Now switch over to Xcode. You should still have the project open. If not, go to File ➤ Open Recent,
and select the project from the list, or double-click the .xcodeproj in Finder as mentioned earlier.

Select the "Source" group in the project, and perform File ➤ New ➤ File from the menu, or
right-click and select New File from the context menu. Select the Cocoa Touch Class (Xcode 5:
Objective-C Class) template from the list of items shown in Figure 2-10 before clicking **Next**.

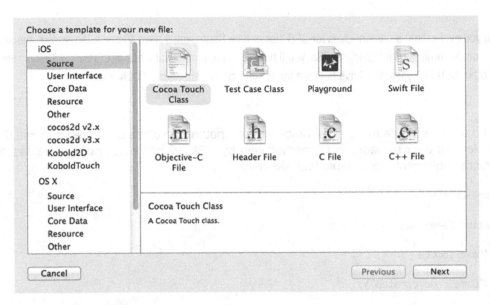

Figure 2-10. *Xcode file templates dialog*

Name your class exactly as you did in SpriteBuilder. In this instance, it must be named GameScene as shown in Figure 2-11. Make it a subclass of CCNode, not CCScene, because even in CCB files of type Scene, the root node is a CCNode instance. Click **Next** and save the file.

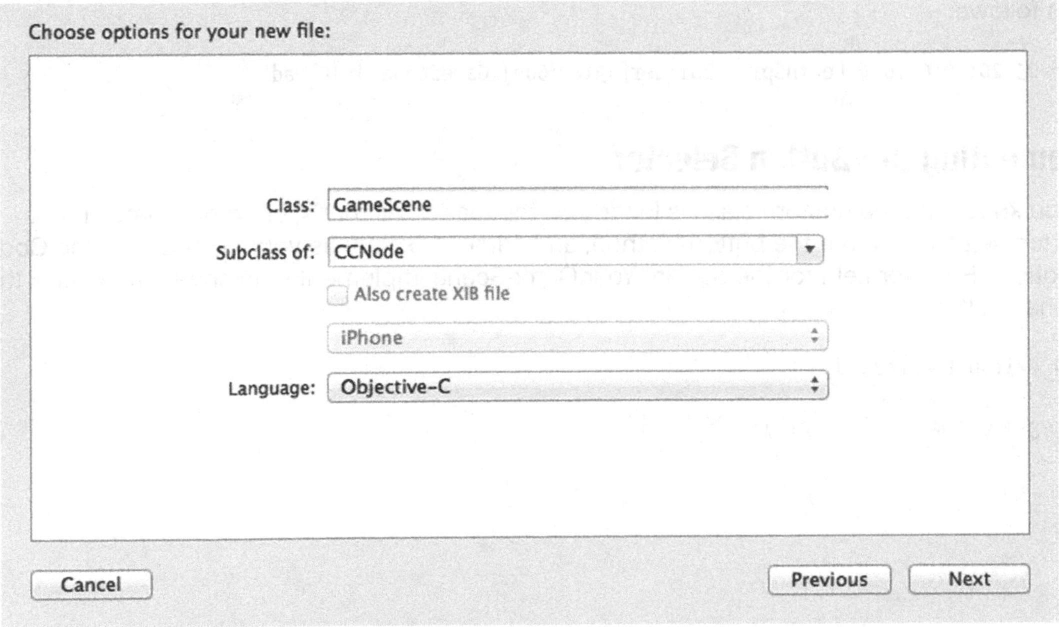

Figure 2-11. *Creating a new Objective-C class named GameScene*

> **Tip**   If you ever create a custom class for CCB files of type Sprite, you'll have to make the class a subclass of `CCSprite`. Accordingly, for Particles CCBs, you'll have to make them a subclass of `CCParticleSystem`. For all other CCB file types, you have to make the custom class a subclass of `CCNode`.

Now select the GameScene.m file. As a quick test of whether the class is created and initialized, you can implement the `didLoadFromCCB` method sent by `CCBReader` to every node it creates. Your GameScene.m implementation should look like this:

```
#import "GameScene.h"

@implementation GameScene

-(void) didLoadFromCCB
{
    NSLog(@"GameScene created");
}

@end
```

When you build and run the app now, you'll find the following log message in the Xcode Debug Console, located at the bottom of the Xcode window in the debug area. See Figure 2-3, the Debug Console is the right half of the area labelled with 4. If you can't see the Debug Console, go to View ➤ Debug Area ➤ Activate Console to show it. The message in the Debug Console should read as follows:

```
2014-06-05 20:00:01.014 LearnSpriteBuilder[49183:60b] GameScene did load
```

Implementing the Button Selector

Now you know that the custom class is loaded by the reader. All that's left to do is implement the button selector. Create the button method, and name it exactly as you entered it on the Code Connections Selector field for the button. Your GameScene implementation should now have this additional method:

```
-(void) exitButtonPressed
{
    NSLog(@"Get me outa here!");
}
```

> **Tip**   You can optionally set up the selectors for Button, Text Field, and Slider nodes so that they receive the
> sending node as a parameter. To do so, you would simply append a colon to the selector name—for instance,
> `exitButtonPressed` would become `exitButtonPressed:` in the Selector field on the Code Connections
> tab for the node. Then update the method signature accordingly, for brevity, in a single line:
>
> ```
> -(void) exitButtonPressed:(CCControl*)sender {  NSLog(@"Sender: %@", sender);  }
> ```
>
> Instead of `CCControl*`, you can use the sending node's specific class—for instance, `CCButton*`. `CCControl`
> is the super class which Button, Text Field, and Slider nodes inherit from and is guaranteed to work for all
> of them.

Run the app, tap the button, and you'll see a message like this in the Debug Console:

```
2014-06-05 20:24:02-959 LearnSpriteBuilder[49437:60b] Get me outa here!
```

Changing the Scene on Button Tap

Would be even nicer if tapping the button actually did change to the menu scene, don't you think?
Connecting scenes is a task that you have to code, but it's really straightforward and the same
procedure for all scene transitions. See Listing 2-1.

Listing 2-1. Changing the scene on button press

```
-(void) exitButtonPressed
{
    NSLog(@"Get me outa here!");

    CCScene* scene = [CCBReader loadAsScene:@"MainScene"];
    CCTransition* transition = [CCTransition transitionFadeWithDuration:1.5];
    [[CCDirector sharedDirector] presentScene:scene withTransition:transition];
}
```

> **Caution**   You should not append the .ccb file extension when loading CCBs. It's a common and
> understandable mistake, but CCBReader will fail to load files where you specify the .ccb extension. Published
> CCB files are converted to a binary format optimized for fast loading and compact storage. This binary file
> format carries the extension .ccbi—that's .ccb with a trailing *i*. The plain text format .ccb files aren't actually
> in the bundle. Therefore, it's important to omit the file extension in calls to CCBReader. Or, perhaps to remind
> you of the differing extensions, you can also append the .ccbi extension.

First, CCBReader is used to load a SpriteBuilder CCB file as the scene with the loadAsScene: method. The loadAsScene method is a convenience method. It returns a CCScene object with your CCB file's root node as the only child. To better understand this, here's the equivalent code to loadAsScene but implemented using the load: method:

```
CCNode* ccbRootNode = [CCBReader load:@"MainScene"];
CCScene* scene = [CCScene node];
[scene addChild:ccbRootNode];
```

Here scene is what the method returns. To access the MainScene's root node, you would have to write

```
CCNode* rootNode = scene.children.firstObject;
```

Now that you have an instance of a CCScene, it can be presented with an optional transition:

```
CCTransition* transition = [CCTransition transitionFadeWithDuration:1.5];
[[CCDirector sharedDirector] presentScene:scene withTransition:transition];
```

A transition is a way to animate the scene change. The fade transition fades one scene to black before fading the new scene in. You can also use cross-fade, fading to color and a variety of moving and pushing transitions.

What are these transition methods' exact names? This information is always at your fingertips with Xcode code completion suggestions—if you don't get suggestions, check that the option is turned on under Xcode Preferences ➤ Text Editing ➤ Suggest completions while typing.

Once you start typing parts of a class or method name, you should see a list of the available completion suggestions like in Figure 2-12. If not, try pressing the ESC key at this point.

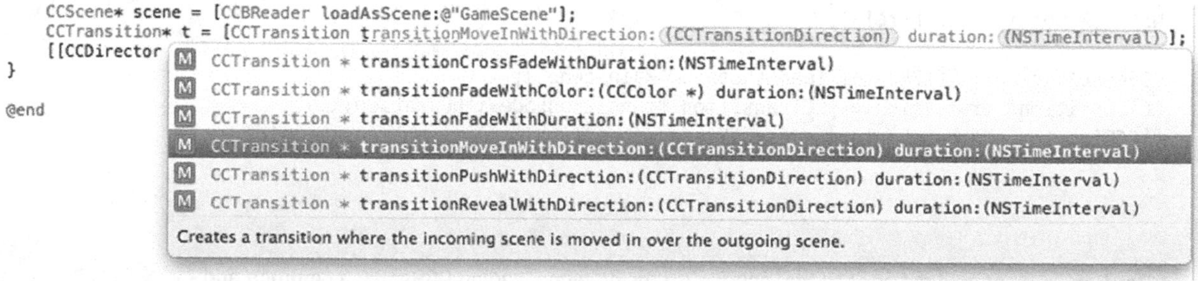

Figure 2-12. Taking advantage of Xcode auto-completion suggestions

Tip   You can also find a list of transitions in the Cocos2d class reference: http://www.cocos2d-swift.org/docs/api/Classes/CCTransition.html. Or type *CCTransition* anywhere in Xcode, and then right-click the text and select Jump to Definition. (Alternatively, put the cursor anywhere on the text and select Navigate ➤ Jump to Definition from the menu.) This will open the interface for CCTransition, where you'll find, along with documentation, the names of methods and properties and other details of the class.

Now that you know how to the start scene in AppDelegate and how to change scenes when tapping a button, run the app and try it if you haven't done so yet—I'll leave it as an exercise to change the starting scene back to the MainScene and to add another button on the MainScene. So that, when the button in the MainScene is tapped, it transitions to the GameScene. An example of this project state is provided with the book in the *01 - Change Scenes with Buttons* folder.

Creating a Level Sub File Node

Back to SpriteBuilder—specifically, the GameScene.ccb file. The game we're building should support multiple levels. Because each level will have the same basic game play, it makes sense to reuse the GameScene.ccb for each level so that you don't have to re-implement common features in each level separately. For instance, the HUD or heads-up display—a misnomer, but a commonly used term that refers to any nonscrolling content, like pause buttons and score labels in a scrolling world.

This is where the Sub File node comes in handy. It allows you to create template CCB files that can be instantiated multiple times and edited in a single file. Consider the Sub File node being the equivalent of a class in Objective-C. The GameScene will have three Sub File nodes, one for the actual level contents, one for the HUD layer, and one for any popovers like the pause and "game over" menus.

Since re-organizing resources at a later point is tedious and error prone, it's important to start with a project structure that can grow with the project. For this exercise, start by adding a new folder named *Levels* to the project, where all the game's level files will be added to. You can create a folder via the File ➤ New ➤ Folder menu or by right-clicking in the Resource Navigator view on the lower left half of the File View tab—that's where the CCB files and other resources are listed.

First, create a CCB that will contain the level's nodes. Since a level needs a specific size, in this case to determine the scrollable area of the world, the Layer document type is the right choice. Select the Levels folder before you issue the File ➤ New ➤ File command, and before you right-click the Levels folder and select New File. This will display the dialog in Figure 2-13.

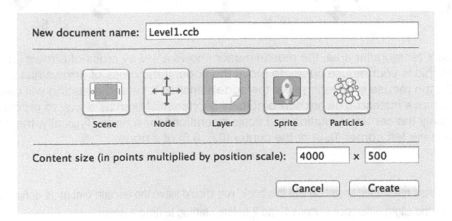

Figure 2-13. Level1.ccb is of type Layer and uses a custom content size

Name the new layer *Level1.ccb*, and give it a size of 4000 by 500. Then click Create. Initially, the new CCB will be empty (black).

The Level1.ccb file should be in the subfolder named Levels. If it isn't, move it to the Levels folder by dragging the Level1.ccb onto the Levels folder. The project's file hierarchy should be exactly like the one shown in Figure 2-14.

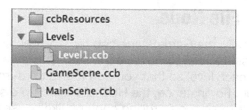

Figure 2-14. Level1.ccb should be in the folder named Levels

Switch to the Node Library View, and drag and drop a Gradient Node onto the stage or onto the root node in the timeline.

The Node Selection Handles

Now before you make this gradient fill the entire level, have a look at the selection handles for a node. You can easily spot the selected node in the stage because its corners are marked with tiny circles, the selection handles.

As you move your mouse over a selected node in the stage, the mouse cursor will change to one of the following icons, and its corresponding action can be performed through clicking and dragging:

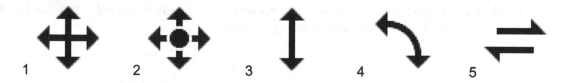

Within the node's rectangular area, the mouse cursor shows a 4-way cross of arrows (1). Click and drag when this is your mouse cursor to move the node. If the cross of arrows has a circle at its center (2), the mouse is hovering near the node's anchorPoint and dragging will cause the anchorPoint to move instead. The anchorPoint itself is often mistaken as a way to reposition a node, but alas it's mainly the center of rotation and scale operations for a node. Typically, the anchorPoint is either at the lower left corner (0, 0) or the center (0.5, 0.5) of a node.

Caution   Unless mentioned specifically in this book, you should leave the anchorPoint at its default value. Watch out for the slight difference in icons 1 and 2 before starting to drag a node.

The two-way arrow handle (3) allows you to scale the node and becomes visible when hovering over one of the four selection handles. It can be mistaken for resizing the node, but except for Color Node and Gradient Node, changing a node's size by changing its scale will result in reduced image quality, in particular when enlarging the node through scaling. If you move the mouse cursor slightly outside the node but hover near a selection handle, its shape will change to a bent 2-way arrow (4), which allows you to rotate the node when dragging.

Finally, the two split-in-half arrows (5) indicate the skew action. You can grab a node between two selection handles to move that edge along its axis, forming a trapezoid-shaped node.

Editing Node Properties

For precision changes, the mouse drag operations are unsuitable. You can use the Nudge, Move, and Align commands from the Object menu for finer control, but this doesn't suit every situation either. Most of the time, when you know the exact value of a property you'll want to use the Item Properties view on the right side of Detail View. All node types present the same basic properties at the top, labeled **CCNode**, as seen in Figure 2-15.

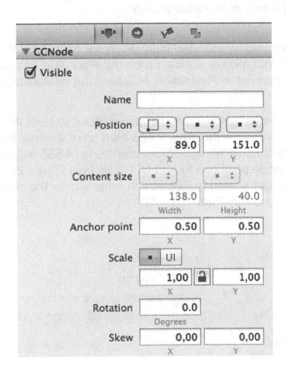

Figure 2-15. CCNode properties are used by all nodes

The Visible check box is self-explanatory, and the Name text field can be used to give a node a custom name to identify it in code.

The Position setting is in points, not pixels. A Retina and non-Retina iPad, for instance, have the same point dimensions of 1024 x 768 points. This makes the position universal for all devices. To further support alignment and perhaps personal preference, you can change a node's reference corner. (See Figure 2-16.) By default, it is set to Bottom-left, which means the node's position is relative to the lower left corner of the root node. Change it to Top-left and the node's position will be the same as that of a UIView, which also considers views to be positioned relative to the upper-left corner of the view, layer, or screen.

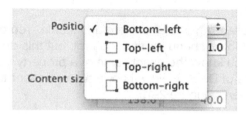

Figure 2-16. *The Corner Alignment settings for the Position property*

The position's scale type can also be adjusted individually for each axis. By default, coordinates are considered to be *X in Points*, but always scaling up on the iPad. This has the effect that when you change the document to Document ➤ Resolution ➤ Tablet, the relative position of the node remains the same on tablet devices.

By default, SpriteBuilder assumes that Universal apps will want to treat the iPad screen essentially as a roughly two times larger screen—the 1024 x 768 iPad point extents are 1.8 times wider and 2-4 times higher than a widescreen iPhone 5C/5S dimensions of 568 x 320. If that is not what you wish, you'll have to change node positions to *X in UI Points* (see Figure 2-17) to actually allow you to cram more nodes onto the larger screen real estate. In other words the player would actually be able to see more of the same world on an iPad.

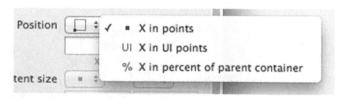

Figure 2-17. *The Position Type settings*

The same UI point scaling type can also be applied to a node's scale property.

Finally, the *percent of parent container* settings is the most important and the most frequently used setting for positions. It allows you to completely ignore most resolution-dependent considerations. The most common use is to quickly center a node on the screen regardless of the target device being a 3.5" or 4" iPhone or an iPad. Simply set the position types for both coordinates to percent of parent container and enter 50% x 50%.

The Content Size property extends this scale type list by two additional settings: Width inset in points and Width inset in UI points, shown in Figure 2-18. The difference between regular and UI point scaling is the same as mentioned above. The inset changes the contentSize from defining the actual width and height of the node to defining the distance from the edges of the parent node.

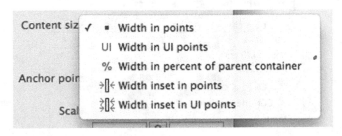

Figure 2-18. Size types available for the Content Size property

Assuming an example node is centered on the layer with Position 50%, 50% and AnchorPoint 0.5, 0.5, an inset of 100 x 40 would change the node's contentSize so that it is 100 by 40 points smaller than its parent. In this particular instance, the node is perfectly centered so its size would be 50 points smaller on both the left and right sides, and 20 points smaller on the top and bottom. The same effect can be achieved by editing the position and content size, though less conveniently.

Changing Node Draw Order

One last but important property is the draw order, in Cocos2d often referred to as zOrder. Sprite Kit users know it as zPosition. But alas, there is no such property under the CCNode properties or anywhere else. The trick here is that, in SpriteBuilder, draw order is solely defined by the order of children in their parent container. In SpriteBuilder, the only way to change draw order is by reordering nodes in the Timeline View.

Drag and drop a Color Node onto the stage, on top of the existing Gradient Node. The Timeline will look like Figure 2-19.

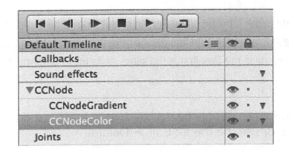

Figure 2-19. The Timeline lists a CCB file's nodes in a hierarchical view

Now if you want the Color Node to be drawn behind (under) the Gradient Node, you just drag and drop it in the Timeline outline view above the Gradient Node. The result should be the same as in Figure 2-20.

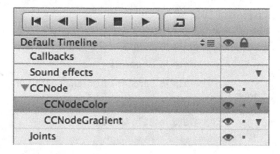

Figure 2-20. CCNodeColor moved upwards via drag and drop to reverse the draw order

In the stage, the color node should now slide under the gradient node if you move it. See Figure 2-21 for an example.

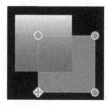

Figure 2-21. Color node is now drawn behind the gradient node

The drag-and-drop operations in the Timeline are also used to move a node so that it becomes a child of another node, essentially changing the node's parent. It is worth noting that child nodes are always drawn in front of their parent node.

> **Tip**   Double-clicking a node in the Timeline allows you to give it a descriptive, purely informational name within SpriteBuilder. A node's name in the Timeline can be different from its Name property but it's good practice to ensure a node's name in the Timeline is the same as its Name property, to avoid confusion.

Finally, delete the Color Node again, it only served to demonstrate the draw order. Select the color node, and press Backspace, or use the menu: Edit ➤ Delete.

Filling the Layer with a Gradient

Armed with that knowledge, it becomes easy to fill the entire layer with the gradient node. Change the content size scale types to Width in percent of parent container and Height in percent of parent container. Enter 100 and 100 for both content size Width and Height fields. Provided that both position and anchor point are both set to their default values of 0, 0, (scale being 1, 1 and rotation being 0), this will make the gradient fill the entire layer. See Figure 2-22 for reference.

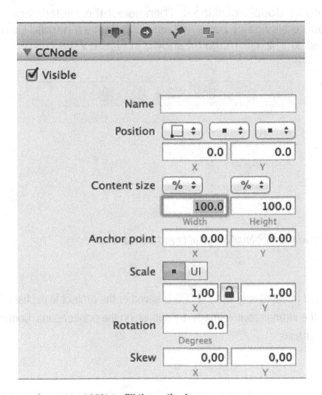

Figure 2-22. Gradient node content size set to 100% to fill the entire layer

Because the Level1 layer is likely wider than the screen, you may want to zoom out to see the entire layer to confirm this. The Zoom In, Zoom Out, and Reset View commands are found in the Document menu—though the keyboard shortcuts Cmd +, Cmd – and Cmd 0 are far more convenient to use. You can also pan the layer around by holding down the Cmd key and dragging the stage with the left mouse button.

Feel free to experiment with the CCNodeGradient properties before moving on. For instance, change the gradient colors and the Vector property that determines the direction of the gradient. Doing so will also help you to better see the early version of the scrolling effect you'll be implementing in the next chapter.

Creating a Sub File Reference

As the last step, you need to actually reference this new Level1.ccb in the GameScene. This is done with the Sub File node.

You could just drag a Sub File node onto the stage and then edit its CCB File property to point to the desired CCB file. But there's an easier way. Here's where the Tileless Editor View on the left-hand Resource Navigator comes in handy.

Open the GameScene.ccb by double-clicking it. Then select the Tileless Editor View tab (second from the left) in the Resource Navigator pane. It'll list a single item named Level1—that's the Level1. ccb—along with a preview thumbnail image as shown in Figure 2-23.

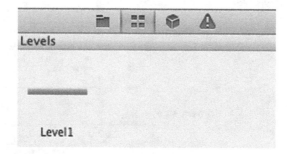

Figure 2-23. Tileless Editor View with a thumbnail image of Level1.ccb contents

> **Note**   The thumbnails are updated only when a CCB is saved or the project is published. If you don't see a thumbnail or it shows the wrong preview image, try publishing the project once. Confirm to Save All documents if SpriteBuilder asks.

You should drag and drop the Level1 item from the Tileless Editor View to create a Sub File node that references the Level1.ccb file's contents. If you inspect the new node's Item Properties tab, you'll see a CCB File entry that references Levels/Level1.ccb. In the Timeline, this new node is labeled CCBFile. You may want to double-click it and give it a recognizable name—for instance, "level content."

Because the Sub File node has a position of its own and the referenced Level1.ccb is treated like a child of the Sub File node, you need to change the new node's position to 0,0 so that the dummy Level is properly aligned with the lower-left corner of the screen. Also, the "change scene" button is now being drawn underneath the level content—just drag the CCButton entry in the Timeline below the "level content" node as described earlier.

As you create more and more CCB files representing individual elements of your game, they will all become available in the Tileless Editor View. They will become your game's custom library of prefabricated content nodes, sometimes called *prefabs* (short for "prefabricated") or templates.

Adding the Player Sprite

The first prefab will be the player character, and it will be a sprite. Sprites need an image resource.

Moreover, as much as possible, sprites should be packed into *atlas textures* to improve rendering performance. Cocos2d refers to atlas textures as "spritesheets," but they are the same thing: a large texture containing multiple images with meta information that tells Cocos2d where inside the atlas texture to find the image for a given name. Fortunately, SpriteBuilder automates both Sprite Sheet generation and loading images from a Sprite Sheet for you.

> **Tip** The more often a particular image is used in the same scene, the more it will benefit from being in a spritesheet. However, if you add too many or too large images, the dimensions of the resulting Sprite Sheet may become greater than the maximum of 4096 x 4096 pixels. If that is the case, SpriteBuilder will generate a warning message, and to fix it you'd have to remove some images, preferably by adding them to a new Sprite Sheet.

Creating a Sprite Sheet

You should create a new folder in the File View now, and name it *SpriteSheets*. Then add a subfolder to it and name it *Global*. Then right-click the Global folder to bring up a context menu (see Figure 2-24), and select *Make Smart Sprite Sheet*.

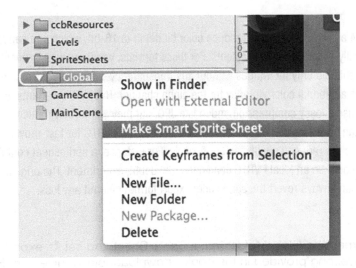

Figure 2-24. Make it so! Turning a folder into a Smart Sprite Sheet

You'll notice the Atlas folder icon turned pink. And above it, in the preview area, you get a few extra options to change the sprite sheet's publishing format. For now, you can leave the format as PNG (uncompressed, no dithering), but the recommended format is PVR RGBA8888 with Compress selected to conserve memory and to load these images significantly faster. There is no downside to using compressed PVR. Cocos2D users may recognize this texture format by its .pvr.ccz extension.

> **Tip**   A common misconception is that image file size equals memory usage, but nothing could be further from the truth. An image.png file that's 100 KB in size could easily consume 16 megabytes of memory as a texture. The maximum, uncompressed size of a texture in bytes is calculated from the image properties: width x height x (bpp / 8) where bpp stands for "bits per pixel." Simply reducing color bit depth from 32-bit (4 bytes per color) to 16-bit (2 bytes per color) already halves a texture's memory usage. The compressed PVR format further decreases memory usage without affecting image quality, while the lossy PVRTC reduces memory usage even further at the expense of image quality.

It shouldn't matter which atlas type you use for the rest of the book, but if you run into an out of memory situations in your app, the atlas type is how you can most easily and quickly reduce memory usage and even increase performance. To do so, simply select one of those cute pink sprite sheet folders with a smiley icon and change the texture type. For instance, the sprite sheet in Figure 2-25 uses PVR RGBA8888—a texture in PVR format with 8 bits for each RGB color channel and another 8 bits for the alpha channel (transparency).

Figure 2-25. Sprite sheet publish format settings

> **Tip**   The RGBA4444 and RGB565 formats reduce color bit depth to 16-bit, which can cause "color-bleeding"—specifically, in images with gradients. For these formats, you may want to enable the Dither check box. The RGB565 is suitable only for images without any transparency—for instance, opaque background images—as it trades additional color vibrancy for the alpha channel. The PVRTC variants are a "last-resort" measure since they use a lossy compression, much like JPG, but they will further reduce memory usage and improve rendering performance. You should only consider using PVRTC for fast-moving, short-lived, or small images—where the reduced quality isn't noticeable. For instance, a spritesheet containing nothing but variations of bullets could be an ideal PVRTC candidate. If in doubt, experiment. The original images will be left untouched, you can always revert the spritesheet export format without any loss.

Now that you have turned the Global folder into a Sprite Sheet and set its export format, you should drag and drop the player.png provided in the book's downloadable archive from Finder onto the *Global* sprite sheet folder. Be sure to drag the image itself, not the folder containing the images. The other images will be used at a later time.

If you want to use your own player image, you should create an image that's 256 x 256 pixels in size and its contents circular in shape, and name it *player.png*. The player is circular because later in the book it will become a deformable soft-body physics object, and a circular shaped image is easiest to draw onto a deformable body.

> **Tip**   Dragging and dropping files from Finder onto SpriteBuilder's File View is the only way to add external resource files to SpriteBuilder.

Creating the Player Prefab

Now create another folder named *Prefabs* in the root of the File View.

Select the folder, and choose File ➤ New ➤ File from the menu, or right-click it and select New File. Name the new document *Player.ccb*, and click the Sprite button to create the document with a CCSprite as its root node. See Figure 2-26.

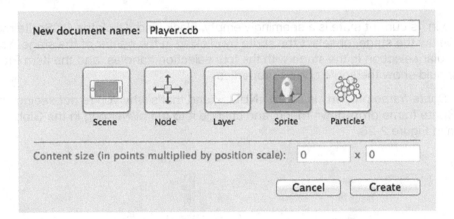

Figure 2-26. Creating the Player.ccb as a Sprite

Your project's File View should now look like in Figure 2-27.

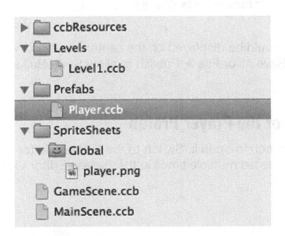

Figure 2-27. The project's file and folder structure so far

If any of the files are not where they are supposed to be, simply drag and drop them now to move them to the correct location.

> **Caution**   Moving resources to different folders, or even renaming them, will cause SpriteBuilder to lose any existing references to that resource. It is crucial to create resources in the right place and therefore to come up with a sound folder structure for the given project as early as possible, and then stick with it. Resource files should be in an appropriate location and named appropriately before making first use of them. It's not impossible to move or rename resource files at a later time, but the more often you have used that file, the more changes you'd have to make to update references so they point to the new path or name.

The Player.ccb in its current state is a seemingly empty, black void. Click the CCSprite root node in the Timeline below the stage, or select the sprite by clicking in the center of the stage. You should now see a circular selection in the stage with the four selection handles, and the Item Properties tab on the right should show the sprite node's properties.

Currently, the *Sprite frame* property is set to <NULL>, and that's why you're not seeing anything. Click on the Sprite frame drop-down menu, and change it to the player.png in the Global sprite sheet folder as seen in Figure 2-28.

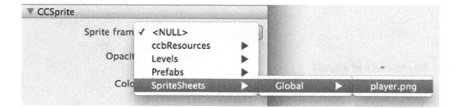

Figure 2-28. Selecting the correct Sprite frame image for the player

Now the player.png image should be displayed on the center stage. For now, that's it for the Player.ccb. Choose File ➤ Save All or File ➤ Publish to allow SpriteBuilder to update the project's preview images.

Creating an Instance of the Player Prefab

Now double-click the Level1.ccb to open it. Switch to the Tileless Editor View (the second tab from the left). You'll see the player listed multiple times in the Tileless Editor View like in Figure 2-29.

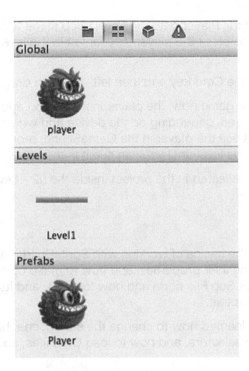

Figure 2-29. Tileless Editor View with curiously duplicate entries

Actually, the list is showing both the image in the Global sprite sheet folder as well as the Player.ccb in the Prefabs folder.

To avoid accidentally using the player's image rather than its Player.ccb prefab, you should uncheck the Global check box in the list below the Tileless Editor View, see Figure 2-30. You should also uncheck the Levels folder since you won't drag and drop a level CCB file to another CCB again—at least not during the course of this book, since changing levels will be done by code.

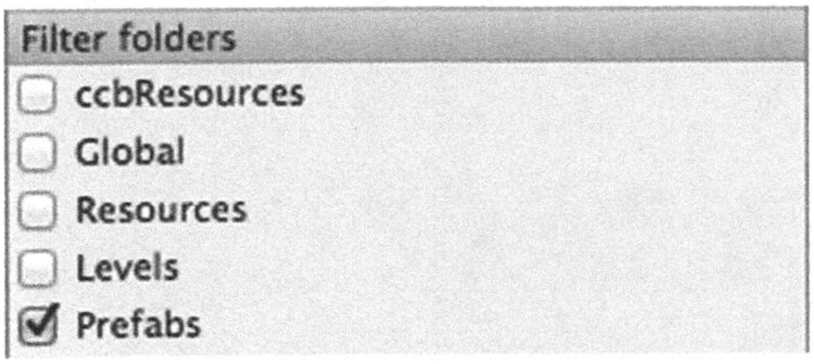

Figure 2-30. Filter check boxes change which folder's contents appear in the Tileless Editor View

Once you've unchecked the Global and Levels folders, their contents should no longer appear in the Tileless Editor View.

You should now drag and drop the Player onto the Level1.ccb stage to create a Sub File node referencing the Player.ccb. Try to place the player very far left in the level as the game will scroll from left to right.

To move the stage, hold down the Cmd key and then left-click and drag.

If you publish, build, and run the game now, the player instance you added to the Level1.ccb may or may not be visible on the screen, depending on the device and where exactly you positioned the player instance. If you can't see the player in the GameScene, move its position in Level1.ccb toward the lower-left corner of the level until you can see it in the app.

This state of the project is also reflected in the project inside the *02 - Level with Player Prefab* folder.

Summary

In this chapter, you've learned the basics of working with SpriteBuilder and Cocos2d, how to create CCB files and nodes, how to edit their properties, and how to make code connections. Specifically, you learned about the important Sub File node and how to use it, and its benefits will become even more obvious in the coming chapters.

On the programming side, you learned how to change the start scene, how to create custom classes, how to react to button selectors, and how to load CCB files, and how to do transitioning between scenes.

You now have a skeleton app with two scenes between which you can change back and forth with a tap of a button. In the next chapter, you'll scroll the level to ensure the player stays centered on the screen. And you'll add touch controls and movement to the player.

Chapter **3**

Controlling and Scrolling

Most games need some way to control the player character. You'll learn to use Cocos2D actions to move the player through the level you designed. Due to this project's levels being larger than the screen, and to add the impression of depth to the world, you'll also implement parallax scrolling as well.

Touch and Go: Moving the Player

The first order of business is to add code that reacts to touch events. You'll use that to move the player around. To do so, you first have to establish a reference to the player node in the *GameScene* class.

Finding the Player Node by Its Name

In the GameScene.m class, add the brackets and variable declarations of Listing 3-1 just below the class' @implementation section.

Listing 3-1. Add these ivars to the GameScene class

```
@implementation GameScene
{
    __weak CCNode* _levelNode;
    __weak CCPhysicsNode* _physicsNode;
    __weak CCNode* _playerNode;
    __weak CCNode* _backgroundNode;
}
```

This code declares private variables (known as *ivars*) named _levelNode, _physicsNode, _playerNode, and _backgroundNode. They are private because they are being declared in the @implementation section of the class. Private variables are not visible to other classes, not even subclasses.

The _playerNode is declared as CCNode, not CCSprite. This is mainly because we don't need its sprite-specific functionality here, so it's okay to reference it by its super class. If at a later time you need to use its CCSprite functionality, you can change the variable definition to __weak CCSprite* _playerNode or simply cast it like so:

```
CCSprite* playerSprite = (CCSprite*)_playerNode;
```

> **Tip**   If you have little experience with Objective-C, you can get a good understanding of the language and object-oriented programming concepts by reading through Apple's "Programming with Objective-C" guide: https://developer.apple.com/library/mac/documentation/cocoa/conceptual/ProgrammingWithObjectiveC. Apress also has several Objective-C titles in its library at www.apress.com.
>
> If you are an experienced programmer and you're mainly facing syntactical squabbles, you'll find Ray Wenderlich's "Objective-C Cheat Sheet" helpful: http://www.raywenderlich.com/4872/objective-c-cheat-sheet-and-quick-reference.

The __weak keyword signals the compiler that this variable should not retain the object assigned to it. If you were to send the removeFromParent message to the _playerNode instance, it would be allowed to deallocate and the _playerNode reference would automatically become nil, both because of the __weak keyword.

In general, it is good practice to declare object pointer ivars not created or owned by a class as __weak. In Cocos2D specifically, you should always declare references to nodes as __weak when the reference is either a parent (or grandparent, etc.) or a sibling of the node. Omitting the __weak keyword creates a strong reference, and in the worst case a retain cycle—a situation where in its simplest form, node A strongly references node B while B also holds a strong reference to A and both never let go of each other, and therefore both can't deallocate. In cases where __weak is inappropriate, you'll quickly notice it because the reference generally becomes nil earlier than expected.

> **Tip**   To learn more about weak and strong variables, and when and why to use them as well as general memory-management guidelines, you'll find that information in Apple's "Advanced Memory Management Programming Guide": https://developer.apple.com/library/ios/documentation/Cocoa/Conceptual/MemoryMgmt, specifically the "Practical Memory Management" section. The guide is amended by the "Transitioning to ARC Release Notes" found here: https://developer.apple.com/library/mac/releasenotes/ObjectiveC/RN-TransitioningToARC. Note that the book's projects, SpriteBuilder, and Cocos2d-Swift all use ARC (automatic reference counting) to make memory management a lot easier.

With the preceding variables declared, you should get a reference to the player node and assign it to _playerNode. The simplest way to get a node reference is by its name. To do so, open the Level1.ccb within SpriteBuilder and select the player node. On the Item Properties tab, enter **player** (all lowercase) into the Name text field.

> **Caution**   Only the Name property of a node can be used to obtain the node by its name. Changing the name of a node in the Timeline alone will not make it accessible by this name. The Timeline names are only for clarity in SpriteBuilder.

Publish the project and go back to Xcode. In GameScene.m, add the code highlighted in Listing 3-2 to the already existing didLoadFromCCB method.

Listing 3-2. Enable user interaction

```
-(void) didLoadFromCCB
{
    // enable receiving input events
    self.userInteractionEnabled = YES;

    // load the current level
    [self loadLevelNamed:nil];
}
```

The first line allows the GameScene class to receive touch events. Add the Listing 3-3 code shown next to the didLoadFromCCB method. It will be expanded upon later in the book; it doesn't currently load levels yet.

Listing 3-3. Getting the player node by its name

```
-(void) loadLevelNamed:(NSString*)levelCCB
{
    // get the current level's player in the scene by searching for it recursively
    _playerNode = [self getChildByName:@"player" recursively:YES];
    NSAssert1(_playerNode, @"player node not found in level: %@", levelCCB);
}
```

Here the first child node that goes by the name "player" is returned. The search is performed recursively, which means search covers the entire node hierarchy, including all child and grandchild nodes of all children in the self node. The result is assigned to the _playerNode ivar.

If the _playerNode couldn't be found by its name, the NSAssert here will throw an exception and spit out a message in the log. Safety measures like these are good practice because they allow you to catch issues the moment something doesn't appear to be as expected, rather than leaving you wondering why the player won't move. For the rest of the book, I'll leave out the safety checks for brevity and readability, but you can learn more about debugging strategies and defensive programming techniques in this book's chapter 14: Debugging and Best Practices.

There's but one thing that you ought to do in every Xcode project: add an exception breakpoint as shown in Figure 3-1. To do this, click on the Breakpoint Navigator tab in Xcode (the right-facing arrow-like icon highlighted in tab bar). At the bottom of the pane is an Add button (a + symbol). Click it and choose Add Exception Breakpoint. You can optionally edit the breakpoint by right-clicking it. In Figure 3-1, it is set to catch Objective-C exceptions only. The exception breakpoint will halt the program at the offending line of code so that you know exactly where a program error occurred, rather than Xcode always jumping to the main method. Exception breakpoints are an essential debugging aid.

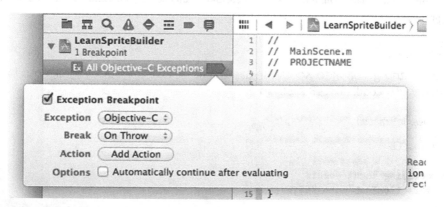

Figure 3-1. Adding an exception breakpoint to every project is an essential debugging aid

Now that touch events are enabled and the _playerNode reference is assigned, you can move the player to a touch location easily. For the moment, the code in Listing 3-4 will do. Add the Listing 3-4 code to the GameScene.m implementation file below the loadLevelNamed: method.

Listing 3-4. Teleporting the player to the touch location

```
-(void) touchBegan:(UITouch *)touch withEvent:(UIEvent *)event
{
    _playerNode.position = [touch locationInNode:self];
}
```

This takes the location of the touch and transforms it from the touch's Cocoa coordinate system (origin in the upper-left corner) to the OpenGL coordinate system used by Cocos2D (origin in the lower-left corner). It also converts the position to the local coordinate space of the supplied node, in this instance self. The result is directly applied to the _playerNode, which will now, when you build and run, instantly zap to where you tap on the screen.

Assigning the Level-Node ivar

For the next steps, you need to have a reference to the level node. Instead of getting it by name like the player, you can also have SpriteBuilder assign it to the GameScene class directly, provided that the class already declares an ivar or property of the same name. Which it already does since Listing 3-1.

Assigning a variable via SpriteBuilder and obtaining a node by name are equally fine. For the most part, it's a matter of personal preference, though it's recommended not to use the getChildByName: method frequently in a scheduled method or in update: methods, in particular with recursive searches and a deep-node hierarchy.

> **Caution**   At the time of this writing, assigning variables from within SpriteBuilder works only for nodes that are direct descendants of a given CCB file. It cannot be used to assign nodes to ivars or properties where the node is in another CCB imported via a Sub File (CCBFile) node. This is the reason why the player node was obtained by name.

Open the GameScene.ccb within SpriteBuilder, and select the CCBFile instance that references the Levels/Level1.ccb. Then, on the Details Inspector on the right side, switch to the Item Code Connections tab. In the second row's text field, enter **_levelNode**, which is the name of the ivar you already declared in Listing 3-1. Do leave the drop-down menu set to "Doc root var" as shown in Figure 3-2.

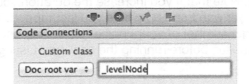

Figure 3-2. A doc root var assigns a node to a correspondingly named ivar or property declared in the CCB root node's custom class

If you publish, build, and run, the _levelNode ivar will be assigned by CCBReader before it sends the didLoadFromCCB message. That's the easiest, most efficient way to create a reference to a node contained within a CCB.

If you want to confirm that the variable has been assigned, you could add this log statement to didLoadFromCCB:

```
NSLog(@"_levelNode = %@", _levelNode);
```

Run the project and you'll find the preceding line logged in the Xcode Debug Console. If necessary, open the Console in Xcode under View ➤ Debug Area ➤ Activate Console. If you see _levelNode = (null) , the variable name in Figure 3-2 probably doesn't match the ivar's name. Otherwise, the message in the log will be similar to this:

```
LearnSpriteBuilder[54443:70b] _levelNode = <CCNode = 0x9f77b30 | Name = >
```

Moving the Player with CCActionMoveTo

To move the player smoothly to the desired location, you can replace the contents of the `touchBegan:withEvent:` method with the action-based movementcode in Listing 3-5.

Listing 3-5. Moving the player smoothly with a move action

```
-(void) touchBegan:(UITouch *)touch withEvent:(UIEvent *)event
{
    CGPoint pos = [touch locationInNode:_levelNode];
    CCAction* move = [CCActionMoveTo actionWithDuration:0.2 position:pos];
    [_playerNode runAction:move];
}
```

First, the touch location is converted relative to the _levelNode. This is important to allow the player to move about the full extents of the _levelNode (4000x500 points) rather than being confined to the screen space (568x320 points on 4-inch iPhones or 1024x768 points on iPads). However, this isn't reflected by the game yet because there is no scrolling; hence, the player can't move further than the initial screen position.

Next, a CCActionMoveTo is created that moves a node to a given coordinate over time. This action is then run on the _playerNode. Note that if you increase the duration you will notice that the move actions don't stack and the player won't end up where you last tapped. To fix that, you'd have to assign a tag—an arbitrary integer number of your choice—to the action. Using this tag, you can stop the existing action with the same tag before running the new one. Listing 3-6 shows the updated code with this improvement.

Listing 3-6. Stop an action by tag to avoid having multiple move actions running simultaneously

```
-(void) touchBegan:(UITouch *)touch withEvent:(UIEvent *)event
{
    [_playerNode stopActionByTag:1];

    CGPoint pos = [touch locationInNode:_levelNode];
    CCAction* move = [CCActionMoveTo actionWithDuration:20.2 position:pos];
    move.tag = 1;
    [_playerNode runAction:move];
}
```

> **Tip** You can find all available action classes in the Cocos2d-Swift class reference. Their class names always begin with *CCAction*: http://www.cocos2d-swift.org/docs/api/index.html.

If you build and run the project now, you should see the player moving smoothly across the screen when tapping. But the player won't be able to "leave" the initial screen. That's where scrolling comes into play.

Scrolling the Level

Now, when I say scrolling, many developers naturally assume that it's the camera panning over the background that creates the scrolling effect. Some engines and toolsets actually do it this way, mainly if 3D development tools are at the core. But in 2D game engines, it is a lot more common and practical to move the content layer in the opposite direction of the movement.

In fact, in Cocos2D and many other 2D engines, there is no concept of a camera. Not even OpenGL, the rendering technology Cocos2D is based on, has a camera. There's just the device screen. In order to change what's visible on the screen, you'll have to move the contents of the scene as the camera view that the screen represents stays fixed—fixed relative to the virtual world, that is. Of course, you can move, tilt, and drop your phone freely in the real world, but that doesn't affect what's displayed on screen.

Actually, if you drop your phone, it may affect its screen. But that's something else entirely.

Scheduling Updates

In our case, if the player moves to the right and up, for example, what we're really going to do is to move the _levelNode toward the left and down to keep the player centered on the screen. That gives the impression of the player moving toward the right and up, but really the player stays centered on the screen while the entire level's content moves to the left and down.

Still, the player's position is going to be what you would expect: limited to the confines of the level node and in an absolute position. The player's position will range from the level node's origin (lower-left corner at 0,0) to the full extents of the level node, here: 4000x500 points.

To set this up, add the update: method from Listing 3-7 just above the @end line at the bottom of the GameScene.m file.

Listing 3-7. The update: method is automatically called once per frame

```
-(void) update:(CCTime)delta
{
    // update scroll node position to player node, with offset to center player in the view
    [self scrollToTarget:_playerNode];
}
```

The update: method is called automatically by Cocos2D when implemented in a node class. It runs every frame before rendering the nodes to the screen. We need to use that method for scrolling because our player's position is currently updated over time by the CCActionMoveTo. Later, the player's position will be modified by the physics engine. In both cases, we don't know exactly when or where the player position update occurs; therefore, the scroll position is simply recalculated every frame.

Unlike you did with previous Cocos2D versions, you no longer have to explicitly schedule the update: method. You can still schedule other methods or blocks using the node schedule and unschedule methods as documented in the CCNode class reference: http://www.cocos2d-swift.org/docs/api/Classes/CCNode.html. For example, to run a selector once after a delay, you would write

```
[self scheduleOnce:@selector(theDelayedMethod:) delay:2.5];
```

Then implement the corresponding selector in the same class. The selector must take one parameter of type CCTime:

```
-(void) theDelayedMethod:(CCTime)delta
{
    // Your code here ...
}
```

> **Caution**   You should never use NSTimer, any performSelector variant, or Grand Central Dispatch methods like dispatch_after in a Cocos2D game to schedule timed events. These timing methods do not pause automatically when the node or Cocos2D is paused, and with the exception of NSTimer you can't even manually pause and resume them. You also don't know when exactly in the update/render loop these timing methods will run, or whether they'll reliable run in the same order. You should solely rely on the CCNode scheduling methods mentioned earlier, or use a CCActionSequence that contains both a CCActionDelay and either a CCActionCallBlock or CCActionCallFunc to run code after a given time or at specific intervals.

The delta parameter is the delta time, or difference in time, since the last call to the update: method. At 60 frames per second, delta time is usually around 0.0167. This value is in seconds.

Delta time is generally used to move nodes at the same speed regardless of frame rate; however, there are severe drawbacks to doing so. We won't be using delta time in this book because we're using Cocos2D's physics engine for movements. Physics games in particular should slow down as the frame rate decreases rather than skipping frames and moving ahead, thus leaving objects to advance greater distances per individual frame.

Moving the Level Node in the Opposite Direction

Of course, you'll also have to add the scrollToTarget: method in Listing 3-8 to the GameScene.m as well complete the basic scrolling. The target parameter is our _playerNode but instead of using the _playerNode ivar directly, I decided to pass it in as a parameter. This enables you to scroll to different target nodes after you've completed the book and are ready to extend the project.

Listing 3-8. Scrolling to target requires a tiny bit of math

```
-(void) scrollToTarget:(CCNode*)target
{
    CGSize viewSize = [CCDirector sharedDirector].viewSize;
    CGPoint viewCenter = CGPointMake(viewSize.width / 2.0, viewSize.height / 2.0);

    CGPoint viewPos = ccpSub(target.positionInPoints, viewCenter);

    CGSize levelSize = _levelNode.contentSizeInPoints;
    viewPos.x = MAX(0.0, MIN(viewPos.x, levelSize.width - viewSize.width));
    viewPos.y = MAX(0.0, MIN(viewPos.y, levelSize.height - viewSize.height));

    _levelNode.positionInPoints = ccpNeg(viewPos);
}
```

This looks like math. Smells like geometry. And it's good for your health! Okay, I guess I need a more convincing argument. Okay: it's really simple! Better?

The first two lines are just setup code to assign the size of the view to `viewSize`, which is equal to the size of the screen in points. And then the center point of the view is calculated and assigned to `viewCenter`. No troublesome math there.

The `viewPos` variable is initialized with the target's `positionInPoints` with the `viewCenter` subtracted from it. This subtraction with the `ccpSub` function is what keeps the target node centered in the view. If you didn't do that, scrolling would still function but the target node would appear at the lower-left corner of the screen.

> **Tip**   The `ccpSub` function along with others carrying the *ccp* prefix are declared in the `CGPointExtension.h` header file. You will find this file in the Xcode project under `libs/cocos2d-ios.xcodeproj/cocos2d/Support/Math`. The `ccp` functions perform many commonly needed vector math operations, like add, subtract, multiply, dot product, or calculate the distance between two points.

Worth noting is the use of `positionInPoints` rather than `position`. The position values are interpreted differently based on a node's `positionType` property—for instance, if the node's `positionType` is set in SpriteBuilder to "percent in parent container," the position value range is typically in the order of 0.0 to 1.0. The `positionInPoints` property converts the position based on `positionType` and returns the absolute position in points, and vice versa during assignment. The `contentSize` and `scale` properties both have equivalent `contentSizeInPoints` and `scaleInPoints` methods that you should prefer whenever you calculate in points.

The `levelSize` variable is assigned from `_levelNode.contentSizeInPoints`. It is used in the two following lines, which clamp the `viewPos` to the level's size using the `MIN` and `MAX` macros.

The `viewPos` coordinates are first clamped to the level extents using the inner MIN macro. Here `viewSize` is subtracted from the `levelSize`. This is an inset calculation because the screen should never scroll closer than `viewCenter` to the level's borders, on both sides for both axes. The insets on all four borders of the level are visualized as two-faced arrows, which are shown in Figure 3-3. Both border distances added together are conveniently equal to `viewSize`. Or, in other words, the scrollable area is two times `viewCenter` or one `viewSize` smaller than the level area.

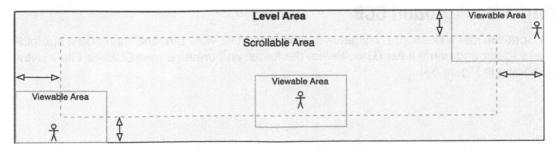

Figure 3-3. Relation of Level Area to Scrollable Area. Arrows depict the Scrollable Area inset. Note the player is not tied to its center position when near level borders. The diagram is not drawn to scale

The smaller of the two candidates, `viewPos` or `levelSize` minus `viewSize`, is returned by the `MIN` macro to the enclosing `MAX` macro, which in turn ensures that the `viewPos` is always equal to or greater than 0.0. Together, this prevents the `_levelNode` from scrolling past its borders.

Finally, the `viewPos` is negated (multiplied by –1.0) and then assigned to the `_levelNode.positionInPoints`. Remember what I said earlier about moving the level node in the opposite direction? That's what this line does. For instance, if the calculated `viewPos` is 850,340, the `ccpNeg` method would change the coordinates to –850,-–340 so that movement of the `_levelNode` goes in the opposite direction of where the player is going.

Publish the SpriteBuilder project. Then build and run the Xcode project. You are now able to scroll over the level's area, but no further.

If you're having trouble noticing the scrolling motion, go back to SpriteBuilder and change the Vector property of the `Level1.ccb` Color Gradient node to make its gradient slanted. Or simply add more Color Node or Gradient Node instances to `Level1.ccb` as you see fit in order to see something visual scroll by as you move the player. Then publish and re-run the project.

Parallax Scrolling

While you're enjoying scrolling, why not make it better with parallaxing background layers?

Parallaxing is a way to create the impression of depth in 2D games by moving background layers slower than the actual game layer. Some games even add foreground layers that move faster to give the impression of some objects being even closer to the camera than the game characters are.

There are multiple ways to implement parallax scrolling, the simplest being just moving the layers at different speeds given a specific speed factor for each layer. But this approach has the drawback that you never quite know how large each layer needs to be, and it's hard to judge which parts of what background layer will be visible when the player arrives at a given point in the level.

The parallaxing approach I used for this book derives the scrolling speed factor for each layer based on each background layer's size in relation to the level's size. That way, the background layers also align perfectly with the level borders. If the player is in the far-left corner of the level, the background layer's lower-left corners will align with the level's lower left corner. The same goes for the other three corners. The background layers neither "overshoot" nor will they be "too short," and their scrolling speed is solely determined by their content size relative to the level node's content size.

Adding a Background CCB

First, in SpriteBuilder's Resource Navigator, switch to the File View tab, and then add a subfolder in the `Levels` folder and name it **Parallax**. Select the folder, and create a new CCB via File ➤ New ➤ File, as shown in Figure 3-4.

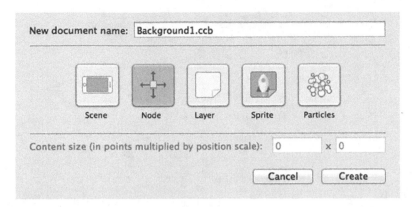

Figure 3-4. Create a new Node CCB file for the background layers

This time select Node as the CCB type, and enter **Background1.ccb** as the document name. Then click Create. Your File View should look like Figure 3-5.

Figure 3-5. Current state of the File View in SpriteBuilder

Now switch to the Node Library View tab also in the Resource Navigator, and drag and drop a Gradient Node onto the stage. Feel free to change the gradient colors. The important part is that the node position should be set to 0,0 and its Content size should be large enough to fill both iPhone and iPad screens. At the time of this writing, this means the content size of the gradient layer should be 568x384 at a minimum to cover the entire visible area on all current devices. Figure 3-6 shows the Gradient Node's properties.

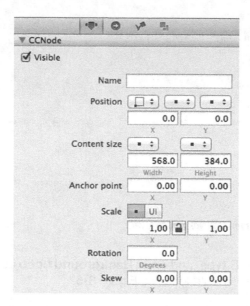

Figure 3-6. Background gradient node properties

> **Note**   When you create a CCB of type Layer, you'll notice it defaults to the same 568x384 dimensions. 568 points is the width of a 4-inch iPhone, while the iPad's screen is only 512 points wide—or more precisely, SpriteBuilder considers the iPad screen to be half its points size at 512x384, not its actual 1024x768 point size. That's because SpriteBuilder will scale up node positions and sizes by a factor of 2 on iPads by default. The height of 384 points stems from the fact that, at half its 768-point height, the iPad screen is still slightly higher than the 4-inch iPhone screen with 320 points. The somewhat odd 568x384 content size is the lowest common denominator that fits all iPhone and iPad screen sizes. It can be scaled with factors 2x and 4x to match iPhone Retina, iPad, and iPad Retina resolutions—not perfectly, but close enough.

As for the gradient colors, if you do want to get them exactly the same as those used by the book's graphics, click on the color rectangle next to the "Start color" property. This will open the OS X color selection dialog. On the Color Palettes tab (the third tab in the floating color wheel dialog), set the Palettes drop-down menu to Web Safe Colors. Then select the orange-yellowish color with the FFCC33 code next to it. Do the same for the End Color, but choose the pinkish color with the color code FF6699.

Note that you could also use a sprite with a gradient image; however, if you don't need any more details other than the gradient itself, the Gradient Node is likely faster and definitely consumes a lot less memory.

Adding the main Background Sprite

There's also a background sprite provided with the book's downloadable archive, named
level1_background_Cerberus.png. It's depicted in Figure 3-7. It will be drawn over the gradient and
is slightly larger than the gradient. The larger a background layer or image is, the faster it will parallax
as the player moves across the level. As before, if you prefer you can provide an image of your own
creation provided that the image size matches.

Figure 3-7. Cerberus background image

Speaking of image sizes. Since SpriteBuilder assumes all images to be designed for iPad Retina
resolution by default, the image has to be correspondingly huge: 2375x1625 pixels. SpriteBuilder
will automatically create downscaled versions of the image for non-Retina iPads and
Retina iPhones (1188x813 pixels) and non-Retina iPhones (594x406 pixels). As you can see, when
scaled down to non-Retina iPhone point dimensions, the image is just barely larger than the 4-inch
iPhone's dimensions of 568x320 points.

> **Tip**   This image is not sized ideally for downscaling because you'll end up with fractional dimensions like
> 1187.5 x 812.5 when dividing by 2 or 4. There can't be fractional pixels in an image, so the image size is
> rounded to the next nearest integer value. It doesn't make a difference for huge background images like this
> one, but for smaller images it's important to choose an iPad Retina image size that is divisible by 4 without a
> remainder. Otherwise, artifacts may appear due to minimal differences in the image aspect ratio on devices
> where the app uses downscaled versions of the image.

Before adding the Cerberus image, create a folder named **Sprites** and inside it a subfolder named **Level1** in the File View. This is where you'll store images for that particular level, which should not be in a SpriteSheet. Why shouldn't it be in a SpriteSheet? Quite simply, because the image is far too big to benefit from being in a SpriteSheet, and it's used only once in a level, anyway. It would take up way too much space and leave little room for other images that are used more than once.

Now drag and drop the level1_background_Cerberus.png file from Finder into the Sprites/Level1/ folder. Then drag it from the File View onto the Background1.ccb stage. Change the Cerberus sprite's position to 0,0. Because the anchor point for sprites defaults to 0.5, 0.5 the sprite is centered on the lower-left corner of the background layer. This is not what you need, so change the Anchor point property to 0,0. Now the Cerberus sprite should be above and slightly larger than the gradient.

Working with Images

The background gradient and sprite layers aren't enough to see the parallaxing effect, but first I want to digress into image and project settings because it's important to familiarize yourself with the available options before adding more images. When they are used correctly, you can easily improve performance or reduce the bundle size of your app, and you're probably already wondering what these image settings do.

Select the level1_background_Cerberus.png image in the File View. Above the File View, you'll see the preview area showing a thumbnail of the image along with additional settings as seen in Figure 3-8.

Figure 3-8. Image Preview with settings

If for some reason you have only 2x scaled versions of an image, suitable for use on iPhone Retina and non-Retina iPads, you could change the "Scale from" setting from Default to 2x. This does not conserve memory; instead, SpriteBuilder will now create both a downscaled 1x version and an upscaled 4x version from the 2x image. This means the 4x image has the same level of detail as the original 2x version. Changing the "Scale from" setting will also be reflected in stages where the image is used, where it will become twice or four times as big if you change the "Scale from" setting from 2x and 1x, respectively.

You can also drag and drop an image onto one of the 4 squares, labeled AUTO in Figure 3-8. This will replace the image for the particular scale with the image you dropped onto it so that, for instance, the iPad Retina (tablethd) would display a different image or just a differently sized version of the same image. A good example for this is a title screen that has an additional "HD" callout when the app launches on an iPad.

It is highly recommended that you create all images for the highest resolution your app supports. Although SpriteBuilder gives you all the freedom, it boils down to just two choices: create all images at 4x the 568x384 point resolution if you want your app to run on all iPad models, or create images at 2x the iPhone point resolution of 568x320 if your app is designed *only* for iPhone-sized devices and doesn't run on iPads as a native iPad app.

For instance, a background image that fills an iPad Retina screen (default 4x scale in SpriteBuilder) must be at least 2048x1536 pixels, and 2272x1536 pixels is even better to also cover the entire 4-inch iPhone screen when downscaled by factors 2 and 4. If your app is designed only for iPhones (using 2x scale for all images in SpriteBuilder), a background image that fills the entire Retina screen must be 1136x640 pixels (568x320 points). But if you wanted to have the option to make an iPad version at a later time, you should definitely design your images for the iPad Retina resolution, anyway.

Tip   Though SpriteBuilder gives you full control over messing with the scale settings, I say "mess" with a wee bit of resignation. You see, SpriteBuilder offers a clear 1x, 2x, 4x scale for iPhone, iPhone Retina, iPad, and iPad Retina devices that just makes it super-easy to develop for iOS. If you leave this path, you're setting yourself up for a ton of extra coding and testing. Please don't go there!

But let's face it, iPad Retina images are frickin' huge. They significantly increase your bundle size, which you don't want, understandably. Instead, you should experiment with the export formats and the Compress settings as seen in Figure 2-25 in Chapter 2. Even 16-bit color depth is still good quality for most images, but it cuts down memory usage and file size by up to 50%. PVRTC goes even further at the expense of image quality. And if that's not enough, read the next section, "Project Settings," for more options to reduce app size.

Now there's a third option as well, and that's using 2x resolution images for most, if not all, game elements in a universal iPhone plus iPad app, and changing the scale type to UI points for relevant nodes. This gives you an iPad version where the visible area of the world is roughly twice as large as on iPhone devices, with the world seemingly zoomed out (game objects appear smaller). Of course, your game design needs to respect that;it needs to be fair and playable on both devices— specifically, considering unfair advantages in multiplayer as well as greatly differing difficulty levels. Not many games use that approach, and for good reason—it can drastically alter the play experience between iPhone and iPad versions.

Project Settings

If you're developing an iPhone-only app, SpriteBuilder gives you the option to change the default scaling from 4x as well as to change which resources to publish. Open the File ➤ Project Settings dialog, which is shown in Figure 3-9.

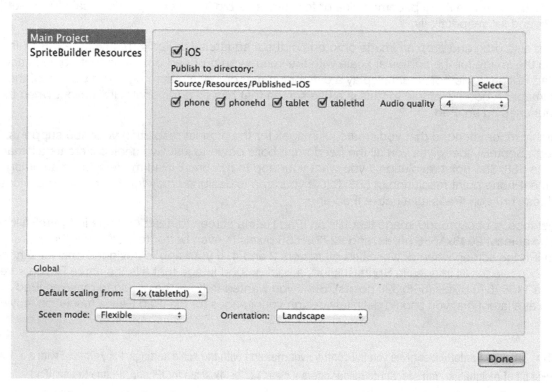

Figure 3-9. Project Settings dialog

If your app shouldn't run natively on iPad devices, or you want the iPad version to show a proportionally larger portion of the game world, you can change the "Default scaling from:" setting to 2x (phonehd). Note that changes to the default scaling are not applied to existing images, only to new images added to SpriteBuilder henceforth. For our project, leave this setting at 4x (tablethd).

> **Caution**   Apple requires app developers to support Retina resolutions. Apps have reportedly been rejected for looking "blurry" because they weren't using Retina-sized images on Retina devices, although Apple seems to be less strict when it comes to games. Still, I strongly advise against using the *Scale from* setting 1x for any image, because it will have noticeably low quality on iPad Retina devices. The only exception is if you are designing a pixel-art game.

When you later find your app download size has increased too much, consider unchecking one or more of the publishing target check boxes labeled phone, phonehd, tablet, or tablethd as needed to reduce the size of the bundle. Here's a quick overview of which iOS device will load resources from which category:

- ▪ *phone*: Used only by iPhone 3GS

- ▪ *phonehd*: Used by iPhone 4 and newer iPhones

- ▪ *tablet*: Used by non-Retina iPads: iPad 1 and 2, iPad mini first generation

- ▪ *tablethd*: Used by iPad third and iPad mini second generation and newer iPads

If your minimum deployment target is iOS 7 or newer, definitely uncheck phone. There is no non-Retina iPhone device supported by Cocos2D other than the iPhone 3GS, and the 3GS' highest supported operating system is iOS 6. If your app is for iPads only, uncheck both the phone and phonehd check boxes. Likewise, if your app is for iPhone only, you should uncheck the tablet and tablethd check boxes. Unchecking unneeded publish targets can significantly reduce your app's download size.

> **Note** SpriteBuilder apps will not run on the original iPhone and the iPhone 3G as well as corresponding iPod touch models (first and second generation, and third generation with 8-GB flash memory).

As for the other options, leave them as is for the book's project, I'll quickly go over the more elusive options:

- ▪ *Audio quality*: This affects the size and quality of published audio files. The effect on app size varies depending on the audio files. Quality level 1 creates the smallest files but also low quality audio.

- ▪ The *Screen mode* setting if changed to Fixed disables SpriteBuilder's scaling to adapt CCBs to the device resolution. It's main use case is when your game is iPhone-only and you want to treat the 3.5-inch and 4-inch iPhones as essentially the same devices, with the widescreen iPhones being slightly (88 points) wider. In that case, it may be a little easier to use fixed mode, but it's generally not recommended because it makes screen layouts more difficult.

- ▪ Last, the *Orientation* setting should be self-explanatory. Change it when your game is supposed to run in portrait mode. The book's project uses landscape orientation.

Adding Additional Background Layers

Back to parallaxing layers. You obviously need more than one layer to get the desired depth effect. Moreover, it's not a good idea to compose each parallax layer out of a single image like the Cerberus sprite. The closer a layer appears to the viewer, the larger its size needs to be. It would be wasteful for texture memory usage, and there comes a point where textures simply won't work anymore: a texture can be at most 4096x4096 pixels. This is a hardware limitation.

Instead, you should compose such large layers out of multiple individual nodes, sprites mostly. In order to scroll multiple sprites at once, you need to add them to the same layer, where "layer" refers to a regular node acting as a container for these sprites.

> **Note**   If you've used Cocos2D before, you may be thinking "CCLayer" whenever I say "layer." But there is no special Layer node anymore. The CCLayer class itself was never more than just a plain CCNode with the added capability of handling user input. Now the user input functionality is in the CCResponder class, which all node classes inherit, including CCNode. That means you simply use a CCNode whenever you used to use a CCLayer.

Drag and drop three additional Node instances from the Node Library onto the stage. You may want to rename these nodes in the Timeline View (double-click a node to edit its name) like in Figure 3-10.

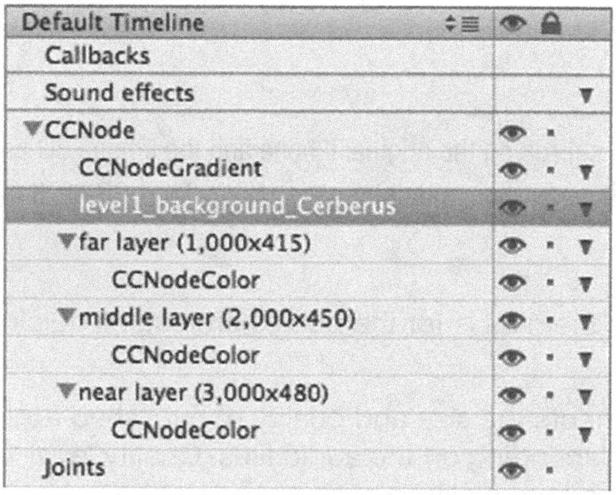

Default Timeline	⇕≡	👁 🔒
Callbacks		
Sound effects		▼
▼CCNode		👁 ▪
CCNodeGradient		👁 ▪ ▼
level1_background_Cerberus		👁 ▪ ▼
▼far layer (1,000x415)		👁 ▪ ▼
CCNodeColor		👁 ▪ ▼
▼middle layer (2,000x450)		👁 ▪ ▼
CCNodeColor		👁 ▪ ▼
▼near layer (3,000x480)		👁 ▪ ▼
CCNodeColor		👁 ▪ ▼
Joints		👁 ▪

Figure 3-10. The initial layer nodes in Background1.ccb

Now select each of these three nodes, and make sure their position is set to 0, 0. Since the goal is to derive the parallax scrolling factor based on each parallax layer's size, change each node's "Content size" property to a value that's greater than or equal to 568x384 but smaller than or equal to the level's size (4000x500 points). Each node's "Content size" should be larger than the one above it in the Timeline. If that was too confusing, just copy the content size values in Figure 3-10, where I set the layer sizes to 1000x415, 2000x450, and 3000x480, respectively.

> **Tip**   You could also create a CCB file of type Node and use those as parallax layers. I added them to the same CCB because it's mainly static content that is not being re-used for other backgrounds, and it makes it easier to see each layer's relative size.

When you select each layer node, its selection rectangle will show you the size of the background layer. Nodes added to a layer must be within this area to be seen in the game. However, the selection rectangle goes away as soon as you select another node. To permanently see the layer's size visually while adding nodes to it, you should drag and drop a color node onto each layer node in the Timeline. Each color node should be a child of one layer node. If, after dropping, the color node didn't become a layer's child, simply drag it in the Timeline View and drop it onto a layer node. The result should look like that shown in Figure 3-10.

Perform the following steps for each color node in sequence:

1. Set the Content size type to % .. *in percent of parent container* for both width and height.

2. Set the Content size width and height to 100% to expand the color node to its parent layer's size.

3. Set the color node's Opacity property to a low value like 0.1 to better see the nodes of other layers behind it.

4. Change the color property to a color of your choice.

Figure 3-11 shows the Item Properties of one color node; its properties are representative of all three color nodes.

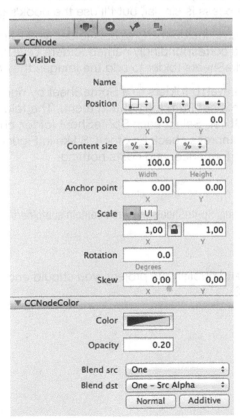

Figure 3-11. Properties of color nodes visually highlighting each layer's size

When you've made these changes to all three color node instances, the result will look like a multicolored, multilayered image like in Figure 3-12.

Figure 3-12. Background layers highlighted with color nodes

The color nodes will be a permanent visual size indicator for each layer. By unchecking their Visible check box (see Figure 3-11), you can later hide these helper nodes in both SpriteBuilder and in the app. You can leave these color nodes in the CCB because their memory consumption is negligible, and invisible nodes don't impact rendering performance either.

Adding SpriteSheets for Background Graphics

At this point, you should add the background images provided with the book. You can also add your own background images. The process is similar, but I'll use the book's graphics as an example.

In the book's downloadable archive, inside the Graphics folder, you'll find PNG image files whose names begin with level1_ inside correspondingly named folders Level1a and Level1b. Drag and drop these folders onto the SpriteSheets folder to add the images they contain to the project.

Then change both Level1a and Level1b folders to a SpriteSheet by right-clicking one after the other and selecting *Make Smart SpriteSheet* from the context menu. The folder will turn pink with a smiling icon, just like the Global SpriteSheet. Select each SpriteSheet folder, change the export format to PVR RGBA8888, and select the Compress check box for iOS like in Figure 2-25 in Chapter 2. Doing this saves memory, improves performance, and costs nothing.

Caution   At the time of this writing, SpriteSheets must not contain subfolders.

After you make these changes and publish the project, you should end up with a File View and preview as shown in Figure 3-13.

Figure 3-13. SpriteSheets with Level1 graphics

Note   The reason why there are two SpriteSheets is because the images are too large to fit in a single SpriteSheet. A SpriteSheet's dimensions for `tablethd` scaled images must not exceed the texture size limit of 4096x4096 pixels.

Designing the Background Layers

You can now add these images as sprites to the layers in Background1.ccb. You can just drag the images from the SpriteSheets or from the Tileless Editor View onto the stage.

> **Tip**   I recommend placing a copy of each image in the desired layer first, optionally renaming them in the Timeline, and editing any shared properties such as Opacity or Scale. Then you can select one of these template sprites and use copy and paste to add more sprites of the same type using the same name. The advantage of this workflow is that copies of a node automatically share the same parent; they will be siblings. That spares you the trouble of accidentally adding images to the root node or the wrong layer. Plus, they're easily identifiable because each copy takes over the source sprite's name.

I can't possibly describe how to precisely arrange these images—feel free to be creative. Should you not have any images available, you can simply use Color Node and Gradient Node instances as placeholders for real images. The resulting timeline might resemble the one in Figure 3-14.

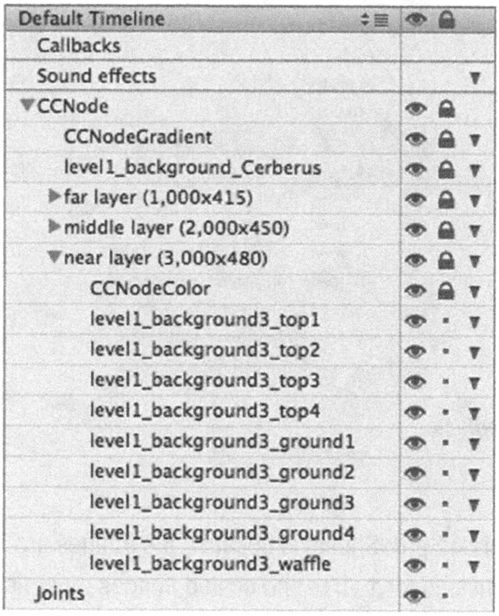

Default Timeline		
Callbacks		
Sound effects		▼
▼CCNode	👁 🔒	
CCNodeGradient	👁 🔒 ▼	
level1_background_Cerberus	👁 🔒 ▼	
▶ far layer (1,000x415)	👁 🔒 ▼	
▶ middle layer (2,000x450)	👁 🔒 ▼	
▼ near layer (3,000x480)	👁 🔒 ▼	
CCNodeColor	👁 🔒 ▼	
level1_background3_top1	👁 · ▼	
level1_background3_top2	👁 · ▼	
level1_background3_top3	👁 · ▼	
level1_background3_top4	👁 · ▼	
level1_background3_ground1	👁 · ▼	
level1_background3_ground2	👁 · ▼	
level1_background3_ground3	👁 · ▼	
level1_background3_ground4	👁 · ▼	
level1_background3_waffle	👁 · ▼	
Joints	👁 ·	

Figure 3-14. Timeline of the Background1.ccb parallax layers with sprites

> **Tip**   To avoid accidentally moving or otherwise editing a layer and the nodes it contains, you can click in the Lock column in the Timeline so that a Lock symbol appears to the right of the node's name. When the lock is active, all of the node's properties will not be editable, all Item Properties fields are grayed out, and the same applies to the locked node's children.
>
> To further ease editing, click on the eye column just left of the lock column to hide a node and its children. Contrary to a node's Visible property check box on the Item Properties pane, the eye column can be used to hide nodes within SpriteBuilder. When you publish and run the app, nodes without the eye symbol will still be visible in the app.

Whether you use your own images, the one's provided with the book, or just color nodes, keep this in mind: it's important to add a couple visible nodes to each layer and position them so that they are at least partially inside each layer's extents, as visualized by the color nodes you've added in the previous step. Otherwise, you won't be able to enjoy the parallaxing effect.

The result of your background layer editing operation might resemble something like what's shown in Figure 3-15.

Figure 3-15. Background1.ccb contents after adding graphics to parallax layers

Before you get to program the parallax scrolling, open Level1.ccb in SpriteBuilder.

At this point, you should remove any extraneous nodes from Level1.ccb that you may have added while testing scrolling. Also, remove the original background gradient node since that's now part of the Background1.ccb. To delete a node, select it and use Edit ➤ Delete or press Backspace. You should end up with an empty stage with just the player node on it. If you accidentally removed the player, just drag and drop it from the Tileless Editor View onto the stage once more.

Switch to the Tileless Editor View. In the list should be a section labeled *Parallax*, which contains a preview image of Background1.ccb. For brevity, I've unchecked all the Filter folders currently not needed in Figure 3-16.

Figure 3-16. *Tileless Editor View shows a preview image of Background1.CCB*

Now you can drag and drop the Background1 from the Tileless Editor View onto the Level1 stage to create a Sub File node referencing Background1.ccb. Then change its position to 0,0 to align it perfectly with the stage borders. Make sure you set its Name property to "background" because you'll soon add code to get a reference to the node by this name. The Name property is on the Item Properties tab in the Details Inspector. Changing the node's name in the Timeline will *not* make it accessible by name via code.

Oh, hey! The player's gone. Hmmm...it's probably behind the background now.

Select the player node in the Timeline, and drag and drop it so that it is below the background node in the Timeline hierarchy. Make sure it doesn't become a child of the background; it should be on the same level as the background. Figure 3-17 is what the Level1 Timeline should resemble now, with the background node above the player node.

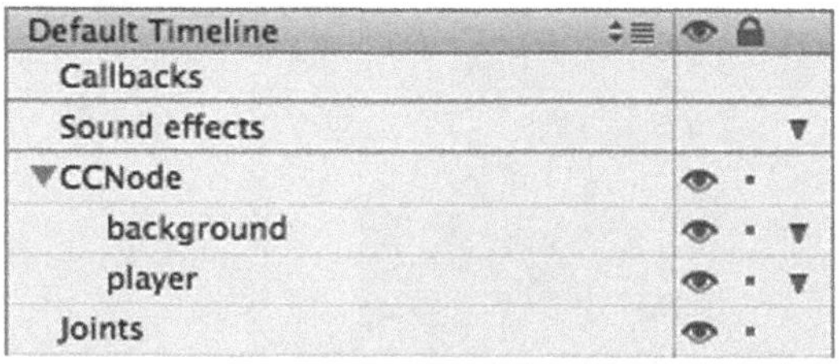

Default Timeline			
Callbacks			
Sound effects			▼
▼CCNode		👁	•
background		👁	• ▼
player		👁	• ▼
Joints		👁	•

Figure 3-17. *Timeline of Level1.ccb at the current stage*

You can publish, build, and run now to check out the new background. Notice that there's no parallaxing effect yet, and as you move from left to right the background layers seem to disappear one by one.

> **Caution**   If you notice the game running slowly in the iOS Simulator at this point, there's no need to worry. The iOS Simulator is terribly slow when it comes to rendering graphics—it's a software renderer that doesn't use your Mac's powerful graphics hardware at all! Apple chose to sacrifice performance in order to have the iOS Simulator's output match exactly what you would see on a device. If you want to verify performance of an app **always** test by running the app on a device.
>
> The same goes for memory usage—the iOS Simulator can take advantages of all the free memory available on your Mac, so it's very unlikely to run into low memory situations in the iOS Simulator. On the other hand, iOS devices have at most 1 GB of RAM, of which only a fraction is available to apps. The earlier and more often you start testing on an actual device, the better.
>
> While I'm at it, know that the iPhone 4's performance is significantly behind all other devices, including its iPhone 3GS predecessor. The iPhone 4 has to render four times as many pixels due to its Retina screen, yet its technical specs clock it in at just about 33% faster CPU and GPU compared to the iPhone 3GS.

Prepare to Parallax in 3, 2, 1...

To get the background layers to parallax requires some setup steps. The very first thing to do is introduce a physics node into the equation, and then change the player node to become a child node of the physics node. From then on, the physics node will be the level's content container rather than the Level1.ccb itself.

> **Note**   I'll explain the use of the physics node in the next chapter. Technically, you could use any other node type for the time being, but you'll need a physics node in the next chapter. Because replacing a node with one of a different type isn't currently possible in SpriteBuilder, it makes sense to use the physics node right away.

The main reason for adding the player (and other game objects) as the child of another node is to be able to move the level contents independently from the parallaxing background. If you were to continue using the Level1.ccb root node as the player's parent node, the changes made to the player's parent position would offset all of the Level1.ccb child nodes, including the background. That would make the background scrolling code more complicated and harder to understand, and it would be difficult to add stationary nodes, such as the in-game pause button to the level.

From the Node Library View, drag and drop a physics node onto the Level1.ccb stage. Set its position to 0,0, and change its Name property to "physics" (that's for the next chapter). In the Timeline view, drag and drop the player node so that it becomes a child of the CCPhysicsNode as in Figure 3-18 by dropping it exactly on the CCPhysicsNode.

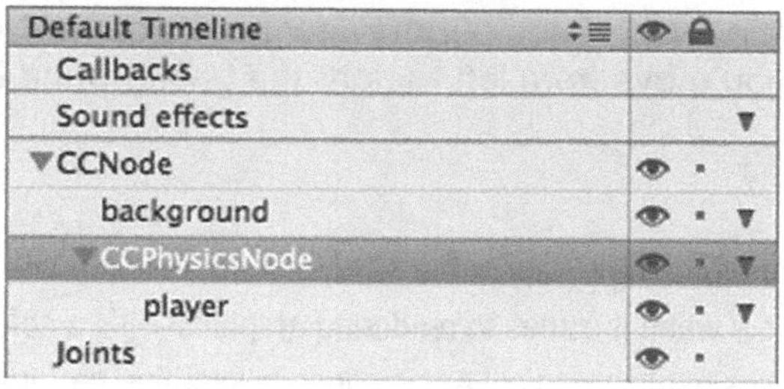

Figure 3-18. The player node is now a child of a CCPhysicsNode

> **Note**   You may have noticed that you can't drag and drop the player node onto the background node. This is because the background node is a Sub File (CCBFile) node, which does not accept child nodes. There are other nodes that can't have child nodes: Particle System, Label TTF, Label BM-Font, Button, Text Field, Slider, and Scroll View. This limitation is imposed on nodes that create or manage their branch of the node hierarchy. For instance, a button actually contains a sprite and a label node as children, while Scroll View and Sub File nodes "inherit" the nodes of a CCB file, even though these nodes aren't shown in the Timeline.

You'll now need to assign the `CCPhysicsNode` reference to the `_physicsNode` ivar in order to make the scrolling code work with the newly introduced physics node. Because `getChildByName:` returns a reference to a `CCNode` class, you have to cast the returned node if it is of another class. Add this code at the top of the `loadLevelNamed:` method in `GameScene.m`:

```
_physicsNode = (CCPhysicsNode*)[self getChildByName:@"physics" recursively:YES];
```

Note that casting an object reference to another class like this never generates a compile error. That doesn't mean it's always correct, however. At runtime, if the particular object is cast to a class of which the object isn't a member of, sending messages to this object is prone to crashing with "unrecognized selector sent to instance" or other errors. Only use casts when you are absolutely sure that an object is of a given class. If you can't be sure of this at compile time, it is customary to verify the class membership with the `isKindOfClass:` method before performing the cast, as in the following code:

```
CCNode* node = [self getChildByName:@"physics" recursively:YES];
if ([node isKindeOfClass:[CCPhysicsNode class]])
{
    _physicsNode = (CCPhysicsNode*)node;
}
```

While you're at it, add the following line to assign the `_backgroundNode` reference, also in the `loadLevelNamed:` method:

```
backgroundNode = [self getChildByName:@"background" recursively:YES];
```

To summarize, your `loadLevelNamed:` method should be like the one in Listing 3-9, excluding any comments and error-checking code.

Listing 3-9. Assigning physics, background, and player node in loadLevelNamed

```
-(void) loadLevelNamed:(NSString*)levelCCB
{
    _physicsNode = (CCPhysicsNode*)[self getChildByName:@"physics" recursively:YES];
    _backgroundNode = [self getChildByName:@"background" recursively:YES];
    _playerNode = [self getChildByName:@"player" recursively:YES];
}
```

You can optionally add statements like `NSAssert(_physicsNode);` to verify that these nodes were indeed found and assigned. If they aren't found and `nil` is returned, you either forgot to add them to the level or you named them incorrectly. Both issues are a common source of (human) error when working with SpriteBuilder, so it makes sense to verify references using `NSAssert`.

> **Tip**   If you want to learn more about assertions, breakpoints, and resolving issues in general, please refer to the debugging chapter at the end of the book. Learning to debug issues properly is absolutely worth investing the time in because it'll quickly pay back in improved productivity, which is much better than banging your head for days over a seemingly inexplicable issue. I'll shut up about it until then, I promise, but please do yourself the favor and check it out.

Looking at Listing 3-9, it seems rather unnecessary to search through the entire node hierarchy starting with `self` when you know that the background and physics nodes are children of the _levelNode, and the player is a child of the physics node. A slightly better (but entirely optional) version of the preceding code is shown in Listing 3-10.

Listing 3-10. This version of loadLevelNamed: avoids searching recursively where it isn't necessary

```
-(void) loadLevelNamed:(NSString*)levelCCB
{
    _physicsNode = (CCPhysicsNode*)[_levelNode getChildByName:@"physics" recursively:NO];
    _backgroundNode = [_levelNode getChildByName:@"background" recursively:NO];
    _playerNode = [_physicsNode getChildByName:@"player" recursively:YES];
}
```

Note that in Listing 3-10 it is crucial to get the reference to the _physicsNode first because it's being used to search for the player, so it must be assigned by that point. The version in Listing 3-10 also doesn't use a recursive search for the _physicsNode and _backgroundNode because they should always be direct children of the _levelNode.

Now in the `scrollToTarget:` method, you need to locate the last line:

```
_levelNode.positionInPoints = ccpNeg(viewPos);
```

Replace it with the line in Listing 3-11 in order to reroute the position updates from the _levelNode to the _physicsNode.

Listing 3-11. Replace _levelNode with _physicsNode in scrollToTarget

```
_physicsNode.positionInPoints = ccpNeg(viewPos);
```

This will decouple the _backgroundNode position so that it can be updated independently from the _physicsNode position, whereas the _levelNode position will now remain fixed at 0,0. If you publish, build, and run now, you will notice that the background layers stay fixed.

To visualize the current layout, look at Figure 3-19. This is the node hierarchy as returned by a call to [CCBReader loadAsScene:@"GameScene"]. In brackets are the CCB files where the content of certain nodes originates from. Note that GameScene, despite its name, is a regular CCNode subclass and not a subclass of CCScene.

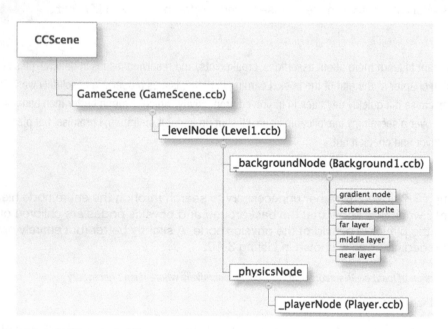

Figure 3-19. The game's node hierarchy in its current state

> **Tip**   You can dump the entire node hierarchy in its current state to the console by writing
> `[self walkSceneGraph:0]` anywhere in your code. This can be useful if you suspect a node may not be in the correct location in the node hierarchy. Also note that *scene graph* can be used synonymously with *node hierarchy*.

Before you get the background layers to scroll again, let's recap the code from the `scrollToTarget:` method. Listing 3-12 includes the change made in Listing 3-11.

Listing 3-12. Version of scrollToTarget: that assigns position to _physicsNode

```
-(void) scrollToTarget:(CCNode*)target
{
    CGSize viewSize = [CCDirector sharedDirector].viewSize;
    CGPoint viewCenter = CGPointMake(viewSize.width / 2.0, viewSize.height / 2.0);

    CGPoint viewPos = ccpSub(target.positionInPoints, viewCenter);

    CGSize levelSize = _levelNode.contentSizeInPoints;
    viewPos.x = MAX(0.0, MIN(viewPos.x, levelSize.width - viewSize.width));
    viewPos.y = MAX(0.0, MIN(viewPos.y, levelSize.height - viewSize.height));

    _physicsNode.positionInPoints = ccpNeg(viewPos);

    // Parallax scrolling code will be added here ...
}
```

The preceding code does the following:

- Assigns `viewPos` the `target.positionInPoints` offset by `viewCenter`
- Clamps `viewPos` so that scrolling stops at level borders inset by `viewCenter`
- Assigns negated `viewPos` to the `_physicsNode`

Somehow you'll have to derive a parallax position for each of the background layers every time the `_physicsNode`'s position has been updated.

The inset part is most important part to understand to comprehend the following parallax scrolling code. Since you want each layer's position to be relative to the position of the `_physicsNode` (aka `viewPos` in this method), it's crucial to consider that `viewPos` (the center of the view) should keep a distance from the level's borders. This minimum distance must be at least `viewCenter.width` in the horizontal direction and `viewCenter.height` in the vertical direction, to prevent the viewable area from showing the outside of the level borders (ie empty space).

Figure 3-3 helps to understand this if you imagine that viewPos is at the center of each Viewable Area. The actual Scrollable Area rectangle (ie allowed positions for viewPos) must be larger than the left and bottom of the Level Area, and smaller than the top and right side of the Level Area. This smaller sized Scrollable Area rectangle is said to be an inset of the larger Level Area rectangle.

Therefore, the relative position of each background layer can't be relative to the full extents of the level's size, which is 4000 by 500 points. Instead, only the scrollable area must be considered when calculating the parallax factor. If you're having trouble imagining this, have another look at the diagram in Figure 3-3.

Here's an example: On an iPhone 5, `viewCenter` would be 284x160. Therefore, the scrollable area ranges from the following:

```
284x160 to 4000 - 284 x 500 - 160 = 3716x340 points
```

In other words, the scrollable area is the size of the level minus the size of the view. Hence, dividing the `viewPos` by the scrollable area (`levelSize` minus `viewSize`) gives you the percentage of where the `_physicsNode` position within the scrollable area currently is:

```
CGPoint viewPosPercent = CGPointMake(viewPos.x / (levelSize.width - viewSize.width),
                                     viewPos.y / (levelSize.height - viewSize.height));
```

You now have the `_physicsNode`'s position in a range of 0.0 to 1.0, where *0,0* refers to the lower-left scrollable area position of 284x160 and *1,1* refers to the top-right position 3716x340. Next you have to apply this percentage to every layer, taking into account the layer's own size.

Try to do the calculation in Listing 3-13 in your head or on paper once, using 568x384 as the `layerSize` width and height and 568x320 as the `viewSize` width and height and tell me what values you get for `layerPos` when viewPosPercent is 0.5, 0.5.

Listing 3-13. Calculating the layer's position relative to viewPosPercent

```
for (CCNode* layer in _backgroundNode.children)
{
    CGSize layerSize = layer.contentSizeInPoints;
    CGPoint layerPos = CGPointMake(viewPosPercent.x * (layerSize.width - viewSize.width),
                                   viewPosPercent.y * (layerSize.height - viewSize.height));
}
```

If neither you nor I made a mistake, you should have noticed that where `layerSize` and `viewSize` are the same, the result is 0. And 0 multiplied by whatever remains 0. Thus, on the x axis you get 0 as `layerPos.x`, while `layerPos.y` is calculated to be the following:

```
0.5 * (384 - 320) = 32 points
```

In English: this layer can move vertically within a range of 64 points and its Y position is currently offset by 32 points.

After the `layerPos` has been calculated, it is negated just like `viewPos` and assigned to the layer:

```
layer.positionInPoints = ccpNeg(layerPos);
```

Be sure to use `positionInPoints` so that the position is properly converted from points to other position types, if needed. To put everything in context, Listing 3-14 shows the updated `scrollToTarget:` method again in full.

Listing 3-14. Scrolling with parallaxing layers

```
-(void) scrollToTarget:(CCNode*)target
{
    CGSize viewSize = [CCDirector sharedDirector].viewSize;
    CGPoint viewCenter = CGPointMake(viewSize.width / 2.0, viewSize.height / 2.0);

    CGPoint viewPos = ccpSub(target.positionInPoints, viewCenter);

    CGSize levelSize = _levelNode.contentSizeInPoints;
    viewPos.x = MAX(0.0, MIN(viewPos.x, levelSize.width - viewSize.width));
    viewPos.y = MAX(0.0, MIN(viewPos.y, levelSize.height - viewSize.height));

    _physicsNode.positionInPoints = ccpNeg(viewPos);

    CGPoint viewPosPercent = CGPointMake(viewPos.x / (levelSize.width - viewSize.width),
                                         viewPos.y / (levelSize.height - viewSize.height));

    for (CCNode* layer in _backgroundNode.children)
    {
        CGSize layerSize = layer.contentSizeInPoints;
        CGPoint layerPos = CGPointMake(viewPosPercent.x * (layerSize.width - viewSize.width),
                                       viewPosPercent.y * (layerSize.height - viewSize.height));
        layer.positionInPoints = ccpNeg(layerPos);
    }
}
```

One last thing, remember how you used the _levelNode in the touchBegan:withEvent: method to convert the touch location relative to the _levelNode? You'll have to replace this use of _levelNode with _physicsNode as well, as seen in the code fragment in Listing 3-15.

Listing 3-15. Replace _levelNode with _physicsNode in touchBegan:withEvent

```
CGPoint pos = [touch locationInNode:_physicsNode];
```

If you were to keep using the _levelNode, you would notice that you're prevented from scrolling further than approximately half a screen size. That's because the _levelNode no longer changes its position during scrolling, with the _physicsNode having taken its place.

Publish, build, and run. You can now see the background layers parallaxing like in Figure 3-20.

Figure 3-20. Player moving toward the right and up shows the effect of parallaxing background layers

Summary

In this chapter, you learned how to control the player with touches and actions, and how to scroll the level contents and background layers as the player moves about the level. You also learned a lot about images, SpriteSheets and the settings related to image conversion and publishing.

The current state of the project can be found in the *03 - Parallax Scrolling* folder.

In the next chapter, you'll learn more about CCPhysicsNode and how to create impenetrable level borders to keep the player from falling outside the level.

Chapter 4

Physics & Collisions

In this chapter, you'll learn more about editing physics properties with SpriteBuilder and how to control the player through physics rather than actions. You'll add impenetrable physics bodies as level borders to prevent the player character from moving outside the level boundaries.

You'll also learn about how to run code when a collision occurs—in this case, to trigger game events like ending the current level—and how to set up collision categories and masks to allow certain physics bodies to pass through each other.

Player Physics

In the previous chapter, you already added a Physics node to the Level1.ccb and made the player node a child of the newly introduced Physics node. This instance of CCPhysicsNode acts as the physics world that controls global physics behaviors—most of all, gravity. Any node that should move and interact like a physics object must be a child or grandchild of a CCPhysicsNode.

Let's give this a try right away and enable physics for the player.

Enabling Physics for the Player Sprite

First try this: open Level1.ccb, select the player, and try to switch to the Item Physics tab—the third tab in the Details Inspector on the right. You'll notice it's grayed out—it can't be selected. This is always the case for Sub File nodes: they do not support physics.

Instead, open the Player.ccb in the Prefabs folder and select the CCSprite root node. Now you can switch to the Item Physics tab and select the Enable Physics check box. Behind the scenes, when the CCB is being loaded, the CCBReader will create an instance of the CCPhysicsBody class and assign it to the node's physicsBody property. When discussing nodes with physics, I will use the term "body" synonymously for "node," primarily when the context refers to the physics properties and behavior of the node.

While you're on the Item Physics tab for the player, change the Physics shape to a circle and give it a Corner radius of 32 points. Leave the other settings as they were, in particular the Dynamic setting should be selected. The settings should be the same as in Figure 4-1.

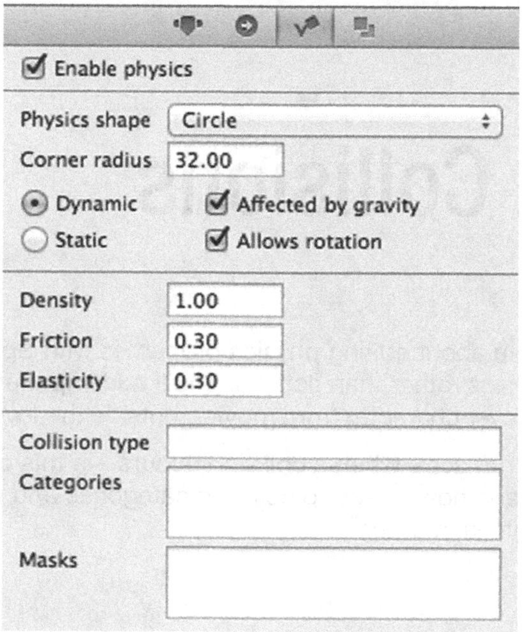

Figure 4-1. The player sprite's physics settings

Now you can have some fun: publish, build, and run the app. You'll notice the player immediately starts falling due to physics-imposed gravity. Nevertheless, you can also tap the screen to make the player move to that location. But you can't prevent the player from continuously falling down ever faster. What's going on here?

Move and Rotate Actions Conflict with Physics

Internally, gravity accumulates and increases the body's velocity even while the node is being moved by the move action. Eventually, the move action stops and physics takes over again.

This is a side-effect of combining actions with physics. More precisely, actions affecting a node's position or rotation properties should not be used on dynamic bodies. They override the physics properties for position and rotation, while ignoring the body's velocity, at least temporarily.

In some cases, move and rotate actions seem to move but the resulting collision behavior won't be what you'd expect, because the movement imposed by the action is not reflected by the node's internal state or conflicts with it. For instance, a move action won't stop because there's a collision in the way; instead, it'll continue to move the node through the collision step by step and the physics engine will try its best to resolve the situation every frame, causing all sorts of issues.

Moving a physics-enabled node, therefore, should be done exclusively by applying forces to the node, or by using joints. An exception to this rule are static bodies. Those you can actually animate using move and rotate actions—and even the SpriteBuilder Timeline—and they'll show correct physics behavior. I'll say more on this topic in chapter 5: *Timelines and Triggers*.

There are also purely visual or functional actions like tinting the node's color or running a block. Those actions can still be used on a node with a physics body indiscriminately.

> **Note**   If you are curious as to why move and rotate actions cannot be combined with physics, consider a leaf blowing in the wind. Normally, a light object such as a leaf will stop when it hits any other object. The leaf has a low mass, so it will not exert noticeable force on colliding bodies. However, if you told the leaf to move on a straight line from A to B with a move action, this would keep it going into and over heavier or impenetrable objects. What should the correct physics behavior be in this case?
>
> Should the leaf eventually topple over the wall it hits? Should it be allowed to penetrate objects to get to the intended location? Or should it stop at the wall but stick to it because it tries to keep going to its destination until it arrives there? Or until the action ends, which means the leaf may never reach its destination?
>
> There is not one right way to solve this. In fact, all of the possible workarounds are wrong. Some just seem more correct than others when considering only a narrow set of conditions or a specific set of expectations, but there is no generally acceptable solution.

Moving the Player Through Physics

Because a physics-enabled node with a dynamic physicsBody should not run any move, rotate, scale, or skew actions, you need to replace the move action with proper physics movement.

The touch events need to change from executing a move action as soon as a touch begins to merely changing a flag. If this flag is set, it will cause a function called from the update: method to accelerate the player in a given direction.

In GameScene.m, add the following four ivars within the @implementation brackets, as seen in Listing 4-1.

Listing 4-1. Additional ivars needed for physics movement

```
@implementation GameScene
{
    __weak CCNode* _levelNode;
    __weak CCPhysicsNode* _physicsNode;
    __weak CCNode* _playerNode;
    __weak CCNode* _backgroundNode;

    CGFloat _playerNudgeRightVelocity;
    CGFloat _playerNudgeUpVelocity;
    CGFloat _playerMaxVelocity;
    BOOL _acceleratePlayer;
}
```

Now locate the touchBegan:withEvent: method and replace its body with the following:

```
-(void) touchBegan:(UITouch *)touch withEvent:(UIEvent *)event
{
    _acceleratePlayer = YES;
}
```

This enables the "user is currently touching the screen" mode.

Of course, you also need to end this mode. To do so, you have to add the touchesEnded: and touchesCancelled: methods as seen in Listing 4-2.

Listing 4-2. Stopping acceleration when there's no active touch

```
-(void) touchEnded:(UITouch *)touch withEvent:(UIEvent *)event
{
    _acceleratePlayer = NO;
}

-(void) touchCancelled:(UITouch *)touch withEvent:(UIEvent *)event
{
    [self touchEnded:touch withEvent:event];
}
```

The cancelled variant is sent rarely—for instance, when a gesture recognizer recognizes a touch pattern. But when it does get called, it's important that it behaves the same as touchEnded: or else the player will be stuck in the acceleration mode even though the user may not have a finger on the screen.

Tip   Instead of replicating the functionality of touchEnded: in touchCancelled: I just forward the message. In this case, it's a one-liner either way, but generally it's good practice to avoid writing the same code more than once. It's called the *DRY principle*: Don't Repeat Yourself. It's single-handedly the most important programming principle, even more important than premature optimization, which is the root of all evil, in case you didn't know. Premature optimization can be paraphrased as follows: Make it work—make it right—make it fast. In that order. But I'm digressing. If you want to conduct an exercise, do a web search for these phrases and read some of the top articles.

Now the update: method also needs to be amended by calling the accelerateTarget: method as long as the _acceleratePlayer ivar is YES. This is shown in Listing 4-3.

Listing 4-3. Accelerate the player node as needed

```
-(void) update:(CCTime)delta
{
    if (_acceleratePlayer)
    {
        [self accelerateTarget:_playerNode];
    }

    [self scrollToTarget:_playerNode];
}
```

Here, it is important to accelerate the player before scrolling because scrolling needs the player's updated position. If you did it the other way, it would still work in general, but the scrolling would lag one frame behind the player's actual position. This would have the view follow the player with a minimal but possibly noticeable delay, as if it were dragging behind the player's position.

Also notice that both methods take the _playerNode as an input parameter, rather than just relying on the _playerNode ivar being accessible within the method. The exercise here is to make methods as flexible as possible at no extra cost. Consider that you may want to accelerate a second player node the same way. You'd just call accelerateTarget: twice with different nodes. Or what if your player has exited the level but the camera should still continue to scroll to a predefined location in the level? You'd change the parameter sent to the scrollToTarget: method from the _playerNode to a node that is at or moving to the desired destination position.

Accelerating the Player

Now add the code in Listing 4-4 just below the update: method. The accelerateTarget: method will move the player sprite by changing the velocity of its physicsBody component.

Listing 4-4. Moving a target node by changing its velocity

```
-(void) accelerateTarget:(CCNode*)target
{
    // Temporary variables
    _playerMaxVelocity = 350.0;
    _playerNudgeRightVelocity = 30.0;
    _playerNudgeUpVelocity = 80.0;

    CCPhysicsBody* physicsBody = target.physicsBody;

    if (physicsBody.velocity.x < 0.0)
    {
        physicsBody.velocity = CGPointMake(0.0, physicsBody.velocity.y);
    }

    [physicsBody applyImpulse:CGPointMake(_playerNudgeRightVelocity,
                                          _playerNudgeUpVelocity)];
```

```
    if (ccpLength(physicsBody.velocity) > _playerMaxVelocity)
    {
        CGPoint direction = ccpNormalize(physicsBody.velocity);
        physicsBody.velocity = ccpMult(direction, _playerMaxVelocity);
    }
}
```

The variables prefixed with _player are assigned some values at the top. You will soon replace them with custom properties to make them editable right within SpriteBuilder. For now, these assignments just exist to make the code functional.

Let's dissect the core of the method:

```
CCPhysicsBody* physicsBody = target.physicsBody;
```

The target's CCPhysicsBody instance is stored in a local variable. This makes the code easier to read, shorter, and minimally faster compared to using target.physicsBody.velocity every time you need to read from or assign to velocity, for instance. The main benefit here is clearly readability; improved performance is only a very, very minor but nevertheless positive side-effect.

Since the game is all about moving from left to right, any already inherent "leftward" movement in a negative x axis direction is canceled when in movement mode by setting the x component of the physicsBody.velocity to 0:

```
if (physicsBody.velocity.x < 0.0)
{
    physicsBody.velocity = CGPointMake(0.0, physicsBody.velocity.y);
}
```

The node may very well be moving to the left—for instance, because external forces pushed it to the left or simply because it is rolling down a slope that's slanted toward the left. The user isn't always touching the screen, and while she isn't, the player's body is free to go wherever it wants to go. But once the user touches the screen, you don't want her having to tap for longer than usual just to cancel out a possible leftward-oriented velocity. At the same time, repeated or continued taps should be allowed to increase the horizontal speed toward the right.

> **Caution**   It's worth noting that the velocity is a CGPoint data type. CGPoint is a C struct, not an object reference (pointer). The same is true for CGSize and CGRect data types. This is why it is required to use CGPointMake rather than just assigning physicsBody.velocity.x = 0.0;. That code would generate a compile error: "Expression is not assignable." That's because a struct field like velocity.x isn't a property in the Objective-C sense—it has no property setter method.

The `applyImpulse:` method uses the previously defined nudge variables as the impulse vector. Internally, `applyImpulse:` updates the body's `velocity` by multiplying the impulse with the inverse of the body's mass:

```
[physicsBody applyImpulse:CGPointMake(_playerNudgeRightVelocity,
                                      _playerNudgeUpVelocity)];
```

You can think of an impulse to be like the impact of a billiard queue on the cue ball. You can do it gently, or you can do it with force. Essentially, an *impulse* is force applied at a specific point in time. The effect of an impulse depends solely on the body's mass—if you increase the body's mass, the same impulse will accelerate the body less than it did before.

If you want to apply an impulse that ignores the body's mass, you simply alter the `physicsBody.velocity` property directly.

A related concept to applying an impulse is applying a force. A *force* is an impulse applied continuously. Taking the previous billiard example, if hitting the cue ball is akin to applying a force, the cue ball would continue to accelerate over time. A force should be met with an opposing force such as friction or an on/off switch (for example, a rocket accelerates until it's out of fuel) to keep the physics simulation reasonably balanced. You don't often see things continue to accelerate past supersonic speeds in the real world. Unless you work in the aerospace industry, of course.

> **Note** In this example, the `CCPhysicsNode` (the player's parent node) has a default gravity force set in its properties. Default gravity will continue to accelerate the player downward, unless you combat the effect by applying an upward-oriented impulse.

Imposing a Speed Limit on the Player

The last block of code checks whether the `physicsBody.velocity` has exceeded a safe value, and if it has, changes the velocity to the maximum speed while preserving the direction:

```
if (ccpLength(physicsBody.velocity) > _playerMaxVelocity)
{
    CGPoint direction = ccpNormalize(physicsBody.velocity);
    physicsBody.velocity = ccpMult(direction, _playerMaxVelocity);
}
```

Normalizing the velocity turns it into a unit vector; a vector whose length is 1 but keeps pointing in the same direction as the original. Multiplying this vector by _playerMaxVelocity makes velocity's length equal to _playerMaxVelocity while still pointing in the same direction. This effectively prevents the speed from exceeding _playerMaxVelocity. Without this code fragment, the user could keep a finger on the screen to make the player accelerate indefinitely.

> **Tip**   The `ccpLength`, `ccpNormalize` and `ccpMult` C functions are all declared in the `CGPointExtension.h` file, alongside other 2D vector functions. To quickly access their declaration, right-click anywhere on a keyword in the Xcode editor and select "Jump to Definition" from the context menu. Try it now with whatever keywords, variables, properties, etc. you're interested in. You'll notice it doesn't just reveal the origins but also brings you to related code fragments and documentation comments. This is a great way to learn more about the code you're using.

By now, you may be wondering what unit velocity is. It's measured in points per second (pt/s). If you wanted to move a body from the left to the right side of a landscape iPad game in one second over a distance of 1024 points, the *x* velocity of that body would have to be, you guessed it, 1024.

Give this a shot now. Publish, build, and run the project. You can now move the player in a parabola curve. Up and down, up and down. Gravity keeps pulling the player down. Tapping the screen will move the player upward and to the right. You can move over the full extent of the level, but the player character can still leave the level's boundaries and vanish.

Expose Design Values as Custom Properties

Now, about those temporary variable assignments. Remove the four lines shown in Listing 4-5 from the `accelerateTarget:` method.

Listing 4-5.   These variable assignments are no longer needed

```
// Temporary variables
_playerMaxVelocity = 350.0;
_playerNudgeRightVelocity = 30.0;
_playerNudgeUpVelocity = 80.0;
```

> **Note**   Keep the ivars declared just below the @implementation of the GameScene—the ones shown in Listing 4-1. You'll still need those.

It's a good idea to make design parameters like the preceding one nudge and to make maximum velocities editable in SpriteBuilder. This is especially true if you plan on doing as little programming as possible, or if you want a nonprogramming person (sometimes referred to as *designer* or *artist*) to be able to modify design values.

To make custom properties editable in SpriteBuilder, go to SpriteBuilder and open the `GameScene.ccb`. Then select the root node in the Timeline. If you look at the `Item Properties` tab, you should see a horizontal divider that reads `GameScene` next to a downward-pointing triangle. That triangle, by the way, allows you to expand and collapse sections of properties, much like folders in Finder. Figure 4-2 shows the collapsed `CCNode` properties section above the `GameScene` section, where you'll find the goal of this exercise: the Edit Custom Properties button.

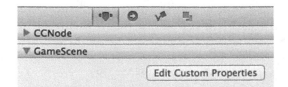

Figure 4-2. *The ominous Edit Custom Properties button*

Note The Edit Custom Properties button does not appear on every node. It is available only on nodes that have their Custom class field on the Item Code Connections tab set to a specific class name. Custom properties will be assigned to the custom class of a node. Without a custom class, there can't be custom properties.

If you click on the Edit Custom Properties button, a dialog will appear. It's empty at first, with no properties defined, but otherwise it looks the same as in Figure 4-3.

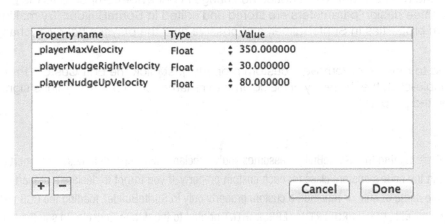

Figure 4-3. *The custom properties editing dialog with some properties defined*

By clicking on the + button, you can add properties that will be assigned to ivars or properties of the same name in the node's custom class. Since you are editing the properties of the GameScene.ccb root node whose custom class is set to GameScene, the variables entered here must be declared in the GameScene class. This part you already completed earlier in Listing 4-1.

Now you need to add three custom properties. Name them exactly like the three ivars in Listing 4-1 that start with _player. Change each property's type to Float, and give them the same values as in Figure 4-3 or Listing 4-3. Click Done and notice how SpriteBuilder has added these properties at the bottom of the Item Properties tab, as seen in Figure 4-4. You can now edit these properties like any other node property.

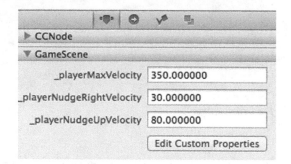

Figure 4-4. Custom properties are editable on the Item Properties tab

> **Note**   SpriteBuilder makes no distinction between properties and ivars. For SpriteBuilder, custom properties are all termed "properties" although, like in this example, they can be declared as ivars as well.

Publish, build, and run as usual. You'll notice no change in behavior compared to the previous run. But now these three design parameters are stored and edited in SpriteBuilder. Try making changes to these custom properties in SpriteBuilder, and observe how the player's behavior changes accordingly.

If you ever need to rename or remove a custom property, just click the Edit Custom Properties button and double-click the Property name column to rename, or click the – (minus sign) button to delete the selected property.

> **Caution**   Keep in mind that SpriteBuilder assumes you've declared corresponding ivars or properties of the same name in the node's custom class for each custom property. If you forgot to declare a property or ivar, misspelled the name of one, or renamed a custom property only in SpriteBuilder, loading the CCB will fail with errors beginning with *** [PROPERTY] ERROR HINT printed to the debug Console. To see the Console, go to View ➤ Debug Area ➤ Activate Console in Xcode.

Constructing the Level Physics

I think gravity is a bit on the low side. Feels too moon-ish, it should be more earth-like. Or just stronger. Newton would have rejoiced if he'd been able to change gravity as easily as in SpriteBuilder.

Then you'll create borders enclosing the level, preventing the player from leaving the playable area as well as funneling toward the exit.

Changing Gravity

To change gravity, open the Level1.ccb and select the physics node (if it was not renamed, it's listed as CCPhysicsNode) in the Timeline. On its Item Properties tab, there is a section labeled CCPhysicsNode that has the Gravity property, as seen in Figure 4-5. Change the gravity Y value from its default value of –100 to –200. The value is negative because the positive Y axis in Cocos2D extends upward, but gravity is a force pointing downward.

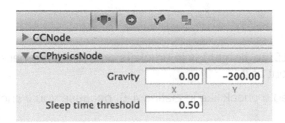

Figure 4-5. Increase CCPhysicsNode gravity to –200

Note that gravity is not a single value but a vector with x/y components. There's nothing stopping you from adding a little sideways gravity, although that would be rather unusual.

Once more, publish, build, and run. See how you like the new gravity. Feel free to go back to the GameScene.ccb root node and play around with the three _player values as well as gravity to get a feel for more or less extreme values. When you are done experimenting, you may want to revert the values to the values in Figure 4-4 and Figure 4-5, respectively. Otherwise, different values may introduce unpredictable behavior later in the book, or simply prevent you from completing the level.

You should leave the Sleep time threshold property as is. It determines how quickly physics bodies will go to sleep, a state where they rest without moving to reduce the load on the CPU. Sleeping bodies will awake when forces are applied to them, and a body must have very little velocity and angular momentum to start sleeping. This setting does not come into effect for bodies that leave the screen and continue to fall forever in a big empty void.

Interlude: Dealing with Lost Bodies

Cocos2D will never remove nodes automatically. Nodes not currently visible on screen are still part of the scene hierarchy; they remain in memory and perform actions though they will not be rendered.

If you were to program a game where nodes are created but never deleted as they move outside the playable area, eventually the game's frame rate is going to decrease over time. In such instances, you have to have code in place that checks periodically whether each node's position has crossed an imaginary boundary—for instance, in the update: method. If a node is determined to be outside the allowed boundary, that node is sent the removeFromParent message in order to remove it. An example is given in Listing 4-6.

Listing 4-6. Example for removing a node based on its Y coordinate

```
-(void) update:(CCTime)delta
{
    if (_playerNode.position.y < (-_playerNode.contentSize.height))
    {
        [_playerNode removeFromParent];
    }

    // more code here ...
}
```

The (-_playerNode.contentSize.height) is in brackets only for clarity because there's an easily overlooked minus sign in front of it.

In this project you don't need a check like in Listing 4-6, because you'll enclose the level with impenetrable walls.

Creating Static Level Borders

You may remember from earlier in this chapter that physics bodies have two modes: Dynamic and Static. Dynamic allows a body to move freely about the world, and it will react to impulses and forces, including gravity. For immovable physics bodies, you would instead choose the Static mode.

Bodies that are set to Static will never, ever change their position or rotation by themselves or through forces, no matter how hard other bodies impact it. You can still manually change a Static body's position and rotation, however. But for this exercise you just need some nonanimated, rigid walls.

Creating the Wall Templates

You'll find all wall images for the first level in the Level1b spritesheet. The images are named level1_foreground_top1.png through level1_foreground_top7.png. You can also use images you create yourself or download from the Internet—the process is the same.

With the images at hand, add a subfolder in the Prefabs folder by right-clicking the Prefabs folder and choosing the New Folder option. Name the new folder Borders. Right-click the Borders folder, and create a New File.

Actually, you're going to create several files with wall templates, but I'm only going to describe the creation of the first. The rest are created and edited in the same way and left for you as an exercise.

In the New File dialog, consecutively name the file, starting with Border1.ccb, and choose Sprite as its type. Then click Create.

After creating the Border1.ccb, select the CCSprite root node in the Timeline. Change the sprite's Sprite frame property to SpriteSheets/Level1b/level1_foreground_top1.png on the Item Properties tab in the Details Inspector on the right.

> **Tip** If you are working with very dark, if not black, images, you may not be able to make out the sprite's outline. If that is the case, you can go to Document ➤ Stage Color and select a background color that gives you good contrast. Gray usually works well. Try Green if you have masochistic tendencies.

You may want to zoom in on the sprite to make it easier to edit its shape. Choose the Zoom In and Zoom Out commands from the Document menu to do so.

In the Details Inspector on the Item Physics tab, select the "Enable physics" check box. Then change the body's type to Static and ensure "Physics shape" is set to Polygon. See Figure 4-6 for reference.

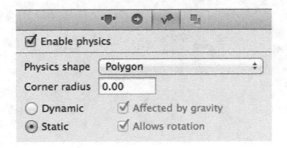

Figure 4-6. A static border image's physics settings

Editing Physics Shapes

With the Physics shape set to Polygon, you can manually modify the body's shape. Notice how the selection rectangle's corner handles have changed color? Previously, they were a grayish blue, but now they are pinkish, uhm, pink. Who picks these colors, anyway?

The pink handles tell you that you can drag and drop individual corner points to change the polygon shape. Try clicking and dragging some of the selection corners to create a shape like the one shown in Figure 4-7.

Figure 4-7. Border image's physics shape rectangle slightly modified

> **Tip**   When you switch to another Details Inspector tab other than the Item Physics tab, the regular selection rectangle will appear and you can no longer edit the physics shape. In order to view and edit a node's physics shape, you have to be on the Item Physics tab.

It's obvious that four edges don't suffice to model the outline for the image in Figure 4-7. You can add points by clicking anywhere on or near a line segment. Try to trace the image's outline as seen in Figure 4-8 by adding more points and dragging them to their desired position. It doesn't need to be perfect—far from it.

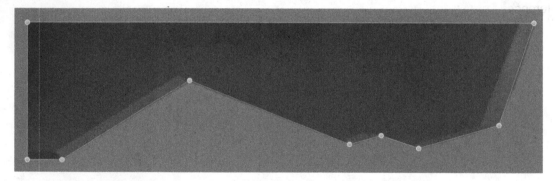

Figure 4-8. *The final version of the shape using as few points as possible to trace the image's outline*

> **Note**   A *line segment*, or just *segment*, is a line with two defined end points. Though commonly you would refer to it as a *line* as well, technically a line has infinite length. A *segment* is a line between two points, having finite length. I'll be using *segment* when I refer to the line between two points, but feel free to read the word as "line" if you prefer.

For the best performance, try to minimize the number of polygon-shaped points. As a rule of thumb, most shapes can be reasonably outlined with anywhere between 6 to 12 points. Where more vertices are required, you should consider tracing the image outline more roughly. Complex shapes are computationally more expensive as the number of polygon points increases. Too-elaborate shapes can also introduce more or less subtle issues, like objects getting stuck or bouncing off of each other in unrealistic ways.

If you need to delete a point on the shape, just right-click the point and it's gone. And if you want to completely start over, deselect and reselect the "Enable physics" check box. This will reset the polygon shape to a rectangle. However, this will also reset the body to Dynamic as well as resetting all other physics properties to their default values; so use this only as a last resort.

When editing polygon shapes, there are two things to watch out for: segments must never cross, and segments must not be parallel or close to being parallel to each other. SpriteBuilder will highlight invalid segments in red.

You can still publish and use shapes with invalid segments, but they will not behave correctly when it comes to collision detection and collision responses. Figure 4-9 shows an example of two invalid segments: in the upper half two segments are intersecting (overlapping), while in the lower half two segments are too close to each other, forming a very sharp edge.

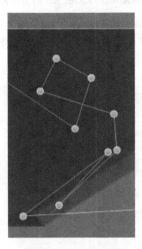

Figure 4-9. This shape has some invalid segments and will likely behave improperly during collisions

Now repeat creating border CCB files and editing their collision shapes for the remaining border sprites. If you like, you can cut it short and do only one additional border CCB sprite, so you have at least a little variety.

Tip   Keep in mind that you can always go back to the border CCBs at any time and change their collision shapes and other properties. All changes to a border CCB will be reflected by all Sub File instances of that CCB—for instance, the possibly dozens of borders you are going to add to the level.

Adding Level Borders

With the border elements set up, you can now add them to the level.

Open Level1.ccb. Start by dragging a regular Node from the Node Library View onto the CCPhysicsNode in the Timeline so that it becomes a child node of the CCPhysicsNode. Then rename this new node as **borders**. You can then group all the border nodes under this borders node. This, in turn, allows you to expand and collapse its children, effectively using the borders node like a folder in Finder.

Once you're done editing the level's borders, you will be glad to be able to collapse the borders node and not have the border nodes clutter up the Timeline. Moreover, you can click on the eye or lock symbols on the borders node in order to hide all of its child nodes respectively to make them read-only.

Now switch to the Tileless Editor View tab and start dragging and dropping border elements onto the stage. It's best to drag and drop the first one directly onto the borders node in the Timeline so that it becomes a child node of the borders node. With the newly added border node selected, you can then drag and drop all other border nodes directly onto the stage. Dropped nodes will automatically become siblings of the selected node, as in they share the same parent.

Be sure you add each border type exactly once. Then change the name of each in the Timeline to something like **border1** through **border7** so that you can easily identify their type in the Timeline. See Figure 4-10 for reference.

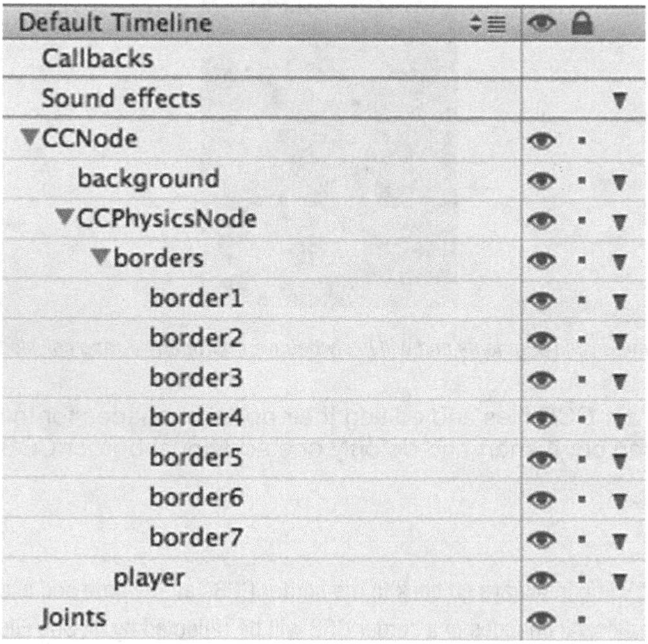

Default Timeline			
Callbacks			
Sound effects			▼
▼CCNode		👁	·
background		👁	· ▼
▼CCPhysicsNode		👁	· ▼
▼borders		👁	· ▼
border1		👁	· ▼
border2		👁	· ▼
border3		👁	· ▼
border4		👁	· ▼
border5		👁	· ▼
border6		👁	· ▼
border7		👁	· ▼
player		👁	· ▼
Joints		👁	·

Figure 4-10. *Level1.CCB Timeline with borders added*

You can then select any one of the border nodes in the Timeline, and just copy and paste it (Edit ➤ Copy and Edit ➤ Paste) to create a sibling with the same name as the source. The copy, unfortunately, will be at the exact same position as the original, meaning you don't instantly see that you did create a copy. You'll have to drag the copy away. Still, copying and pasting is the fastest way to fill a level with multiple nodes of the same type and preserve at least categorizable names for the nodes.

You should now cover up the walls with borders as you see fit by copying and arranging them until there aren't any "holes" left where the player might be able to squeeze out, eventually leaving the level area.

You can also rotate the borders freely to make up the bottom and side borders. The physics shapes will be rotated accordingly and behave correctly in the game. The same goes for scaling, though this will blur the images, especially if the scale factor for at least one axis is 2 or more.

> **Caution**   I mentioned earlier that physics shapes can't be scaled. Now I'm saying you can scale them. So which is it? Well, the scale property of a node with a physics body truly can't be animated or changed at runtime. Still, you can set the initial scale of a physics-enabled node in SpriteBuilder, so it will create an appropriately scaled version of the physics collision shape when the project is published.

If you are impatient and want to quickly get back to reading this book, just scale up the borders significantly along the *x* axis so that you need only a few border nodes to completely surround the level with impenetrable borders. You can go back and create a decent-looking level at a later time, something like what you see in Figure 4-11.

Figure 4-11. *Don't count the calories: Level1.ccb with delicious chocolate borders*

Publish, build, and run the project. If you can't see or move the player, make sure the player isn't overlapping with a border.

If you notice any of the borders falling down, you forgot to set them to Static. In that case, open the corresponding CCB file and check that Static is selected on the Item Physics tab.

> **Tip** You can quickly open a CCB file by double-clicking on its thumbnail in the Tileless Editor View.

If it's done correctly, the player should no longer be able to move or fall outside the level. Congratulations! You now have collisions in your level.

Interlude: Physics Debug Drawing

There's one important aspect about collision shapes you have to memorize: the physics engine couldn't care less about what's drawn on the screen. It considers only its internal state.

Image and collision shapes, for instance, may not always match up exactly, perhaps caused by an editing accident in SpriteBuilder or simply because you've modified the image contents without adapting the sprite's collision shape. To debug such issues, it is very helpful to turn on physics debug drawing once in a while.

> **Caution** Debug drawing will slow down your game. If you want to assess your game's performance or simply play the game, be sure to have physics debug drawing turned off.

To turn debug drawing on, add a new BOOL to the GameScene.m in Xcode as seen in Listing 4-7.

Listing 4-7. Add the debug draw ivar

```
@implementation GameScene
{
    // Other variables omitted

    BOOL _drawPhysicsShapes;
}
```

Locate the loadLevelNamed: method in the same class, and insert the highlighted line in Listing 4-8 after the _physicsNode is assigned.

Listing 4-8. Add the highlighted line to the loadLevelNamed: method

```
_physicsNode = (CCPhysicsNode*)[_levelNode getChildByName:@"physics"
                                                 recursively:NO];
_physicsNode.debugDraw = _drawPhysicsShapes;
```

So...where to set this ivar's value? In SpriteBuilder, of course. Open the GameScene.ccb and select its root node in the Timeline. On the Item Properties tab, click the Edit Custom Properties button. Add a property of the same name as the _drawPhysicsShapes ivar, but this time use Bool as the type and set its value to 1, as seen in Figure 4-12.

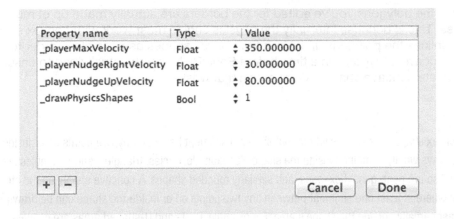

Property name	Type	Value
_playerMaxVelocity	Float	350.000000
_playerNudgeRightVelocity	Float	30.000000
_playerNudgeUpVelocity	Float	80.000000
_drawPhysicsShapes	Bool	1

Figure 4-12. Add a custom property to toggle physics debug drawing on or off

Now you can publish, build, and run to see what physics debug drawing does. Or allow me to direct your attention to Figure 4-13, which provides an example.

Figure 4-13. Screen shot from the game with physics debug drawing enabled

You may notice the polygons you've edited for the borders are actually made up of multiple smaller shapes. This is because internally the physics engine must work with convex shapes, so SpriteBuilder splices the polygons up into as few convex shapes as possible in order to represent non-convex (concave) polygons. In a time before SpriteBuilder, you actually had to ensure you didn't accidentally create concave shapes. What a pain that was!

> **Note**   Convex shapes are shapes where, put simply, a segment between any two points on or inside the shape is always wholly contained inside the shape. For example, circles, triangles, and rectangles are always convex, and so are pentagons, hexagons, and similarly rounded shapes. A concave shape, on the other hand, is a shape where at least one segment between any two points on or inside the shape can be drawn so that it runs at least partially outside the shape's area. For example, L-, T- and U-shaped areas are concave.
>
> Try to create convex shapes for dynamic bodies whenever you can to improve collision stability and performance. Decomposing a concave shape leaves tiny "cracks" in the shape, which can sometimes cause dynamic bodies to respond to collisions unexpectedly, like getting stuck for instance. Collision tests performed against dynamic bodies with decomposed concave shapes are also computationally more expensive.

The state of the project at this point can be found in the "04 - Physics Movement and Level Borders" folder.

Collision Callback Methods

Now it's time to fire up Xcode once more to add code that runs a so-called *callback method* whenever specific collision events occur.

Implementing the Collision Delegate Protocol

Before you can receive contact callback messages, there's a little setup necessary in order to register the GameScene class with the CCPhysicsBody of the level, as referenced by the _physicsNode ivar.

Open GameScene.h, which you'll find looks pretty basic, like in Listing 4-9.

Listing 4-9. The GameScene interface

```
#import "CCNode.h"

@interface GameScene : CCNode

@end
```

In order to allow the class to be used as a receiver of physics collision messages, it must implement the CCPhysicsCollisionDelegate protocol. This is done by simply appending the protocol in angle brackets at the end of the @interface, as seen in Listing 4-10.

Listing 4-10. GameScene is now said to adhere to the CCPhysicsCollisionDelegate protocol

```
#import "CCNode.h"

@interface GameScene : CCNode <CCPhysicsCollisionDelegate>

@end
```

In GameScene.m, you can now register self as the collision delegate of the _physicsNode. In the loadLevelNamed: method, add the line highlighted in Listing 4-11.

Listing 4-11. Assign the GameScene instance as the _physicsNode's collision delegate

```
-(void) loadLevelNamed:(NSString*)levelCCB
{
    _physicsNode = (CCPhysicsNode*)[_levelNode getChildByName:@"physics"
                                            recursively:NO];
    _physicsNode.debugDraw = _drawPhysicsShapes;
    _physicsNode.collisionDelegate = self;
    _backgroundNode = [_levelNode getChildByName:@"background" recursively:NO];
    _playerNode = [_physicsNode getChildByName:@"player" recursively:YES];
}
```

This in itself doesn't do anything yet. But it allows you to implement one or several of the four collision delegate methods shown in Listing 4-12 in the GameScene class. Each type of method can appear multiple times, with different collision type parameter names in the class implementing the CCPhysicsCollisionDelegate protocol.

Listing 4-12. Example method declarations of the four collision delegate messages

```
-(BOOL) ccPhysicsCollisionBegin:(CCPhysicsCollisionPair *)pair
                collisionTypeA:(CCNode *)nodeA
                collisionTypeB:(CCNode *)nodeB;

-(BOOL) ccPhysicsCollisionPreSolve:(CCPhysicsCollisionPair *)pair
                collisionTypeA:(CCNode *)nodeA
                collisionTypeB:(CCNode *)nodeB;

-(void) ccPhysicsCollisionPostSolve:(CCPhysicsCollisionPair *)pair
                collisionTypeA:(CCNode *)nodeA
                collisionTypeB:(CCNode *)nodeB;

-(void) ccPhysicsCollisionSeparate:(CCPhysicsCollisionPair *)pair
                collisionTypeA:(CCNode *)nodeA
                collisionTypeB:(CCNode *)nodeB;
```

Note that the methods in Listing 4-12 are nonfunctional examples; there's a trick to naming the parameters collisionTypeA and collisionTypeB that decides which colliding bodies call which method. I'll explain this shortly.

Upon closer inspection, you'll notice that all four collision callback methods take the same parameters as input, and two of them return a BOOL. Following is a list that explains under which circumstances and in which order each of these methods is called:

- **Begin** methods are called when two bodies first come into contact. It's always the first method called in a collision event between two bodies. By returning NO, the collision is ignored, bodies are allowed to pass through each other, and PreSolve and PostSolve methods for this collision event will not be called.

- **PreSolve** methods get called repeatedly for as long as two bodies are in contact, and before the collision has been resolved. This allows you to tweak the collision response by (temporarily) modifying the contacting body's properties, such as friction or restitution. Returning NO will not resolve the collision so that the two bodies are allowed to penetrate for this particular point in time.

- **PostSolve** methods get called after the collision has been resolved, meaning the bodies have been moved apart and their velocities updated. PostSolve can be used to reset any temporarily modified properties from the PreSolve step. But more importantly, other collision-based properties like totalKineticEnergy and totalImpulse have now been calculated. This allows you to break joints or play sounds as necessary, perhaps when the impact force exceeds a given threshold.

- **Separate** methods get called the moment two previously contacting bodies are no longer in contact.

Tip A Begin method is always followed by a corresponding Separate method, even if the Begin method returned NO. You can rely on counting the number of Begin and End calls to determine how many, or if any, two bodies of the given collision types are currently in contact with each other.

Collision Types and Callback Parameter Names

The collision callback methods in Listing 4-12 all take the same parameters as input. The names of the collisionTypeA and collisionTypeB parameters actually play an essential role in determining which collision callback method runs when two objects collide.

If you take another look at the Item Physics tab shown in Figure 4-1, you'll notice there's a "Collision type" field. You can enter any name there, but it must be a legal Objective-C identifier—meaning it should be all letters and digits, with no spaces or special characters except an underscore, and the name must not start with a digit.

The Collision type identifier can then be used as the name of either or both collisionTypeA and collisionTypeB parameters in collision callback methods.

> **Caution**   Setting or changing the "Collision type" setting does not affect whether any two bodies can collide or not. The "Collision type" is solely used to determine which callback method, if any, runs when a collision between two bodies occurs where at least one has a non-empty `Collision type`.

Give it a shot: open the `Player.ccb` and select the player sprite. Then switch to the Item Physics tab and enter **player** in the "Collision type" field. You can then implement the wildcard callback method in Listing 4-13 to be notified whenever the player starts colliding with another shape.

Listing 4-13. Collision callback that runs when the player collides with any other body

```
-(BOOL) ccPhysicsCollisionBegin:(CCPhysicsCollisionPair *)pair
                         player:(CCNode *)player
                       wildcard:(CCNode *)wildcard
{
    NSLog(@"collision - player: %@, wildcard: %@", player, wildcard);
    return YES;
}
```

This method will just print a message to the debug Console. Note that the second parameter's name is `player`, the same string you entered as the body's "Collision type." The third parameter's name is the special identifier `wildcard`, which stands literally for "any body."

The `wildcard` parameter refers to any node with a physics body, regardless of its collision type. Because no other body has a "Collision type" value except the player, the preceding method will be called whenever the player touches any other body in the level.

You should know that you can't have a callback method with two wildcard parameters. The second parameter should always be named the same as a `Collision type` identifier; otherwise, the callback method will never run to begin with. You can't use `wildcard` as the second parameter's name, though.

In other words, there is no way to run a callback method every time any two bodies collide. If you've used Cocos2D or physics engines before, you may be used to doing just that. Then, within the method, decide which types of bodies are colliding and how to proceed from there. The approach using the `Collision type` identifier and naming the callback method parameters allow you to sort out these collision notifications more efficiently and will automatically distribute collision event-handling code to different methods, based on the bodies' collision types.

The third method parameter in Listing 4-13 could also have been the name of another body's `Collision type`, such as *exit*. For instance, the following method signature will be used shortly to determine collisions between the player and the exit node:

```
-(BOOL) ccPhysicsCollisionBegin:(CCPhysicsCollisionPair *)pair
                         player:(CCNode *)player
                           exit:(CCNode *)exit;
```

> **Tip** The method parameter's name before the colon and the local variable's name after the colon need not be identical like in Listing 4-12. But it is a best practice to use the same identifiers in collision callback methods, like in Listing 4-13, to avoid any confusion.

The collision callback methods always return a BOOL value. If you return YES, you tell the physics engine that the colliding bodies should collide. If you return NO, the colliding bodies will pass through each other unaffected. It is, however, more efficient to use the Categories and Masks to sort out unwanted collisions and thus not even run the collision callback method. This is preferable in situations where you don't need to process additional collision code for the bodies in question.

Ignoring Collisions with Categories and Masks

Before a collision callback method is sent, the physics engine first evaluates a body's `Categories` and `Masks` properties. These are used to sort out collisions before the actual collision detection, resolve, and callback code is performed.

It is preferable to use collision `Categories` and `Masks` to filter out any noncolliding bodies whenever you can because it's more efficient than returning `NO` from the *Begin* contact callback method.

The masks use the same identifiers as the categories. To you better understand this, it may help to think of *Masks* as a short name for "collides with categories" in the rest of the text.

There can be up to 32 unique category identifiers, which are simply arbitrary strings that you enter in SpriteBuilder. Both `Categories` and `Masks` fields can contain multiple identifiers. An example of these settings is shown in Figure 4-14.

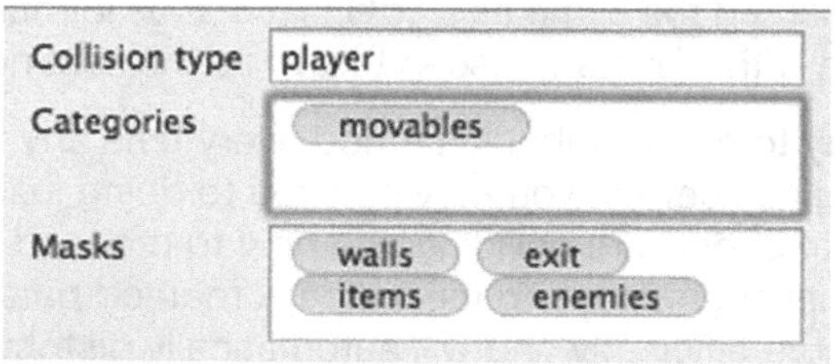

***Figure 4-14.** Example usage of collision categories and masks*

> **Tip** While working on your game, you should make note of the category identifiers and their exact names in a list. This helps you avoid mistakes like incorrectly naming an identifier, and you can keep track of how many of the 32 identifiers you've already used. You should also stick to either plural or singular names, so you never have to wonder whether the identifier was *enemy* or *enemies*. This makes it easier to recall them.

Categories and Masks are both empty by default. The confusing bit here is that an "empty" category means that this body is actually a member of all previously defined categories. Likewise, an "empty" mask means that the body is set up to collide with all previously defined categories. That means physics bodies default to colliding with all other bodies unless their categories and masks are set to specific identifiers.

Further adding to the confusion is the fact that both a body's category and a body's mask are considered in a cross-reference test, and only one of the two tests need to be true in order for collision to occur.

If you have two bodies, A and B, one of A's categories must also be in B's mask or one of B's categories must be in A's mask for both of them to collide. Keep in mind what I said earlier: an empty field is treated as if all identifiers are set in that field. That means if you set A's category and mask to *ACat* but only B's category to *BCat*, leaving its masks field empty, the two bodies will still collide because body B's empty mask field matches any and all categories of body A.

If you expressly want to prevent two bodies A and B from colliding, you will have to fill in both the Categories and Masks fields for both bodies and ensure that A's category is not included in B's mask, and B's category is not included in A's mask. Hold your breath, there's Table 4-1 coming up, which illustrates this.

Table 4-1. Categories and masks used by an imaginary shoot 'em game where bullets should not collide with each other and their respective owners

	Player	Player Bullets	Enemy Bullets	Enemy
Categories	player	playerBullet	enemyBullet	enemy
Masks	enemy	enemy	player	player

The simplest form of creating two noncolliding bodies A and B would be to set both the Categories and Masks fields for body A to *ACat* and both the Categories and Masks for body B to *BCat*. The actual strings used in place of *ACat* and *BCat* are not relevant; the important part is that each body's category identifiers must not be in the other body's Masks list, nor should any of the fields be empty.

Tip   Because any body can have up to 32 identifiers in both its Categories and Masks fields, the collision filtering can easily get pretty confusing. It is best to draw out a chart ahead of time to determine which types of bodies ***should not collide*** with what types of other bodies rather than which ones should collide. Determining what bodies should not collide requires you to use category identifiers, but not vice versa, because bodies collide by default.

It's going to be a lot more tedious trying to use identifiers to map out what bodies ***should be colliding***. You are likely to end up using a lot more identifiers, too. Simply because you would have to model collision behavior that is already working without identifiers.

For instance, in an imaginary shoot 'em up game, you may want to prevent the player's bullets from colliding with the player and other enemy bullets, but the player bullets should collide with enemies—and vice versa for enemies and enemy bullets. And, of course, enemies and players should collide.

Table 4-1 shows you how the identifiers would be set up using Categories and Masks.

If you want to allow bullets to hit each other, all you need to do is change the bullet's Categories from playerBullet and enemyBullet to player and enemy, respectively. If you want the bullets to be able to hit their owners as well, you simply clear the Categories field for both player and enemy bullets.

The *playerBullet* and *enemyBullet* identifiers exist solely to avoid collisions, these identifiers aren't even used in any other Masks fields in Table 4-1. Hence, you can combine them into a generic NoCollision category identifier, reducing the total number of identifiers used by one.

> **Tip**   It's pretty common and understandable to go with category identifiers that closely model the types or classes of objects used. If you ever find yourself running into the 32-identifiers limit, do map out your identifiers and try to find cases where you can combine category identifiers of multiple types of nodes. I can almost guarantee there'll be room for reducing the number of identifiers if you think closely about what the actual collision behavior should be.
>
> Setting up Categories and Masks can get pretty hairy real quick. I strongly recommend you draw them on paper or in a diagram application, and draw connecting arrows to visually see who is supposed to be colliding with whom. Such a table or diagram helps you keep track of your collision setup, and it will make it easier to spot whether you need an additional category, or whether you could combine two categories into one.

Keep in mind that if two bodies' Categories and Masks prevent them from colliding, their corresponding collision callback methods will not fire either. Likewise, if you are mainly interested in determining which types of bodies have collided in order to run custom code, all you need to set up is the Collision type identifier.

> **Tip**   Editing Categories and Masks is required only when it comes to *preventing collisions* with certain types of bodies. But once you start editing them for one or more bodies, it may be required to edit Categories and Masks of seemingly unrelated bodies to ensure certain bodies will still be colliding.

Letting the Player Leave

Since this game requires the player to move from A to B, where A is left and B is right, there's got to be something at B that brings the player to a new level. This is where you'll need an exit of sorts and a collision callback method that triggers the exit-level code. This should be straightforward with what you just learned.

Creating an Exit Node

In SpriteBuilder, right-click the Prefabs folder in the File View and create a New File. Name the file **Exit1.ccb**, and change its type to Sprite before clicking the Create button. Then select the root CCSprite in the Timeline, and on the Item Properties tab, click the "Sprite frame" drop-down menu. You can use any image, but when you are using the book's example graphics you should select the SpriteSheets/Level1a/level1_foreground_doughnut.png. The doughnut will act as the exit object for the first world.

With the sprite still selected, switch to the Item Physics tab. Select the "Enable physics" check box, and change the body type to Static; this prevents the exit node from moving or rotating due to gravity or other forces. Then enter **exit** in the "Collision type" field. This will allow you to easily determine when the player collided with this specific object. Leave the Categories and Masks fields empty so that the player surely collides with the exit node.

Last, edit the doughnut's polygon shape to approximately match the doughnut's outline, but try to use no more than eight points or so. The doughnut doesn't need to have a very precise collision shape. Something like the one shown in Figure 4-15 absolutely suffices.

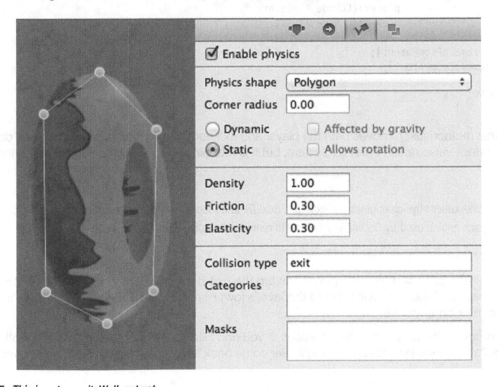

Figure 4-15. This is not an exit. Well, not yet

Then switch over to the Player.ccb, select the player sprite, and switch to the Item Physics tab. Here you need to enter **player** in the "Collision type" field. Also, check that both Categories and Masks fields are empty here as well.

The last thing to do in SpriteBuilder before you'll write some code is to open the Level1.ccb and drag and drop the Exit1 node from the Tileless Editor onto the CCPhysicsNode in the Timeline. The Exit1 doughnut needs to be a child node of the CCPhysicsNode. This is important; if it isn't, the exit node's physics behavior, including collisions, will not work.

You can then freely rotate and position the exit doughnut where you want it to be, normally somewhere near the right end of the level. However, for testing it may be a better idea to position it in the vicinity of the player to be able to test the upcoming code more quickly. You can later move it into its intended place.

Implementing the Exit Collision Callback

Switch over to Xcode, and open the GameScene.m file. Add the code in Listing 4-14 at the bottom of the file, just above the @end line.

Listing 4-14. This exit collision handler just removes both the player and exit node

```
-(BOOL) ccPhysicsCollisionBegin:(CCPhysicsCollisionPair *)pair
                         player:(CCNode *)player
                           exit:(CCNode *)exit
{
    [player removeFromParent];
    [exit removeFromParent];

    return NO;
}
```

For now, this method just removes both the player and exit nodes from their parent, effectively deleting them. The return value doesn't play a role here, but it is returning NO to allow the two bodies to intersect.

Tip   Unlike other physics engines (for example, Box2D), and respectively earlier versions of Chipmunk2D (the physics engine used by Cocos2D), it is legal to remove a colliding node during a collision callback method.

Build and run the project. Move the player toward the exit doughnut. Once they intersect, they will both disappear and the view will jump to the level's lower-left corner simply because there's no player to center on anymore.

For now, removing the player is all the exit does. If you don't like it, feel free to comment out both removeFromParent lines in Listing 4-14. You'll later come back to this method to create a popover menu.

Summary

Your game is now set up to move the player through the level using physics forces and gravity, while impenetrable static physics walls prevent the player from leaving the level boundaries.

You can even exit the level, sort of, by implementing a specific physics collision callback method. You also learned about customizing these callback methods with the Collision type property, and how to prevent bodies from colliding in the first place via the Categories and Masks identifiers.

Chapter 5

Timelines & Triggers

One of SpriteBuilder's major features is its ability to create Timeline animations using keyframes. It can even animate static physics bodies through keyframes while providing proper physics collisions, a feature that is unheard of in other 2D game engines.

This chapter explains how to create Timeline animations with SpriteBuilder and how to play such animations using `CCBAnimationManager`. At the end, you'll have rotating physics gear and saw objects that can push the player forward.

You'll also create a reusable trigger node that you can place in the level with a corresponding `Trigger` class. This allows you to run code when the player enters the trigger area—for instance, playing a Timeline animation on target nodes.

What Are Timelines and Keyframes?

So far you've known the Timeline as a view in SpriteBuilder (see Figure 5-1) and as the area where the hierarchy of nodes in a CCB is presented. You mainly used it to change the draw order of nodes and to rename them. But the Timeline can also animate properties of nodes using keyframes.

A keyframe animation simply records the values of properties of a node at a given keyframe. Say you have three keyframes and, for example, the rotation property is being animated. As the Timeline animation moves from one keyframe to the next, the node's rotation property is continuously updated. The difference between the most recent keyframe's rotation value and the next keyframe's rotation value, as well as the easing mode, determines how the rotation value changes over time. The entire animation is called a *Timeline* in SpriteBuilder.

Keyframe animations enable you to create smooth animations with relatively few keyframes because the in-between values are interpolated. Furthermore, the interpolation can be changed from a linear progression to an equation that computes the values between two keyframes dynamically. This is typically referred to as *easing*, and it allows for effects like the rotation slowing down or speeding up as it nears a keyframe.

Have a look at the various control areas as highlighted in Figure 5-1.

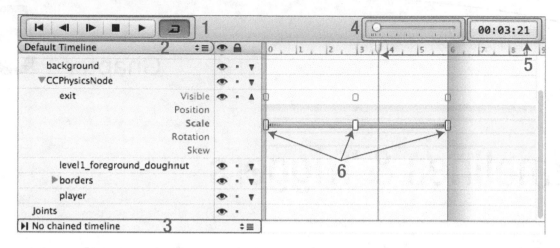

Figure 5-1. The Timeline animation editor view and its controls

Let me run you through the various editing controls in the Timeline that are important to creating keyframe-based animations.

1. **Timeline Controls:** These controls allow you to reset, fast forward, reverse, stop, and play an animation. The rightmost button toggles whether or not the animation loops during playback, but it does not affect playback in the game. (See **3. Timeline Chain**.)

2. **Timeline List:** A CCB file can contain multiple timelines. With the drop-down menu, you can add, remove, duplicate, and rename a timeline, and select the currently edited timeline. In Figure 5-1, *Default Timeline* is selected.

3. **Timeline Chain:** This control allows you to specify the Timeline that should be played when the current timeline playback has ended. If this is set to *No chained timeline*, the Timeline will play only once. In order to loop a Timeline in the game, you set this drop-down menu to the Timeline currently being edited. To loop the Timeline in Figure 5-1, the chained Timeline would have to be changed to *Default Timeline*.

4. **Timeline Scale:** This control scales the keyframe view underneath it.

5. **Timeline Cursor:** This shows the point in time where the animation currently is. You can drag the handle to manually play the animation back and forth.

6. **Keyframes:** Those rectangular handles represent the keyframes. You can drag them left and right to change their position. If you drag the handle so it is centered on a keyframe of a selected node, you can edit this keyframe's property value on the Item Properties tab. Between two keyframes is the keyframe segment, which you can right-click to change the easing mode.

Table 5-1 is a list of animatable properties. Note that not all properties are animatable in all nodes. Whether or not they are depends, for one thing, on the type of the node and whether that node is the root node of a CCB file. Root nodes cannot be animated at all, except for Sprite CCB files where you can at least animate the Color, Opacity, and Sprite Frame properties of the CCSprite root node.

Table 5-1. Animatable properties, their keyboard shortcut for creating keyframes, and their availability

Property	Shortcut	Availability
Color	C	Sprite, Sprite 9 Slice, Label TTF and BM-Font, Color and Gradient nodes.
Opacity	O	Sprite, Sprite 9 Slice, Label TTF and BM-Font, Color and Gradient nodes.
Position	P	All node types.
Rotation	R	All node types.
Scale	S	All node types.
Skew	K	All node types. Not to be used with physics-enabled nodes.
Sprite Frame	F	Sprite and Sprite 9 Slice nodes.
Visible	V	All node types.

> **Caution**   At the time of this writing, the Chipmunk physics engine does not support skewed and scaled nodes. If this still holds true, nodes with physics enabled should not animate both the Skew and Scale properties.

Using the Timeline Editor

Enough theory, let's try something specific. Switch to the Tileless Editor View tab, and drag and drop the doughnut image from the Level1a Sprite Sheet onto the CCPhysicsNode in Level1.ccb.

The new doughnut image must be a child of the CCPhysicsNode so that it scrolls along with the other level nodes. Since there's already an exit node using the doughnut image, think of this doughnut as the imaginary place where the player enters the level. You might want to move it to a position on the far left of the level so that you see it right when the game launches.

With the doughnut image selected in the Timeline, you can now start to add keyframes to create a Timeline animation. But first change the Timeline duration from its overly lengthy default of 10 seconds to, say, 6 seconds. To do so, click on the timestamp digits in the upper right area of the Timeline, which shows the timestamp of the Timeline Cursor in Minutes:Seconds:Frames format. Clicking on this digit counter opens up the *Timeline duration* editing dialog seen in Figure 5-2. Enter 6 seconds and click Done.

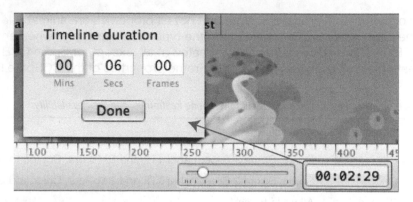

Figure 5-2. Changing the duration of the current Timeline

You may be wondering what the Frames field represents. SpriteBuilder plays back animations at a rate of 30 frames per second. So whenever you need a Timeline duration of less than a second, or perhaps a second and a half, you'll have to edit the Frames field. It accepts values between 0 and 29. For instance, if you wanted a Timeline duration of 1.5 seconds, you would have to enter **1** in the Secs field and **15** in the Frames field.

> **Note**   You can't change the 30 frames per second (fps) playback speed in SpriteBuilder. Changing the frame rate is not necessary, however. A keyframe animation interpolates between two keyframes on a frame-by-frame basis. Assuming that the game actually runs at 60 fps, Timeline animations will also run at the game's frame rate of 60 fps. If the game's frame rate is high, there will be more interpolated in-between states and thus the animation will run more smoothly than in SpriteBuilder.

Make sure that the entire duration of the animation is visible in the Timeline. Use the Timeline Scale slider or resize the SpriteBuilder window to have all 6 seconds of the animation visible. You'll notice that to the right of the 6 seconds marker is a shadow drawn toward the right—this marks the end of the current animation.

Then move the Timeline Cursor to the far left. Click and drag the Cursor handle—that's the blue-ish downward-facing arrow located on the timescale bar from which a vertical line extends downward. The timestamp digits should display the values 00:00:00. Finally, make sure the doughnut image that's supposed to visualize the level-entry point is still selected.

Adding Keyframes

With the correct node selected and the Timeline Cursor at the desired location, you can begin adding keyframes. You'll find one way to do this is by going through the menu via Animations ➤ Insert Keyframe and selecting the corresponding keyframe type,—for instance, Position or Scale. However, this is not too comfortable. Instead, you should get in the habit of using the keyboard shortcuts listed in Table 5-1.

Since the level-entry doughnut should scale a little over time, press the S key now to add a keyframe for the Scale property. You'll notice that like in Figure 5-3 the doughnut item expanded to show the list of animatable properties, with the Scale property drawn in bold to signal that this property has at least one keyframe in the current timeline.

Now move the Timeline Cursor to the 3-seconds mark. It doesn't need to be precisely at 00:03:00; a fraction of a second either way won't make a noticeable difference. Press S one more time to add a second Scale keyframe.

Notice how the two keyframes are now connected with a pink, horizontal line? I'll refer to the space between two keyframes as the *Keyframe Segment*, where the pink line visualizes the form of interpolation between two keyframes. There's the Instant interpolation mode which, when set, actually hides the pink line in a Keyframe Segment.

Finally, move the Timeline Cursor to the far right to 00:06:00 and press S once more to add a third keyframe. You now have a keyframe animation of the Scale property that spans the Timeline's full duration of 6 seconds. It should look like the one shown in Figure 5-3.

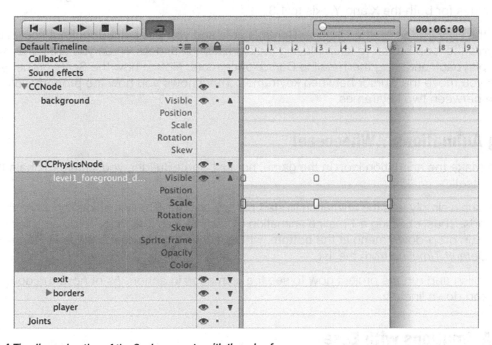

Figure 5-3. A Timeline animation of the Scale property with three keyframes

Caution   If you were to animate the Scale property of a node that has physics enabled, this would trigger an assertion in debug builds. The problem is that one naturally assumes the physics shape would scale along with the node, but it does not.

Editing Animation Settings

Okay, but how does the animation determine which values to interpolate? Right now, nothing happens when you play this animation.

The important point here is that the keyframes allow you to edit the given property at the given point in time. Right now, the Scale property is set to 1,1 for all keyframes, so even though the animation runs, it doesn't alter the Scale property values.

With the doughnut image still selected, switch to the Item Properties tab. Then move the Timeline Cursor back and forth anywhere between 0 and 6 seconds and notice how the Scale property is grayed out most of the time. In fact, you can change the values of an animated property only when the Timeline Cursor is exactly on top of a keyframe for the given property.

Move the Timeline Cursor so that it is exactly on the middle keyframe. You'll know the correct position when the Scale property values become editable on the Item Properties tab. Use the Timeline Scale slider to zoom out the Timeline to make it easier to position the Cursor. Once the Cursor is on top of the middle keyframe and the Scale property is editable, change the scale property values for both the X and Y axis to 1.3.

Now click the Play button on the Timeline Controls area and you'll see the doughnut scales up and down. Toggle the loop button to keep playing the animation in a loop. When you are done, stop the animation playback and drag the Timeline Cursor once more. Notice how the Scale property values change as you move the Cursor between keyframes. That shows you how the property values interpolate between two keyframes.

Looping Animations…Wheeeeee!

In order to make the animation loop in the game, not just SpriteBuilder, you'll have to chain the Timeline to itself.

A Timeline Chain simply tells the animation to start playing another Timeline animation when the timeline playback ends. Thus, chaining a Timeline animation to itself causes it to loop. To do so, click on the Timeline Chain drop-down menu at the bottom, where it says *No chained timeline* in Figure 5-1, and select the *Default Timeline* from the list.

You can publish and run the project now to see the animation in action. As of now, the doughnut scales up and down linearly.

Easing Animations with Ease

You can smooth out the animation using easing modes. Easing affects how the values between two keyframes change over time. Different kinds of easing can be applied to each Keyframe Segment.

To edit the easing mode, right-click in the Keyframe Segment. Usually there will be a pink line between the two keyframes. This brings up a context menu with all the available easing modes, as seen in Figure 5-4.

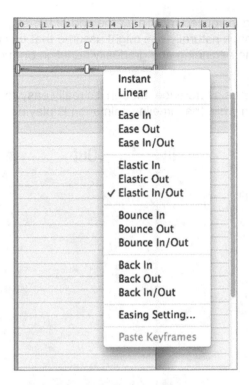

Figure 5-4. Right-click the keyframe segment to bring up the easing context menu

Pick one easing mode from the list by right-clicking each of the two Keyframe Segments. Feel free to try various combinations of easing modes.

Notice that after selecting an easing mode the pink line changes slightly. The line is a flat-colored pink line for the default Linear easing mode. The pink line disappears completely if you select the Instant easing mode. Technically, Instant is not an easing mode; it simply sets the animated value to that of the keyframe the moment the Timeline Cursor reaches the keyframe. For all other easing modes, the pink line becomes slightly shaded at one or both ends, depending on whether you picked an In, Out, or In/Out easing mode.

The In, Out, and In/Out modes determine where in the Keyframe Segment the easing is applied:

- **In:** Applied at the beginning of the Keyframe Segment
- **Out:** Applied at the end of the Keyframe Segment
- **In/Out:** Applied at both the beginning and end of the Keyframe Segment

The terminology may be slightly confusing. Take, for example, the Elastic In easing mode seen in Figure 5-5: first column; second row.

You might think that the easing is applied most near the end of the segment because that's where the amplitude is greatest. Perhaps naturally one might assume that this is an easing Out mode, but truly the easing starts at the beginning and gradually hones in on the target value in ever larger amplitudes.

When in doubt, take Figure 5-5 as a reference, though it's really easy to experiment because you can change the easing modes even while the Timeline animation is playing.

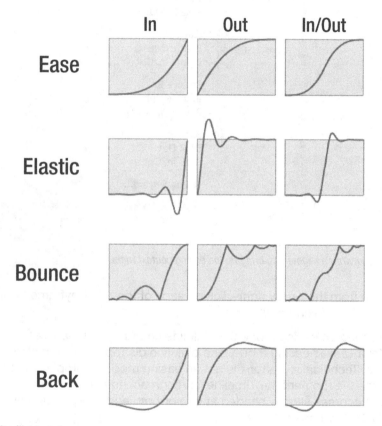

Figure 5-5. *Easing modes illustrated*

The diagrams in Figure 5-5 illustrate how an animated property's value changes over time. Take the Back In/Out easing diagram at the bottom right, for instance, and consider that each horizontal side of the diagram represents a keyframe. If you were to animate, say, the rotation property between the values 100 to 200 using a Back In/Out easing mode, the diagram tells you that the rotation value would first fall slightly below 100 before increasing to a value slightly above 200 and finally closing in at 200. The duration between two keyframes determines over how many frames this animation is interpolated. The longer the animation is, the smoother the interpolation can be.

Caution   If there's very little time between two keyframes—for example, 10 frames or less—you will hardly notice the easing effect. Say the rotation animation had three frames to interpolate between, the first frame would start the rotation property at 100, and the second frame would set it to 150 even for the Back In/Out mode because the third frame rotation property has to be at the other keyframe's value of 200. An easing mode is only effective and will only resemble the curves in Figure 5-5 when there's at least half a second between the two keyframes and the game runs at 30 fps or more. For sequences shorter than half a second, you may want to avoid using easing modes other than Linear or Instant.

The various easing modes are best seen in action, so you should definitely experiment a lot, especially with the combination of various easing modes along several Keyframe Segments and at varying durations. As an exercise, try adding another sequence animating the doughnut's rotation property (R key) over three or more keyframes so that the doughnut sways slightly from left to right and back.

If adding a keyframe fails, possibly with an error sound, you may not have a node selected.

If you need to remove a keyframe, select its handle and press Backspace or right-click the keyframe handle and select Delete from the context menu.

Clicking and dragging is the way to move keyframes to lengthen or shorten the duration to the previous and next keyframes.

Tip   In order to smoothly loop an animation, you'll need one keyframe at both ends of the timeline, with both having the exact same values for the animated property. This ensures that the animation transitions smoothly when it passes over the last keyframe and continues with the first.

If an animation acts erroneously when passing over a keyframe, check whether there are two or more keyframes at the exact same location. Try moving the keyframe where the animation seems to "jump" to see if there's another keyframe underneath it.

Keyframe Animations for Physics Nodes

Now that you know the basics of keyframe animations and how to edit them, you are ready to add some animated game-play elements. The astonishing part here is that you'll be animating nodes with physics enabled, and they'll behave properly in the game despite being animated by actions.

However, keyframe animations of physics-enabled nodes are possible only if the node's physics body is set to Static.

Adding the Gear and Saw

In SpriteBuilder's `File View`, select the `Sprite Sheets` folder. Right-click it to create a `New Folder`, and name it **GameElements**. Right-click the `GameElements` folder, and select `Make Smart Sprite Sheet`. Optionally, you may want to change the Sprite Sheet's publish format to the recommended `PVR RGBA8888` format with `Compress` selected.

In the book's downloadable archive, you'll find an identically named `GameElements` folder, with `circularsaw1.png` and `gear1.png` files in it, among others. Drag and drop all of the files in the `GameElements` folder from Finder onto the `GameElements Sprite Sheet` in SpriteBuilder.

Now repeat the following steps twice, once for the gear and the other time for the circular saw game element to create two new ccb files, named Gear1.ccb and Saw1.ccb.

1. Right-click the `Prefabs` folder, and select `New File`.

2. Name the document `Gear1.ccb` and `Saw1.ccb`, respectively, and change its type to Node. I'll explain why it's a Node and not a sprite after this list. Then click `Create`.

3. Switch to `Tileless Editor View`. Open Gear1.ccb, and then drag and drop the gear1 onto the stage. Open Saw1.ccb, and drag and drop the saw1 onto the stage. Alternatively, you can drag the gear1.png and circularsaw1.png from the GameElements Sprite Sheet onto the respective stages. There should now be a gear sprite in Gear1.ccb and a saw sprite in Saw1.ccb.

4. On the `Item Properties` tab, set the gear/saw sprite's position to 0, 0. Leave the anchor point at 0.5, 0.5. This ensures the gear/saw sprite is centered on its pivot point when placed in the level.

5. Switch to the `Item Physics` tab. Select the *Enable physics* check box. Change the body type to `Static`. Leave `Categories` and `Masks` empty.

6. In the *Collision type* field, enter **gear** when editing the gear object, and **saw** when editing the circular saw object.

7. Only for the gear sprite: leave the *Physics shape* drop-down menu set to Polygon. Edit the Polygon shape as explained in Chapter 4 so that the polygon outline coarsely matches the gear and its gear teeth as shown in Figure 5-6.

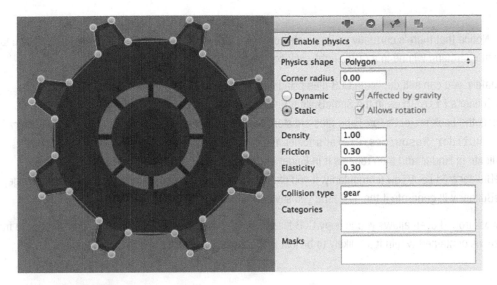

Figure 5-6. Gear polygon shape and properties

8. Only for the saw sprite: change the *Physics shape* drop-down menu to
    Circle. Change the suggested radius from 208 to 190, about 10% smaller.

Remember how I mentioned earlier that root nodes typically can't be animated, and only CCSprite root nodes can animate a few visual properties: sprite frames, opacity, and color?

That's why I didn't use a Sprite CCB document but instead chose to use a Node CCB document with a sprite as child node. That way, you can fully animate the sprite within the CCB file, because the sprite is not the root node. The alternative of editing and animating each gear and saw instance in the level separately simply wouldn't be feasible.

Animating the Gear and Saw

You can move on to animate the gear and saw objects. As before, I'll explain it once for the Gear1.ccb and you should apply the same steps to the Saw1.ccb as well. You don't necessarily have to, but I recommend doing it twice to get in the habit.

Feel free to create additional duplicates of Gear1.ccb and Saw1.ccb with essentially the same content but different rotation animations. You could alter the speed, or make the object rotate only by 180 degrees and then change direction. If you do that, you should pick sensible names for the additional CCB files that describe what the object does. For instance, Gear1_180AndBack.ccb might be a good name for the behavior I just described.

Tip   Notice that there's currently no Duplicate command. But when there will be, the most likely place to find that command will be in a CCB's right-click context menu.

Fortunately, you can still duplicate CCB files using Finder. In Finder, you will find all files listed in SpriteBuilder's `File View` in the SpriteBuilder Resources folder under the project's root folder. For instance, the book project's `Prefabs` files are stored in the `LearnSpriteBuilder.spritebuilder/SpriteBuilder Resources/Prefabs` folder. You can simply copy and paste a .ccb file to create a duplicate in Finder, and then rename it in Finder or SpriteBuilder. Copied CCB files will appear in SpriteBuilder's `File View` momentarily. If you did not duplicate the corresponding .ppng preview image, SpriteBuilder will generate it the next time you save or publish the project.

This workaround even allows you to copy CCB files between projects, though Sub File nodes and Sprite frame references contained within it are likely to be lost in the process and will need to be set again.

Don't worry about creating too many duplicates—the published CCBi files are tiny (a few kilobytes at most), and if the sprites all use the same image there's hardly any increase in memory usage either. A sprite instance, excluding the texture memory, is less than a kilobyte.

For the following descriptions, open the Gear1.ccb and the Saw1.ccb in your second pass.

Select the gear/saw sprite node, depending on whether you are in Gear1.ccb or Saw1.ccb, and change the duration of the `Default Timeline` to 4 seconds, like in Figure 5-2. Those 4 seconds will be how long it takes to complete a full revolution. Feel free to vary the duration a little if you like.

With the gear/saw sprite selected and the Timeline Cursor moved to the `00:00:00` location on the far left, press the R key to create a keyframe. Then move the Timeline Cursor to the far right of the Timeline and press R again to create a second keyframe. With the Timeline Cursor still on the second keyframe, set the Rotation property to 360 on the `Item Properties` tab. This will make the object rotate 360 degrees clockwise. To test this out, press the Play button in the Timeline Controls. See Figure 5-1.

Finally, the Timeline Chain needs to be changed from *No chained timeline* to *Default Timeline* in order for the rotation animation to loop indefinitely. Be sure to left-click the Timeline Chain drop-down menu because right-clicking won't work.

Repeat the preceding steps as many times as you like to create as many variations of rotating objects as you want.

Tip   To create a counter-clockwise rotation animation, simply set the Rotation property to –360 for the second keyframe. Alternatively, set Rotation in the first keyframe to 360 and in the second keyframe set it to 0. Either way works fine. You may want to create a duplicate CCB file with a different name so that you can use both clockwise and counter-clockwise rotating objects in the level.

Theoretically, you could also change the x scale of selected gear or saw objects in the level from 1 to –1, effectively flipping it and reversing the rotation animation. But at the time of this writing that did not correctly rotate the physics collision shape. Generally speaking, keep a scale of –1 in the back of your head as an easy way to not only flip images along one or both axes, but also as a way to reverse the direction of the rotation and position animations.

Adding Gears and Saws to the Level

You should now place one or more gear and saw objects in the Level1.ccb. But first, drag and drop a Node object from the Node Library View onto the CCPhysicsNode. Rename the new node to **gears** and **saws** or something similar. This allows you to change the draw order of the gear and saw nodes all at once. You will also be able to hide the gears and saws in the Timeline, which becomes increasingly important the more nodes you add to the level.

You can then drag and drop gear and saw objects from the Tileless Editor View into the gears and saws node. For the book's graphics, I also recommend you change the draw order of the gears and saws node so they are drawn behind the chocolate borders. Drag and drop the gears and saws node so it is above the borders node in the Timeline. It might look like what is shown in Figure 5-7.

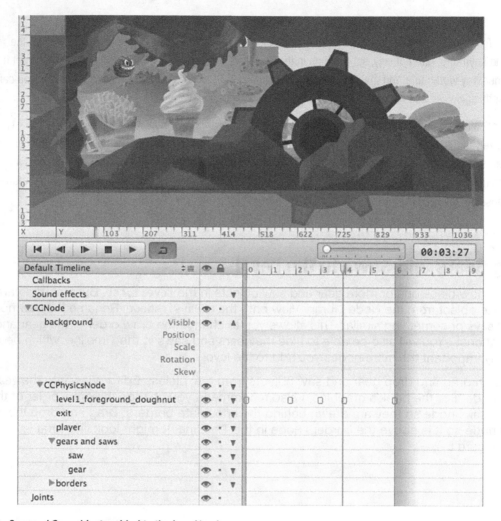

Figure 5-7. Gear and Saw objects added to the Level1.ccb

Just for kicks: while you're in the Level1.ccb, press the Play button in the Timeline Controls. You'll notice not only that the level-entry doughnut animates, but the gear and saw objects will also play their respective timelines. This allows you to preview and fine-tune animations, even if some animations were edited in other CCB files.

For instance, imagine you wanted two gear objects to interlock their teeth while rotating, with one rotating clockwise while the other rotates counter-clockwise. To do so, you would have to change the Rotation property of one gear instance in the level to get the gear teeth to interlock. The Rotation property of the Sub File node will define the starting point (or offset) for the animations of the referenced CCB file—much like a node's position defines the initial starting point of a position (move) animation. You can then position the two gears and press the Timeline Play button to see whether they are interlocking. If they are not, select the gear Sub File node again—each time you press Play, it will deselect all previously selected nodes—and change the gear's Rotation property. Repeat this until the gears interlock perfectly in motion.

At this point, you may be wondering the following: When editing a Timeline animation, you previously could not edit the properties of the animated node unless the Timeline Cursor was exactly on a specific keyframe. But now you can play and stop the animation, and no matter where the Timeline Cursor is located, you can always edit the node's properties and they're always the same, too. How come?

To understand that, consider that you were editing the keyframes of a particular node in a CCB file—for instance, Gear1.ccb. Here you tell the node what to do exactly during an animation by adding keyframes for specific properties and editing property values for each keyframe. For position, rotation, and scale animations specifically, these properties have to be considered relative to the node's current state.

Then you placed an instance of Gear1.ccb in the Level1.ccb. That created a Sub File node that references Gear1.ccb. This Sub File node represents a particular instance of the Gear1.ccb. The Sub File node allows you to specify the referenced node's initial position, rotation, and scale. During playback, the Timeline of the gear plays relative to the Sub File node's position, rotation, and scale. Once again, this proves the utility of working with multiple CCB files and Sub File nodes by allowing a greater variation of animations simply by tweaking the starting values of the animation for individual Sub File node instances.

With at least one gear or saw object placed in the level, you should publish and run the Xcode project. If you notice an animation stopping after a single revolution, check that the Timeline Chain is set to loop by setting it to Default Timeline.

How Not to Autoplay Animations

Have you noticed that the animations so far are playing automatically when you launch the game? Sooner or later there will be a time where you don't want that. Like, for instance, right now.

Assuming you'd like to play back an animation at an appropriate time while the game is running, that's something you need to set up and code. To create an initially inactive saw, you should create a duplicate of Saw1.ccb. If it is available, you should prefer to use SpriteBuilder's Duplicate command; otherwise, make the copy using Finder as described earlier. Rename the duplicate to **Saw1_noautoplay.ccb**, and open it in SpriteBuilder.

Editing Timelines to Uncheck Autoplay

First, you will want to prevent the animation from starting right away. Click on the Timeline List—that's the bar just below the Timeline Controls that currently reads "Default Timeline." See Figure 5-1 for reference. If the context menu won't show up or doesn't look like the one shown in Figure 5-8, I'm pretty sure you're trying to right-click it. Use the left mouse button instead, just like with the Timeline Chain.

Figure 5-8. *Clicking the Timeline List brings up the Timelines context menu, from where you can select, create, duplicate, and edit Timelines*

From the Timelines context menu, choose Edit Timelines. This will bring up a dialog like in Figure 5-9 but with just the Default Timeline entry.

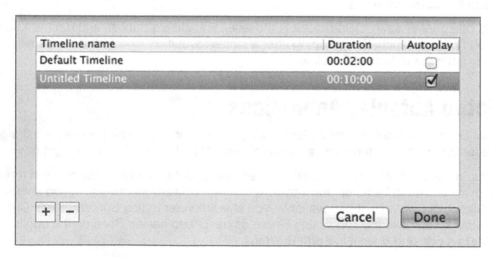

Figure 5-9. *Creating a new, unused Timeline just to prevent the Default Timeline from playing automatically*

You'll notice that the Default Timeline's Autoplay check box is initially checked. First, try to uncheck it to prevent this Timeline from playing automatically. If this works, all is good and fine.

But if you can't uncheck it (it's a bug), simply add another Timeline using the + button and check the Autoplay check box for the new Timeline. This will create a second Timeline just so that you can check its Autoplay check box to get rid of Autoplay for the Default Timeline. This workaround was necessary in the SpriteBuilder version I was working with but may no longer be necessary in the version you are using.

The important aspect here is to uncheck the Autoplay check box one way or another.

Playing Animations Programmatically

Place an instance of the Saw1_noautoplay.ccb in the Level1.ccb, preferably as a child of the gears and saws node, but in any case under the CCPhysicsNode branch. On the Item Properties tab, change the saw's Name to sawNoAutoplay. I'm well known for bad puns, but this one was truly unintentional.

Build and run the app, you will notice the saw won't animate. That's good. Now how to play it when the time comes?

SpriteBuilder comes with a set of utility classes. You already got acquainted with CCBReader, which is responsible for loading CCB files. The other most commonly used SpriteBuilder class is the CCAnimationManager. It's perhaps better known as *CCBAnimationManager*, but it has since become an internal class of the Cocos2D engine. It is responsible for storing and playing animation timelines, which Cocos2D refers to as *sequences*.

> **Note** Sequences and Timelines are closely related terms, though not exactly identical. Cocos2D uses the term sequence for any set of CCAction classes wrapped in a CCActionSequence class that runs the actions it wraps in sequential order. For instance, when a node moves from A to B, then rotates 90 degrees, then moves to C, that's a sequence. A Timeline in SpriteBuilder can then be considered a composite of multiple sequences because, for example, you could also animate a node's opacity and scale while performing the move and rotate actions. Generally speaking, a Timeline is one or more sequences playing in parallel.

Every node instance has an animationManager property through which you can access the CCAnimationManager and thus play back animations by name. For a quick test, add the code in Listing 5-1 at the end of the loadLevelNamed: method in GameScene.m.

Listing 5-1. Running an animation using CCAnimationManager

```
CCNode* sawNoAutoplay = [_physicsNode getChildByName:@"sawNoAutoplay" recursively:YES];
[sawNoAutoplay.animationManager runAnimationsForSequenceNamed:@"Default Timeline"];
```

The first line you should be familiar with. You obtain a reference to the node by name. The animation manager is then instructed to run the sequence named Default Timeline, which must be the exact name of the Timeline in SpriteBuilder, including case. If you build and run this, you'll notice the non-autoplaying saw is now animating again.

> **Note**   It's important to note that each CCB file has its own CCAnimationManager instance where only that specific CCB file's timelines are stored. All Timeline animations edited in a CCB file are stored in the CCAnimationManager of the CCB's root node, while each of the CCB's child node's animationManager instances forwards animation requests to the root node's animationManager instance.
>
> Therefore, in Listing 5-1 it wouldn't work if you used, say, the `animationManager` of `self` (GameScene.ccb), `_physicsNode` or `_levelNode` (both `Level1.ccb`). You have to use a reference to either the `Saw1_noautoplay.ccb` root node or one of its child nodes.

Animation Playback Completion Callback

The `CCAnimationManager` class allows you to get notified when playback of an animation has ended and a looping animation is repeating. To receive these notifications, you have to implement the `CCBAnimationManagerDelegate` protocol in the `GameScene.h` by adding the protocol in the angle brackets as shown in Listing 5-2.

Listing 5-2. Adding the CCBAnimationManagerDelegate protocol to GameScene.h

```
#import "CCNode.h"

@interface GameScene : CCNode <CCPhysicsCollisionDelegate, CCBAnimationManagerDelegate>

@end
```

Then update the `GameScene.m` code from Listing 5-1 with the highlighted line in Listing 5-3, which assigns `self`, the `GameScene` class instance, as the animation manager's `delegate`.

Listing 5-3. Assigning the animation manager delegate

```
CCNode* sawNoAutoplay = [_physicsNode getChildByName:@"sawNoAutoplay" recursively:YES];
sawNoAutoplay.animationManager.delegate = self;
[sawNoAutoplay.animationManager runAnimationsForSequenceNamed:@"Default Timeline"];
```

Below the `loadLevelNamed:` method, you should then add the `completedAnimationSequenceNamed:` callback method as seen in Listing 5-4.

Listing 5-4. This callback method runs whenever an animation has ended

```
-(void) completedAnimationSequenceNamed:(NSString*)name
{
    NSLog(@"completed animation sequence: %@", name);
}
```

Every time this method runs, it will log the name of the animation whose playback ended. The method also runs whenever a looping animation has reached the end of its animation cycle and starts over. This allows you to wait for a looping animation to play back to complete before stopping or replacing it with another animation, in order to prevent nasty jumps in the animation playback.

Alternatively, you can also set a block that runs whenever an animation ends. The advantage is that you do not have to implement the `CCBAnimationManagerDelegate` protocol in the current class to do so; the disadvantage is that you get the `CCAnimationManager` as input, so you have to refer to the `lastCompletedSequenceName` property to get the name of the Timeline that ended. It's also slightly more verbose to set an animation callback block as you can see in Listing 5-5.

Listing 5-5. Using an animation callback block to be notified of "animation ended" events

```
[sawNoAutoplay.animationManager setCompletedAnimationCallbackBlock:^(CCAnimationManager* sender)
{
    NSLog(@"completed animation sequence: %@", sender.lastCompletedSequenceName);
}];
```

Deciding whether to implement the `CCBAnimationManagerDelegate` protocol or use the callback block variant is a matter of personal preference.

Differentiating Between Animations

Note once again that each CCB file has its own `CCAnimationManager` instance. In this instance, only the animations in `Saw1_noautoplay.ccb` will call the callback method in Listing 5-4.

Likewise, if you were to use `self.animationManager.delegate = self;`, the method in Listing 5-4 would run every time a Timeline animation of the `GameScene.ccb` ends. However, it would not run, for example, when a Timeline animation of `Player.ccb` or `Background1.ccb` ends.

Note that it's possible to use the same class as a delegate of multiple animation-manager instances. If you needed to be informed in GameScene about other CCBs' animation events, you could do it like this:

```
self.animationManager.delegate = self;
_levelNode.animationManager.delegate = self;
_playerNode.animationManager.delegate = self;
_backgroundNode.animationManager.delegate = self;
```

Notice, though, that the callback method in Listing 5-4 receives only the name of the sequence that ended. So unless you renamed each Timeline animation, you would have no way of discerning which CCB's `Default Timeline` ended. You would have to edit the Timelines as seen in Figure 5-8 and rename them by double-clicking their name in the dialog shown in Figure 5-9.

Triggering Animations on Collision

Since it doesn't make much sense to prevent an animation from playing automatically, only to play it when the level loads, you're going to trigger the playback of the animation when the player enters a certain area.

Adding Trigger Targets to the Level

First things first: remove the temporary animation playback code in Listing 5-1 from the `loadLevelNamed:` method.

Next, open `Level1.ccb` in SpriteBuilder. Assuming you have already added one instance of `Saw1_noautoplay.ccb` to the gears and saws node, add another one. You should have at least two of them.

You should rename the existing saw instance in the Timeline, and then make a copy of the saw and arrange it as you see fit. Just be sure the saws don't overlap the player and the player can't touch them right away, as you're going to make them deadly in a while.

Select each `Saw1_noautoplay` prefab instance in turn, and change its name property on the `Item Properties` tab to `triggerSawRotation`. The trigger node will get the same name—that will make the connection between the trigger area and the to-be-triggered nodes.

Creating a Trigger CCB

What would be a good trigger node? Color nodes are arguably the best option, though in general you can use any type of node. Trigger areas should be visible while editing but see-through (transparent). The node color can be used to highlight different types of triggers with different colors.

Once again, you should create the trigger object as a template. You should be familiar with the process by now, so I'll keep the instructions short and to the point.

Create a `New File` in the `Prefabs` folder, name it `TriggerOnce.ccb`, and change its type to Layer. The Layer type allows you to specify an initial size. It shouldn't be too small or too large, and the actual size isn't that important—it will only determine the trigger node's initial size in the level. A size of 128x128 works fine. Then click `Create`.

> **Note**   The Layer type is important because it will give you a rectangular selection handle when placed in the level. You may have noticed that the saw and gear instances have rotational selection handles. Rectangular selection handles are simply easier to work with when you need to resize the node often, which you'll need to do in order to adjust the trigger area's size and rectangular shape.

Drag and drop a `Color` node from the `Node Library View` onto the `TriggerOnce.ccb` stage. On the `Item Properties` tab, set the position to 0, 0. Then change the `Content size` type for both width and height to the same width and height of the root node (128x128) so that the color node fills the layer's entire area. Also, pick a color of your choice and set the opacity to 0.3—though the actual value doesn't matter. You may want to come back later and change opacity and color to more appropriate values because this depends a lot on the graphics used, the number and size of trigger areas and, above all, personal preference.

> **Note**   You can also set the color node's Content size type to % and width and height to 100 in order to fill the entire level. However, in the SpriteBuilder version at the time of this writing, this would create a 1x1 sized polygon collision shape when enabling physics. Hence, I refrained from doing so. Both ways are going to work equally well—after all, the size of the TriggerOnce.ccb layer and its color node doesn't need to be changed.

On the Item Physics tab for the color node, check Enable physics, change the type to Static, and as the Collision type enter **trigger**. This will allow you to handle collisions with triggers separately. Categories and Masks can be left empty—currently, there aren't any other dynamic objects that might activate triggers besides the player.

On the Item Code Connections tab for the color node, enter **Trigger** as the Custom class name. This will create an instance of the (soon to be added) Trigger class for every TriggerOnce.ccb added to the level.

Since this particular trigger should trigger only once, switch to the Item Properties tab once more. At the bottom, click the Edit Custom Properties button and add a custom property named **triggerCount** of type Int with value 1. This will make the trigger activate only once before removing itself. If you omit adding this property or set it to 0, it will create a Trigger instance that triggers every time the player enters it. Values greater than 1 will make the trigger activate the given number of times before removing itself from the level.

> **Tip**   Feel free to add another trigger CCB in the same way, name it TriggerForever.ccb, and omit the triggerCount parameter or set its value to 0. I'm sure you will find a use for a repeatedly activatable trigger area eventually.

Note that it's also possible to create triggers with polygon shapes as opposed to purely rectangular shapes. However, a polygon shape will not be reflected visually in SpriteBuilder because the color node fills a rectangular area. You would have to use a sprite node with a corresponding trigger image if you wanted to visually display a polygon trigger area in SpriteBuilder.

On the other hand, you can almost always model more complex trigger areas with multiple rectangular triggers. Trigger collision areas also rarely need to be very precise either. So it's best to avoid using polygon-shaped triggers altogether and instead combine multiple rectangular trigger areas.

Adding Triggers to the Level

Before you add any triggers to Level1.ccb, you should first drag another plain Node from the Node Library View onto the CCPhysicsNode in the Level1.ccb Timeline. Then rename this node to **triggers**. This will be the container for all the trigger nodes.

Now you can drag a TriggerOnce from the Tileless Editor View onto the triggers node in the Timeline. Change the trigger's Name property on the Item Properties tab to **triggerSawRotation**. The name connects the trigger with nodes of the same name—the saw nodes you've added earlier also have *triggerSawRotation* as their name. The target nodes will receive a message when the player (or other nodes) cause the trigger to activate.

Change the trigger's position, and use the selection handles to resize (scale) the object to best match the desired size of the trigger area. Just make sure the player will be able to collide with it.

You can also create copies of this new trigger if you want to form a more complex trigger shape. Multiple triggers can overlap without issues.

Creating the Trigger Class

If you were to build and run the Xcode project now, you would receive an error originating from CCBReader that states that the custom class Trigger cannot be found. You may want to try and run the project just to get acquainted with the error message, as you'll probably encounter it from time to time.

To fix this error, you'll need to add a class of the same name as you've entered under the Item Code Connections tab in the Custom class field of the trigger's color node. That class' name is *Trigger*, in case this wasn't obvious.

In Xcode, select the Project Navigator tab. That's the leftmost tab where the files, groups (yellow folder icons), and folders (blue folder icons) are shown in a hierarchical view not unlike Finder displays files and folders. Right-click the Source group and select New File. This will open the same dialog as in Figure 2-9. From the iOS Cocoa Touch section, select Objective-C class, and then click Next, which will show the dialog you see in Figure 2-10. Enter **Trigger** in the Class field, and make it a Subclass of *CCNode* before clicking Next. You'll end up with two new files in the Xcode project, named Trigger.h and Trigger.m.

Again, try to run the project, and once more you'll receive an error message regarding a missing property named triggerCount. The Trigger class is still missing this property or ivar.

Let's use a proper @property this time because you may possibly want to access or change this value at runtime from other classes. Open Trigger.h and add the @property like in Listing 5-6, as well as the @protocol that defines the method that target nodes need to implement. Also, add the declaration of the triggerActivatedBy: method.

Listing 5-6. Adding the triggerCount property to Trigger.h

```
#import "CCNode.h"

@protocol TriggerDelegate <NSObject>
-(void) didTriggerWithNode:(CCNode*)activator;
@end

@interface Trigger : CCNode

@property int triggerCount;

-(void) triggerActivatedBy:(CCNode*)activator;

@end
```

This allows you to run the project without errors, although the trigger itself doesn't work yet.

Programming the Trigger Class

The Trigger.m implementation will be a tad more complex, but it's also a reusable class that you may want to use in your own projects. It collects all the trigger and target nodes upon loading. The Trigger class forwards the trigger collision event to all target nodes, updates the triggerCount and, if necessary, removes the trigger nodes when they are no longer needed.

Initializing Trigger and Target Arrays

Start by updating Trigger.m so that it resembles Listing 5-7.

Listing 5-7. Trigger implementation initializing trigger and target storage dictionaries

```
#import "Trigger.h"

static NSMutableDictionary* targetArrays;
static NSMutableDictionary* triggerArrays;

@implementation Trigger
{
    BOOL _repeatsForever;
}

-(void) didLoadFromCCB
{
    if (targetArrays == nil)
    {
        targetArrays = [NSMutableDictionary dictionary];
        triggerArrays = [NSMutableDictionary dictionary];
    }

    [targetArrays removeAllObjects];
    [triggerArrays removeAllObjects];

    _repeatsForever = (_triggerCount <= 0);
}

@end
```

At first, two static NSMutableDictionary variables are declared. The keyword static means these variables will be shared with all instances of the Trigger class. Essentially, they are global variables, but because they are declared in the scope of the implementation file they are accessible only to code in the Trigger.m file.

The @implementation section declares an ivar _repeatsForever, which will be used to determine whether this particular trigger instance will never remove itself.

The didLoadFromCCB method contains initialization and cleanup code for the two global dictionaries. If targetArrays is nil, it will create an NSMutableDictionary instance and assign it. The same is done for triggerArrays because it can simply be assumed that if targetArrays is nil then triggerArrays will be nil, too.

Next, both dictionaries are instructed to `removeAllObjects`. That's kind of odd on first sight, right?

Here's to foresight: eventually you'll be able to change levels. Given that the two dictionaries are global (`static`) variables, they and their contents will remain in memory as you switch levels and present other scenes. So in every new level that contains at least one Trigger instance, those dictionaries need to be cleared of any remaining references.

> **Note** It may seem kind of inefficient to have every trigger `removeAllObjects` when doing so once would suffice, but I find it's not enough to justify adding extra code to check whether `targetArrays` and `triggerArrays` are empty every time a `Trigger` instance is created. Whether you do that or simply issue the `removeAllObjects` method for every instance amounts to the same work anyway, but it'll be more code.

Finally, `_repeatsForever` is set to the result of `_triggerCount` being equal to or less than 0. This means the trigger will be repeating if `_triggerCount` is initially 0 or a negative value. This would be the case if you'd simply omit adding the `triggerCount` custom property in SpriteBuilder because ivars are initialized to 0.

> **Tip** In Objective-C, all `static` variables and all ivars are always initialized to 0. For BOOL ivars, 0 equals NO; for `id` and Objective-C class pointer variables, 0 equals `nil`. Furthermore, since automatic reference counting (ARC) is enabled in every SpriteBuilder project, each local variable of type `id` and Objective-C class pointers are initialized to `nil` as well. The only variables you have to assign a value before reading from them are local variables that are primitive data types (i.e., BOOL, `int`, `CGFloat`, `double`, `NSUInteger` and similar) and C structs and C pointers like `void*`.

This version of the project should build and run without errors, but triggers won't be functional yet.

Finding Triggers and Targets

The next step is to collect a set of targets for each trigger. Triggers connect to targets simply by using the same name for trigger and target nodes. Not only can there be multiple targets for a single trigger, there can also be multiple triggers of the same name activating the same target(s).

Finding and Storing Triggers

You should add Listing 5-8 to `Trigger.m` just above the @end line.

Listing 5-8. Storing the trigger and target nodes in onEnter

```
-(void) onEnter
{
    [super onEnter];

    self.parent.visible = NO;

    NSAssert1(_parent.name.length > 0, @"Trigger node has no name: %@", self);
    self.name = _parent.name;

    NSPointerArray* triggers = [triggerArrays objectForKey:_name];
    if (triggers == nil)
    {
        triggers = [NSPointerArray weakObjectsPointerArray];
        [triggerArrays setObject:triggers forKey:_name];
    }

    [triggers addPointer:(void*)self];

    if ([targetArrays objectForKey:_name] == nil)
    {
        NSPointerArray* targets = [NSPointerArray weakObjectsPointerArray];
        [targetArrays setObject:targets forKey:_name];

        [self addTargetsTo:targets searchInNode:self.scene];
        NSAssert1(targets.count > 0, @"no target found for trigger named '%@'", _name);
    }
}
```

Notice that you can't use didLoadFromCCB to find all triggers and targets; instead, you have to use onEnter. Since didLoadFromCCB runs immediately after each individual node has been loaded, there likely will be target or trigger nodes that haven't been loaded yet if you were to run the code in Listing 5-8 in didLoadFromCCB. The soonest you can start searching for all target and trigger nodes in the node hierarchy is when onEnter runs. The onEnter method is sent to each node instance after it has been added as a child to another node.

> **Caution**   Notice that onEnter requires calling its [super onEnter] implementation. The compiler will warn you if you omit calling [super onEnter]. If you don't call the super implementation, scheduling and input events will not work or won't work correctly. Always heed compiler warnings! Warnings are there to improve your code quality and to make you aware of potential issues. Search for the exact warning or error text if you want to find out more about a specific warning and how to fix it.

The first order of business in Listing 5-8 is to set the visible status of the trigger node to NO. Actually, it's setting the trigger's parent node. That's because the color node representing the trigger area visually is the node with the custom class Trigger. But the color node is a child node of the TriggerOnce.ccb root node. I prefer to hide the root node in case I want to design more complex triggers with multiple color nodes, for instance.

Next the node takes over its parent's name. That is because in Level1.ccb the Name property is assigned to the Sub File node instance that references the TriggerOnce.ccb. That ends up assigning this name to the TriggerOnce.ccb root node, the color node's parent. Assigning self.name from _parent.name is merely a convenience because it allows you to use the _name ivar declared in the CCNode class.

> **Tip**   Since forgetting to give a trigger a name can be a common mistake, I decided to add an assertion here that warns you if the _parent.name.length is 0—meaning the parent's name is either nil or an empty string. This assertion will fail in both cases: if _parent.name is nil, the entire test will also return nil (aka 0) because messages sent to nil objects return 0 by default.

You may be wondering why I did not assign directly to the _name ivar or why I got the name via _parent.name rather than self.parent.name.

As a rule of thumb, you should prefer to use an ivar, where available, when merely reading its value. It makes the code shorter and, as a side-effect, slightly faster. However, when assigning a value to a property, it is best practice to assign to the property via self.name rather than assigning to the _name ivar directly. The rationale here is that self.name = @".." internally runs the property setter method [self setName:@".."], which may perform additional code. Bypassing the property setter can result in all kinds of issues. If you have the slightest doubt about possible side-effects of assigning directly to an ivar, always assign to the property or run the property setter method instead.

The next code fragment of Listing 5-8 is reprinted in Listing 5-9 to allow you to focus on just the code discussed next.

Listing 5-9. Creating a triggers NSPointerArray and assigning self to it

```
NSPointerArray* triggers = [triggerArrays objectForKey:_name];
if (triggers == nil)
{
    triggers = [NSPointerArray weakObjectsPointerArray];
    [triggerArrays setObject:triggers forKey:_name];
}

[triggers addPointer:(void*)self];
```

In the first line, an NSPointerArray is obtained by looking up the object using the trigger's _name in the triggerArrays. Initially, there will be no such object, resulting in triggers being nil. If that is the case, the if block will create an NSPointerArray and assign it to triggers, as well as storing it in the triggerArrays dictionary using the trigger's _name as the key.

The curious part is definitely the NSPointerArray. It sounds like a regular NSArray or NSMutableArray, but it's actually not a subclass of either. It does behave much like a trimmed-down variant of NSMutableArray, though. And its specialty is storing pointer references and allowing you to store zeroing weak references to objects—meaning the triggers array does not retain the trigger nodes added to it. If a trigger node stored in the triggers array deallocates, the Objective-C runtime will automatically set the corresponding pointer to nil in the array rather than leaving a dangling pointer (which, when used, will cause crashes or bugs). The weakObjectsPointerArray initializer configures the array to behave this way.

But why? Consider that both the trigger and target nodes could be removed from the node hierarchy at any given point in time, whether they have been triggered or not. Trigger nodes should not be kept from deallocating simply because you maintain a list of triggers in a global array. Hence, storing them weakly (not retaining) in an NSPointerArray allows triggers that are removed from the node hierarchy to deallocate.

> **Caution**   NSPointerArray is available only on devices running iOS 6.0 or newer.

With the triggers array set up, all that's left to do is pass in self in the call to addPointer:, but not without casting it to (void*) because NSPointerArray stores generic void* pointer values. The (void*) cast doesn't alter the object reference in any way; it's merely a way of stating to the compiler that the self object can safely be represented as a void* pointer.

Finding and Storing Targets

The remaining lines of Listing 5-8 that we haven't discussed so far are reprinted in Listing 5-10 for the sake of clarity, focus, and zen.

Listing 5-10. Searching for targets

```
if ([targetArrays objectForKey:_name] == nil)
{
    NSPointerArray* targets = [NSPointerArray weakObjectsPointerArray];
    [targetArrays setObject:targets forKey:_name];

    [self addTargetsTo:targets searchInNode:self.scene];
}
```

Notice that targets are searched only when there's no corresponding entry of the given _name in the targetArrays dictionary. This is to prevent searching the same targets multiple times in cases where you have multiple triggers of the same name. Only the first trigger needs to search for targets because the other triggers will refer to the same targets.

If there's no array with the given _name in targetArrays, the code in Listing 5-10 will create an NSPointerArray storing weak pointer references and assign it to targets. The same array is also assigned to targetArrays using the trigger _name as its key. Next a method is called that performs the actual search recursively, starting with the self.scene node. It adds all the target nodes of the same name to the targets array.

The addTargetsTo:searchInNode: method is shown in Listing 5-11—you should add this method to your Trigger.m file just below the onEnter method.

Listing 5-11. Recursively searching for and gathering target nodes

```
-(void) addTargetsTo:(NSPointerArray*)targets searchInNode:(CCNode*)node
{
    for (CCNode* child in node.children)
    {
        if ([child.name isEqualToString:_name])
        {
            if ([child conformsToProtocol:@protocol(TriggerDelegate)])
            {
                [targets addPointer:(void*)child];
            }
        }

        [self addTargetsTo:targets searchInNode:child];
    }
}
```

The addTargetsTo:searchInNode: method runs recursively and tries to collect all instances of nodes given a specific name and whose class conforms the TriggerDelegate protocol. You can't use getChildByName: here because that will return only the first child node with the given name, but you need a list of all nodes of the same name.

If a target node has the correct name and conforms to the TriggerDelegate protocol, a reference to the target node is added to the targets array.

The last line continues the recursive search by calling the addTargetsTo:searchInNode: method again, but with child as the parameter. This ensures that every node in the scene is processed once and not a single one will be missed.

It also means the trigger system in its current version won't recognize nodes added after loading the GameScene.ccb file. If you need this, I'll leave it as an exercise for you to do.

You could add a +(void) addTarget:(CCNode*)target method to the Trigger class that assigns the target node, based on its name, to the correct targets array stored in targetArrays. You should verify that the target node conforms to the TriggerDelegate protocol before adding it. To add a target node, you could then call [Trigger addTarget:aTargetNode] from any other class, provided that you did add #import "Trigger.h" to that class' implementation file.

Forwarding Trigger Events to Targets

What's left is to inform target nodes when the trigger is activated. This is where the triggerActivatedBy: method in Listing 5-12 comes into play.

Add the code in Listing 5-12 to Trigger.m below the addTargetsTo:searchInNode: method.

Listing 5-12. Sending trigger messages to targets

```
-(void) triggerActivatedBy:(CCNode*)activator
{
    NSPointerArray* targets = [targetArrays objectForKey:_name];

    for (id target in targets)
    {
        [target didTriggerWithNode:activator];
    }

    if (_repeatsForever == NO)
    {
        NSPointerArray* triggers = [triggerArrays objectForKey:_name];
        [self updateTriggers:triggers];
        [self cleanupTriggers:triggers];
    }
}
```

Based on the trigger's _name, the list of targets is obtained from targetArrays. All targets are enumerated to send the didTriggerWithNode: message to each target, which allows each target to run custom code when triggered.

Declaring the target variable with the id keyword in the for loop allows you to send the didTriggerWithNode: message without the compiler complaining that the selector is not declared. If for some reason you need to declare target as CCNode*, you will have to include the TriggerDelegate protocol to tell the compiler that you are certain that this reference implements the TriggerDelegate selectors. The alternative for loop would then have to look like this:

```
for (CCNode<TriggerDelegate>* target in targets)
```

Also note that individual target variables may be nil because targets is an array storing its pointers weakly. Fortunately, you don't need to perform an extra nil check because sending messages to nil objects is legal in Objective-C, effectively skipping all nil targets.

> **Caution**   As with casting, adding a protocol to a variable declaration does not automatically make the object implement the protocol's selectors. So this can still raise an undeclared selector runtime error if a target node's class doesn't implement the didTriggerWithNode: method.

Cleaning Up Triggers and Targets

Unless the trigger is repeating—meaning its initial triggerCount was set to 1 or more—the NSPointerArray containing all triggers of the same name needs to be updated and possibly cleaned up. That's what the last two methods are for.

Add the updateTriggers: and cleanupTriggers: methods in Listing 5-13 below the triggerActivatedBy: method.

Listing 5-13. Update and cleanup triggers

```
-(void) updateTriggers:(NSPointerArray*)triggers
{
    for (Trigger* trigger in triggers)
    {
        trigger.triggerCount--;
    }
}

-(void) cleanupTriggers:(NSPointerArray*)triggers
{
    if (_triggerCount <= 0)
    {
        for (Trigger* trigger in triggers)
        {
            [trigger.parent removeFromParent];
        }

        [targetArrays removeObjectForKey:_name];
        [triggerArrays removeObjectForKey:_name];
    }
}
```

The updateTriggers: method simply reduces the triggerCount property of each trigger by one. It assumes that all triggers of the same name start with the same triggerCount; otherwise, some triggers may trigger more often than others, which is probably not what you want. Specifically, it doesn't allow you to combine TriggerOnce.ccb and TriggerForever.ccb to trigger the same targets. If that's what you need, you would have to update cleanupTriggers: so that it only removes triggers whose triggerCount has reached 0 and where the trigger isn't set to repeat forever.

The cleanupTriggers: method then tests the current trigger's _triggerCount, which has just been decreased. If it is 0 or less, it can be assumed that all the triggers have done their job and can be removed. As I said earlier, each trigger is the child of a CCNode, the root node of the TriggerOnce.ccb, so it is best to remove the trigger's parent by sending it the removeFromParent message. Removing the parent will also remove any child nodes, including the trigger node itself.

Considering that these triggers have done their job, neither the targets' nor the triggers' NSPointerArray are needed anymore. Hence, they are being removed from the targetArrays and triggerArrays.

Informing Triggers About Collisions

What's left at this point is to actually send the triggerActivatedBy: message to a Trigger instance on collision, and implement a class that conforms to the TriggerDelegate protocol that then runs custom code when its didTriggerWithNode: selector runs.

This is where the Collision type of the color node in the TriggerOnce.ccb comes into play. You've set this field to trigger. Therefore, you should add a collision method to GameScene.m whose third parameter is named trigger.

Add the code in Listing 5-14 at the end of GameScene.m, just above the @end keyword.

Listing 5-14. Responding to collisions between player and trigger nodes

```
-(BOOL) ccPhysicsCollisionBegin:(CCPhysicsCollisionPair *)pair
                        player:(CCNode *)player
                        trigger:(Trigger *)trigger
{
    [trigger triggerActivatedBy:player];

    // return NO to allow the bodies to pass through each other
    return NO;
}
```

Notice that the third parameter is a pointer to a Trigger instance rather than a CCNode instance. You can declare the parameter to be a Trigger* instead of CCNode* under the assumption that the trigger parameter will always be a Trigger class instance. If it is not, it will result in a "unrecognized selector sent to instance" error.

You will also have to import the Trigger.h in the GameScene.m file. Add the following line at the top of the GameScene.m file, just below the other #import lines:

```
#import "Trigger.h"
```

Importing the Trigger.h file will make the Trigger class known to the GameScene class. This will get rid of the "Use of undeclared identifier 'Trigger'" error.

Triggering Target Nodes

Every target node that's supposed to be activated by a trigger needs to have the following:

- A custom class assigned to the node in SpriteBuilder.
- The custom class' header needs to #import "Trigger.h".
- The custom class' @interface needs to adopt the TriggerDelegate protocol.
- The custom class' @implementation needs to have a -(void) didTriggerWithNode:(CCNode*)activator method with the desired functionality.

Since playing an animation when activated by a trigger will be a common use case, it makes sense to write a generic class PlayTimelineWhenTriggered. But before you write this class, open Saw1_noautoplay.ccb in SpriteBuilder, and then select the root node. Do **not** select the saw sprite. Switch to the Item Code Connections tab, and enter **PlayTimelineWhenTriggered** in the Custom class field.

> **Caution**   The PlayTimelineWhenTriggered class inherits from CCNode. This is why it won't work as a custom class of a sprite node that inherits from CCSprite. Custom classes for sprite nodes need to inherit from the CCSprite class. The same is true for other node types—for instance, the custom class of a button needs to inherit from CCButton.

You should return to Xcode now to add the `PlayTimelineWhenTriggered` class.

Right-click the `Source` group and select `New File`. Once again, you'll go through the dialogs in Figure 2-9 and Figure 2-10. Name the class **PlayTimelineWhenTriggered**, and make it a `Subclass` of `CCNode` before clicking `Next` to create the files. Open the `PlayTimelineWhenTriggered.h` file, and enhance it with the code highlighted in Listing 5-15.

Listing 5-15. Extending the PlayTimelineWhenTriggered class to become a TriggerDelegate

```
#import "CCNode.h"
#import "Trigger.h"

@interface PlayTimelineWhenTriggered : CCNode <TriggerDelegate>

@property NSString* timelineName;

@end
```

Adopting the `TriggerDelegate` protocol is necessary to allow instances of this class to be used as a target by the `Trigger` class. The `timelineName` property is just to allow more flexibility for this class.

If `timelineName` is nil or an empty string, the class will play the `Default Timeline` when activated; otherwise, it will attempt to play the Timeline whose name is given by `timelineName`. In any node where you set the `PlayTimelineWhenTriggered` class as its `Custom class,` you can then add a custom property `timelineName` of type `String` that allows you to specify the name of the Timeline to be played. Refer to Figure 4-2 and Figure 4-3 if you don't remember how to add custom properties to a node.

Let's move on to the `PlayTimelineWhenTriggered.m`, shown in its entirety in Listing 5-16. I suppose I needn't say this anymore: make your `PlayTimelineWhenTriggered.m` look like the one in Listing 5-16.

Listing 5-16. Playing a Timeline when triggered

```
#import "PlayTimelineWhenTriggered.h"

@implementation PlayTimelineWhenTriggered

-(void) didLoadFromCCB
{
    if (_timelineName.length == 0)
    {
        _timelineName = @"Default Timeline";
    }
}

-(void) didTriggerWithNode:(CCNode*)activator
{
    [self.animationManager runAnimationsForSequenceNamed:_timelineName];
}

@end
```

The `didLoadFromCCB` method is used to assign the `@"Default Timeline"` string to `_timelineName` if `_timelineName` is initially either an empty string or nil. The `_timelineName` ivar is automatically created by the compiler just by adding the `@property` to the class' `@interface`. The `didTriggerWithNode:` method plays the animation specified by `_timelineName` when a `Trigger` activates it.

Quite simple, isn't it? You will probably need to create many variants of classes implementing the `TriggerDelegate` protocol to perform all kinds of different things when triggers are activated. But for each class, you should strive to use custom properties to allow yourself or your team to alter the class' behavior.

If you publish, build, and run the app and move the player into a trigger area that activates the `Saw1_noautoplay.ccb`, it will crash.

Avoiding the "Physics Space Locked" Error

Wait, did I just say "crash"? Unfortunately so:

```
Aborting due to Chipmunk error: You cannot manually reindex objects while the space is locked.
Wait until the current query or step is complete.
    Failed condition: !space->locked
```

This error is representative of a known issue with most physics engines: during collision events, you can't modify certain aspects of the physics world (known as *space* in Chipmunk). In this instance, playing the animation will change the node's rotation, and thus the rotation of the node's physics body. Chipmunk doesn't like this because the physics world (space) is *locked*, meaning the bodies in it are currently processed and need to be in a coherent state where only the physics engine itself is allowed to make changes.

Consider where playing the animation came from: a `Trigger` instance sent the `didTriggerWithNode:` message, which in turn had its `triggerActivatedBy:` method run by the `GameScene.m` collision callback method `ccPhysicsCollisionBegin:player:trigger`.

Fortunately, there's a quick and simple fix for such issues. It's so simple you can try this whenever you merely suspect such a *u can't touch this* issue. I'm terribly sorry about the earworm.

Update the `didTriggerWithNode:` method in `PlayTimelineWhenTriggered.m` as shown in Listing 5-17.

Listing 5-17. Fixing the Chipmunk space ➤ locked error

```
[self scheduleBlock:^(CCTimer *timer) {
    [self.animationManager runAnimationsForSequenceNamed:_timelineName];
} delay:0.0];
```

Scheduling a block with a 0 delay defers executing the contents of the block until the next time the Cocos2D scheduler runs scheduled blocks. At the latest, this will run in the next frame.

> **Tip** If you find that you often need to use the `scheduleBlock:` trick to prevent `space locked` errors, you should consider updating the `triggerActivatedBy:` method in `Trigger.m` so that the call to `didTriggerWithNode:` is already deferred to a scheduled block. If you do that, you no longer have to schedule blocks in `TriggerDelegate` classes, but on the other hand all `didTriggerWithNode:` messages will be deferred.

If you run the project now, the saws start rotating as soon as the player enters a trigger area. The current state of the project can be found in the folder `06 - Triggered Animations`.

Summary

In this chapter, you've learned how to create keyframe animations using the Timeline editor and how to play back these animations via `CCAnimationManager`.

You then added a generic `Trigger` class that allows you to run code whenever the player enters a given trigger area. Trigger and target nodes are connected simply by giving them the same name.

Chapter **6**

Menus & Popovers

By this point, you have a level and game elements that make the game playable in principle. Before expanding upon more game elements and additional levels, I would like to take some time to connect the dots...the menus to be precise.

The saws should probably kill the player, but this requires a *Game over* menu to allow the player to retry or end the level. You can't pause the game either, nor does it pause automatically when the app is sent to the background.

You'll learn how menus can be designed to scale easily with varying screen resolutions, as well as how to present them as popovers or full-screen views without having to change scenes. You will also find use for the *Callbacks* feature of the Timeline.

Static In-game Menus

For user interface elements such as a pause button or score display, you'll need a way to fixate these elements on the screen so that they don't move along when the level scrolls. But before you do that, you should add the prepared user interface graphics.

Adding Menu Graphics

In the book's downloadable archive in the Graphics folder, you'll find the *Menu* and *UserInterface* folders. You should drag both folders onto the *SpriteSheets* folder in SpriteBuilder. Then turn these two folders into Sprite Sheets by right-clicking them and selecting *Make Smart Sprite Sheet*. As usual, you should change the format to *PVR RGBA8888* with *Compress* checked.

If you want to use your own menu and UI images, you can do so. There are no fixed sizes for the individual images except for the menu background, which should fill the entire screen. Though if you use custom graphics, you may need to use different values for certain property values (position, content size) to make your images fit.

Adding a Static Game Menu Layer

The game menu layer will be the node that contains all of the in-game user interface controls and labels. For now, you need it just to add a pause button, but it could also contain a score label, a countdown timer, the player's health bar, a virtual joypad, buttons to activate special abilities, or just about any other user interface element that shouldn't scroll along with the level.

All of the user interface elements should be in their own folder, just like the prefabs. Your first task is to add a new folder in SpriteBuilder's *File View* and name it **UserInterface**. Then right-click the *UserInterface* folder and select *New File* to create a new CCB document. Name this document **GameMenuLayer.ccb**, and set its type to *Layer*. Leave the size at the default 568x384, and click *Create*.

Aligning a Button with Reference Corners

Drag and drop a *Button* node from the *Node Library View* onto the *GameMenuLayer.ccb* stage. Drag and move the button so that it is very close, if not touching, the upper-left corner of the layer.

Next, open *GameScene.ccb* and drag and drop the *GameMenuLayer* from the *Tileless Editor View* onto the stage. Then verify that its position property is set to 0,0.

Switch to Phone resolution by pressing Cmd+1 in case you are viewing *GameScene.ccb* in iPad resolution. Notice how the button is only partially visible or not visible at all.

> **Caution** When viewing a CCB file that includes another CCB file via a Sub File node, you must save the CCB file referenced by the Sub File node in order to see its most recent edits.
>
> In this instance, the *GameMenuLayer.ccb* is included via a Sub File node in the *GameScene.ccb*. Whenever you make a change to *GameMenuLayer.ccb*, you have to do File ➤ Save while viewing the *GameMenuLayer.ccb* or publish the project in order to see its current state in the *GameScene.ccb*.

Use the Document ➤ Resolution ➤ Tablet Landscape and Document ➤ Resolution ➤ Phone Landscape menu items to switch between iPad and iPhone screen sizes on the fly. Or more easily, just press Cmd+1 and Cmd+2 to toggle between the available resolutions. CCB files of type *Scene* also offer a *Phone Landscape (short)* (Cmd+3) resolution representing 3.5-inch iPhones up to iPhone 4S.

You'll see the button is fully visible on iPad but not on iPhone due to the *GameMenuLayer.ccb* content size being the default 568x384 size. This size is a compromise that scales up well on an iPad, but the 384 points height make the layer slightly higher than the iPhone screen.

Open the *GameMenuLayer.ccb* again, and select the root node. Change its *Content size* property types for both width and height to % by selecting the *% in parent container* items from the drop-down lists. The width and height values should automatically change to 100 for both width and height; if not, make sure the value is 100 for both. This makes the layer scale with the size of its parent node. In this instance, that would be the *GameScene.ccb* root node, which in turn is already set to have a content size of 100% because that's the default setting for CCBs of type *Scene*.

In essence, the size of *GameMenuLayer.ccb* now equals the size of the screen on all devices. The % content size setting is effectively passed down from parent nodes, allowing child nodes to take on the size of the screen or a size proportional to the screen size if all of their parents do the same.

Scaling *GameMenuLayer.ccb* to the size of the screen won't automatically scale the positions and sizes of the nodes it contains, however. Therefore, select the button and change its reference corner drop-down menu to the *Top-Left* setting. The reference corner drop-down menu is highlighted in Figure 6-1. Then change the button's position so that it is about 50 by 20 points away from its reference corner.

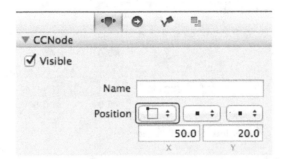

Figure 6-1. The button's reference corner is set to Top-Left to make its position relative to the top left corner of the layer

Changing the reference corner will position the button so that it is always relative to the top-left corner of the layer. As the layer's height increases and decreases on devices with different screen sizes, the button's position will remain at 50 points inwards horizontally and 20 points below the top-left corner of the screen.

Changing the reference corner and making the layer scale with the dimensions of the scene is the best way to align nodes to each corner of the screen regardless of the device. Though you can achieve a similar effect using the % position type and without changing the reference corner, doing so can cause noticeable layout problems when switching between iPhone and iPad devices.

For instance, assume the button's reference corner was still set to *Bottom-Left* and the Y position was set to *95%*. That would make the button appear at a distance of *320 – 320 * 95% = 16* points below the top screen edge on iPhones. While on iPads, the button would be *768 – 768 * 95% = 38* points below the screen. Not quite: taking into account that SpriteBuilder applies a 2x scale to positions when switching from iPhone to iPad, that gives you an absolute distance of 19 points below the top screen edge on iPad.

Such % positions would result in a difference of 3 points (16 points vs. 19 points) in Y position between iPhone and iPad screens. While that may be *close enough* for many cases, where you need precise positioning you must change the reference corner and specify the position in points.

Editing Button Properties

The button you've added to *GameMenuLayer.ccb* is a tad ugly and nondescript at the moment. Select the button, switch to the *Item Properties* tab, and stand in awe of its many, many properties divided into four sections: *CCNode*, *CCControl*, *CCButton*, and *CCLabelTTF*. Where to start?

You've already completed editing the *CCNode* properties, and you should be familiar with them from editing any other node. No need to change them any further. So then let's have a look at the remaining properties sections.

CCControl Properties

The *CCControl* properties shown in Figure 6-2 need no changes. Nevertheless, I'll give you a quick explanation because you just want to know anyway. Am I right?

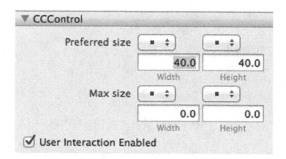

Figure 6-2. CCControl properties define the minimum and maximum sizes of a CCControl node

Note that all nodes that inherit from *CCControl* offer these properties. The *CCControl* nodes are *Button*, *Text Field*, and *Slider*.

Preferred size should have been named *minimum size*, because it determines the smallest possible size of a control—in this case, the button. Correspondingly, *Max size* determines the maximum size, unless it is set to 0 to allow the button's size to grow without limits.

These settings are mainly useful for buttons whose title will change programmatically because a button's size grows and shrinks with the size of the label printed on it.

User Interaction Enabled should be self-explanatory. If unchecked, the button will not respond to touches or clicks unless user interaction is enabled programmatically by setting the userInteractionEnabled property to YES. All nodes inherit this property from *CCResponder*, which controls whether the node's custom class will receive touch and accelerometer events.

CCButton Properties

The *CCButton* properties is where you need to apply some editing love. Above all, the *Title* should reflect what the button does; change it to *PAUSE* as seen in Figure 6-3. Ignore the *Localize* check box for now, it will be explained in the "Labels & Localization" chapter.

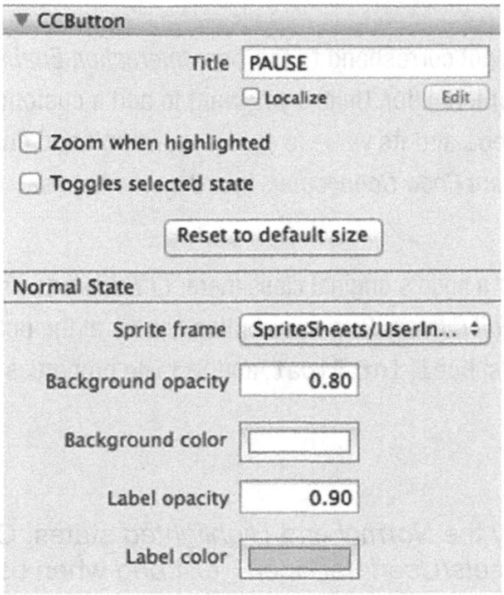

Figure 6-3. CCButton properties with proper title and custom graphics

When selected, *Zoom when highlighted* will zoom in the button (both background and label) when the user taps and holds. This is a legacy feature because Cocos2D used to do that to all menu buttons, for better or worse. I think it's a crude effect, so try to avoid it. Instead, I'll shortly explain neat tricks with which you can give the user visual cues without resorting to zooming or changing the background image.

Checking *Toggles selected state* makes the button a toggle button, changing from its normal state to its selected state and back every time it is tapped. When the button is in the selected state, the properties for the *Selected State* section are used. So if you want to make a toggle button, be sure to use different properties for *Normal State* and Selected State; otherwise, you won't be able to tell whether the button is on or off, normal or selected.

The *Normal State* section in the bottom half of Figure 6-3 is representative of all of the button's possible state properties. All button states have the same *Sprite frame*, *Background*, and *Label* properties. There are four button states:

- **Normal:** The default state.

- **Highlighted:** Takes effect for the duration the button is touched (tap and hold).

- **Disabled:** In effect when the button's enabled property is set to NO programmatically or by adding a custom property (see Tip box that follows) to signal that the button currently does not function.

- **Selected:** Used when *Toggles selected state* is checked and the button has been tapped once, and for every other tap following that.

Tip The Disabled state does not correspond to the *User Interaction Enabled* check box, and you can't edit the enabled property in SpriteBuilder. Unless you want to add a custom property to the button, name it **enabled**, and set its type to Bool and its value to 0. Alas, you can't add custom properties unless you specify a *Custom class* on the *Item Code Connections* tab. But who is to say this class has to be a truly *custom* class?

As a matter of fact, you can enter a node's original class (here: *CCButton*) as provided by Cocos2D in the *Custom class* field to make the *Edit Custom Properties* button appear at the bottom of the *Item Properties* tab. Then you can add any of the class' Bool, Int, Float, and String properties that are not normally editable in SpriteBuilder.

In this case, the button uses only the *Normal* and *Highlighted* states. Click on the *Sprite frame* drop-down menu and select *SpriteSheets/UserInterface/P_exit.png* when using the book's graphics. Do so for both normal and highlighted sprite frame properties. When using your own graphics, just make sure the sprite frame is set to the same image for both states.

To give the user a visual cue that she is currently touching the button, it suffices to change the *Background opacity* and *Label opacity* of the normal state to a value slightly below 1.0, say 0.8. This makes the button slightly transparent and only becoming fully opaque when touching it.

Another option for a visual highlight is to leave both normal and highlighted state settings at their default values except for one or both color properties of either the normal or highlighted state. The button's background and/or label would then change color when highlighted—for instance, lit up with a bright white as opposed to a light gray in the normal state. In this instance, that effect is also used by making the button's *Label color* a light gray in the normal state.

Tip When using colors for highlights, the best effects are achieved with only subtle color variations. For instance, you could use lighter and darker versions of the same color. Changing the background or label color from green to red...well, that's just going to look ugly.

CCLabelTTF Properties

The button's *CCLabelTTF* properties are the same as those for a regular *Label TTF* node. The image in Figure 6-4 does not show the *Font Effects* section; this will be discussed in detail in the "Labels & Localization" chapter.

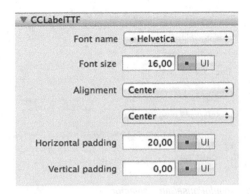

Figure 6-4. CCLabelTTF properties

The label's *Font name*, *Font size*, and *Alignment* properties should be self-explanatory. Clicking the *UI* button for Font size as well as the padding properties prevents these properties from scaling by a factor of 2 when running on iPad, effectively keeping the button the same size as on an iPhone rather than scaling it up. You can give this a try and then toggle screen sizes with Cmd+1 and Cmd+2 to see the effect. But revert it back to point scaling by clicking the dot icon as shown in Figure 6-4.

The *Horizontal padding* and *Vertical padding* settings allow you to declare the button's label to be twice this many points wider and higher. The horizontal padding of 20 shown in Figure 6-4 makes the label 40 points wider in total, which will also expand the button's background image accordingly. Padding is mainly used to control how far the label is inset from the background image's borders.

In this case, set *Horizontal padding* from its default 10 to 20 to ensure that the label's letters are printed entirely on the solid gray area of the background image rather than drawn over or close to the background image's unevenly shaped borders.

Assigning the Button Selector

On the *Item Code Connections* tab for the button, enter **shouldPauseGame** as the button's *Selector* in the *CCControl* section. See Figure 6-5 for reference. The *Target* drop-down menu should be set to *Document root*.

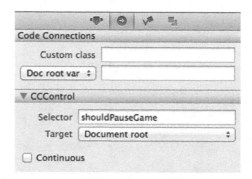

Figure 6-5. *The pause button will run the shouldPauseGame selector*

There's also a *Continuous* check box that you should not check; if you check it, the button would run the selector once every frame as long as the user keeps a finger on the button. This can be useful for a rapid fire or d-pad button, but here it is undesirable.

Tip   I like to prefix user-initiated actions with "should" because they can be seen as a request, not a command that must be obeyed indiscriminately. If that sounds contradictory, consider a platformer game where you can jump and double-jump, with the jump button always being active. The user requests a jump by having the jump button run the `shouldJump` selector. The method first checks if the player is on ground, and if so, initiates the jump. If the request is sent when the player is in the air, the `shouldJump` selector will either initiate a double-jump or ignore the request.

It is best practice to double-check all user interactions for validity. For instance, if you didn't instantly disable the pause button when pressed, the user might tap the pause button a second time accidentally, potentially causing issues like running the animation twice. Naming selectors with the "should" prefix is therefore a nice indicator that an action should be performed but can also be denied or interpreted differently based on certain conditions.

Assigning the GameMenuLayer Class and Ivar

The button's `shouldPauseGame` selector is sent to the *Document root*. The document root is the root node of *GameMenuLayer.ccb*. Therefore, the root node of *GameMenuLayer.ccb* needs to have a custom class where the selector can be implemented.

> **Caution**   It's a common mistake to set the custom class of the button itself, consequently creating a subclass of *CCButton* to handle the button selectors. Buttons are never the receivers of their own selectors.

Select the root node in *GameMenuLayer.ccb*, and switch to the *Item Code Connections* tab. In the *Custom class* field, enter **GameMenuLayer**.

Furthermore, you'll want access to the *GameMenuLayer* root node from within the GameScene class. Open *GameScene.ccb*, select the sub file node referencing *GameMenuLayer.ccb*, and then set Doc root var to _gameMenuLayer. This will assign a reference to the *GameMenuLayer.ccb* root node to the *GameScene* ivar named _gameMenuLayer, which you'll add next.

> **Caution**   Another common mistake is to edit the Doc root var field of the *GameMenuLayer.ccb* root node rather than its reference in *GameScene.ccb*. Doing so will literally create a self reference in a *GameMenuLayer* ivar. Changing the variable type to Owner var will not work either because the owner is a reference you specify in code when using the *CCBReader* method load:owner:.

Programming the GameMenuLayer

It's time to fire up Xcode again to add the GameMenuLayer class and the shouldPauseGame method.

Your first goal should always be to make new code connections technically functional as soon as possible and verify that they work. It's a potential waste of time to start writing code without first confirming that the connected selectors actually run and the ivars or properties are being assigned properly. You may be inclined to find the flaw in your logic instead, possibly wasting time looking for issues in all the wrong places. It's the programming equivalent for "Did you plug it in?" issues.

Implementing and Confirming Code Connections

Create a new Objective-C class just like you did in the last chapter with the Trigger and PlayTimelineWhenTriggered classes. This time, name the new class **GameMenuLayer** and make it a subclass of *CCNode*. Look at Figure 2-10 and Figure 2-11 if you need to refresh your memory.

Adding the class satisfies the requirement created by assigning GameMenuLayer as the custom class of the *GameMenuLayer.ccb* root node. You can confirm that the class is instantiated at least once by adding the code in Listing 6-1 to merely log whenever a node with this class has been loaded by *CCBReader*.

Listing 6-1. Logging confirms that at least one node using the GameMenuLayer class is loaded

```
#import "GameMenuLayer.h"
#import "GameScene.h"

@implementation GameMenuLayer

-(void) didLoadFromCCB
{
    NSLog(@"YAY! didLoadFromCCB: %@", self);
}

-(void) shouldPauseGame
{
    NSLog(@"BUTTON: should pause game");
}

@end
```

To satisfy the _gameMenuLayer variable assignment to *GameScene.ccb*'s root node, open *GameScene.m* to import the new GameMenuLayer class and to add the _gameMenuLayer ivar at the top of the file as highlighted in Listing 6-2.

You will also add a _popoverMenuLayer reference that will be used as the reference to the currently displayed popover layer drawn over the current level while the level is paused. The popover layers for this game are displayed when the player dies, the player makes it to the exit, or the pause button is tapped to bring up the pause menu.

Listing 6-2. Adding the _gameMenuLayer ivar to GameScene.m

```
#import "GameScene.h"
#import "Trigger.h"
#import "GameMenuLayer.h"

@implementation GameScene
{
    // existing ivars omitted for brevity ...

    __weak GameMenuLayer* _gameMenuLayer;
    __weak GameMenuLayer* _popoverMenuLayer;
}
```

Now you can build an run the project to confirm that it launches without errors. Check the log for the *YAY!* message upon load to confirm that a GameMenuLayer instance has been created. Clicking the pause button should also log the message in the shouldPauseGame selector of Listing 6-1.

Assigning a GameScene Reference to GameMenuLayer

You've already assigned a reference to the GameMenuLayer class to the _gameMenuLayer ivar in the GameScene class. But you will also need a back reference to the GameScene instance in the GameMenuLayer class. For that, you need a GameScene* property in the GameMenuLayer class.

Open `GameMenuLayer.h`, and add the code highlighted in Listing 6-3 to add a weak reference named gameScene as a property.

Listing 6-3. GameMenuLayer gets a weak GameScene property*

```
@class GameScene;

@interface GameMenuLayer : CCNode

@property (weak) GameScene* gameScene;

@end
```

Note the use of the `@class GameScene;` line. It tells the compiler that `GameScene` is an Objective-C class without having to import it. It is good practice to prefer `@class` in Objective-C headers over `#import` whenever possible. This minimizes the risk of circular imports, which in its simplest form is an interface A that declares a property to class B and imports header B, while interface B declares a property to class A and imports header A. The compiler gets all confused and spits out `unknown type name` errors when you have a circular import.

You still have to `#import` the corresponding class' header file in the `GameMenuLayer.m` implementation file, which was done in Listing 6-1. But being able to move the `#import` from the header (interface) file to the implementation file is the best strategy to prevent circular imports.

> **Note**   For `@property`, the storage identifiers are written without the leading underscores. Hence, it is weak for properties and __weak for ivars. I've also frequently seen developers use the `assign` storage identifiers, perhaps because they were following outdated tutorials. The `assign` keyword for ARC-enabled apps is the same as `unsafe_unretained`, which will not retain the reference nor set it to nil when it deallocates, leaving a dangling pointer and a potential `EXC_BAD_ACCESS` crash. For ARC-enabled apps, you should almost exclusively use weak storage identifiers or no (defaults to `strong`) storage identifiers for properties and ivars.

Now you only need to assign `self` to the gameScene property in `didLoadFromCCB` in `GameScene.m` as seen in Listing 6-4.

Listing 6-4. Assigning self to the GameMenuLayer's gameScene property

```
-(void) didLoadFromCCB
{
    _gameMenuLayer.gameScene = self;

    // remaining code omitted...
}
```

> **Caution**   The `didLoadFromCCB` method runs in reverse hierarchical order. This means a child's `didLoadFromCCB` will always run before the `didLoadFromCCB` of its parent. In this case, `_gameMenuLayer` is a child of the GameScene node. This means that the `_gameMenuLayer.gameScene` property is assigned after GameMenuLayer's `didLoadFromCCB` method runs. Code in GameMenuLayer that requires a valid `_gameScene` reference must be deferred—for instance, until the `onEnter` method runs.

If you quickly need a reference to the GameScene custom class, you can also use this code snippet to get a reference from anywhere except a node's `init` and `didLoadFromCCB` methods, because `self.scene` is still `nil` at that point:

```
GameScene* gameScene = (GameScene*)self.scene.children.firstObject;
```

Showing and Removing Popover Menus

While you're in Xcode, let's move ahead and implement some code before you've actually created the corresponding CCB files. The goal is to show a popover screen by its name—in this case, the pause menu popover when the pause button is tapped.

In GameMenuLayer.m, update the `shouldPauseGame` method as shown in Listing 6-5.

Listing 6-5. Showing the pause popover menu

```
-(void) shouldPauseGame
{
    [_gameScene showPopoverNamed:@"UserInterface/Popovers/PauseMenuLayer"];
}
```

This calls a yet-to-be-defined method, `showPopoverNamed:` in the GameScene class. Since we'll also need to remove a popover menu, update the GameScene.h interface with the method declarations highlighted in Listing 6-6.

Listing 6-6. Declaring methods for showing and removing popovers

```
#import "CCNode.h"

@interface GameScene : CCNode<CCPhysicsCollisionDelegate,CCBAnimationManagerDelegate>

-(void) showPopoverNamed:(NSString*)popoverName;
-(void) removePopover;

@end
```

Declaring methods in the @interface section of a class allows these methods to be called from other classes without raising a compiler warning.

Now add the showPopoverNamed: method in Listing 6-7 to GameScene.m. Add it at the very bottom of the file, just above the @end line.

Listing 6-7. Showing a popover menu

```
-(void) showPopoverNamed:(NSString*)name
{
    if (_popoverMenuLayer == nil)
    {
        GameMenuLayer* newMenuLayer = (GameMenuLayer*)[CCBReader load:name];
        [self addChild:newMenuLayer];

        _popoverMenuLayer = newMenuLayer;
        _popoverMenuLayer.gameScene = self;

        _gameMenuLayer.visible = NO;
        _levelNode.paused = YES;
    }
}
```

Checking that _popoverMenuLayer is nil ensures there can be only one visible popover menu at a time, even if the method runs twice in succession by accident. Then the CCBReader load: method is used to load the CCB by its name. The return value is cast to GameMenuLayer*, which assumes that all popover menus use GameMenuLayer as their custom class. The newMenuLayer is then added as a child before it is assigned to the ivar _popoverMenuLayer.

You may wonder, "Why not assign directly to _popoverMenuLayer and remove the local variable newMenuLayer?" The reason is that _popoverMenuLayer is declared __weak, so it will not retain any references assigned to it. But when CCBReader load: returns, there is, if only for a short time, no strong reference holding on to the returned node. Therefore, ARC is going to release the node and set the _popoverMenuLayer reference to nil even before the next line with addChild: runs! To be precise: it may or may not work, depending on the device in debug configurations, but it will certainly not work in release configurations.

> **Tip**   I recommend adding an NSAssert line directly before the addChild: line to verify that newMenuLayer is not nil. The popover might be in a different folder, there might be a typo in the CCB's name, or the popover CCB file simply wasn't created or published yet. Those are common and often repeatedly occuring issues, not just in this example game. It's a good idea to try and catch those early.

Like the _gameMenuLayer.gameScene before, the _popoverMenuLayer.gameScene is assigned to self, to allow methods inside the GameMenuLayer class to send messages back to the GameScene instance.

When a popover menu is shown, the pause button and other static user interface elements should be hidden. Setting the _gameMenuLayer.visible to NO effectively hides the layer and thus the pause button, which in turn makes the button inactive. A button you can't see is a button you can't touch, so to speak.

Pausing the _levelNode prevents the game from advancing by pausing all of the child nodes of the levelNode. Pausing a node pauses its Timeline animations, running actions, and scheduled selectors. Because the _physicsNode is a child of the _levelNode, the physics world will also be paused.

In order to remove a popover menu, you also need to add the removePopover method from Listing 6-8 just below the showPopoverNamed: method. It just removes the node from its parent (the GameScene node) and sets the _popoverMenuLayer ivar to nil to allow a new popover to appear. Even though the _popoverMenuLayer should become nil automatically right away, it's a good idea to remind yourself that this is intentional by explicitly assigning nil.

Listing 6-8. Removing a popover

```
-(void) removePopover
{
    if (_popoverMenuLayer)
    {
        [_popoverMenuLayer removeFromParent];
        _popoverMenuLayer = nil;

        _gameMenuLayer.visible = YES;
        _levelNode.paused = NO;
    }
}
```

Finally, the _gameMenuLayer with the pause button is made visible again and the _physicsNode is unpaused.

With this setup, you can show and hide popover menus quite neatly. There's only one thing left to prepare. In GameMenuLayer.m, you should add the two methods of Listing 6-9 just below the shouldPauseGame method.

Listing 6-9. Enabling the GameMenuLayer to resume the game by playing a specific timeline animation

```
-(void) shouldResumeGame
{
    CCAnimationManager* am = self.animationManager;
    if ([am.runningSequenceName isEqualToString:@"resume game"] == NO)
    {
        [am runAnimationsForSequenceNamed:@"resume game"];
    }
}

-(void) resumeGameDidEnd
{
    [_gameScene removePopover];
}
```

The idea here is that shouldResumeGame runs a Timeline with a specific name: *resume game*. But only if this specific Timeline isn't currently running, to prevent the user from tapping the resume button multiple times in quick succession and thus unintentionally restarting the Timeline.

> **Caution**   Timeline names are case sensitive. Because of this, it's recommended to follow a common rule for all Timeline names—for instance, no uppercase letters at all or camel casing, where each word begins with an uppercase letter.

Pausing the Game

What's left to do is to create the actual pause menu popover as a Layer CCB. In it, a Timeline animation with the name *resume game* is created that has a *Callbacks* keyframe that will run the resumeGameDidEnd selector.

Creating the Pause Menu Popover

For this and the following popover menus, add a subfolder named *Popovers* to the *UserInterface* folder in SpriteBuilder's *File View*. Then right-click the *Popovers* folder, select *New File* to create a CCB document of type *Layer*, named *PauseMenuLayer.ccb*.

The first thing you should do to this and all other popover CCBs is to set the root node's *Content size* property to *100%* for both width and height, in order to scale it up to match each device's screen size. With the root node still selected, select the *Item Code Connections* tab and enter **GameMenuLayer** as the *Custom class*. That's the same class as for the GameMenuLayer.

> **Note**   The reason for using the same class for all popover menus, including the GameMenuLayer itself, is that they all share a lot of common code. For instance, all of them will pause the game, and they all have a restart button. Plus the code in GameMenuLayer is short and simple.

Next you'll want to add a background graphic that's somewhat smaller than any device's screen so that it can easily be centered on all devices. About 320x240 is a good size. Using a background that's smaller than any screen size greatly simplifies user interface design. You can just center the content and completely ignore any screen size considerations. Only the distance from the layer's background to the screen edges will vary.

Drag and drop a *Sprite* from the *Node Library View* onto the stage and change its *Sprite frame* to *SpriteSheets/UserInterface/P_bg.png*. Alternatively, you can also drag and drop the P_bg from the *Tileless Editor View*; you may need to check the *UserInterface* check box in the *Filter folders* list below the *Tileless Editor View*. No matter how you create the sprite, you should set its position types to % and both position values to *50* so that the sprite is centered.

> **Tip**   If you're having difficulty seeing the sprite image since it's pretty dark, go to Document ➤ Stage Color
> and select a different background color for the stage.

You have to use % positions for all following nodes as well. The actual layout of labels and buttons is up to you, it's only important to make all nodes in the layer children of the background sprite so that their positions are always relative to the background sprite's lower left corner rather than relative to the screen's lower left corner. This allows you to move the sprites along with the background if you ever decide that the background shouldn't be centered but rather offset a little.

Add a *Label TTF* from the *Node Library View*, make it a child of the P_bg sprite, and change its position types to %. Drag and move it to where you like. Oh, and change the *Label text* field to something like *Game Paused*. You may also want to pick a different font or change the font size.

Proceed by adding three *Button* nodes, one after another, from the *Node Library View*. Make those children of the P_bg sprite, and change their position types to % as well. Then move them to appropriate locations. See Figure 6-6 for a possible result.

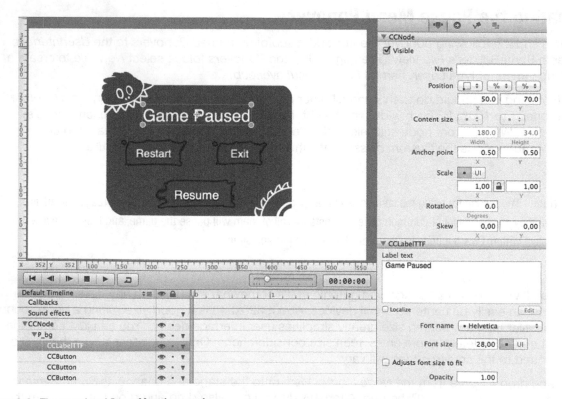

Figure 6-6. The completed PauseMenuLayer.ccb

For each button, perform the following steps on the *Item Properties* tab:

■ Set *Title* to *Restart*, *Exit*, or *Resume*, depending on which button you are editing.

■ Change *Sprite frame* for both *Normal State* and *Highlighted State* to the same image. You may want to use the following images from *SpriteSheets/ UserInterface*: *P_restart.png*, *P_exit.png*, *P_resume.png*.

■ For *Highlighted State*, change both *Background color* and *Label color* to a gray color—for instance, the web color with hex code #999999. This will give a visual cue when touching the buttons: they will appear darker while highlighted.

■ Under the *CCLabelTTF* section, edit the *Font name* and *Font size* as you like. You may need to increase *Horizontal padding*, perhaps even *Vertical padding*, to make the background image slightly larger so that the button's text is wholly contained in the background frame.

After editing the properties, switch to the *Item Code Connections* tab. For each button, enter the corresponding *Selector*: shouldRestartGame, shouldExitGame, and shouldResumeGame.

You can publish, build, and run the project now. Then tap the pause button to see your new popover menu. Note that tapping any button on the layer will cause a crash at this stage.

If nodes aren't where they are supposed to be, verify the parent-child relationship is correct and that position types are set to % for all nodes. See Figure 6-6 for reference.

Interlude: Full-Screen Popovers

An in-game menu that only temporarily replaces the current scene is a frequent request, and developers are often left wondering how to implement that.

Usually, developers are seeking to use push and pop scene methods, or even replace scenes while saving and restoring game states. While there's use for both, it's really simple to create a nondestructive full-screen "scene" on top of the current scene without having to change scenes. You can do that with minor enhancements to the popover layer you've just created. Let's try it.

Drag and drop a *Color Node* from the *Node Library View* onto the *PauseMenuLayer.ccb* stage. Move the color node in the Timeline so that it is above the P_bg background sprite. Be sure the color node is not a child of the background sprite. Then set the color node's position to 0,0 and change *Content size* to use % types and *100* as the value for both width and height. This expands the color node to fill the screen.

If you run this in the game and tap the pause button, suddenly your game view disappears. This is because you are looking at a full-screen popover menu with a solid color background. If you prefer, you can also use a *Gradient Node* instead of the color node.

Tip If you notice lag due to low framerate when displaying such a full-screen popover, simply set the visible property of the _levelNode in the background to NO. This will prevent it from being rendered behind the popover, improving rendering performance.

But wait, there's more to it! In addition to a full-screen popover, you can also dim the level view while the popover is presented. This is easily achieved by changing the color node's `Color` property to black and then setting its `Opacity` to about 0.5.

You can also play with the color node's `Blend src` and `Blend dst` settings to create additional effects. Try setting `Blend src` to `One` and `Blend dst` to `One - Dst Color` to get false colors. Try changing the color node's color and opacity, too.

Or set `Blend src` to `One - Dst Color` and `Blend dst` to `Src Alpha Saturate` with `Opacity` set to 1 and white color to create a photo-negative effect as shown in Figure 6-7.

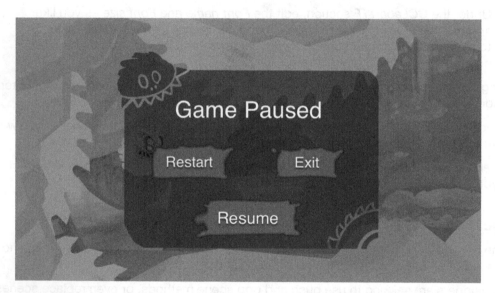

Figure 6-7. The PauseMenuLayer presented in the game with a photo-negative effect applied by using blend modes

> **Note**   The `src` and `dst` abbreviations stand for *source* and *destination*, respectively. These properties refer to OpenGL blend modes, which affect how the colors of pixels in overlapping source and destination buffers are blended together.

The blend modes may work differently or not at all for a gradient node, or any other node for that matter. Changing blend modes in SpriteBuilder will also not show you the actual results as they appear in the game—you have to test blend-mode settings in the Simulator or on a device.

Of course, you can also use a *Sprite* with a background image large enough to cover the largest screen size, either in place of the color node or instead of the P_bg sprite, in order to create a full-screen popover with a full-screen background image.

Changing Scenes with SceneManager

At this point, the restart and exit buttons in the Pause popover menu won't do anything yet. Except maybe crash. The restart and exit buttons simply present a new scene that will remove the current scene, so you won't have to worry about closing the popover or anything.

Since you will be presenting scenes from various places throughout the project, and typically each scene should be presented with the same transition, it makes perfect sense to have only one method that presents a particular scene in a particular way. That way, you won't have to skim all of your code for scene changes in order to change the type of transition used or its duration.

A class that contains only so-called "class" methods (similar to static methods in C++) helps to extract such common, repetitive tasks that are unfitting to any existing class.

Add a new Objective-C class to the Source group in Xcode. Name the new class **SceneManager**, and change the *Subclass of* field to NSObject, the base class of all Objective-C classes. It doesn't need to be a *CCNode* because this class will not be added as a child to the node hierarchy.

Add the code highlighted in Listing 6-10 to the SceneManager.h file.

Listing 6-10. The SceneManager interface declares only class methods

```
#import <Foundation/Foundation.h>

@interface SceneManager : NSObject

+(void) presentMainMenu;
+(void) presentGameScene;

@end
```

The SceneManager.m implements these two class methods—as denoted by the leading + character.

For brevity, I declared the variables in Listing 6-11 to be of type id and gave them only single-letter identifiers just so the lines are short enough to avoid having to add line breaks in the book. Of course, single-letter variable names should generally be avoided except for very short code fragments where there can't be any ambiguities.

Listing 6-11. SceneManager presents each scene with a specific transition and duration

```
#import "SceneManager.h"

@implementation SceneManager

+(void) presentMainMenu
{
    id s = [CCBReader loadAsScene:@"MainScene"];
    id t = [CCTransition transitionMoveInWithDirection:CCTransitionDirectionLeft
                                        duration:1.0];
    [[CCDirector sharedDirector] presentScene:s withTransition:t];
}
```

```
+(void) presentGameScene
{
    id s = [CCBReader loadAsScene:@"GameScene"];
    id t = [CCTransition transitionMoveInWithDirection:CCTransitionDirectionRight
                                              duration:1.0];
    [[CCDirector sharedDirector] presentScene:s withTransition:t];
}
```

@end

> **Note**   Using the generic type *id* in place of a pointer to a specific Objective-C class is perfectly legal, and in fact very useful if you don't actually need to do anything with the particular object except pass it on to other methods.

With the SceneManger methods defined, open GameMenuLayer.m. At the top, below the other #import lines, add the line in Listing 6-12 to make the SceneManager class known to the GameMenuLayer implementation file.

Listing 6-12. Adding the SceneManager import

```
#import "SceneManager.h"
```

Then add the methods in Listing 6-13 just below the shouldPauseGame method.

Listing 6-13. Restart and exit buttons simply present a scene

```
-(void) shouldRestartGame
{
    [SceneManager presentGameScene];
}

-(void) shouldExitGame
{
    [SceneManager presentMainMenu];
}
```

Notice that calling the SceneManager class methods does not require having an instance of the SceneManager class. You can just call them by using the class' name itself as the receiver. The drawback of class methods is that they do not have access to the class' state—for instance, they couldn't access any of the SceneManager class' properties and ivars if it had any.

The SceneManager acts purely as a utility class that runs repetitive, stateless code that needs to be accessible from various other classes to perform a specific purpose (presenting scenes). If you have a task that fits this description, you should consider putting it in a class that has only class methods.

Adding a Callbacks Keyframe

Before resuming the game, it is a good idea to first remove the pause popover menu with an animation. This gives the user some time to prepare herself for resuming play, perhaps introducing a 3..2..1 countdown timer after dismissing the pause menu.

Now, theoretically, you could assign an `animationManager.delegate` and implement the `completedAnimationSequenceNamed:` method to find out if the *resume game* Timeline is done playing.

However, I haven't explained how to use the *Callbacks* keyframes in the Timeline, and I haven't explained how they can be used to run custom selectors at any point in the Timeline. This situation is a good use for a *Callbacks* keyframe. In fact, any time you need to call a selector at a specific point in time during a Timeline animation, you would use a *Callbacks* keyframe.

In SpriteBuilder, open the *PauseMenuLayer.ccb*. Left-click on the *Timeline List* (see Figure 5-1), and select *New Timeline*. This will create and select a new timeline named *Untitled Timeline*. Left-click the *Timeline List* again, and then select *Edit Timelines* to bring up the same Timelines editing dialog as shown in Figure 5-9. Double-click the *Untitled Timeline* text to edit it, and rename this Timeline **resume game**. Leave the *Autoplay* check box unchecked for the *resume game* Timeline, and then click *Done*.

> **Caution**   Once you have more than one timeline in a CCB, it becomes crucial to verify that you are editing the correct Timeline. Check the *Timeline List* before making edits, especially if you're wondering why an edit wouldn't change anything. It may take some time to get used to the idea of switching Timelines, which you can do by left-clicking the *Timeline List*, and then select the desired Timeline from the *Timelines* submenu.

Next, edit the Timeline duration by clicking on the digits box in the upper right corner of the Timeline. (See Figure 5-2 for reference.) Make the Timeline two seconds long; this should be enough time. Now move the Timeline Cursor to the end of the timeline at the 2-seconds mark. Here's where you should add a *Callbacks* keyframe.

If you tried to add a *Callbacks* keyframe before you probably couldn't. The trick is to hold the *Option* key, and then click on the *Callbacks* segment to add a *Callbacks* keyframe.

With a *Callbacks* keyframe added, it still won't do anything yet—you'll have to edit the keyframe's properties. To do so, double-click the keyframe. A popover like the one shown in Figure 6-8 will appear, where you should enter **resumeGameDidEnd** in the *Selector* field.

> **Tip**   The sound effects keyframes are also added by Option-clicking on the sound-effects segment, and they're editable by double-clicking a keyframe.

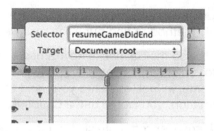

Figure 6-8. Editing a Callbacks keyframe

As with other keyframes, you can also right-click a *Callbacks* or *Sound effects* keyframe to *Cut*, *Copy*, or *Delete* it. You can also delete keyframes by selecting a keyframe with a left-click and pressing the *Backspace* key.

> **Note**   If you receive a message that says "the root node cannot be removed" when trying to cut or delete a *Callbacks* or *Sound effects* keyframe, just deselect the root node by selecting any other node or by clicking on the stage, outside any node, to deselect the currently selected node(s).

You've already added the necessary code to handle resuming a game in Listing 6-9. The `shouldResumeGame` method runs the *resume game* Timeline, which in turn will eventually run the `resumeGameDidEnd` selector.

If you build and run the app now, pause the game, and then click resume, the pause menu popover will disappear after two seconds and the game continues.

You can also restart the level and exit to the menu now, as the `SceneManager` will change scenes. (See Listing 6-13.) As an exercise for you, you may want to add another `SceneManager` class method that presents the `GameScene` but without using a transition. Then update the `shouldRestartGame` method to use your new `SceneManager` method.

Animating the Pause Menu on Resume

Having no visual feedback at all after tapping the resume button on the pause menu is kind of dreadful. How exactly you animate the *resume game* Timeline of the *PauseMenuLayer.ccb* is up to you, except for the *Callbacks* keyframe at the end that runs the `resumeGameDidEnd` selector. In the following paragraphs, I give just an example and some inspiration as to what you can do in those two seconds.

First, consider that animating the P_bg background sprite will also move, scale, and rotate its child nodes. About the only property that is not inherited is opacity. If you wanted to slowly fade out the popover layer, I'm afraid you would have to add the same opacity keyframes to each individual button, the label, and the background sprite—and on top of that, make them all start and end at the same time stamp with the same opacity values. Therefore, I decided not to fade out the layer.

> **Tip**   If you followed the blend-mode interlude, you may find it difficult to see things on the stage. If that is the case, click the eye symbol in the Timeline to the right of the *CCNodeColor* entry to hide the color node while leaving it visible in the game.

Select the P_bg sprite node and press *V* to insert a *Visible* keyframe. Move this keyframe to the far left, time stamp 00:00:00. The visible property can only be turned on and off; therefore, the *Keyframe Segment* is drawn thicker and it behaves differently, filling the entire segment even though there's just one keyframe so far. Move the Timeline Cursor just past the 1-second mark, and add another *Visible* keyframe with the *V* key. See Figure 6-9 if you need a visual hint.

Next add two *Position* keyframes with the *P* key at the 00:00:00 and 00:01:00 timestamps. Move the Timeline Cursor onto the second keyframe, the one to the right, and then drag and move the P_bg sprite to the upper left corner of the screen. Right-click the *Position Keyframe Segment*, and select the *Ease In* easing mode. This completes the move animation to the upper left corner, and in itself it's rather boring.

Add two *Scale* keyframes with the P_bg sprite selected, also at the 00:00:00 and 00:01:00 time stamps. Move the Timeline Cursor onto the second keyframe, and then change the Scale property to 0.2 and 0.1 for the X and Y axes. Right-click the *Keyframe Segment*, and choose the *Ease Out* easing mode. If you run this animation, the entire pause layer should drop to the back (zoom out) while sliding to the upper left.

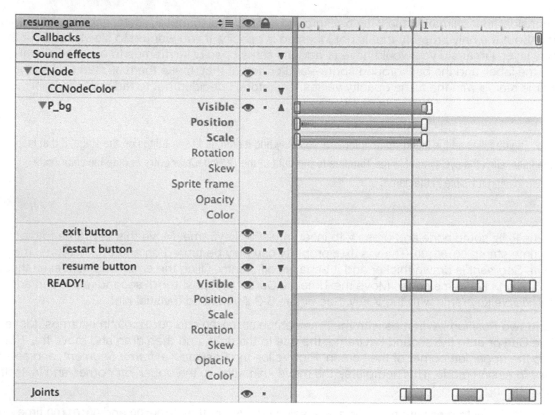

Figure 6-9. An example for the resume game Timeline with a blinking READY! label

If you also want to add some kind of ready indicator, drag and drop a *Label TTF* node from the *Node Library View* onto the stage. This node should be a child of the root node but *not* a child of the P_bg sprite. Change the label's text to **READY!**, and increase its *Font size* to *100*. Feel free to edit any other label properties as you see fit. But do uncheck the label's *Visible* check box at the very top of the properties tab so that it starts out initially hidden. You should also change the label's position types to % and values to *50* so that it is centered on the stage.

With the new label still selected, move the Timeline Cursor to about the 1-second mark, and then press *V*. Move the Timeline Cursor to the right, and press *V* again. Repeat this until you have about three equally spaced and sized *Keyframe Segments* as seen in Figure 6-9. Drag and move the keyframes to even out the spacing, or intentionally make the spacing uneven. The important part is that the last keyframe should set the label's Visible property to NO. There will be a pink *Keyframe Segment* drawn between each two keyframes where the label is visible.

If you play this animation, the menu will zoom out and move to the upper left, at which point the *ready* label starts to blink three times. If you run this in the game, the game will resume when the Timeline reaches the *Callbacks* keyframe.

As an exercise for you, add three additional *Callbacks* keyframes at the same time stamps where the label becomes visible. Use the same selector updateReadyCounter for each keyframe, implement the corresponding method in GameMenuLayer, and add a _readyCounter ivar of type int to the GameMenuLayer class.

The _readyCounter should be set to 3 in the shouldResumeGame method and decreased by one every time updateReadyCounter runs. In the same method, you update the label's text property to 3, 2, and 1, depending on the _readyCounter, to create a countdown label.

You'll need a reference to the label to do so, so either give it a name and get it by name, or more efficiently use the *Item Code Connections* tab to assign the label reference to a _readyLabel ivar of type CCLabelTTF*, which you'll have to add as an ivar in the GameMenuLayer.m file.

Interlude: Pausing the Game When It Enters the Background

Wouldn't it be nice if the game would automatically pause whenever the app enters the background? This happens, for instance, when receiving a phone call or the user taps the home button while playing.

Furthermore, wouldn't it be awesome if any node could implement one of the UIApplicationDelegate methods and receive them as they are sent by iOS without having to manually pass these messages along or registering notifications and what not? Well yes, and in fact it's quite straightforward to implement.

Open the AppDelegate.m file in Xcode. Just below the startScene method, add the method from Listing 6-14.

Listing 6-14. Forwarding UIApplicationDelegate messages to nodes

```
-(void) performSelector:(SEL)selector
                 onNode:(CCNode*)node
             withObject:(id)object
              recursive:(BOOL)recursive
{
    if ([node respondsToSelector:selector])
    {
        [node performSelector:selector withObject:object];
    }

    if (recursive)
    {
        for (CCNode* child in node.children)
        {
            [self performSelector:selector
                           onNode:child
                       withObject:object
                        recursive:YES];
        }
    }
}
```

> **Tip** The method in Listing 6-14 could be added as a category on NSObject instead—in particular, if you find that you have use for it in the future.

The performSelector:onNode:withObject:recursive: method mimics the behavior of other performSelector methods defined by the NSObject class, except that it runs the selector only if the given node implements it by testing for respondsToSelector: first.

> **Note** The performSelector:withObject: line may generate a "may cause a leak" warning. You can safely ignore it as long as the performed selector does not return a pointer or id type. Also note that the selector must take a single parameter—no more and no less. If you need to use other message signatures, you would have to make a variant of the method in Listing 6-14 that takes no object or two objects, and use either the performSelector or performSelector:withObject:withObject: methods to pass the objects along.

If the recursive flag is set, the same method will also be run for each of the node's children and their children. Effectively, every node in the node hierarchy gets a chance to run the given selector merely by having implemented it.

This is not the most efficient way of passing messages to other nodes, so avoid using this for frequent events or as a replacement for properly obtaining references of nodes to which you want to send messages. But it works well as a convenience to distribute rare messages without knowing which nodes may be interested in receiving that message. The alternative would be to register a node with NSNotificationCenter and, of course, properly unregister it as well, which is more cumbersome and error prone than just implementing a specific UIApplicationDelegate selector.

An example use is to forward the applicationWillResignActive: message to any node interested in handling that particular message. Add the code in Listing 6-15 to AppDelegate.m just below the newly added performSelector:onNode:withObject:recursive: method.

Listing 6-15. Forwarding a UIApplicationDelegate message to all nodes in the scene

```
-(void) applicationWillResignActive:(UIApplication *)application
{
    CCScene* scene = [CCDirector sharedDirector].runningScene;
    [self performSelector:_cmd
                   onNode:scene
               withObject:application
                recursive:YES];

    [super applicationWillResignActive:application];
}
```

The currently running scene obtained from CCDirector runs the _cmd selector on the scene and recursively on all of its child nodes, passing along the application object. The CCDirector class is the Cocos2D UIViewController subclass and manager of Cocos2D application states.

What's the _cmd selector here, and where does it come from?

It's a hidden method parameter every Objective-C method receives behind the scenes. It is the selector of the currently running method. In other words, in this example _cmd is identical to writing @ selector(applicationWillResignActive:). The other implicit Objective-C method parameter is one you've already made frequent use of: it's the self keyword.

To actually pause the game when the application will resign, add the method in Listing 6-16 to GameMenuLayer.m, perhaps just below the already existing shouldPauseGame method since it doesn't do anything but run the shouldPauseGame method.

Listing 6-16. The GameMenuLayer class receives applicationWillResignActive: and runs shouldPauseGame

```
-(void) applicationWillResignActive:(UIApplication *)application
{
    [self shouldPauseGame];
}
```

If you build and run the app now, press the Home button once the game is running to close the app. Actually, the app won't close—it will be sent to the background for an indefinite time.

Then tap the app's icon again to relaunch the app. You should see that the app continues from where you closed it, but the game is paused and the pause popover menu is shown.

Killing the Player

The Game Over state can be handled just like pause with a popover menu, with nearly the same functionality, allowing the player either to restart the level or to exit the current game session.

And, of course, the player needs to die! And what better way to kill the player than by slicing it up with a circular saw?

Creating a "Game Over" Popover

In SpriteBuilder, right-click the *Popovers* folder and add a *New File*. Name the new document *GameOverMenuLayer.ccb*, set its type to *Layer*, and then click *Create*. Editing the *Game over* menu follows the same basic principle as the pause menu, so I will only note the differences here.

For instance, the predesigned graphics for the *Game over* menu all start with a G_, though you are free to use other images. And there should be no resume button, only exit and restart buttons. Since there's no resume function, you needn't add the *resume game* Timeline either. And the label's text shouldn't read *Game Paused*, but rather *Game Over*.

Be sure to set the *Custom class* of the *GameOverMenuLayer.ccb* root node to GameMenuLayer; otherwise, none of the buttons will work. Likewise, the exit and restart buttons should have their *Selector* fields set to shouldExitGame and shouldRestartGame, respectively. That's what's important for functionality, the rest is just visual appeal. I'm not saying that visuals aren't important too, but they're not as important for continuing with the book.

But you are free to spend some time to animate the nodes on the menu shown in Figure 6-10. For instance, why not animate the Color property of the *Game over* label? Select the *Game over* label node, and then add multiple *Color* keyframes by pressing *C*. Move the Timeline Cursor onto each keyframe and, on the *Item Properties* tab, click the colored rectangle next to the Color property, which presents the OS X color-picker dialog to let you pick a color. Right-click the individual *Keyframe Segments*, and change the easing modes to whatever you like.

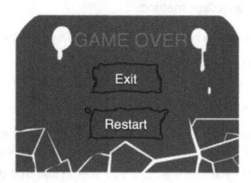

Figure 6-10. What the Game Over menu might look like

Run this animation and you'll weep tears of delight. Such vivid colors. But enough with the sentimentalities. Art really isn't my strong point, so let's move on to kill the player.

Showing the "Game Over" Popover

Go back to Xcode, and open GameScene.m. Locate the ccPhysicsCollision methods, and below the last one, add the collision method shown in Listing 6-17.

Listing 6-17. There will not be blood: responding to a collision between player and saw

```
-(BOOL) ccPhysicsCollisionBegin:(CCPhysicsCollisionPair *)pair
                        player:(CCNode *)player
                           saw:(CCNode *)saw
{
    [self showPopoverNamed:@"UserInterface/Popovers/GameOverMenuLayer"];
    return YES;
}
```

The third parameter is named saw, in line with the Collision type of each saw prefab. If there is a collision between player and saw, the method simply shows the GameOverMenuLayer popover now. It's a pretty harsh ending, but alas, there will *not* be blood. Not now, anyway.

> **Note**   If you find that some or all of the saws do not run the collision method in Listing 6-17, open each saw prefab in the *Prefabs* folder in SpriteBuilder. Each of them should have their *Collision type* set to *saw* on the *Item Physics* tab. You may want to confirm this now, and where the *Collision* type is missing or incorrect, enter *saw*. Be sure to check the sprite node of each CCB, not their root nodes.

Interlude: Fixing the Initial Scroll Position

Wow! Game Over was quick. Is there anything else we could do?

You may have noticed that when you press the restart button or whenever you change from the menu scene to the game scene, the level view isn't centered on the player initially. That's kind of bad, and it's a result of the GameScene updating its scroll position only after the first time the update: method has run. But the very first frame is rendered earlier.

Fortunately, the fix is easy. Open GameScene.m, and locate the loadLevelNamed: method. Add the highlighted line of Listing 6-18 at the end of the method.

Listing 6-18. Fixing the initial scroll position

```
-(void) loadLevelNamed:(NSString*)levelCCB
{
    // existing code omitted ...

    [self scrollToTarget:_playerNode];
}
```

This will ensure the _physicsNode.position is updated according to the player's initial position before the scene is rendered for the first time. If you run the game now and restart or exit to the main menu via the pause menu, the screen will be centered on the player immediately. This will be particularly noticeable when presenting the GameScene with a transition.

> **Tip** Sometimes such inconsistencies or visual glitches in the first or first couple frames of a scene can't be avoided. In that case, you could start the scene with a full-screen popover presented, perhaps one that uses the exact same background as the preceding loading scene so that the user won't even notice the difference. Then just fade out or remove the popover menu after a few frames have been drawn, using a *Callbacks* keyframe in the popover's Default Timeline.

Summary

You can now pause the game and kill the player. Both actions present a popover menu to restart and exit the level or, in the case of the pause menu, resume the game with a *ready* animation. There were a number of cool tricks dispersed throughout this chapter as well.

The project at this stage of the book is also found in the book's downloadable archive in the *07 - Popover Menus* folder.

Getting Down to Business with SpriteBuilder

Chapter 7

Main Scene and Game State

So far we've fully neglected the main scene, where the game's main menu ought to be. The main menu is a good place to add a *Settings* menu that allows you to change the volume of background music and sound effects.

The settings popover requires a grid-based layout, which is why you'll use the *Box Layout* node for the first time. You'll also add a way to store the game state permanently—for instance, unlocked levels and audio volumes—so that it doesn't get lost if the app is terminated.

Main Scene Background

It's time to give the game's main menu a make-over. Right now *MainScene.ccb* is still the pale, blue scene with the SpriteBuilder label and a play button.

Designing the Background Images

In the previous chapter, you already added the Menu and UserInterface Sprite Sheets. Switch to the Tileless Editor View and, at the bottom, check the *Menu* folder so that it isn't filtered out. You should find the Menu images like they are in Figure 7-1.

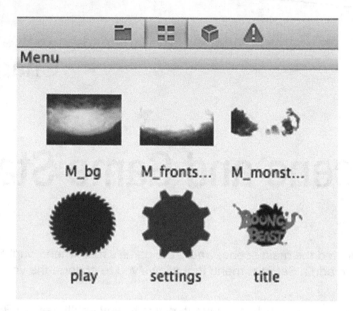

Figure 7-1. The Menu images as seen in the Tileless Editor View

If you want to provide your own images, you should have about three screen-sized images forming the menu's background layers. *Screen-sized* means the lowest common denominator size—that is, 568x384 points if your app should run on both iPhones and iPads. Considering that the iPad is scaled by a factor of two and that there are Retina iPads that add another scale factor of two, the full-screen images should be 2272x1536 pixels in size. If you design your app to run only on iPhones, your reference size should be 568x320 points. Thus, you only need images that fit the iPhone Retina screen—in other words, the full-screen images should be 1136x640 pixels in size. See Chapter 3 if you need a refresher on resolution and image sizes.

You may be wondering why all of the background layer images should be screen-sized. Isn't this a waste of memory and doesn't it increase file size? Actually, no. If you place these images in a Sprite Sheet, SpriteBuilder will cut off any excess transparent areas. It will crop off the transparent parts and store only the smallest possible rectangle that encloses any and all nontransparent pixels. Figure 7-2 illustrates this.

Figure 7-2. SpriteBuilder crops images in Sprite Sheets so that only the smallest possible rectangle enclosing all nontransparent pixels remain. Here the dark gray area at the top is cut off

Figure 7-2 is the *M_frontsmoke.png* image with colorized highlights. The gray rectangle at the top is the area SpriteBuilder cuts off because it contains only transparent pixels. The image also highlights the semi-transparent pixels by using a solid color for any pixel that isn't fully transparent. This emphasizes how even a single or just barely visible pixel can significantly reduce how much SpriteBuilder can crop. The image in Figure 7-2 could be optimized to increase the amount of cropping by removing the semi-transparent clouds of pixels smeared upwards on both sides of the image.

This is a constant struggle for game developers: visual quality vs. memory usage/performance.

Figure 7-3 shows the Menu Sprite Sheet's preview image. You'll notice that the *M_bg.png* image uses about the same space as the two *M_monsters.png* and *M_frontsmoke.png* images. Furthermore, some images are rotated to pack the images more efficiently in the Sprite Sheet.

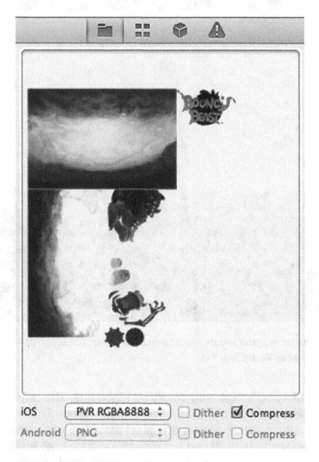

Figure 7-3. SpriteBuilder automatically optimized the Menu Sprite Sheet by cropping transparent, rectangular areas and by rotating individual images

As a result of these Sprite Sheet optimizations, screen-sized or generally large images that contain mainly transparent areas consume just as much memory and occupy just as much space in the Sprite Sheet as if their size had been cropped by an image program.

I'm telling you this because drawing all images on the same-sized canvas while relying on SpriteBuilder to crop transparent areas makes graphics design for games a lot easier.

For one, you can place each screen-sized sprite at the same position (typically 0, 0 or the center of the screen) and they will overlap just like they do in the image program. No fiddling with positions necessary. Cocos2D considers the cropped-off areas and offsets the sprite textures accordingly.

You can then do the entire layout of a scene or layer in the image program. Many artists prefer to do so. The artist will be able to move the elements within this 2272x1536 canvas as she sees fit, and they will appear the same way in the game. Just save the images, publish, and run the app to see the new layout in the game.

Designing the Background CCB

Since you may want to re-use the menu's background layer in other scenes, it's a good idea to design it in a separate layer.

Right-click the *UserInterface* folder—the folder, not the Sprite Sheet of the same name—and select *New File*. Name this new document **MainMenuBackground.ccb**, set its type to *Layer* with the default 568x384 size, and then click *Create*.

As usual, the first thing to do to a Layer CCB's root node is set its *Content size* types to % and *Content size* values to *100*. This ensures the layer properly scales with varying screen resolutions while remaining centered on all devices.

Add a regular *Node* from the Node Library View onto the *MainMenuBackground.ccb* stage. Set the node's position types to % and its values to *50* so that the node is centered on the layer. You may also want to rename the node in the timeline to **background**. The *background* node will be the container for the background images.

You can now drag and drop the background images from the Tileless Editor View onto the *background* node. Add the images in this order (see also Figure 7-4):

- *M_bg*
- *M_monsters*
- *M_frontsmoke*

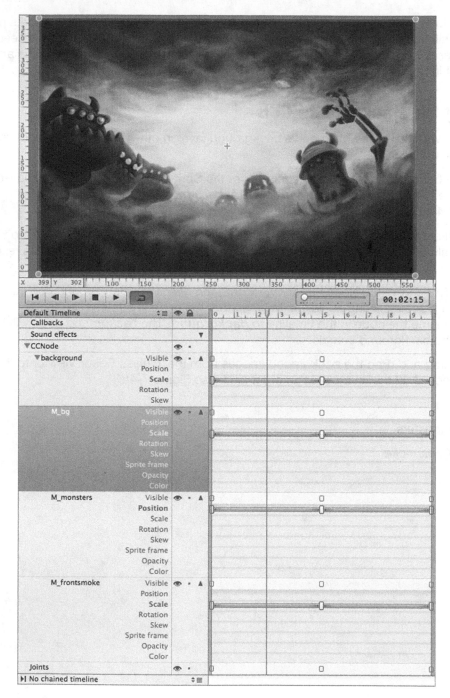

Figure 7-4. *A scary animation. Doesn't look like it. Doesn't look like much either, but it has its effect. It's not shown here because you have to see it in motion*

They should all be children of the centered *background* node so that the sprites will automatically be centered on the layer. The sprites center automatically because the anchor point for sprites defaults to 0.5x0.5, meaning the texture is drawn centered on the sprite's position.

Note   Changing a node's anchor point affects scale and rotate operations, as well as bounding box and collision detection. The anchor point only shifts the visual representation of a node, and this change may not be represented by, say, physics. You should never mistake the anchor point as a way to position nodes. Always use the position to move nodes. In well-designed Cocos2D apps, it should be very rare to find any anchor point having any values other than 0, 0.5 or 1. In general, anchor points set to 0x0 and 0.5x0.5 are by far the most commonly used.

Animating the Background

Nothing is as unexciting as a static background. Anything can be made more attractive with just a bit of motion. And this is even more true if the images were designed with a little motion in mind, which is why the background images are split into separate layers in the first place. Otherwise, you could have just used a single, static, and boring background image.

Consider, for instance, the OS X screen savers—specifically, the Classic screen saver that draws images without animating them. Then compare it with the Ken Burns screen saver, where the images are panning and zooming slowly. Which one looks more lively?

If you need another example, consider TV programs. Any time there isn't a human being or animal in focus and the scene is largely static, if not a photograph, the camera *always* pans or zooms slowly, perhaps both. And they say you can't learn anything from watching TV.

In Figure 7-4, you can see how little it takes to make the background images even scarier through the use of a few scale animations and moving the monsters slowly up and down—of course, with easing.

Specifically, you should add three keyframes to each of the background images and the *background* node. Start by adding three scale keyframes to the *background* node by pressing S. One keyframe should be at either end, and the third should be in the middle at the 5-seconds mark. Move the Timeline Cursor over the keyframe in the middle and, on the *Item Properties* tab, for the *background* node, set both *Scale* values to *1.02*.

It's a miniscule amount of scaling, but once you play the animation, you'll notice the effect already. Then right-click a *Keyframe Segment* and select *Ease In/Out*. Repeat this for the other *Keyframe Segment* too. Play the animation again, and you'll notice it will be even smoother now.

Next, repeat adding three scale keyframes with *Ease In/Out* easing to the *M_bg* and *M_frontsmoke* sprites. For *M_bg*, set the middle keyframe's scale values to *1.01* and *1.02* for X and Y. And for *M_frontsmoke*, set the middle keyframe's *Scale* values to *1.02* and *1.06* for X and Y. I'm sure you'll notice how this enhances the animation further.

Now select the *M_monsters* node and change its Y position property to *–15*. This will move the node down a bit. Then add three position keyframes by pressing the P key—again, one keyframe at either end and one at the center. Move the Timeline Cursor over the center keyframe, and then edit the Y position property to *0*. Don't forget to apply the *Ease In/Out* mode to both Keyframe Segments. This will make the monsters move up and down synchronized with the scale movement.

Last, you'll want this animation to loop forever. To do so, left-click on the bottom bar that reads *No chained timeline* in Figure 7-4 and select *Default Timeline* from the list to chain the animation to itself, thus looping it.

The resulting animation shows the entire background layer slowly coming at you while the monsters rise out of the smoke. As the background recedes, so will the monsters as they drop down into the smoke.

Try to intensify this animation effect or make it even more subtle by increasing the timeline duration and moving the keyframes accordingly. There's a lot to be gained with subtlety in animations. And synchronicity. Therefore, while you may want to try different easing modes for this animation, the best effect is when all nodes use the same easing mode. Otherwise, the movements will not be synchronized, diminishing the desired effect.

Launching with the Menu

To try this animation in the game you need to complete a few more housekeeping steps. For one, you haven't yet added the background to the *MainScene.ccb*, which still contains the original nodes.

Open the *MainScene.ccb*, and remove the gradient and label nodes. In fact, remove any excess nodes except for the play button; otherwise, you won't be able to play a level until the next chapter. But you may want to move the play button out of the way, near the lower-left corner.

With the *MainScene* cleared, drag and drop the *MainMenuBackground* onto the stage, either by dragging it from the Tileless Editor View or by dragging the *MainMenuBackground.ccb* from the File View. Then set the position of the newly created *CCBFile* instance to *0, 0*. You should also rename the *CCBFile* instance to **background** in the Timeline.

The original play button should be drawn in front of the background. It should be underneath the *background* node in the Timeline. If it's not, drag the play button downward in the Timeline to change the draw order.

After you publish the project, you can run Xcode and try it out—though it's a bit awkward to go through the pause menu and then exit the game to the main menu. Open *AppDelegate.m*, and locate the startScene method. Then change the line it contains so that it loads *MainScene.ccb*, as seen in Listing 7-1.

Listing 7-1. Launching the app with MainScene.ccb

```
-(CCScene*) startScene
{
    return [CCBReader loadAsScene:@"MainScene"];
}
```

The game will now launch with the *MainScene*, but it's still missing the logo and buttons.

Main Scene Logo and Buttons

Let's add some buttons and the logo. Since the button images *play.png* and *settings.png* from the Menu Sprite Sheet should have a rotation animation, you need to get a little creative regarding how they work as buttons.

Also, you'll want to use the Timeline Chain to have an intro sequence where the buttons come flying in from the side of the screen.

Designing Logo and Buttons

But first things first. Once more, create a new CCB file for the buttons. Right-click the *UserInterface* folder and select *New File*. Name the document **MainMenuButtons.ccb**, make it a *Layer*, leave the default size, and click *Create*. You should probably change the stage color right away, too. Go to *Document* ➤ *Stage Color* ➤ *White* to better see the images.

Again, the first thing to do on a Layer CCB is to select the root node and change its *Content size* types to % with values of *100* to ensure proper scaling and centering.

As it has so many times before, a grouping node will come in handy for both positioning and animation. Add a regular *Node* from the Node Library View onto the stage. Change the node's position types to % and its values to *50*. Give the node a nice name, let's say **logoAndButtons**. I bet you can do these steps in your sleep after just a few days of working with SpriteBuilder.

From the Tileless Editor View, you can now drag and drop the *play*, *settings*, and *title* images onto the *logoAndButtons* node. The actual position for these sprites are not really important, but I'll give you the values I used.

The title sprite should be slightly above center, so change its position to *0, 50*. The play sprite's position should be at *–50, –60*, and the settings sprite's position at *50, –60*. Negative positions are absolutely okay since the position of a node is always relative to the parent node—in this case, *logoAndButtons*. The three sprites should now have some space between them, as you can see in Figure 7-5.

Figure 7-5. The MainMenuButtons.ccb contents

> **Tip**   If you need to see the background to properly align buttons and logos, you can always drag and drop
> *MainMenuBackground.ccb* onto the stage and move it to the top of the Timeline so that it is drawn in the
> background. However, you should not forget to remove that background layer or at least uncheck its *Visible*
> property. Merely unchecking the eye symbol will only hide it from SpriteBuilder, but it will still render two
> instances of *MainMenuBackground.ccb*. That would be a major drag on performance.

The buttons could use some text on them because the images alone do not really convey meaning.
From the Node Library View, drag one *Label TTF* node onto the play sprite, and then drag another
Label TTF onto the settings sprite. The labels should be child nodes of the play and sprite nodes,
respectively.

For both labels, you first select the label and then change its position type to % and value to *50*.
This centers the label on the respective sprite. Then enter appropriate *Label text*—for example, *PLAY*
(all caps) for the play label and *Settings* for the settings label. The play label could use a *Font size* of
20, while the settings label allows for no more than *Font size* 16 if the text is not supposed to draw
beyond the gear image. The result should look similar to Figure 7-5.

Animating Logo and Buttons

Animating will be a tad more interesting this time. You'll create an intro Timeline that moves the logo
and buttons in place, before they start rotating.

Left-click the *Timeline List* (as shown in Figure 5-1 in Chapter 5), and select *Edit Timelines* to bring
up the dialog shown in Figure 5-9. Click the + button to create a second Timeline and name it **loop**.
Double-click *Default Timeline* in the list to change its name to **entry**. Leave the Autoplay check box
as is. Then click *Done*.

The goal is to have the entry animation play automatically. The entry animation is then chained to run the loop animation, while the loop animation is chained to itself to loop forever. Overall, this is a very convenient way to create a looping animation with a one-time entry animation. Let's set this up first.

The *Timeline List* should read *entry*, showing that the entry Timeline is selected. If it's not, left-click the *Timelines List* and select the *entry* Timeline.

At the bottom of the Timeline, left-click *No chained timeline* and set it to *loop*. Left-click on the *Timeline List* again and, from the *Timelines* submenu, choose the *loop* animation. Again, at the bottom where it says *No chained timeline*, perform a left-click and select *loop*. This will properly chain the *entry* Timeline to *loop*, and *loop* on itself to repeat forever.

> **Note**   SpriteBuilder will not play back chained Timelines in sequence. SpriteBuilder will play only the currently selected Timeline, and optionally loop it. To test chained Timelines, you'll have to actually run the app.

Editing the Entry Animation

Select the entry Timeline again. This is the first one you'll animate. The idea is that the buttons are initially off-screen and come zapping in. This mandates a very short animation—after all, the user will want to use your app quickly and not wait for its animations to finish, no matter how hard you worked on them.

Click the duration box as seen in Figure 5-2 to edit the Timeline duration. Set it to 1 second and 15 frames, or 00:01:15. This equals 1.5 seconds since SpriteBuilder plays back animations at 30 frames per second.

Select the *logoAndButtons* node, and move it just outside the left side of the layer. An X position of –20 (in %) will do fine. Then move the Timeline Cursor to the far left, and press the P key to create a keyframe. Move the Timeline Cursor to the far right, and press P again to create a second keyframe. Edit the *logoAndButtons* node position so it has an X position of 50 (in %). This will create a dull, slide-in motion, but the good thing is that logo and buttons follow suit.

To spice up the movement, right-click the Keyframe Segment and select the *Elastic Out* easing mode. This will be a bit too bouncy initially. Right-click the Keyframe Segment again. With either one of the Elastic or regular Ease modes selected, the *Easing Setting* menu item will be enabled; click it to open a tiny popup window that allows you to set an ambiguous floating-point value.

In this case, the value is called *Period*, and it defines how springy the animation is. The lower the value is, the more the node will move back and forth before coming to rest. In this case, enter a value of *0.9*, click *Done*, and play the animation again. It's less springy now.

> **Caution**   The *Easing Setting* value will be reset to its default value if you change the Keyframe Segment's easing mode to another easing mode. I'm afraid you will have to re-enter the setting value whenever you select another easing mode.

The entry animation can certainly be spiced up some more. A nice effect is to scale in the buttons at the appropriate time. Repeat the following steps for both the play and settings sprite nodes:

1.   Select the sprite node (*play* or *settings*).

2.   Move the Timeline Cursor to about the middle of the timeline.

3.   Add a Scale keyframe by pressing S. Set both Scale X and Y properties to 0.

4.   Move the Timeline Cursor to the far right end of the timeline.

5.   Press S to add another Scale keyframe. Set both Scale X and Y properties to 1.

6.   Right-click the Keyframe Segment, and choose the *Bounce Out* easing mode.

You may want to try moving the first keyframes for the play and settings sprites so that their scale animations start at slightly different time stamps. See Figure 7-6 to see what the entry Timeline might look like.

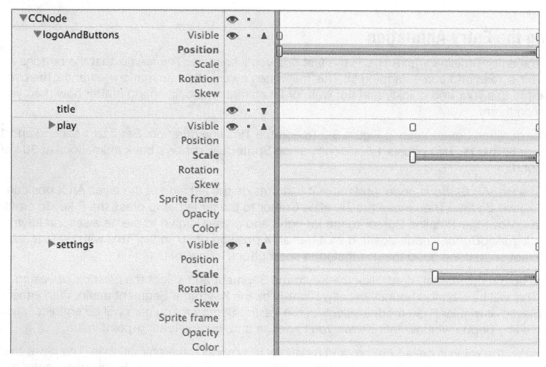

Figure 7-6.   The entry Timeline moves the nodes in from the left and, at some point, scales the buttons in too

Editing the Loop Animation

So much for the *entry* Timeline. Now switch to the *loop* Timeline. You'll notice that, for one, all of the existing keyframes disappeared. You are editing an as-of-yet blank Timeline. In addition, the *logoAndButtons* node—and, with it, both the logo and button sprites—have moved to their original location just left of the layer.

This shouldn't bother you too much, but it's worth considering that whatever you animate in one Timeline is not reflected in another Timeline. So if you want to chain two Timelines, you have to design the start of the next Timeline in exactly the way the previous Timeline leaves the node to prevent the nodes from making any sudden movements.

In this instance, it's an easy fix, just select the *logoAndButtons* node and change its position to 50%x50%. Since you have the loop animation selected, this position change will not affect the *logoAndButtons* position in the entry Timeline.

Change the Timeline duration as described earlier, and make it 2 seconds long. Then, for both the *play* and *settings* sprites, do the following:

1. Select the sprite node (*play* or *settings*).

2. Move the Timeline Cursor to the far left.

3. Press R to create a Rotation keyframe.

4. Move the Timeline Cursor to the far right.

5. Press R to create another Rotation keyframe.

6. Change the value for the *Rotation* property to *360*. This applies the value to the rightmost keyframe.

Play the animation. Notice how the sprites rotate. Also notice how the labels rotate with their parent sprites. Argh. Perhaps, on second thought, it wasn't such a good idea to make the labels child nodes of the play and settings sprites?

Not quite. You could still apply a trick: if you play the same animation of a parent node on the child node, but backwards, the two animations will cancel each other out! So if you rotate each label in the opposite direction of their parent sprites, they will stop rotating! Try this for both labels:

1. Select the label of the sprite node (*play* or *settings*).

2. Move the Timeline Cursor to the far left.

3. Press R to create a Rotation keyframe.

4. Change the value for the *Rotation* property to *360*. This applies the value to the leftmost keyframe.

5. Move the Timeline Cursor to the far right.

6. Press R to create another Rotation keyframe.

7. Change the value for the *Rotation* property to *0*. This applies the value to the rightmost keyframe.

The result is that the sprites now rotate clockwise while their child labels rotate counter-clockwise. Since both animations start and stop at the same time, and both animate a full revolution, the label's rotation cancels out their parent sprites' rotation, and thus the labels remain fixed.

Now I wouldn't have told you to do it in this seemingly dumb way if there wasn't a neat side-effect to it as well. Right-click the Keyframe Segments for each label, and change their easing modes to *Ease In/Out*. You can optionally right-click again and change the *Easing* settings to a slightly lower Rate value—for instance, in the range 1,3 to 1,8.

In any case, since the two animations are no longer synchronized—the label's rotation speeds up and slows down over time thanks to easing—the labels now sway left and right.

Though this is just an odd example you are encouraged to experiment with such stacked animations. You'll find the most curious ways to animate nodes if you animate the parent differently than the child.

For instance, imagine you were to move a regular node 200 points to the right with one easing mode, and move its child sprite node 150 points to the left using a different easing mode so that the sprite ultimately moves 50 points to the right but has the combined effect of two different easing modes.

If you run the app now, you should see the logo slide in from the left. The buttons then appear with their scale animation while the logo is still moving. Once this timeline has ended, the buttons start rotating.

> **Tip**   What if you wanted to have the buttons rotate even while the entry Timeline is running? There are generally two ways to do so.
>
> One is to duplicate the rotation keyframes for the sprites and their labels in the entry Timeline. That works well here but would amount to twice the work, and even more if you ever changed how the buttons rotate.
>
> The alternative is to create a custom CCB document for each button and create the rotation animation there. However, this means you would have to create a Custom class for each button's CCB document, though you can use the same class for both buttons. Obtaining a reference to the *MainScene* class is still possible in more than one way. For instance, the following code in the class' onEnter method obtains a reference to the MainScene object: `MainScene* mainScene = (MainScene*)self.scene.children.firstObject;`

Adding the Buttons to MainScene

If you want to see the new logo and buttons in the game, you still have to add the *MainMenuButtons.ccb* to the *MainScene.ccb*. Do so as described earlier for the *MainMenuBackground.ccb* by either dragging the .ccb file itself onto the *MainScene.ccb* stage or by dragging it from the Tileless Editor View.

Either way, you should change the new CCBFile node's position to 0,0 and give it a proper name—for instance, ***logoAndButtons***.

Creating Buttons Out of Ordinary Sprites

Hmmm, isn't there something amiss? So far the buttons aren't really buttons, just a sprite with a label. How do you make them click?

Easy, by adding a button! And then removing the button's frame and label so that it's just an invisible touch area that runs a selector. The only downside is that you can't animate the button's highlighted state because there's no notification sent by the button when it's merely highlighted. But at least you'll have a way to create buttons without having to make the images play by the rules of the *Button* node.

> **Note**   Try using *play.png* or *settings.png* as the button's normal-state sprite frame and you'll know what I mean by said rules. Or create a Sprite 9 Slice and assign it the SpriteSheets/Menu/play.png. Internally, the *Button* node uses a Sprite 9 Slice, which is responsible for scaling the nine different regions of the sprite, well, differently.

Open *MainMenuButtons.ccb*, and repeat the following steps for both the *play* and *settings* sprites:

8. Drag and drop a *Button* from the Node Library View onto the sprite (play or settings) in the timeline so the button becomes a child of the sprite.

9. Change the button's position types to % and the values to 50 to center the button on the sprite.

10. Clear the button's Title field on the Item Properties tab by removing all characters. This makes the button's label disappear.

11. For both *Normal State* and *Highlighted State*, change the *Sprite frame* property to the <NULL> item. This removes the button's background images. It is now an invisible button.

12. The size of the button will be a bit too small. Change the button's *Preferred size* property to 60x60.

You now have two invisible buttons on both the *play* and *settings* sprites. The fact that the buttons rotate along with the sprites won't matter much since the buttons are square and cover the sprite's circular-shaped images well enough, regardless of rotation. Though you could, of course, apply the same reverse-animation trick you used for the sprite's labels.

Connecting the Buttons

To connect the buttons with selectors, switch to the *Item Code Connections* tab. Then select each button in order and, in the Selector field, enter **shouldPlayGame** for the play button and *shouldShowSettings* for the settings button.

There's one more thing missing though. The selectors need to be sent somewhere, and that somewhere is the *Document root*. This term refers to the root node of the *MainMenuButtons.ccb*. Select its root node, and enter **MainMenuButtons** in the *Custom class* field.

Now open the Xcode project and add a new Objective-C class. Do so as described in Chapter 2, Figure 2-9 and following. The class' name must be MainMenuButtons, and it should be a subclass of CCNode.

Edit the *MainMenuButtons.m* file to add the methods in Listing 7-2.

Listing 7-2. Testing that the button selectors work

```
#import "MainMenuButtons.h"

@implementation MainMenuButtons

-(void) shouldPlayGame
{
    NSLog(@"PLAY");
}

-(void) shouldShowSettings
{
    NSLog(@"SETTINGS");
}

@end
```

This code is just to test that the buttons work. If you run the app and tap the buttons, you'll see the preceding NSLog statements printed to the Xcode console.

Settings Menu

The settings menu will be implemented as a popover, much like the *pause* and *game over* menus of the game. There are several notable new features here. One is a universal close button that closes the overlay it is added to by simply removing the corresponding parent node. To ease creating the settings menu layout, the *Box Layout* node is used to arrange the nodes in rows and columns.

Another feature is the Slider controls, and I'll describe how they can be used to change a property's value—in this case, audio volume levels. Because the audio volumes should be persisted across app launches, the *GameState* singleton class is introduced at the end of this chapter.

Designing the Settings Menu with Box Layout

Right-click the *UserInterface* folder, select *New File* to create a new CCB document named *SettingsLayer.ccb* of type *Layer* with the default size of 568x384. Start by changing the root node's *Content size* types to % for the layer to shrink and expand with its parent node's size and, thus, the screen size. The content size width and height values should be 100, 100.

As you have so frequently done before, drag a *Node* from the Node Library View onto the stage, change its position type to %, and position values to *50*. Then rename the node to settingsLayer. This node will act as the screen-centering container node for the rest of the items.

From the *UserInterface* section in the Tileless Editor View, drag the S_bg image onto the *settingsLayer node*. Alternatively, drag a sprite node from the Node Library View and change its *Sprite frame* to *S_bg.png*. The new sprite must be a child node of *settingsLayer*. It should automatically center on the stage.

Introducing Box Layout Nodes

Now for the *Box Layout* node. It can position nodes in either a horizontal or vertical layout, meaning the nodes will either be stacked vertically or aligned horizontally. The settings menu is supposed to have a label and two volume sliders for music and effects, all aligned vertically. But the sliders will have a label next to them, aligned horizontally.

This grid-like layout can be emulated using the parent-child relationship. A vertical *Box Layout* node has two horizontal *Box Layout* nodes for the sliders as children.

From the Node Library View, drag and drop a *Box Layout* node onto the *settingsLayer* so that it becomes a child of the *settingsLayer* node. On the *Item Properties* tab, change the *Direction* property under the *CCLayoutBox* section from its default *Horizontal* setting to the *Vertical* setting. To differentiate the layout nodes, you should rename the layout node in the Timeline to **verticalLayout**.

Then you should add a Label TTF and two additional *Box Layout* nodes as children of the *verticalLayout* node. You should rename the two *CCLayoutBox* entries in the Timeline to *horizontalLayoutMusic* and *horizontalLayoutSfx*. As for the label, change its *Label text* to **Settings** and increase its *Font Size* to *32*.

Each slider will be added to one of the horizontal layout nodes, together with a label node. From the Node Library View, drag a *Label TTF* and a *Slider* node to the *horizontalLayoutMusic* node, and then repeat this step for the *horizontalLayoutSfx* node. Select each label, and change its text to **Music Volume** or **Effects Volume**, depending on whether the label is a child of the *horizontalLayoutMusic* or *horizontalLayoutSfx* node, respectively.

The initial result will not look too good, just like in Figure 7-7.

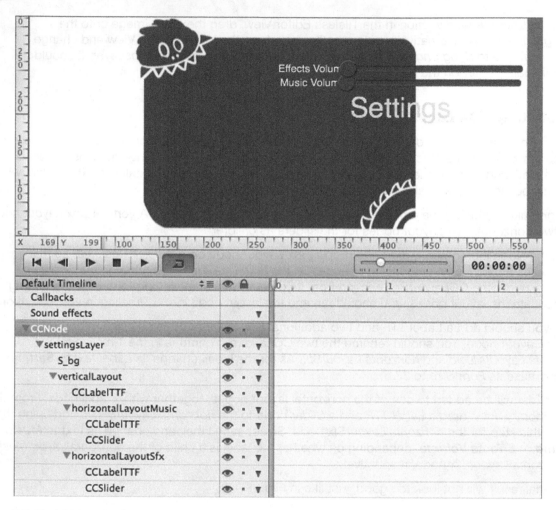

Figure 7-7. The initial result using Box Layout nodes won't look too good

Let's quickly dissect what's happening in Figure 7-7. The *verticalLayout* node vertically aligns its children: the settings label and the two horizontal layout nodes, each of which contains a Label TTF and a *Slider* node.

Alignment and spacing leave a lot to be desired. Also, the contents of the *verticalLayout* node are in reverse order, with the label at the bottom and the *horizontalLayoutSfx* at the top. This is an unfortunate behavior of *Box Layout* nodes whose *Direction* is set to *Vertical*. It can be easily worked around by dragging the *verticalLayout* child nodes in the Timeline so that they are in reverse order as they appear on the layer.

The nodes are also not centered on the layer but offset to the right and up. This is because the anchor point of *Box Layout* nodes defaults to 0, 0. So even though the *verticalLayout* node's position is centered on the stage, its content extends to the right and up because of the anchor point. Select the *verticalLayout* node, and change its *Anchor point* property to *0.5* for both the X axis and Y axis. This will center the nodes. You should also change the *verticalLayout* node's *Spacing* property to *30* to increase the vertical space between the sliders and the labels.

The sliders are still too wide, though, and they are overlapping the labels. You can decrease the slider's size by selecting a slider, and then changing the *Width* of the *Preferred size* property from its default *200* to *150*. Do this for both *CCSlider* nodes.

The labels still overlap with the sliders, however. This is a spacing issue, and fixed by editing the *Spacing* property for both the *horizontalLayoutMusic* and *horizontalLayoutSfx* box layout nodes. Set the spacing to *20* for both.

Left-Alignment with Box Layout

If you have eagle eyes, you may have spotted that the two labels and sliders still do not align perfectly. The music volume label seems to be slightly more indented than the effects volume label, while the sliders do not start and end at the same X position either. If you want to pronounce this effect, select the effects volume label and change its text to **FX Volume**. I bet now you can see it. See Figure 7-8 for an example.

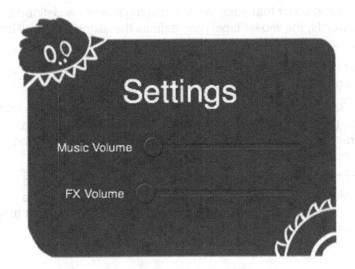

Figure 7-8. The labels and sliders do not align correctly

The problem here is that the size of the labels will be different unless they use the exact same text. Even if both labels had the same number of characters, they might still be different in size unless you are using a fixed-width font such as Courier. But Courier is an ugly font: It looks like this.

Fortunately, this can be fixed easily by ensuring that both the *horizontalLayoutMusic* and *horizontalLayoutSfx* box layout nodes have the same content size. If you select one and the other, you'll notice their *content size* properties differ. The *horizontalLayoutMusic* node has a width of 246, while the width of *horizontalLayoutSfx* is just 230 if you've set its child label's text to *FX Volume*.

This means that the *horizontalLayoutSfx* content size is 16 points less wide. So you merely need to make it 16 points wider. Consider the *Spacing* property that you've set to *20* for both horizontal layout nodes. You need to increase the spacing for the *horizontalLayoutSfx* node only.

Select the *horizontalLayoutSfx* node, and change *Spacing* to *36*—that's the original 20 plus the missing 16 points. That is all: alignment fixed.

Check the content size of the two horizontal layout nodes to confirm that their width is now the same. Both labels are now left-aligned, as are the sliders.

Center-Alignment with Box Layout

But what if you wanted the labels to be center-aligned and not have to worry about adjusting the *Box Layout* node's spacing properties whenever you change a label's text?

As of now, you have each label and slider aligned horizontally in a *Box Layout* node, and the two box layout nodes are aligned vertically in another *Box Layout* node. You can always reverse this setup. In this instance, you could have both labels in a vertically aligned *Box Layout* node, and both sliders in another vertically aligned *Box Layout* node. You would then add both vertical box layout nodes to a horizontally aligned *Box Layout* node.

The result will be different in so far that each vertical column's width is defined by the node with the largest width. In other words, the widest label now defines the alignment of all labels in relation to all sliders next to the labels.

Give this a shot by first removing the *horizontalLayoutSfx* and *horizontalLayoutMusic* nodes. This will also remove their child nodes.

Then drag and drop a *Box Layout* node onto the existing *verticalLayout* node and name it *horizontalLayout*. Drag and drop two more *Box Layout* nodes onto the *horizontalLayout* node, change their *Direction* property to *Vertical* and change their names in the Timeline to *verticalLayoutLabels* and *verticalLayoutSliders*.

Then add two *Label TTF* nodes to the *verticalLayoutLabels* node, and change their label text to *FX Volume* and *Music Volume*, respectively. Also, add two *Slider* nodes to the *verticalLayoutSliders* node. You may want to edit the label and slider names in the Timeline so that they reflect whether they refer to music or effects volume. See Figure 7-9 for reference.

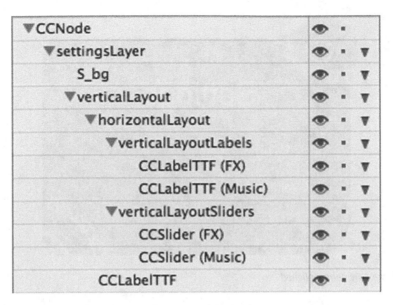

Figure 7-9. Labels and sliders aligned in separate vertical columns

Now you still have the same problem as before: the sliders and labels are positioned too tightly. Therefore, set the *Spacing* property to *25* for the *Box Layout* nodes named *horizontalLayout* and *verticalLayoutSliders*, while *verticalLayoutLabels* should use a *Spacing* of *18*. Observe how each change affects the nodes involved.

The advantage of this setup is that it behaves a little more like auto-layout, at least considering horizontal alignment, which tends to be more important than vertical alignment. You still have the same problem as before, but now with vertical alignment—hence, the spacing of *verticalLayoutLabels* needed to be set to *18* to better align them with the sliders.

It's difficult to get the alignment correct either way when there are *Label TTF* nodes involved.

Still, if you change a label's text or font size, or a slider's width, this new setup will shift the position of the nodes in the other column accordingly. The result will be like those shown in Figure 7-10. Notice the labels are now center-aligned inside their vertical column.

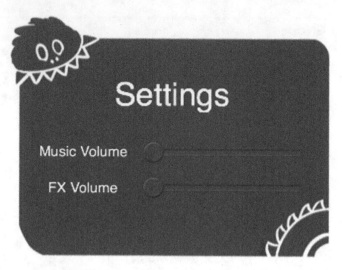

Figure 7-10. The labels are now center-aligned

It's not possible to give a general recommendation as to which type of layout is preferable—columns first, rows second as in the first example, or rows first and columns second as in the second example. Sometimes one is easier to work with; at other times, the other way is easier. It definitely helps if you can make all nodes involved in a grid-based layout the same dimensions.

But, alas, with labels this is almost never possible unless you are using a fixed-width font. Sometimes padding labels with space characters can help, though, if the alignment doesn't have to be perfect.

> **Tip**   There's one thing you can experiment with if you need to specify the dimensions of a label really badly: use *Button* nodes in place of *Label TTF*! You can set the button's sprite frames to <NULL> in order to hide the background sprites, and you'll still be able to change the button's size via the *Preferred size* and *Max size* properties, as well as the label's *Horizontal padding* and *Vertical padding*. You would end up with a label whose extents you can modify.

Changing the Slider Visuals

The default sliders look a bit dull. If you select a slider and go to the *Item Properties* tab, you'll notice the *CCSlider* section shown in Figure 7-11. These settings allow you to change the images associated with the slider's background (the stretchable line) and the slider's handle.

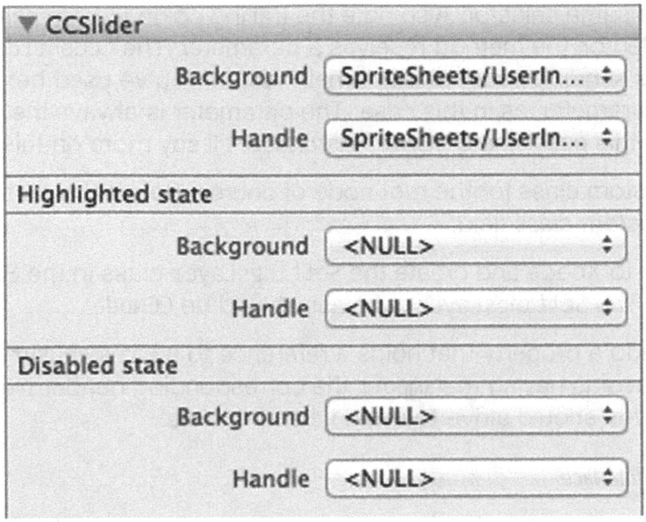

Figure 7-11. Slider image settings

Change the *Background* image to *SpriteSheets/UserInterface/S_bar.png*, and set the *Handle* image to *SpriteSheets/UserInterface/S_ball.png* for the normal state (the topmost setting in Figure 7-11).

Set both the *Background* and *Handle* images to *<NULL>* for the *Highlighted State*. This means the highlighted state—the state while the user is dragging the handle—will use the same images as the normal state.

Note that the slider background image should have a specific size, since it is stretched as needed. This goes for other stretchable *CCControl* images as well, such as the button background image. Internally, the slider and button use the *CCSprite 9 Slice* node for the images; however, that sprite's properties are not exposed. So if you use an incorrectly sized slider or button background image, it will look anywhere between "not quite correct" to abhorrent—or just not what it's supposed to look like.

You will find the default slider and button images in any SpriteBuilder project in the *ccbResources* folder if you need to look up the sizes of the built-in images.

The *ccbSliderBgNormal.png* and *ccbSliderBgHighlighted.png* images are used as the slider's default background images. The images are 28x10 pixels in size but have their *Scale from* property (shown in Figure 3-8 in Chapter 3) set to 2x. You can use the 28x10 size for your own background images and set the *Scale from* property for those images to 2x, or you can design them with a 56x20-pixel resolution and not worry about changing the *Scale from* setting.

Connecting the Sliders

This should be almost second nature by now: Select the effects slider and switch to the *Item Code Connections* tab. Enter **volumeDidChange:** in the *Selector* field, and check the *Continuous* check box. Also enter *_effectsSlider* in the *Doc root var* field.

Repeat this for the music slider: set its *Selector* to **volumeDidChange:**, also check the *Continuous* check box, and then enter *_musicSlider* in the *Doc root var* field.

Yes, both sliders use the same selector. Also note the trailing colon in both selectors—if there's a colon at the end of a selector, the method receives a parameter. The CCControl class that sends these selectors supports sending parameterless methods, as you've used before, as well as methods with a single parameter, as in this case. The parameter is always the CCControl object running the selector—in this case, the CCSlider instances. I'll say more on this shortly.

What's missing? The custom class for the root node of course! Select the root node, and enter **SettingsLayer** in the *Custom class* field.

Now you can move over to Xcode and create the SettingsLayer class in the *Source* group. See Figure 2-9 in Chapter 2. The SettingsLayer subclass should be CCNode.

Edit *SettingsLayer.h* to add a property that holds a reference to a MainMenuButtons instance like in Listing 7-3. The @class avoids having to #import the corresponding header file in the *SettingsLayer.h* header file—something you should strive to avoid when possible.

Listing 7-3. The SettingsLayer interface

```
#import "CCNode.h"

@class MainMenuButtons;

@interface SettingsLayer : CCNode

@property (weak) MainMenuButtons* mainMenuButtons;

@end
```

SettingsLayer.m needs the additions highlighted in Listing 7-4.

Listing 7-4. The slider selectors receive the sender as an input parameter

```
#import "SettingsLayer.h"
#import "MainMenuButtons.h"

@implementation SettingsLayer
{
    __weak CCSlider* _musicSlider;
    __weak CCSlider* _effectsSlider;
}

-(void) volumeDidChange:(CCSlider*)sender
{
    NSLog(@"volume changed, sender: %@", sender);
}

@end
```

The sender parameter is always of type CCControl*, but since you can be certain that only sliders run this selector, you can safely assume the parameter to be of type CCSlider*. CCSlider is, of course, a subclass of CCControl. The two CCSlider ivars will be used to determine which slider performed the volumeDidChange: selector.

Before you can try out the sliders, you need to load and show the settings layer in *MainMenuButtons.m*. Specifically, replace the existing shouldShowSettings method with the one in Listing 7-5.

Listing 7-5. Show the settings layer

```
-(void) shouldShowSettings
{
    SettingsLayer* settingsLayer = (SettingsLayer*)[CCBReader load:
                                          @"UserInterface/SettingsLayer"];
    settingsLayer.mainMenuButtons = self;
    [self.parent addChild:settingsLayer];

    self.visible = NO;
}
```

SettingsLayer is loaded by CCBReader, using the full path to the *SettingsLayer.ccb* file. Then the mainMenuButtons reference is assigned, and the settingsLayer is added as a child not to the MainMenuButtons class but to its parent (the MainScene instance). This is because the MainMenuButtons instance itself is set to invisible—if the settings layer were a child of MainMenuButtons it, too, would be hidden. That would be counterproductive.

You can now run the game and tap the *Settings* button to open the settings popover. If you move the sliders, you will see lines like the following (shortened) lines logged to the Xcode Console:

```
[..] volume changed, sender: <CCSlider = 0x10a13ebf0 | Name = musicSlider>
[..] volume changed, sender: <CCSlider = 0x10a135f70 | Name = effectsSlider>
```

Each sender object is a different instance of CCSlider. If you gave the sliders a name on the Item Properties tab, this name will also be logged.

Dismissing the Settings Popover

You can't currently dismiss the settings popover. You should fix that by introducing a generic close button. You can use the same button for other layers, and you can use the same concept in general for buttons that should instead forward their selectors to a specific parent class.

But in many cases, you can't do that because buttons and other *CCControl* nodes send their selector to the document root—the CCB root node's custom class. Especially if the *Button* would be in its own CCB file, you would have to create a separate button for each specific task—perhaps even separate buttons for the same task but different use cases. There's a simple solution.

Right-click the *UserInterface* folder and select *New File*. Name the new document **CloseButton.ccb** and, for a change, use the *Node* type before clicking *Create*. With the root node selected, switch to the *Item Code Connections* tab and set its custom class. Here it should be named **CloseButton**.

Then drag a *Button* node from the Node Library View onto the stage. On the *Item Properties* tab, you need to change only the button's sprite frame for the normal state and the *Highlighted State* to *SpriteSheets/UserInterface/S_back.png* and change the *Background* color of the *Highlighted State* to a light gray color. And, on the *Item Code Connections* tab, enter **shouldClose** in the *Selector* field. You should also clear the *Title* field to remove all text from the button.

That's all there is to the button's CCB file. You should open *SettingsLayer.ccb* and drag and drop *CloseButton.ccb* onto the *settingsLayer* node. Drag and move the button so that it is in the upper right corner of the *S_bg* background image (position 140x75) as seen in Figure 7-12. Or, if you would rather align it with the corner, you can change the position types to % and use *100, 100* or a little less for the position.

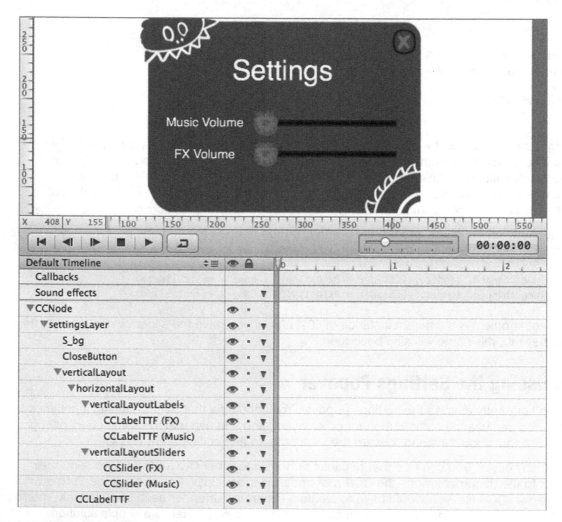

Figure 7-12. The final version of the SettingsLayer.ccb

In Xcode, create yet another Objective-C class with the name **CloseButton** and using CCNode as the subclass. Open the *CloseButton.m* file to add the method highlighted in Listing 7-6.

Listing 7-6. Forwarding the CloseButton message to the nearest parent node

```
#import "CloseButton.h"

@implementation CloseButton

-(void) shouldClose
{
    CCNode* aParent = self.parent;

    do
    {
        if ([aParent respondsToSelector:_cmd])
        {
            [aParent performSelector:_cmd];
            break;
        }

        aParent = aParent.parent;
    }
    while (aParent != nil);
}

@end
```

The shouldClose method takes the button's parent before entering the do/while loop. It checks if the parent responds to the _cmd selector, which refers to the shouldClose selector. The use of _cmd simply makes it easier to use this code in other buttons—you don't have to update the code to use each specific selector. In fact, this code cries out to be added to a class method like in the SceneManager, or maybe a category on CCNode. I'll leave this as an exercise for you.

If the given parent does respond to the same selector, that selector is performed and the loop ends at the break statement. Otherwise, the aParent variable is set to aParent's parent, traversing ever closer toward the CCScene instance in the node hierarchy. If, in fact, the CCScene instance is reached before a parent implementing the given selector was found, the loop will also end because the scene's parent is guaranteed to be nil.

Tip   As with the previous use of performSelector, you can ignore the "may cause a leak" warning since the selector does not return an object. (It returns void.)

You can get rid of the warning by using [aParent performSelector:_cmd withObject:nil afterDelay:0] instead. This tells the compiler to set up a timer which, in turn, performs the selector when it fires. When a timer is involved, there can't be a value returned by the selector; therefore, the compiler stops complaining. The extraneous nil object sent as parameter to the selector is simply ignored if the selector is declared to take no parameters, as in this case. But because there is now a timer involved, and despite the delay being 0, the selector may not necessarily be performed before the current frame gets rendered. So this may introduce an additional delay of a single frame before the selector runs—though that won't be a problem when dismissing a popover.

What's left now is to implement the same shouldClose method in a CCB's custom class that is an ancestor of *CloseButton.ccb*. In this case, we needn't go very far, the SettingsLayer should handle it. Move over to *SettingsLayer.m* to implement the method in Listing 7-7 in its implementation.

Listing 7-7. The shouldClose selector is forwarded to the SettingsLayer instance

```
-(void) shouldClose
{
    [self removeFromParent];
    [_mainMenuButtons show];
}
```

So why not just remove aParent directly in the CloseButton's shouldClose method? (See Listing 7-6.)

> **Note**   Separation of concerns is one of the most fundamental programming principles. The close button should notify and leave the implementation to the affected class, rather than assuming that "close" means removeFromParent and nothing else—and not even giving the removed node a chance to know what is being done to it. That would be rude! For more information on separation of concerns, see http://en.wikipedia.org/wiki/Separation_of_concerns.

In the same light, just as the _mainMenuButtons.visible state could have been set from within the SettingsLayer method in Listing 7-7, it's best to let the MainMenuButtons class handle it in the way it sees fit. Therefore, add the method declaration of Listing 7-8 to *MainMenuButtons.h*.

Listing 7-8. Declaring the show method

```
#import "CCNode.h"

@interface MainMenuButtons : CCNode

-(void) show;

@end
```

And, of course, add the corresponding show method (Listing 7-9) to the *MainMenuButtons.m* file.

Listing 7-9. The show implementation

```
-(void) show
{
    self.visible = YES;
}
```

I've added a suggestion as a comment about what you could be doing when the SettingsLayer closes, besides removing the settings layer and showing the buttons. What if both CCB classes needed to play a Timeline animation of their own, one that animates the SettingsLayer out and the MainMenuButtons in?

Whatever that may look like, they would both need to run the animation using their own `animationManager` instances, and the `SettingsLayer` would have to respond to a `Callbacks` selector in order to properly remove itself for good.

Of course, playing an animation is just one of many reasons why a class might want to respond to an event in its own way, rather than having it dictated by some other class. If you follow the principle of separation of concerns, you will find it a lot easier to re-use classes and individual CCB files, within the same project and even in future projects.

The result of your work can be seen in Figure 7-13. Notice that the settings background image is transparent—that's because the image has been designed to be slightly transparent. You could as well use a fully opaque background and then lower the opacity of the sprite. Same difference.

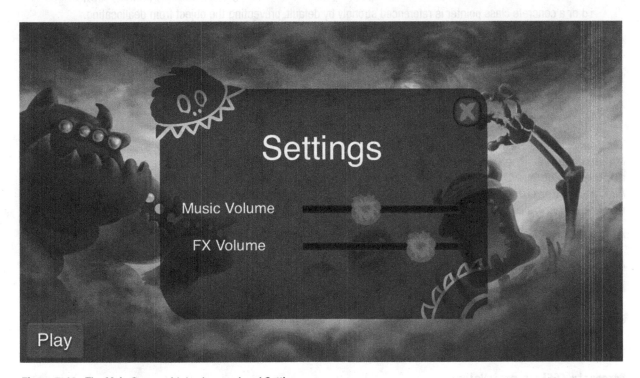

Figure 7-13. The Main Scene with background and Settings menu

Persisting Game States

Since you'll want the app settings to persist across launches, and because you'll soon need to persist other data such as unlocked levels, it's time to introduce the `GameState` class that persists the game's various states.

Introducing the GameState Class

The `GameState` class will be a wrapper for `NSUserDefaults`, in order to avoid injecting the same code with the same string keys all over the code. Just like `NSUserDefaults`, it will be a singleton class. A *singleton* is a class that can be instantiated only once.

Did I hear you think, "Finally!"? Or was it "Eeww!?!"? I am aware that singletons are a hotly debated topic—some people even have extremely subjective opinions about it. Singletons are frequently overused and/or misused, and especially for beginning programmers they are tempting constructs since the global accessibility makes them super-simple workarounds for passing along data and references between objects.

I just have one plea: before you use a singleton, make sure you have exhausted all other options or dismissed them as impractical. Only relatively few variables and methods need to be global.

> **Tip** For object references in particular, avoid having them at all in a singleton class. Any property of type `id` or a concrete class pointer is referenced strongly by default, preventing the object from deallocating. Since the singleton itself will never (normally) deallocate during the runtime of the app, any object reference retained by the singleton will also practically become a permanent instance unless explicitly set to `nil`. And if you have to set a reference to `nil` explicitly, you're back to how programming was before ARC—that is, manual reference counting (MRC) and manual memory management in general.

This said, in this particular case with the class being a wrapper for the already-singleton class `NSUserDefaults`, the use of the `GameState` class is sound and justifiable. So go ahead and create another Objective-C class in Xcode. You know the drill: right-click the *Source* group, choose *New File*, and enter **GameState** as the name, but make it a subclass of `NSObject` since singletons need not be, nor should they ever be, `CCNode` subclasses.

After creating the class, open the *GameState.h* file and add the lines highlighted in Listing 7-10.

Listing 7-10. Declaring the GameState methods and properties

```
#import <Foundation/Foundation.h>

@interface GameState : NSObject

+(GameState*) sharedGameState;

@property CGFloat musicVolume;
@property CGFloat effectsVolume;

@end
```

The `sharedGameState` class is prefixed with a +, which makes it a class method accessible from any other class. It will return, and if necessary create, the single instance of the `GameState` class. The properties will enable you to change and retrieve the volumes as if they were properties of the class, when in fact they will run custom setter and getter methods instead of referring to ivars.

Add the code in Listing 7-11 just below the `@implementation GameState` line in the *GameState.m* file. This creates a single instance of the class if there is no instance yet. It will then return the instance.

Listing 7-11. Creating a single instance of the class and returning it

```
+(GameState*) sharedGameState
{
    static GameState* sharedInstance;
    static dispatch_once_t onceToken;

    dispatch_once(&onceToken, ^{
        sharedInstance = [[GameState alloc] init];
    });

    return sharedInstance;
}
```

> **Note** This version of creating and returning a singleton instance is compliant with ARC. You may have
> seen Objective-C class singletons done differently on the Internet. Those refer to outdated variants, typically
> predating ARC, which shouldn't be used and may not even work anymore.

First, this method declares two `static` (global) variables. Whether you place them inside the method definition or above and outside doesn't make a difference for `static` variables. If it bothers you that they are declared inside the method because that makes them seem like local variables, move them above the method definition. Either way is fine, and in both cases both variables will be initialized to 0 (nil) by default because they are declared `static`.

The `sharedInstance` stores the reference to the single class instance, while the `onceToken` with its funny data type `dispatch_once_t` is nothing else but an integer variable of type `long`.

The `dispatch_once` method runs a block once and only once. The `&onceToken` means to take the address of the `onceToken` variable; in other words, a pointer to `onceToken` is passed in. Only if `onceToken` is 0 will the block run, and when `dispatch_once` has run the block once, it will change `onceToken` to a non-zero value.

The block itself simply allocates and initializes an instance of the class via the familiar `alloc/init` sequence and assigns the created instance to the static `sharedInstance`, which retains the instance indefinitely. Any other time the `sharedGameState` method runs, the block does not run again and the already existing `sharedInstance` is returned.

Now add the `musicVolume` property setter and getter methods of Listing 7-12 below the `sharedGameState` method.

Listing 7-12. The musicVolume property setter and getter methods

```
static NSString* KeyForMusicVolume = @"musicVolume";

-(void) setMusicVolume:(CGFloat)volume
{
    [[NSUserDefaults standardUserDefaults] setDouble:volume
                                   forKey:KeyForMusicVolume];
}
```

```
-(CGFloat) musicVolume
{
    NSNumber* number = [[NSUserDefaults standardUserDefaults]
                         objectForKey:KeyForMusicVolume];
    return (number ? number.doubleValue : 1.0);
}
```

The NSUserDefaults key is declared as a static NSString* variable so that you don't have to write the string twice. If you ever made a typo writing the same thing twice over, you'll understand the value of declaring frequently used strings as static variables.

Property setter and getter methods follow a consistent naming scheme. The getter has the same name as the property; the setter prefixes the property name with set, and the property's first letter is capitalized.

NSUserDefaults is the class that persists any integral data type and so-called property list objects: NSData, NSString, NSNumber, NSDate, NSArray, or NSDictionary. So it won't save your custom class just like that. But you can save individual properties of your classes, like the volumes here.

The standardUserDefaults is a singleton accessor just like sharedGameState. The setDouble:forKey: method stores a value of type double for the given key, which must be an NSString* object. The same key is then used in objectForKey: to receive the NSNumber object associated with that key. NSUserDefaults will always return integral data types wrapped in NSNumber objects so that it can return nil to signal that there's no entry for the given key, which will be the case when you first launch the app.

This fact is used in the return statement in the ?: ternary operator. It reads: if number is nil, return the statement after the question mark (number.doubleValue); otherwise, return the statement after the colon (1.0). So if number is nil, it just returns a safe default value—in this case, the highest possible volume level of 1.0. The parentheses are optional and used only to enhance readability, to clarify that the result of the expression is returned rather than number.

> **Note**   The CGFloat type is defined as float on 32-bit devices (for example, iPhone 5C) but is a double type on 64-bit devices (such as iPhone 5S). It is good practice to use setDouble: and doubleValue when the type involved is CGFloat. This prevents the value from being truncated in NSUserDefaults. It is not an issue to store a float value as double, nor is returning a double that will then be truncated to float. In the same light, it is a best practice to always use CGFloat in place of float and use double only if the type has to be double even on 32-bit devices.

Without further ado, add the methods in Listing 7-13 to *GameState.m* just below the music volume methods. They are the equivalent setter and getter methods for the effectsVolume property.

Listing 7-13. The equivalent setter and getter methods for the effectsVolume property

```
static NSString* KeyForEffectsVolume = @"effectsVolume";

-(void) setEffectsVolume:(CGFloat)volume
{
    [[NSUserDefaults standardUserDefaults] setDouble:volume
                                          forKey:KeyForEffectsVolume];
}

-(CGFloat) effectsVolume
{
    NSNumber* number = [[NSUserDefaults standardUserDefaults]
                        objectForKey:KeyForEffectsVolume];
    return (number ? number.doubleValue : 1.0);
}
```

Persisting the Volume Slider Values

With the GameState class in place, you can now connect the sliders with the two volume properties in the GameState singleton to persist their values.

Add the lines highlighted in Listing 7-14 to *SettingsLayer.m*.

Listing 7-14. Connecting the slider values with GameState properties

```
#import "SettingsLayer.h"
#import "MainMenuButtons.h"
#import "GameState.h"

@implementation SettingsLayer
{
    __weak CCSlider* _musicSlider;
    __weak CCSlider* _effectsSlider;
}

-(void) didLoadFromCCB
{
    GameState* gameState = [GameState sharedGameState];
    _musicSlider.sliderValue = gameState.musicVolume;
    _effectsSlider.sliderValue = gameState.effectsVolume;
}

-(void) volumeDidChange:(CCSlider*)sender
{
    if (sender == _musicSlider)
    {
        [GameState sharedGameState].musicVolume = _musicSlider.sliderValue;
    }
```

```
        else if (sender == _effectsSlider)
        {
            [GameState sharedGameState].effectsVolume = _effectsSlider.sliderValue;
        }
}

-(void) shouldClose
{
    [[NSUserDefaults standardUserDefaults] synchronize];
    [self removeFromParent];
    [_mainMenuButtons show];
}

@end
```

In didLoadFromCCB, the volume values are assigned to the slider values. Coincidentally, both sliderValue and volumes use the same value range between 0.0 and 1.0. Initially, the GameState volumes will return 1.0, which will position both volume slider handles to the far right. Whenever the volumeDidChange: method runs, the received sender is compared with the existing ivars in order to determine whether it was the music or the effects volume that changed. In both cases, the corresponding GameState property is assigned the current sliderValue.

The shouldClose method now also calls the NSUserDefaults method synchronize to ensure the data in GameState is persisted to disk when the settings popover is closed. This is just a precaution. NSUserDefaults does synchronize its data periodically, but it may not do so soon enough if the app were to crash shortly after closing the settings popover—or if you hit the stop button in Xcode.

> **Note**   You certainly should not call synchronize every time an NSUserDefaults value changes, because disk access is a comparatively slow operation. And like I said before about separation of concerns: should a developer really concern himself with the fact that synchronizing NSUserDefaults is required to write the values in GameState to disk? You can certainly improve this by adding a corresponding synchronize method to GameState and call that instead.

If you run the project now and open the settings menu, you'll notice the slider handles start out at the far right. Drag the slider handles, close the settings popover, and then quit the app or hit the stop button in Xcode.

You can then relaunch the app from Xcode, and you'll see the slider positions (and thus their values) will have been persisted. You can also try hitting the stop button in Xcode while the settings popover is still open, and any changes to the sliders will most likely have been reverted to their previous state on the next relaunch.

> **Note**   Connecting the volume sliders with actual audio volumes will be done in the upcoming audio chapter.

Summary

You now have a nicely animated main menu with a functional settings menu. The volume values are persistently stored by the `GameState` class, which will be enhanced in the next chapter to store unlocked levels as well.

You also learned about structuring code in the process, as well as how to turn any node into a button and how to forward button events to classes that actually need to handle the event.

You can find the current state of the project in the *08 - Main Menu and Settings* folder.

Chapter 8

Selecting and Unlocking Levels

For this game, you will want to give users a way to select which level they want to start with. Since the levels are separated into different worlds, you'll use a *Scroll View* node to allow the user to swipe between worlds.

In addition, you'll want a flexible way to add more levels while keeping track of which levels the player has already unlocked. The GameState class will help in that area.

Of course, you'll have to add additional-level CCB files. You'll be adding several dummy levels that you can then update with your own graphics and actual gameplay as you please. You'll even learn how to count the level files currently in the app.

Moreover, and this completes the various menus, you'll add a level-completion popover that will allow the user to play along with the next level.

Adding the Content Node

You'll start by designing the *Scroll View*'s *Content* node. The *Content* node is a container whose content will be scrolled. In this case, you'll want to design each world's level-selection screen as an individual page, and later enable pagination in the *Scroll View* node so that each world menu will be centered on the screen after every swipe gesture. This behavior is similar to flipping through photos in the iOS photo album.

In a scrolling view, the *Content* node's content size determines the size of the scrollable area. The *Scroll View*'s content size determines the area where the user can touch and drag. It also determines the bounds for the *Content* node. The *Content* node's edges are constrained to the edges defined by the *Scroll View*'s position and content size.

> **Note** The content will still be drawn outside the *Scroll View*'s boundaries. If you need the content to draw only within the *Scroll View*'s area, you would have to draw a sprite over it that acts as a frame. Or you could add the *Scroll View* to a CCClippingNode programmatically.

The setup of pagination-enabled content requires you to consider that the *Scroll View* automatically determines the number of pages based on the ratio of the *Scroll View* size in relation to the *Content* node size.

For example, if you wanted five individual, horizontally scrolling pages that are each 100 points in width, the width of the *Scroll View* must be 100 and the total size of the *Content* node must be 500. That's assuming the pages have no margin. With margins between individual pages, you also have to consider the size of the margin and live with the fact that any added margins causes the individual pages to slowly shift their snap positions as you scroll further. The *Scroll View* then behaves as if the first page were left-aligned while the last page is right-aligned.

So here we go. Create a new CCB file in the *UserInterface* folder, and name this document ***MainMenuLevelSelect.ccb***. The CCB type must be set to *Node* before you create the CCB document. Select the root node, and on the *Item Properties* tab, set the content size types to %. Since you'll add three pages to the *Scroll View* and only horizontal scrolling will be allowed, you have to set the content size to 300% width and 100% height. This will make the *Scroll View*'s *Content* node three times as large as the *Scroll View*'s size, no matter what the size of the *Scroll View* will be.

You should also name the root node `levelSelect` so that a reference to it can be obtained easily. On the *Item Code Connections* tab, you need to set a custom class by the name of `MainMenuLevelSelect`. This class will later receive the button events. It will also handle highlighting the levels that have already been unlocked.

On to adding content. On the *Tileless Editor View*, make sure that the *UserInterface* Sprite Sheet is checked at the bottom. You should see a number of images starting with an uppercase W followed by a digit. These are the world-specific, level-selection images. The ones named *W1_bg*, *W2_bg*, and so on are the background images defining a page visually. Drag and drop one of each—you should add three in total. All three images are 411x290 points in size. You will see the importance of this shortly.

Right now, all three images are likely at the same position. You need to space them out evenly in a horizontal direction. The *W1_bg* position should be 0x0. *W2_bg* should be at position 441x0 and *W3_bg* should be at 882x0. These positions add a 30-point-wide margin between the images. The margin is entirely optional, but it is important to consider because it contributes to the size of an individual page. Additionally, set each background sprite's anchor point to 0x0 simply because this will align the first background sprite's lower left corner with the root node's position and thus the *Scroll View*'s lower left corner. The result should look like Figure 8-1.

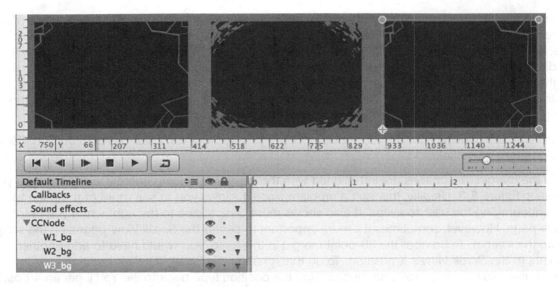

Figure 8-1. Three page-background images spread out evenly

Adding the Scroll View Node

The setup in Figure 8-1 is enough to try out an actual *Scroll View* node. Open *MainScene.ccb*, and switch to the *Node Library View*. From there drag and drop a *Scroll View* node onto the stage.

With the *Scroll View* node selected, edit its properties so that the position types are set to % and values are set to 50. Set the anchor point to 0.5x0.5 so that the *Scroll View* node is centered on the scene.

Now the important bit: the *Scroll View*'s content size. You know that individual background images (pages) are 411 points wide. You've also added a 30-point margin by setting the position of the second and third background images so that there is an added 30 points of horizontal distance on the previous page. This means a single page is 411 points plus 30 points wide. Enter 441x290 as the *Scroll View*'s content size.

Moving on to the properties specific to CCScrollView. They are shown in Figure 8-2. Your first step should be to set the *Content node* value via the drop-down menu to *UserInterface/MainMenuLevelSelect.ccb*. The first background image should immediately appear on the stage within the area defined by the *Scroll View*. If it doesn't, choose File ➤ Save All from the menu or simply click the publish button once.

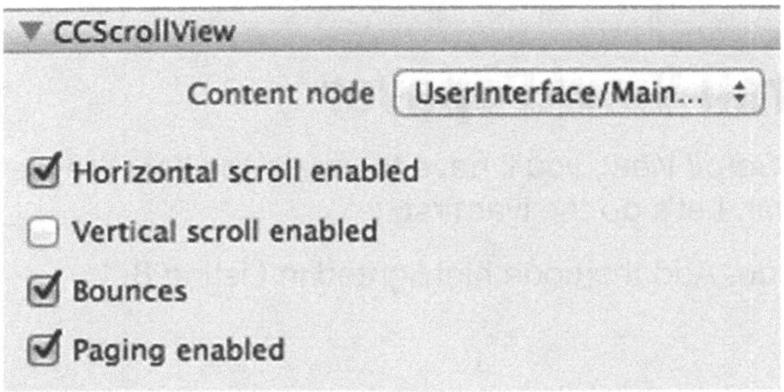

▼ **CCScrollView**

Content node [UserInterface/Main... ÷]

☑ Horizontal scroll enabled

☐ Vertical scroll enabled

☑ Bounces

☑ Paging enabled

Figure 8-2. The Scroll View's properties

The *Scroll View* node should scroll only horizontally; therefore, uncheck *Vertical scroll enabled*. The *Bounces* setting determines the behavior at the edges. That is, if you try to scroll left on the first page, or right on the last page, with *Bounces* checked, you can drag the *Content* node slightly in that direction, but it will keep bouncing back. With *Bounces* disabled, dragging left on the first page or right on the last page simply has no effect. Bouncing is helpful to indicate the borders of the scrolling content to the user. Last, *Paging enabled* will scroll and snap each page in place. Without paging, you can scroll through the *Content* node without any kind of snapping.

On the *Item Code Connection* tab, you should also assign a Doc root var. Enter **_levelSelectScrollView** in the corresponding field.

Due to the margin, the images are left-aligned with the margin extending entirely to the right, as you can see in Figure 8-3. Usually, this isn't a problem since it allows you to see more of the page to the right, encouraging the user to swipe. It also shows more clear space to the right when you reach the last page. However, sometimes it's more important to center the *Scroll View* pages on the stage despite the margin. To combat the 30-point margin in this case, you would have to add another 15 points to the *Scroll View*'s X position. To do that, change the *Scroll View*'s X position type to points, enter **299** (284 plus 15), and then change the position type back to %. You'll get an X position of 52.6%, and the pages are centered on the screen. I'll leave it up to you whether you prefer the pages centered or not.

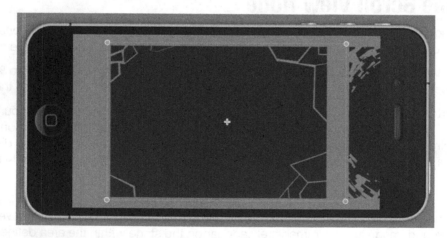

Figure 8-3. The Scroll View node selected in SpriteBuilder. Notice the page image being left aligned within the Scroll View. The background and button nodes have been hidden for visual clarity

Showing the Scroll View Popover

Before you can try out the *Scroll View*, you'll have to create the `MainMenuLevelSelect` class and the `_levelSelectScrollView` ivar. Let's do the ivar first.

Open *MainScene.m* in Xcode. Add the code highlighted in Listing 8-1.

Listing 8-1. Adding the CCScrollView ivar

```
#import "MainScene.h"

@implementation MainScene
{
    __weak CCScrollView* _levelSelectScrollView;
}

-(void) didLoadFromCCB
{
    NSLog(@"scroll view: %@", _levelSelectScrollView);
}

@end
```

The NSLog line exists only to verify the assignment was done properly. It should log something similar to this:

```
LearnSpriteBuilder[67794:60b] scroll view: <CCScrollView = 0x9b54490 | Name = >
```

If there is still a playButtonPressed method in MainScene, you can remove that. It was used by the original play button that you added way back in Chapter 2. You should also check if *MainScene.ccb* still contains that button. If it does, you can remove that as well. If you remove the button and its selector code, you won't be able to play the first level for now, but you'll add this functionality back in shortly.

For now, you don't need to do anything further with the CCScrollView ivar, but it will be used shortly to explain how to react to certain *Scroll View* events.

Next, create a new Cocoa Touch Class as shown in Figure 2-10 and 2-11. Name the class **MainMenuLevelSelect**, and make it a subclass of CCNode. Once the class is created, open the *MainMenuLevelSelect.h* and add the code highlighted in Listing 8-2.

Listing 8-2. MainMenuLevelSelect header

```
#import "CCNode.h"

@class MainMenuButtons;

@interface MainMenuLevelSelect : CCNode

@property (weak) MainMenuButtons* mainMenuButtons;

@end
```

The additions are analogous to those in SettingsLayer, enabling the MainMenuButtons class to assign itself to the MainMenuLevelSelect class so that it can send messages back to it. You'll need it only for closing the level-selection popover, just like you did in SettingsLayer, too.

MainMenuLevelSelect.m does not need any modifications for now.

MainMenuButtons.m, on the other hand, requires several additions. Add the code highlighted in Listing 8-3.

Listing 8-3. Excerpt of MainMenuButtons.m with new additions highlighted

```
#import "MainMenuButtons.h"
#import "SettingsLayer.h"
#import "MainMenuLevelSelect.h"

@implementation MainMenuButtons
{
    __weak MainMenuLevelSelect* _levelSelect;
}

-(void) didLoadFromCCB
{
    _levelSelect = (MainMenuLevelSelect*)[self.parent
                                  getChildByName:@"levelSelect"
                                      recursively:YES];
    _levelSelect.parent.visible = NO;
    _levelSelect.mainMenuButtons = self;
}

// ... remaining methods omitted
```

This imports the new MainMenuLevelSelect class header in order to add an ivar for that class named _levelSelect. So far, so good.

In didLoadFromCCB, you obtain the reference to the MainMenuLevelSelect instance by its name. You've done that a couple times before. But wait, the MainMenuButtons class has no relation to the *Scroll View* or the *Scroll View*'s *Content* node, meaning they aren't children of the MainMenuButtons class. If you take a closer look at the getChildByName: method, you'll notice it is actually sent to the MainMenuButtons parent node. Since MainMenuButtons is a child of the MainScene node, self.parent is a reference to the MainScene instance. The MainScene contains the *Scroll View* as a child, and the *Scroll View* contains the *Content* node as a child. Therefore, the MainMenuLevelSelect instance can be found by its name recursively.

In the same light, _levelSelect.parent.visible = NO hides the CCScrollView because it is the parent of the MainMenuLevelSelect instance. It is important to hide the CCScrollView instance rather than the MainMenuLevelSelect instance because this will disable all touch events for the CCScrollView. If you only made _levelSelect invisible, it has the same effect visually, but the user could still swipe through the various pages unknowingly. Since the CCScrollView is always made invisible, you can optionally select the *Scroll View* node in *MainScene.ccb* and uncheck its *Visible* property to hide it.

Last, the _levelSelect is assigned a reference to the MainMenuButtons instance so that it can later send the show message to the MainMenuButtons instance when the user closes the MainMenuLevelSelect popover.

What remains is to update the shouldPlayGame method to the version in Listing 8-4.

Listing 8-4. Showing the level-selection popover

```
-(void) shouldPlayGame
{
    _levelSelect.parent.visible = YES;
    self.visible = NO;
}
```

This makes the CCScrollView visible and hides the MainMenuButtons instance.

Notice that, unlike with the SettingsLayer, the CCScrollView instance is not removed from the scene and reloaded when it should be shown; rather, you simply change its visible state on and off. Changing visible state is a lot more efficient if you need a given node (or branch of nodes) frequently compared to loading a CCB or even just creating new node instances programmatically. Of course, changing visible states will not free memory. But, again, if you need a node frequently, you have to have enough spare memory to be able to show it at any time, so such nodes also can stay in memory the whole time.

Furthermore, it often requires additional memory to create or load a node during the process of loading or creating it. Specifically, when loading textures it is common that, for just a frame or two, the memory usage increases twofold and immediately drops back down to what the texture really uses. When your app is getting very close to receiving memory warnings, it is better to not remove nodes that you are going to need frequently.

That said, the real reason to keep the CCScrollView and its *Content* node in the scene for the entire time is a pragmatic one. You would have to create an additional CCB file that contains just the *Scroll View* node in order to be able to load the *Scroll View* and its *Content* node with CCBReader. At the moment, only the *MainMenuLevelSelect.ccb* (the *Scroll View*'s *Content* node) is a separate CCB instance while the *Scroll View* node was added directly to *MainScene.ccb*. So you would be able to load only the *MainMenuLevelSelect.ccb Content* node with CCBReader.

If you were to remove the CCScrollView from its parent node, you would have to create another instance of the CCScrollView programmatically, initializing it with a *Content* node loaded with CCBReader or assigning it to the *Scroll View*'s contentNode property—but only the second time and every time after that, further complicating the code.

Tip   Always consider the "Keep it simple stupid," or KISS, principle (not to be mistaken for the band of the same name). See http://en.wikipedia.org/wiki/KISS_principle. The principle translates to this: *If you can create the same behavior with less code, choose to write less code.* Less code has fewer bugs and is easier to understand, change, and reuse. Watch out specifically for duplicated code or code that does essentially the same thing except for a few parameters. This is code that ought to be extracted into its own method.

This setup suffices to try out the *Scroll View* in Xcode. Publish, build, and run. You can now swipe the three background images left and right, and each page will snap to the area defined by the *Scroll View*. Notice also how you can still tap the buttons underneath the *Scroll View*. You can also test the boundaries where the *Scroll View* still accepts touch and drag movements and where it doesn't.

Designing the Scroll View Content Node

What you can't do at this point is actually tap a level to play it, nor can you close the *Scroll View* popover. To be able to do that, let's finalize the design of the level-selection pages so that each page represents a given world.

> **Note**   I'll use the # character as a placeholder for the digits 1, 2, and 3 whenever I want to refer to the entire group of *W#_something* images in the following descriptions.

Start by adding a close button to each page. Open *MainMenuLevelSelect.ccb*. Then drag and drop one *CloseButton.ccb* onto each *W#_bg* sprite. Do so by using either the *Tileless Editor View* with the correct *UserInterface* folder at the bottom checked, or by dragging the *CloseButton.ccb* from the *File View*. It's best to drop each button directly onto a *W#_bg* sprite so that it becomes a child of the page background image.

Select each *CloseButton*, and change its *Position* types to % and its values to 100 on the *Item Properties* tab. That's all that the buttons need.

Now add the logo and title for each world. On the *Tileless Editor View*, make sure the other *UserInterface* folder is checked—the one that refers to the *UserInterface* Sprite Sheet containing all the *W#* images. You can see an excerpt in Figure 8-4.

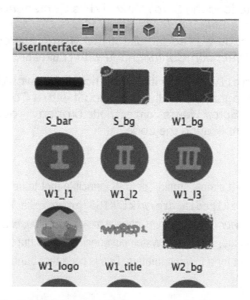

Figure 8-4. The UserInterface Sprite Sheet with the various W# images used for the Scroll View pages

Drag the *W1_logo* onto the *W1_bg* sprite. Then drag the *W1_title* onto the *W1_logo* sprite. *W1_title* should be a child of *W1_logo*, and *W1_logo* should be a child of *W1_bg*. Then repeat this step for the *W2* and *W3* title and logo images, and be sure to add them to their corresponding *W2* and *W3* background sprites. See Figure 8-5 for reference.

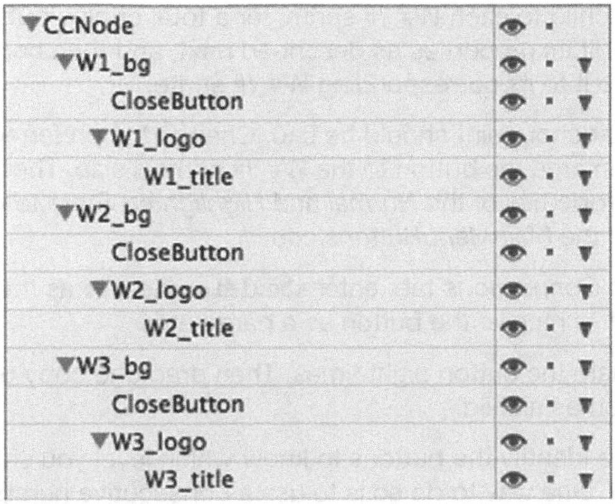

Figure 8-5. Logo and title have been added

Select each logo and title image in turn to change their positions. The logo position types should be % and the values should be 50x85, while the title position types should also be percent and values set to 50x0. This will align the images neatly at the top center of each page.

For the three level buttons for each world, you best use a *Box Layout* node to align them horizontally. Drag one *Box Layout* from the *Node Library View* onto each W#_bg sprite, and then change the *Box Layout* node's position types to % and its values to 50x35. Also, change the anchor point to 0.5x0.5 so that the child nodes will be centered on the *Box Layout* node's position, and *Spacing* should be 30 to keep the level buttons at a fixed distance from each other.

You should then drag the *W#_l1*, *W#_l2*, and *W#_l3* images in that order onto the *CCLayoutBox* node so that each *Box Layout* node has three *W#_l#* sprites as children. See Figure 8-6 for reference, and ignore the *CCButton* nodes for now. Now change the color property of all *W#_l#* sprites except the first (*W1_l1*) to a light gray—color code #999999 works well. This will dim the images, signaling to the user that those levels haven't been unlocked yet. The first level is, of course, always unlocked.

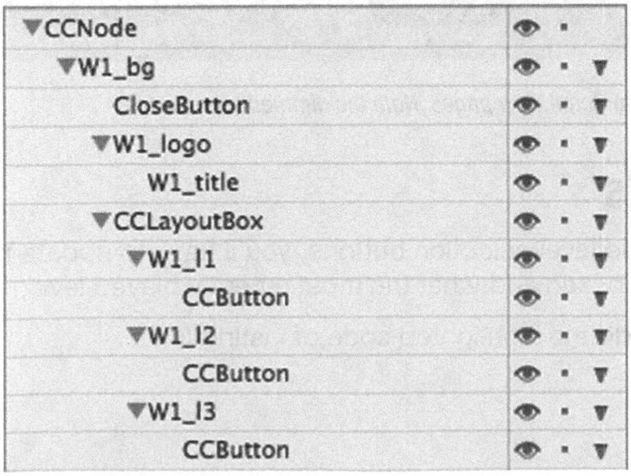

Figure 8-6. The first page's layout. The other page's layout is the same except it uses the corresponding W2 and W3 images

Then add one button as a child to each *W#_I#* sprite, for a total of nine buttons. But you should add only one button for now, edit its properties as described next, and then copy and paste the button eight more times and move it to its corresponding *W#_I#* sprite.

The button's position and anchor point should be 0x0. Change the preferred size types to % and the values to 100x100 to enlarge the button to the *W#_I#* sprite's size. Then clear the *Title* field and change the *Sprite frame* properties of the *Normal* and *Highlighted State* to <NULL>. This gives you the same invisible button as in the *MainMenuButtons.ccb*.

On the button's *Item Code Connections* tab, enter **shouldLoadLevel:** as the selector. Note the trailing colon, because you'll want to receive the button as a parameter.

Now you can copy and paste the button eight times. Then drag one copy of the button so that each *W#_I#* sprite has one button as a child.

Finally, you'll need a way to identify the buttons to know which level you should be loading when a particular button is tapped. One way to do so is to use a consecutive numbering scheme by entering **1** as the name for the first button; **2** would be the name of the second button, and so on until the last button, whose name should be 9. Be sure to enter only digits, and don't pad with zeros. The name property will be the only property unique to each button. The layout of the first page is given as an example in Figure 8-6.

The result can be seen in Figure 8-7, which shows the first two pages of the *Scroll View*.

Figure 8-7. The final design of two Scroll View pages. Note the dimmed level buttons

Unlocking Levels

Before you can program the level-selection buttons, you'll have to update the GameState class to record which levels are unlocked and what the most recently played level is.

Open *GameState.h*, and add the highlighted code of Listing 8-5.

Listing 8-5. Adding level properties to GameState

```
#import <Foundation/Foundation.h>

@interface GameState : NSObject

+(GameState*) sharedGameState;

@property CGFloat musicVolume;
@property CGFloat effectsVolume;

@property int currentLevel;
@property (readonly) int highestUnlockedLevel;
-(BOOL) unlockNextLevel;

@end
```

The currentLevel is the level that is currently being played. This will play a role in the
unlockNextLevel method. The highestUnlockedLevel is what it says, the highest numbered level
the player is allowed to play. This particular property is set to readonly so that it is illegal for other
classes to change this property. Only the unlockNextLevel method should be allowed to change it,
and this is done by implementing both property getter and setter methods. Indeed, you can mark a
property readonly while also overriding the property's setter method.

Add the methods in Listing 8-6 to *GameState.m*, just above the @end line.

Listing 8-6. Setter and getter for the readonly property highestUnlockedLevel

```
static NSString* KeyForUnlockedLevel = @"unlockedLevel";

-(void) setHighestUnlockedLevel:(int)level
{
    int totalLevelCount = 9;
    if (_currentLevel > 0 && _currentLevel <= totalLevelCount)
    {
        [[NSUserDefaults standardUserDefaults] setInteger:level
                                            forKey:KeyForUnlockedLevel];
    }
}

-(int) highestUnlockedLevel
{
    NSNumber* number = [[NSUserDefaults standardUserDefaults]
                        objectForKey:KeyForUnlockedLevel];
    return (number ? [number intValue] : 1);
}
```

The setter method defines the maximum number of levels in the game; this game is intended to have
nine levels. The currentLevel property is tested to be in the range 1 through 9 before it is stored in
NSUserDefaults. The getter method obtains the stored NSNumber and either returns its intValue or
1 if there is no entry for the key KeyForUnlockedLevel yet. It returns 1 because the first level should
always be unlocked.

Unlocking levels is done with the `unlockNextLevel` method, as you can see in Listing 8-7. Add it just after the `highestUnlockedLevel` method.

Listing 8-7. Unlocking the next level

```
-(BOOL) unlockNextLevel
{
    int highest = self.highestUnlockedLevel;
    if (_currentLevel >= highest)
    {
        [self setHighestUnlockedLevel:_currentLevel + 1];
    }

    return (highest < self.highestUnlockedLevel);
}
```

The currently `highestUnlockedLevel` is obtained from the property setter via `self.highestUnlockedLevel` and assigned to the highest variable. If `currentLevel` is equal to or greater than the highest number, the `setHighestUnlockedLevel:` setter is called so that it unlocks the next level following the current level. At the end, the method returns a `BOOL` value that indicates whether the next level was indeed unlocked or not, by comparing the previous highest number with the current `highestUnlockedLevel`.

Highlighting Level Buttons

The level buttons need to be unlocked—that is, their color set to white—if their level is currently accessible. "Accessible" means that the button's level number is less than or equal to `highestUnlockedLevel`. You'll also want to launch the `GameScene` and load the button's corresponding level file.

Add the highlighted code in Listing 8-8 to *MainMenuLevelSelect.m*. The code in `didLoadFromCCB` will enumerate all buttons to compare each button's level number with the current `highestUnlockedLevel`. If the button's level should be unlocked, the button's parent sprite gets its color set to white, removing the dimming effect caused by applying a gray color to it in SpriteBuilder.

Listing 8-8. Level buttons whose level is unlocked should not be grayed out

```
#import "MainMenuLevelSelect.h"
#import "MainMenuButtons.h"
#import "SceneManager.h"
#import "GameState.h"

@implementation MainMenuLevelSelect

-(void) didLoadFromCCB
{
    int count = 1;
    int highest = [GameState sharedGameState].highestUnlockedLevel;
    CCNode* button;
```

```
while ((button = [self getChildByName:@(count).stringValue
                        recursively:YES]))
{
    if (button.name.intValue <= highest)
    {
        CCSprite* sprite = (CCSprite*)button.parent;
        sprite.color = [CCColor whiteColor];
    }

    count++;
}
```

@end

The assignment to the button variable occurs within the while condition. This is legal and safe to do, but it requires you to use double brackets to prevent the compiler from complaining—after all, it's a common mistake to use the assignment operator = instead of the equality operator == in conditions. The brackets ensure that the assignment occurs first, and only afterward is the result (button) used as the condition—which is true as long as button is not nil.

Of note is the @(count).stringValue literal. In modern Objective-C, you can initialize arrays, dictionaries, and numbers using the literal syntax.

```
NSArray* array = @[obj1, obj2, obj3];
NSDictionary* dict = @{key1: obj1, key2: obj2, key3: obj3};
NSNumber* number = @(1234);
NSNumber* number = @(YES);
NSNumber* number = @(count);
```

The literal syntax is easier to read and shorter than using the regular initializers for the preceding classes. The expression @(count) thus takes the count value and returns an NSNumber object. The NSNumber class conveniently creates a string representation of its value via the stringValue property. Therefore, @(count).stringValue is shorthand for converting a number to a NSString object, turning a 1 into @"1". This string can then be compared with the names of the buttons, which should have 1 through 9 as their name string.

> **Note**   Why not use a NSNumber to begin with? That's simple: NSNumber is an immutable class. You have to create a new NSNumber object if the value must change. There is no corresponding NSMutableNumber class, either.

The counterpart, string-to-number conversion, happens in button.name.intValue. The button.name is an NSString object, and NSString has several convenience properties like intValue, which attempt to convert the string to an int value. However, if that fails—for instance, if you used the string @"one"—the property will simply return 0.

The button's parent node is a CCSprite—one of the *W#_l#* sprites. If the button's level is accessible, the sprite gets the whiteColor assigned, which removes any tinting. CCColor is the color class used by Cocos2D; it is very similar to UIColor and NSColor.

> **Note**   Changing the color property applies the so-called *color-tinting* effect to the node. You cannot make a sprite brighter than its original image through tinting because there is no brighter tint color than white. Applying white as the color (the default) will make the node look like its original image.

Since unlocking levels occurs only while playing the *GameScene*, the code in Listing 8-8 does not need to re-run every time the *Scroll View* is shown. This is good because the *Scroll View* simply toggles its visible state to show and hide; therefore, didLoadFromCCB will run only once, when the *MainScene* has been loaded.

Closing the Level-Selection Popover

The level-selection popover can be closed with the CloseButton.ccb instances you've already added to each page. The CloseButton class forwards the shouldClose message to the first parent that implements it. So that's what you'll have to do, meaning that you add the code in Listing 8-9 just below the didLoadFromCCB method in *MainMenuLevelSelect.m*.

Listing 8-9. Closing means hiding the Scroll View

```
-(void) shouldClose
{
    self.parent.visible = NO;
    [_mainMenuButtons show];
}
```

The *Content* node's parent instance is the *Scroll View*. So all it takes is to set the parent's visible status to NO and then let the *MainMenuButtons* node show itself.

Loading Levels

What's left is to register button presses for each level and test if that level is unlocked or not. If it is, load the level; otherwise, well, maybe later you'll play a dismissive sound effect in that case.

Add the method in Listing 8-10 just below the shouldClose method in *MainMenuLevelSelect.m*.

Listing 8-10. Loading a level...or not

```
-(void) shouldLoadLevel:(CCButton*)sender
{
    GameState* gameState = [GameState sharedGameState];

    int levelNumber = sender.name.intValue;
    if (levelNumber <= gameState.highestUnlockedLevel)
    {
        gameState.currentLevel = levelNumber;
        [SceneManager presentGameScene];
    }
    else
    {
        // maybe play a 'access denied' sound effect here
    }
}
```

As before, the button's name property is converted to int via the intValue property of NSString. The only difference here is that the button is passed to the method as the sender object. So depending on which level button the user taps, the sender will be the button that was tapped.

If the levelNumber obtained from the button's name is less than or equal to the highestUnlockedLevel, the user can play that particular level. At this point, the GameState singleton's currentLevel property is updated so that it is readily available from within the SceneManager. SceneManager then presents the GameScene with the current level—which is a method that you'll update shortly. And if the user tapped a level button whose level is currently locked, the shouldLoadLevel: method simply ignores the request.

Now open *SceneManager.m*. First import the GameScene and GameState headers. Add them at the top of the file where the other import line is. See Listing 8-11.

Listing 8-11. Importing the GameScene header

```
#import "SceneManager.h"
#import "GameScene.h"
#import "GameState.h"
```

Locate the presentGameScene method. Replace its contents with Listing 8-12.

Listing 8-12. Presenting GameScene and loading the current level

```
+(void) presentGameScene
{
    CCScene* scene = [CCBReader loadAsScene:@"GameScene"];
    GameScene* gameScene = (GameScene*)scene.children.firstObject;

    int levelNumber = [GameState sharedGameState].currentLevel;
    NSString* level = [NSString stringWithFormat:@"Levels/Level%i",
                       levelNumber];
    [gameScene loadLevelNamed:level];
```

```
    id t = [CCTransition transitionPushWithDirection:CCTransitionDirectionLeft
                                            duration:1.0];
    [[CCDirector sharedDirector] presentScene:scene withTransition:t];
}
```

The *GameScene* is loaded, as usual, using the CCBReader's loadAsScene: method. I've mentioned this before, but it's worth noting again: the loadAsScene: method returns a generic CCScene object whose only child is always the root node of the CCB that was loaded. In this case, it's an instance of the GameScene class.

The current level number is then converted to a string of the format Levels/Level%i. For example, the resulting string will be Levels/Level1 for the first level or Levels/Level2345 for the 2,345[th] level.

> **Tip** Developers still frequently pad file names with additional zeros to fight a long-won battle: numeric sorting. If you feel tempted to format numbered items by padding with zero—for instance, Level0001—because you might have up to a thousand levels, please don't! Modern operating systems are well aware of the numeric sorting problem. You will no longer see numbered files sorted in this particular order: Level1 - Level10 - Level2. At the same time, the string-formatting code Level%i fits all numbers, from one to gazillions. Having to consider padded zeros makes every format string more complex than it needs to be.

With the reference to the GameScene instance, you can send it the loadLevelNamed: method, passing in the generated level string. You should do so before presenting the scene so that the scene is fully prepared before it is rendered. The loadLevelNamed: method is the same one you've already used before, except you haven't been using it from another class. To prevent the compiler from complaining about a missing selector declaration, you have to open *GameScene.h* and add the declaration as shown in Listing 8-13.

Listing 8-13. Declaring the loadLevelNamed: selector

```
#import "CCNode.h"

@interface GameScene : CCNode <CCPhysicsCollisionDelegate,
                               CCBAnimationManagerDelegate>

-(void) showPopoverNamed:(NSString*)popoverName;
-(void) removePopover;

-(void) loadLevelNamed:(NSString*)levelCCB;

@end
```

In *GameScene.m*, you should now remove the line [self loadLevelNamed:nil]; from the didLoadFromCCB method.

Although this will now successfully load the first level, it's a fallacy. After all, the first level is already referenced by the GameScene.ccb, yet you aren't loading the particular level passed in to the loadLevelNamed: method. You should change that now by updating the loadLevelNamed: method in *GameScene.m*. As highlighted by Listing 8-14, all the new lines are at the top of the method.

Listing 8-14. The actual level-loading procedure

```objc
-(void) loadLevelNamed:(NSString*)levelCCB
{
    [_levelNode removeFromParent];

    CCNode* level = [CCBReader load:levelCCB];
    [self addChild:level];

    _levelNode = level;

    _physicsNode = (CCPhysicsNode*)[_levelNode getChildByName:@"physics"
                                                   recursively:NO];
    _physicsNode.debugDraw = _drawPhysicsShapes;
    _physicsNode.collisionDelegate = self;

    _backgroundNode = [_levelNode getChildByName:@"background" recursively:NO];
    _playerNode = [_physicsNode getChildByName:@"player" recursively:YES];

    [self scrollToTarget:_playerNode];
}
```

The _levelNode is the reference to the *Sub File* node currently referencing Level1.ccb. Loading a level should first remove the existing level. Then CCBReader loads the levelCCB string originally generated by the shouldLoadLevel: method in *MainMenuLevelSelect.m*. The level is then added as a child to the GameScene.

Finally, the _levelNode reference is replaced by the new level. Note that because _levelNode is a __weak reference, you couldn't assign the node returned from CCBReader load: directly to it. It would likely be set to nil by the Objective-C runtime because at that point there would be no strong reference to the level node until the next line, where it is added as a child.

If you run this now, press Play, and then tap the first-level button, you should enter the GameScene with the first level loaded as before. Or wait. There's no pause button anymore.

Silly me. I totally forgot one thing. Take a look at Figure 8-8.

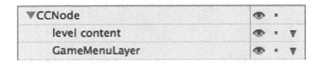

Figure 8-8. The default node order in GameScene.ccb

So far, the GameScene has relied on the ordering of nodes in SpriteBuilder to determine the draw order. The level content (_levelNode) is drawn first, and then the GameMenuLayer is drawn on top of the level.

However, now you are removing the _levelNode, loading a new one, and adding it as a child node to the GameScene. Adding a node will always put it at the end of the list; therefore, the draw order is now reversed, and you can no longer see the pause button.

To fix this, replace the addChild: line of Listing 8-15 with the one in Listing 8-15.

Listing 8-15. Fixing the draw order

```
level.zOrder = -1;
[self addChild:level];
```

The zOrder property determines the node's draw order. Nodes with a lower zOrder are drawn before nodes with a higher zOrder, but only if they have the same parent. Nodes with the same zOrder are drawn in the order they were added to the parent. Note that the preceding code can be shortened to a single line:

```
[self addChild:level z:-1];
```

Now loading levels works! But you want proof? Okay, there's one thing to consider, anyway: right now the GameScene references the *Level1.ccb* in the *GameScene.ccb* file. So when you load the GameScene, it will actually load the *Level1.ccb* along with it, and then replace it with a newly loaded instance of whatever level you chose to load. That's kind of inefficient, having two levels loaded one after the other and having both in memory at the same time.

Adding a Dummy Level

To fix this, go into SpriteBuilder and right-click the *Levels* folder. Select *New File*, and name it **DummyLevel.ccb**. Set its type to *Node*, and click *Create*. That's all. You just need an empty CCB.

Now open the *GameScene.ccb*, and select the level *Content* node. On the *Item Properties* tab, click the *CCB File* drop-down menu. Select the newly created *Levels/DummyLevel.ccb* as the *Sub File* node's reference. The GameScene will be empty now except for the pause button in the upper left corner.

> **Note**   If GameScene still contains a button that changes scenes, you should remove it, because it is no longer needed.

You should now publish, build, and run the app. Tap play, and load the first level. This should present the GameScene with the first level. This proves that the level was loaded correctly; if it hadn't been, the GameScene would have been a black screen with just the pause button on it.

Winning Levels

What happens if you play through the level and reach the exit? That's right, the view resets to the lower left corner and you're stuck. It's time to fix that and unlock the next level at that point.

In SpriteBuilder, right-click the *UserInterface/Popovers* folder to add a *New File*. Name the document **LevelCompleteLayer.ccb**, and set its type to *Layer* before creating it. Then change the root node's content size types to % and values to 100x100. Then switch to the *Item Code Connections* tab, and enter GameMenuLayer as the class name. That's your collective popover class shared by the other in-game popover layers.

You need a background image, label, and button. From the *UserInterface* section in the *Tileless Editor View*, drag any image that ends in *_bg* onto the stage. For instance, I used *W2_bg*. Change the background sprite's position types to % and its values to 50x50 and you're done with it.

Then switch to the *Node Library View*, and drag a *Label TTF* node onto the background sprite so that the label becomes a child of the sprite. Change the label's position types to % and its values to 50x66. Set the label's *Title* to something that indicates level completeness—for instance, "Level Complete" sounds fine. Feel free to change the label in any way you like.

Last, add a *Button* from the *Node Library View* and drop this onto the background sprite, also making it a child. Change the button's position types to % and its values to 50x30. A preferred size of 170x50 enlarges the button image slightly. The button's *Title* should read *Next Level* or something similar. Also, change the *SpriteFrame* of both *Normal State* and *Highlighted State* to SpriteSheets/UserInterface/P_resume.png, and change both *Background* and *Label* color of *Highlighted State* to a light gray (#999999) for visual feedback when the button is pressed.

Don't forget to set the selector on the *Item Code Connections*, and enter **shouldLoadNextLevel** in the *Selector* field. That completes the wonderfully minimalistic *Level Complete* popover seen in Figure 8-9.

Figure 8-9. Level complete: Everything is awesome

> **Tip** If you want to make this popover more complete, consider adding retry and exit buttons to it. After all, the popover uses the same GameMenuLayer class as the other popovers, so it's only a matter of connecting the button's selectors to shouldRestartGame and shouldExitGame.

Back to Xcode. You'll want to show this popover when the player collides with the exit object. Open *GameScene.m*, and import the GameState header by adding the highlighted line in Listing 8-16 just below the other import lines.

Listing 8-16. Importing the GameState header

```
#import "GameScene.h"
#import "Trigger.h"
#import "GameMenuLayer.h"
#import "GameState.h"
```

Then locate the physics collision method with player and exit as parameters, and replace it with the version in Listing 8-17.

Listing 8-17. Colliding with the exit object shows the Level Complete popover and unlocks the next level

```
-(BOOL) ccPhysicsCollisionBegin:(CCPhysicsCollisionPair *)pair
                        player:(CCNode *)player
                          exit:(CCNode *)exit
{
    [[GameState sharedGameState] unlockNextLevel];
    [[GameState sharedGameState] synchronize];

    [self showPopoverNamed:@"UserInterface/Popovers/LevelCompleteLayer"];

    return NO;
}
```

This unlocks the next level. Thanks to the checks performed in Listing 8-6 and Listing 8-7, you can call this method every time a level is completed. Even if you are replaying level 1 again, it won't reset the highest unlocked level back to level 2. The GameState is synchronized, and the changes are written back to disk because you really don't want the player losing an unlocked level even if the app were to crash a second later.

Note that the synchronize method may or may not be defined, depending on whether you followed my earlier advice to add it to GameState. If it is undefined, you can add it to *GameState.h* and *GameState.m* now or just replace the call to synchronize with the following line:

```
[[NSUserDefaults standardUserDefaults] synchronize];
```

It's the same thing. And, of course, the LevelCompleteLayer is shown as a popup.

Which brings you to the GameMenuLayer class already. In GameMenuLayer.m, add an import for the GameState header just below the other import lines, as seen in Listing 8-18.

Listing 8-18. Adding the GameState header

```
#import "GameMenuLayer.h"
#import "GameScene.h"
#import "SceneManager.h"
#import "GameState.h"
```

You then just need to add the selector shown in Listing 8-19. Add it just above the @end line.

Listing 8-19. Loading the next level

```
-(void) shouldLoadNextLevel
{
    [GameState sharedGameState].currentLevel += 1;
    [SceneManager presentGameScene];
}
```

This should be pretty straightforward. The current level is increased by one because the player is going to the next level. The presentGameScene method then presents a new GameScene instance and instructs the instance to load the current level.

This is pretty much it. However, you don't have any additional levels yet. But you can still try one thing: play the first level and reach the exit. Confirm that the Level Complete popover is shown, and then tap the *Next Level* button. Doing this will most certainly cause a crash because there's simply no *Level2.ccb* in your project yet. But if you relaunch the app and tap the play button you should notice that the Level 2 button is no longer grayed out. So, in principle, the unlocking part works.

> **Tip**   If you ever need to reset the highest unlocked level, just delete the app from the device and simulator. This will also delete all items stored by the app, including its User Defaults dictionary.

Adding More Levels

There's a shortcut to adding more levels. Open Finder, and locate the *LearnSpriteBuilder. spritebuilder* project folder. Inside that folder, you'll find the *Packages/SpriteBuilder Resources. sbpack* folder, which contains all the files SpriteBuilder shows in its *File View*. Therefore, if you move into the *Levels* folder, you'll find your *Level1.ccb* and *DummyLevel.ccb* files, among others.

> **Note**   The *.sbpack* folder is a so-called *package* and looks like a file rather than a folder. Finder allows you to browse into package contents by right-clicking the package and then selecting *Show Package Contents* from the context menu.

You can then just duplicate the *Level1.ccb* (by copying and pasting) eight more times and rename the copies so that they are called *Level2.ccb*, *Level3.ccb*, and so on, up to *Level9.ccb*.

This won't make the game very interesting to play through, but at least you can confirm that it works technically. Don't forget to publish it in SpriteBuilder before you try it out.

You can then start modifying each duplicated level as you see fit. If you prefer to start each level from scratch, here's a checklist of things that a level has to have in order to function technically:

- Create a CCB using the *Level#.ccb* naming scheme. The CCB must be of type *Layer*.

- The CCB's root node defines the level's size. The default level size is 4000x500.

- Optionally, add a parallaxing background—for instance, *Background1.ccb*.

- Add a Physics Node whose name property must be set to "physics."

- Add one *Player.ccb* prefab instance to the *Physics* node. The player's name property must be set to "player."

- Add an *Exit.ccb* prefab instance to the *Physics* node.

You may want to consider adding special code for the very last level. Obviously, it can't load another level yet. So in the collision delegate method with the `player` and `exit` parameters, check if `currentLevel` is equal to or greater than the `GameState` level count. You will have to create a `levelCount` property in `GameState` with a custom property getter that just returns a constant value.

The alternative would be to not have an exit in the last level, and instead add a different type of exit that runs a different kind of physics collision delegate method. That way, you can most easily handle this special case and present a Game Won popover.

Counting Level Files

Since the number of levels is hardly ever predetermined in a game, you may be wondering if you couldn't just count the levels? Well yes, you can!

You would have to count the number of *Level#.ccbi* files in the bundle's *Published-iOS/Levels* directory. Adding Listing 8-20 to *GameState.m* (just above @end) is entirely optional. Take note, however, that if you do add it, unlocking more levels will work only if you have consecutively named *Level#.ccb* files in SpriteBuilder.

Listing 8-20. Counting the levels in the game

```
-(int) levelCount
{
    NSBundle* mainBundle = [NSBundle mainBundle];
    NSString* path;
    int count = 0;

    do
    {
        count++;
        NSString* level = [NSString stringWithFormat:@"Level%i", count];
```

```
        path = [mainBundle pathForResource:level
                                 ofType:@"ccbi"
                            inDirectory:@"Published-iOS/Levels"];
    } while (path != nil);

    count--;
    return count;
}
```

This do/while loop starts counting with one, generating a level string "Level1". This is passed into the pathForResource method of the NSBundle class. It doesn't look for a file directly; rather, it requires you to pass in the individual path components: file name, extension (here, called *type*) and path (*directory*). The file name is "Level1". The extension is "*ccbi*" because published CCB files are converted to the binary *ccbi* format. And the directory is " "Published-iOS/Levels". Therefore, it will look for the file "Published-iOS/Levels/Level1.ccbi" in the root of the bundle.

> **Note**   A *bundle*, which is sometimes called a *package*, is just a folder structure that OS X and iOS treat like a single file. Every app is a bundle, and you can peek inside its contents in OS X if you right-click an .app file and select *Show Package Contents*.

You can see and browse the bundle files in Xcode: just locate the *Resources* group, and you'll see a *Published-iOS* folder with a blue icon. That folder and all of its contents will be added to the compiled app bundle as is. However, you shouldn't manually add files to that folder or edit them because the *Published-iOS* and *Published-Android* folders are managed by SpriteBuilder, meaning your changes may be lost when publishing the SpriteBuilder project.

This loop is repeated until the first *Level#.ccb* file returns a path string that is nil, indicating that the file couldn't be found. Because the level file that wasn't found was already counted, the count variable is reduced by one just after the loop before returning the value.

In order to use the levelCount method, edit the setHighestUnlockedLevel: method and replace the first line with the one highlighted in Listing 8-21.

Listing 8-21. Assigning the levelCount result

```
-(void) setHighestUnlockedLevel:(int)level
{
    int totalLevelCount = [self levelCount];

    if (_currentLevel > 0 && _currentLevel <= totalLevelCount)
    {
        [[NSUserDefaults standardUserDefaults] setInteger:level
                                       forKey:KeyForUnlockedLevel];
    }
}
```

Showing the Correct Level-Selection Page

Last but not least, let's return to the *Scroll View* one more time. When you've played through the first three levels, you've unlocked the first level of the second world. Yet when you open the level-selection popover in the *MainScene*, it will always show the first page. This ought to be fixed.

Open *MainScene.m*, and import the GameState header just below the other import, as shown in Listing 8-22.

Listing 8-22. Importing GameState

```
#import "MainScene.h"
#import "GameState.h"
```

Then go to the didLoadFromCCB method, and replace it with the version in Listing 8-23.

Listing 8-23. Switching to the page with the highest unlocked level

```
-(void) didLoadFromCCB
{
    int numPages = _levelSelectScrollView.numHorizontalPages;
    if (numPages > 0)
    {
        int highest = [GameState sharedGameState].highestUnlockedLevel;
        int worldPage = (highest - 1) / numPages;
        worldPage = MIN(worldPage, numPages - 1);

        _levelSelectScrollView.horizontalPage = worldPage;
    }
}
```

The numHorizontalPages returns 3 in this case, because there are three pages (worlds). By dividing the highestUnlockedLevel minus 1 by the number of pages, the result is a value in the range of 0 to 3—for instance, (1 - 1) / 3 = 0, which is what happens when you first run the app. Consider that (3 - 1) / 3 = 0, so if you happen to have unlocked all three levels of the first world, the first page (index 0) would still be shown. Unlocking another level, such as (4 - 1) / 3 = 1, will then show the second page (world).

> **Note**   If you were to uncheck the *Scroll View*'s *Paging enabled* property, numPages will be 0. Hence, you conduct the test to ensure numPages is greater than 0. This prevents a division-by-zero error with paging disabled.

The MIN macro ensures that worldPage is always in the range 0 to numPages - 1 because highestUnlockedLevel may be set to 10 after completing the ninth level. The resulting worldPage index is then assigned to the *Scroll View*'s horizontalPage index property to have the *Scroll View* show that particular page. Now if you have a couple levels and you unlocked the first six levels, you'll immediately see the second page of the *Scroll View* as shown in Figure 8-10.

Figure 8-10. The level-selection Scroll View in action and showing the second page

Implementing Scroll View Delegate Methods

There's one last bit to understanding the CCScrollView class. It provides a CCScrollViewDelegate protocol defining callback methods sent to a delegate if it implements the protocol methods. There's no real use for it at the moment, but it can't hurt to implement the protocol methods to see what *Scroll View* events you can react to.

Still in *MainScene.m*, you should add the highlighted code of Listing 8-24 to the didLoadFromCCB method.

Listing 8-24. Switching to the page with the highest unlocked level

```
-(void) didLoadFromCCB
{
    // Code in Listing 8-23 omitted ...

    id levelSelect = _levelSelectScrollView.contentNode;
    _levelSelectScrollView.delegate = levelSelect;
}
```

This takes the *Scroll View*'s *Content* node and assigns it as the *Scroll View*'s delegate instance. The delegate object receives the CCScrollViewDelegate methods. The use of id here is important because if you didn't use it, the compiler would warn that you are trying to assign an incompatible type, unless you were to cast it to an object conforming to said protocol: (id<CCScrollViewDelegate>).

Note that you could have assigned the delegate just as well in the `MainMenuLevelSelect` class. For instance, the following would work in the `didLoadFromCCB` method of *MainMenuLevelSelect.m*:

```
CCScrollView* scrollView = (CCScrollView*)self.parent;
scrollView.delegate = self;
```

It amounts to the same code, and I leave it up to you which you should use. But it serves to illustrate there's almost always more than one way to do the same thing.

Next, open *MainMenuLevelSelect.h* to make the class conform to the `CCScrollViewDelegate` protocol, as highlighted in Listing 8-25.

Listing 8-25. Conforming to the CCScrollViewDelegate protocol

```
#import "CCNode.h"

@class MainMenuButtons;

@interface MainMenuLevelSelect : CCNode <CCScrollViewDelegate>

@property (weak) MainMenuButtons* mainMenuButtons;

@end
```

The protocol defines the following methods as optional, so you don't have to implement all (or any) of them. I added comments to Listing 8-26 to explain when each method runs.

Listing 8-26. The CCScrollViewDelegate protocol messages

```
// Sent repeatedly while scrolling (dragging).
- (void)scrollViewDidScroll:(CCScrollView *)scrollView;

// Sent each time the user begins touching & dragging the scroll view.
- (void)scrollViewWillBeginDragging:(CCScrollView *)scrollView;

// Sent each time the user lifts the finger to stop dragging.
// decelerate parameter is YES when view will move to the nearest page.
- (void)scrollViewDidEndDragging:(CCScrollView * )scrollView
                willDecelerate:(BOOL)decelerate;

// Sent immediately after didEndDragging (only if paging is not enabled)
- (void)scrollViewWillBeginDecelerating:(CCScrollView *)scrollView;

// Sent when the scroll view stopped moving.
- (void)scrollViewDidEndDecelerating:(CCScrollView *)scrollView;
```

You can see for yourself when each of these delegate methods run. Open *MainMenuLevelSelect.m*, and add the methods in Listing 8-27 just above the `@end` line.

Listing 8-27. Implementing CCScrollViewDelegate stub methods

```
-(void) scrollViewDidScroll:(CCScrollView *)scrollView
{
    NSLog(@"%@", NSStringFromSelector(_cmd));
}
-(void) scrollViewWillBeginDragging:(CCScrollView *)scrollView
{
    NSLog(@"%@", NSStringFromSelector(_cmd));
}
-(void) scrollViewDidEndDragging:(CCScrollView * )scrollView
                willDecelerate:(BOOL)decelerate
{
    NSLog(@"%@%@",
          NSStringFromSelector(_cmd), decelerate ? @"YES" : @"NO");
}
-(void) scrollViewWillBeginDecelerating:(CCScrollView *)scrollView
{
    NSLog(@"%@", NSStringFromSelector(_cmd));
    // This delegate method will only run when paging is not enabled
}
-(void) scrollViewDidEndDecelerating:(CCScrollView *)scrollView
{
    NSLog(@"%@", NSStringFromSelector(_cmd));
}
```

Use these methods as you see fit. For this project you won't need them. But for instance `scrollViewWillBeginDragging:` and `scrollViewDidEndDecelerating:` can be used to determine a page change. This would allow you to start and stop animations on the individual pages as the user navigates through the pages.

Summary

You can find the current state of the project in the *09 - Level Selection Scroll View* folder.

You now know how to use the *Scroll View* node and how to unlock and add more levels to the project. In the next chapter, you'll beef up the game with more physics game objects so that you can design levels with greater variation.

Chapter 9

Physics Joints

In this chapter, you'll add more game elements to make the levels more fun to design and play. Many complex physics objects require the use of joints. *Joints* are a means of keeping individual bodies together, and they define the freedom of movement between the connections.

Physics objects like chains, ropes, and springs all require joints to operate. Joints are also used to model soft-body physics. You will learn about this advanced technique in the next chapter after I lay the foundation for joint editing in this chapter.

Joints can also be difficult to tame. They are the reason for most physics glitches observed in games. Be it a horse and carriage suddenly launching high up in the air, ragdolls not coming to rest and limbs constantly jittering, or complex bodies seemingly stretching to infinity or compressing to a fraction of the original size. Examples are aplenty.

What Are Joints?

A *joint* is an invisible physics object that connects exactly two bodies together. The joint defines the connection points between the two bodies, called *joint anchors*. These anchors should not be confused with a node's anchor point, which determines the node's texture offset. The joint anchor is the point where the joint applies force to a body, which need not be within the node's collision shape or texture.

Joints add constraints to two physics bodies. These constraints can force, for example, the bodies to keep a fixed distance or a relative angle to each other.

The constraint parameters also determine how rigid the constraint is. Some constraints are soft, allowing the bodies to move apart or closer to each other with only little force applied to get them to their intended distance or rotation. Other constraints may be very rigid, allowing very little tolerance in distance variation and thus applying a potentially enormous amount of force to the bodies.

> **Caution**   The more rigid a constraint is, the more likely or severe physics glitches can be. Imagine a soft rubber band and a metal spring connecting two bodies—for instance, two buckets filled with water. The soft rubber band hardly pulls the two objects together when pulled, because there is very little force applied to the bodies even if the band is stretched out by twice its original length. A metal spring, on the other hand, requires a large amount of force to extend it even by just a little bit. If you let go of the metal spring, its reaction will be much more violent than the rubber band stretched by the same distance.

A *constraint* means that the physics engine is applying forces to the bodies of the joint in an attempt to keep the bodies positioned within the limits defined by the joint constraints, rather than just changing their positions. This has the effect that joints may never move bodies to a precise location that satisfies all constraints. This means two bodies connected with a joint are unlikely to ever come to rest at the exact same relative positions they originally had when you designed them in SpriteBuilder.

Joints can also be used as a means of moving objects through the world. Just entertain the following thought: Thus far, the game world scrolls by keeping the player centered. What if you add another invisible node with a physics body and connect that body with a soft spring joint to the player. Then let the camera follow the invisible node. The camera will then smoothly accelerate and decelerate depending on the player's movement. If you want the camera to look ahead rather than lag behind, you could reverse the setup by moving the invisible node that drags the player behind.

Types of Joints

In SpriteBuilder, three different joint types are available from the *Node Library View* as shown in Figure 9-1.

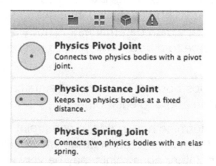

Figure 9-1. Joints in the Node Library View

> **Tip**   These joints can also be created in code by using the `CCPhysicsJoint` class methods. Even though `CCPhysicsJoint` exposes eight joint-creation methods in SpriteBuilder, they are only variations of the three joint types: pivot, distance, and spring. The only joint type `CCPhysicsJoint` exposes that is (currently) not editable in SpriteBuilder is the ratchet joint, a kind of pivot joint that rotates smoothly in one direction but rotates in discrete angles in the opposite direction.

Here is a description of the three joint types:

- **Pivot joint**   This is also known as a pin, hinge, or revolute joint. The pivot joint has only one anchor, which is the point the two bodies will rotate around. Consider that, unlike in reality (that is, with gears), the pivot joint does not have to be directly on top of either of the two connected bodies in order to rotate the connected bodies around its anchor.

- **Distance joint**   This type of joint keeps two bodies at a fixed distance from each other, while allowing them to revolve freely around each other. Optionally, you can enforce a minimum and maximum distance that the two bodies must not exceed; otherwise, they are allowed to stretch and contract their distance to a small degree if a large force is applied.

- **Spring joint**   This is a variation of the distance joint in that stretching and contracting is the desired behavior. You can adjust the rigidity (stiffness) of the spring as well as how much it springs back and forth (damping).

While three joint types may not sound like much, there's a lot you can do with them—especially if you consider that you can combine the various joints. Many specialized joint types of physics engines are built on these three basic joint types.

The same two bodies can be connected with different kinds of joints, and multiple bodies can be interconnected with joints. This is usually done to create bodies with a "soft" feel to them. However, you have to be careful in doing so, because interconnected joints add constraints that can end up fighting against each other. In the worst case, the object will behave erratically, folding in on itself or "exploding" and possibly triggering an assertion.

Creating a Chain

You are probably eager to get going, so let's dive right in.

Right-click the *Prefabs* folder in SpriteBuilder's *File View* and select *New File*. Create a document of type *Node*, and name it **Chain.ccb**. Now switch to the *Tileless Editor View*, ensure the *GameElements* entry below the *Tileless Editor View* is selected, and confirm it contains the images shown in Figure 9-2.

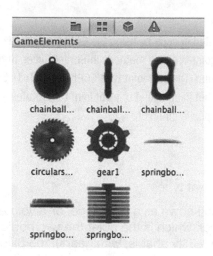

Figure 9-2. The chain and spring images

If the chain and spring images aren't there, you'll find them in the *GameElements* folder of the *Graphics* archive. Drag and drop the PNG images whose names start with *chainball* and *springboard* into the *GameElements* Sprite Sheet in SpriteBuilder before proceeding. Alternatively, use your own images. Just to give you a size reference, the chainball image is 416x416 pixels and the springboard is 254x234 pixels, making these images much smaller than the gear and saw.

Setting Up the Chain Sprites

Drag and drop two chainball chain images onto the *Chain.ccb* stage, one of each kind. One looks like the lowercase letter l (*chainball_chain1.png*), and the other looks like an 8 (*chainball_chain2.png*). I will refer to them as simply the *letter l chain* and *letter 8 chain* images. They are the two rightmost images in the first row in Figure 9-2. Also, drag and drop one chainball_ball.png (the leftmost image in the top row in Figure 9-2) onto the stage.

Make sure all sprites are children of the root node, because you don't want them to be children of each other. Positions don't matter yet—you'll first edit the physics properties.

Select the letter-8 chain, and on the *Item Physics* tab, select the *Enable Physics* check box. You should leave all physics properties at their default values. You may want to edit the physics shape to make the rectangle slightly smaller, but don't add any vertices—there's no need to make the chain's collision shape more detailed than a rectangle. With this done, you can copy (Cmd+C) and paste (Cmd+V) the node twice so that you have a total of three chains that look like an "8".

Proceed to do the same for the letter "l" chain node. Select it, select *Enable Physics*, and definitely edit its collision shape to make it smaller. Zoom the view in and out with Cmd+ and Cmd− to be able to edit the collision shape more precisely. After editing the collision shape, create two additional copies of the sprite. You should now have a total of six chain sprites, three of each kind.

Now select the ball sprite and also select its *Enable Physics* check box. But in this case change its *Physics Shape* to *Circle*, and set the *Corner radius* to *42*. Since the collision shape is offset slightly from the ball's center, click and drag its center handle to move the collision circle so that it is wholly contained within the ball and just about centered. It doesn't need to be perfectly centered. You should also change the ball's density to *0.5*; otherwise, the player will have a hard time pushing the ball out of the way.

Finally, go to the *Node Library View* and drag and drop a plain node onto the stage, making it a child node of the root node like the others. This will become the "hook" node for the chain, marking the spot where the chain will be affixed to the world so that the chain won't simply fall down.

Move the *hook* node slightly upward by changing its position to *0x10* so that the topmost chain element will correctly revolve around the hook. On the *Item Physics* tab for the *CCNode*, check *Enable Physics* and change the body's type to *Static*. Also, set the *Physics Shape* to *Circle*, and change the *Corner radius* to *8*. You should also rename this node to **hook** in the Timeline.

Now arrange these images in the pattern shown in Figure 9-3.

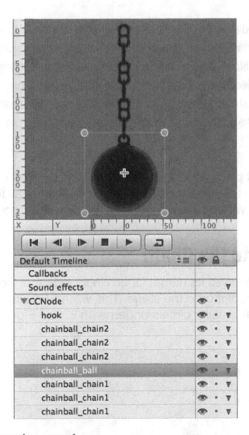

Figure 9-3. The chain with the ball properly arranged

Select a *chainball_chain2* in the Timeline, and set its position to *0x0*. This will be the topmost chain element. Now select a *chainball_chain1* sprite in the Timeline, and set its position to *0x–24*. This should make it look like it hooks perfectly into the first chain. Repeat this process for the remaining four chains, alternating *chain1* and *chain2* so that they look like Figure 9-3 and decreasing the Y position for every chain element by another –24 points. The chain element's Y positions from top to bottom should be 0, –24, –48, –72, –96, and –120. The ball's Y position should be –178.

Since the *chain1* sprites should be drawn on top of all *chain2* sprites, you need to move the *chain1* sprites below the *chain2* sprites in the Timeline to ensure their draw order is correct. The ball is supposed to be drawn underneath the last *chain1* sprite, so it's best to move the ball just between the *chain2* and *chain1* sprites. Also, just because it seems more natural, you may want to move the *hook* node to the very top.

Note that the physics simulation is blissfully unaware of the node draw order. Despite the ball being sorted in between the two types of chain elements, it will still dangle perfectly fine at the end of the chain.

Caution   Physics-enabled bodies ignore their node's parent-child relationship. This means a physics-enabled child node will not move if its parent moves. The physics engine knows no parent-child concept and will therefore treat all physics-enabled bodies as independent of one another. I strongly recommended that you design all complex physics objects without any parent-child relationships, except where the child items do not have physics enabled and should follow along with their physics-enabled parent node. You will see an example in the discussion of the *Spring* object, which you'll add later in this chapter.

Now open the *Level1.ccb*, and place an instance of *Chain.ccb* somewhere near the player's starting position. If you publish and run this now, the chain will not behave at all like a chain. Instead, it will fall down and its individual pieces will come apart because you haven't connected them with joints yet.

Adding Pivot Joints to the Chain

Let's make this a chain that deserves its name. Open *Chain.ccb* and, from the *Node Library View*, drag and drop a *Physics Pivot Joint* onto the stage. This will add a pink circle object that, when selected, shows two additional, smaller circles underneath it. See Figure 9-4.

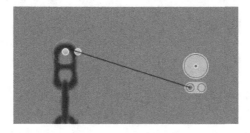

Figure 9-4. Dragging a connection from the pivot joint on the right to the hook node on the left

Notice that the new joint added itself as a *CCPhysicsJoint* in the Timeline under the *Joints* group. You can select a joint like other nodes by clicking on it either in the stage or in the Timeline. Likewise, you can drag and drop joints like nodes, too. Unfortunately, at least at the time of this writing, you can't copy and paste joints.

The two smaller circles underneath a joint, as shown in Figure 9-4, indicate that the joint hasn't been connected with other bodies.

You can click and drag on one of the two small circles to draw out a line. If you have some experience with Interface Builder, you'll find this behavior is similar to connecting IB outlets and actions. You can drag the line over a physics-enabled node onto the stage or on the timeline, and when you release the mouse button the connection is made if the highlighted drop target was a valid physics-enabled node. This makes a connection with the physics body and the joint.

In this instance, drag from the left circle and drop the line onto the *hook* node. You may find it easier to drop the line onto the *hook* node in the Timeline rather than trying to locate it on the stage as shown in Figure 9-4. That's mainly because the hook is invisible and has only a small collision shape.

Drag a line from the right circle below the joint onto the first chain element and then drop the line. Again it may be easier to drop the line on the node in the Timeline. Once this is done, the two smaller circles will be gone, indicating that this joint is properly connected to two bodies.

> **Note** Not connecting one or both joint connectors to physics bodies will generate a warning when publishing the SpriteBuilder project, indicating that the joint will not be functional.

Editing Common Joint Properties

With the pivot joint still selected, go to the *Item Properties* tab. You'll see a host of new properties.

Figure 9-5 shows the properties common to all joints, except for the *Reference* property (which exists only on pivot joints), while the other joints have an additional *Anchor B* setting. The pivot joint is the only joint with a single anchor point.

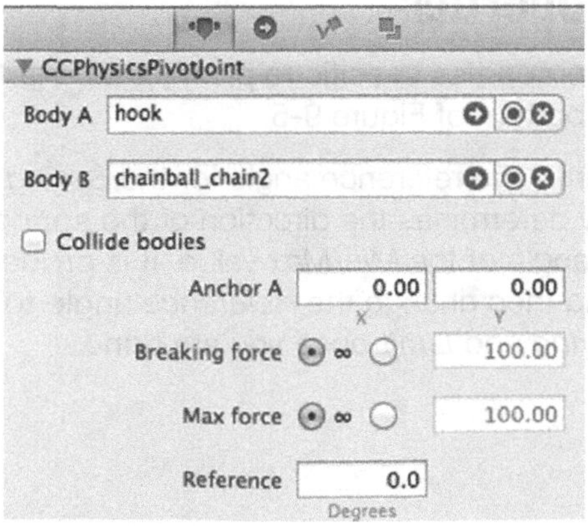

Figure 9-5. Joint properties common to (almost) all joints

The *Body A* and *Body B* fields show the Timeline names of the connected nodes. The right-facing arrow allows you to conveniently select that particular node. The X icon lets you remove the current connection, while the circle icon to the left of it allows you to drag a line and reconnect the joint with a body. The circle buttons are equivalent to the same icons displayed underneath the joint shape on the stage if the joint is connected to just one body or no body.

The *Collide bodies* check box is not selected by default, because in most cases you don't want bodies connected via a joint to be colliding with one another. In this case, the chain elements are overlapping, so if they did collide with each other it would be a problem. You'll find a good use for selecting *Collide bodies* when designing the *Spring* object.

Anchor A (and, for other joints, *Anchor B* as well) determines where the connection between the two bodies is made. The coordinates are in points and always relative to the *Body A* node, which in this case is the *hook* node. Since you want the first chain to be pinned to the hook, set *Anchor A* to *0x0*.

Breaking force and *Max force* are set to infinity by default, meaning the joint will never sever its connections and it is allowed to use maximum force to resolve its constraints.

Max force can be used specifically to get restless joint connections under control. To avoid applying and accumulating too much force, you can limit the maximum force the joint applies to resolve its constraints. Doing this prevents a large amount of force from corrupting the complex object or from propelling objects touching it away at high speeds.

With *Breaking force*, you can determine the maximum amount of force the joint will be able to withstand. If that amount of force is exceeded, the joint will be removed, separating the connection between the two bodies. You will have to find an appropriate breaking force for each joint through experimentation. If the bodies come apart even when the joint is at rest, you'll know that the breaking force is too low.

> **Caution**   If a discrete *Breaking force* is set, its value should be equal to or smaller than *Max force* to avoid accuracy issues when resolving collisions.

Editing Pivot-Joint Properties

Let me run down the remaining properties specific to pivot joints, starting with the *Reference* property, which is shown at the bottom of Figure 9-5.

The *Reference* property determines the reference angle for the *Spring* and *Limit* sections. If *Spring* is enabled, the *Reference* property determines the direction of the spring; for the *Limit*, the *Reference* property determines the center angle of the *Min/Max* value. It is probably more instructive to just enable either *Spring* or *Limit*, and then change the *Reference* angle to see its effect. Be sure to reset *Reference* to *0* and uncheck *Spring* and *Limit* once you are done.

The remaining properties are shown in Figure 9-6.

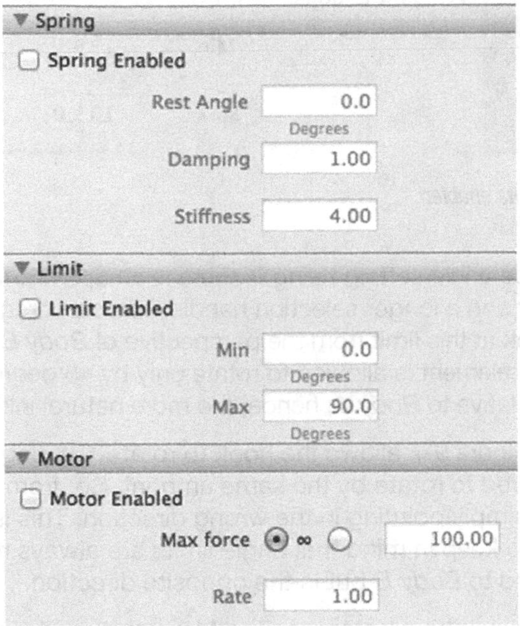

Figure 9-6. Properties specific to the pivot joint.

Spring Enabled allows the connected bodies to separate and bounce back rather than being rigidly confined to the pivot joint's anchor. It is like combining a pivot joint with a spring joint. The *Reference* angle determines the natural direction of the spring, but it does not rigidly constrain the movement of the bodies along this very angle. The *Rest Angle* setting allows you to further offset the spring angle in case you need to enable both *Spring* and *Limit*, but the spring needs to point in a different direction than the *Reference* angle. Note that negative angle values are perfectly okay.

The *Spring Damping* and *Stiffness* values are the same as for the spring joint. Damping comes into effect when the two bodies are either moving toward or away from each other. The default damping of 1 does not change the bodies' velocities at all. But a value of 0.9 would reduce the two bodies' velocity pointing away from or toward each other by 10% every second. A damping value of 0 would allow the two bodies to move away or toward each other only at very low speed. If you want a spring that deserves its name, you'll want to use a damping value somewhere between 0.5 and 1.

A spring's stiffness essentially determines how strong the spring is. A high stiffness value will have the two bodies apply a lot of force to quickly take their intended positions, while a low stiffness value would only gradually pull the two bodies together or away from each other.

The *Limit Enabled* setting allows you to determine the *Min* and *Max* angles the two bodies are allowed to rotate around each other. To be precise, it determines the angle limits relative to *Body A*. Since the pivot joints for the chain should have an angle limit, select the *Limit Enabled* check box and enter a range from –135 to 135 in the *Min* and *Max* fields, as shown in Figure 9-7. This prevents the chain elements from overlapping each other too much and specifically prevents them from making a complete revolution, an impossible behavior for a real-world chain.

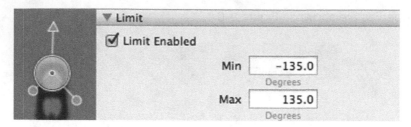

Figure 9-7. Pivot joint with angle limits enabled

Notice how, with the *Reference* angle setting being 0, there is an upward-facing arrow on the joint on the stage, as well as a shorter and a longer selection handle. You can drag these handles to change the *Min/Max* values. If you look at this limit from the perspective of *Body B*, the first chain element, you might think that the first chain element is allowed to rotate only by 45 degrees to either side. But like I said before, angle limits are relative to *Body A*; hence, the more natural initial observation is incorrect.

Instead, the setup shown in Figure 9-7 allows the hook to rotate 135 degrees to either side. In turn, the other *Body B* is also allowed to rotate by the same amount. So, from the perspective of *Body B*, the selection handles are simply pointing in the wrong direction. This is probably going to be confusing for a while, so try to keep in mind that angle limits are always relative to *Body A*, and the angle limits are equally applied to *Body B* but in the opposite direction.

Also, take note that *Min* can never be greater than the *Max* value, and vice versa. This may lead to some odd editing behavior where you enter a value and SpriteBuilder changes it back to make it the same as the other value. Or, if you drag the *Min/Max* selection handles, they may suddenly flip to the other side or overlap one another to adhere to the "Min must be smaller or equal to Max" rule.

Finally, the mysterious *Motor*. (See Figure 9-6.) Only pivot joints currently provide a *Motor* property. This is not actually a motor; rather, it is a constraint that applies a constant rotational force (torque) to the connected bodies. The mysterious *Rate* property is the desired angular velocity the bodies should take on. Higher values result in more torque. In order to reverse the direction of the rotation, simply enter a negative value. A motor's *Max force* may need to be set to prevent the objects from spinning too fast.

A motor works best if one of the two bodies either has a high density or is a static body, while the other has a low density and has a circle collision shape (wheel). But, of course, you are not limited to creating motorized vehicles with wheels. You could also use it to create a bear trap that snaps open and shut, though any type of motor that needs to be turned on and off or sped up and slowed down requires writing code.

Connecting the Chain Elements

You are now tasked with adding the six pivot joints to *Chain.ccb*. Unfortunately, you can't copy and paste the existing joint, but please do try it in case this feature has been added by the time you are reading this.

If you can't copy and paste the existing joint, drag and drop six more pivot joints from the *Node Library View* onto the stage. Connect the joints one by one to the chain elements and the ball. Connect the *Body A* of each joint to the *Body B* of the previous joint, and connect *Body B* to the next element in the chain.

Don't forget to check *Limit Enabled* for each joint and then set the *Min/Max* values to *–135* and *135*, respectively.

If you need help finding good anchors, you can set the anchor for joints whose *Body A* is a *chain2* element to 9.5x6 and, for those joints where *Body A* is a *chain1* element, set the anchor to 6.5x4. Yes, you need only two different anchor values because the anchors are relative to *Body A*, and you only have the aforementioned two different types of chain elements that have already been moved in place. The ball doesn't need to be considered because it's attached as *Body B* to the last joint.

The result of this editing operation should look like Figure 9-8.

Figure 9-8. Ball and chain are hooked up, and the selected joint shows the angle limits

You can now try out your "ball on a chain(TM)". Feel free to add additional *Chain.ccb* instances to *Level1.ccb*. Definitely try rotating the chains so that they start out swinging.

> **Note**   You may observe strange behavior with the chains at this time—for instance, collisions with invisible areas. You'll fix the collision categories and masks later. For now, just ignore the fact that the chains will behave erratically when they intersect walls or triggers. For now, just move the chains to a collision-free area to test them.

Creating a Rope

How to create a physics rope is a frequently asked question, yet the solution is not nearly as complex as you might imagine. In fact, if you observed the behavior of the chain, you may have noticed that it isn't too far from how a physics-simulated rope should behave.

Turning the Chain into a Rope

In fact, you're just going to modify the chain to make a rope. To do so, create a duplicate of *Chain.ccb* and rename it to **Rope.ccb**.

> **Note**   If SpriteBuilder has no duplication functionality yet, you can make a copy with Finder. Locate the project's .spritebuilder folder and browse into the SpriteBuilder Resources/Prefabs folder in order to make a duplicate of the *Chain.ccb*. You should then rename the duplicate to **Rope.ccb**. In SpriteBuilder's *File View*, the *Rope.ccb* should automatically appear in the *Prefabs* folder.

Open the *Rope.ccb*. Several modifications to the chain are necessary to turn it into a rope.

First, select all the *chain2* sprites, and on the *Item Properties* tab, change their *Sprite frame* to *SpriteSheets/GameElements/chainball_chain1.png* in order to replace the 8-shaped chain elements with the I-shaped ones. This step is added only to improve the visual appearance of the rope.

Because changing the sprite frames also changes the locations of the pivot joints, you should select the joints that are offset from the rope and change their anchor to 6.5x4 so that all pivot joints are on the rope and spaced evenly. Also, if you switch to the *Item Physics* tab and select the former *chain2* sprites, you'll notice their collision shape is too big for the image. So you should also edit the collision shape to more closely match the *chain1* images that you are using as rope segments.

Also, change the *Scale* property of the ball to *0.5x0.5* to make it smaller. Change its Y position to –156 to make it connect with the rope. And, on the *Item Physics* tab, change its density to *0.15* to make the ball lighter. These new settings will reduce stress on the rope and allow it to swing more easily.

The former chain segments will feel more like a rope if you tweak the joints so that the spring is enabled and the angle limit is smaller than before. Perform the following steps on all pivot joints with the exception of the first one, the one that connects to the *hook* node.

For each joint, select the *Spring Enabled* check box and then change *Damping* to *0.5* and *Stiffness* to *8.0*. Also, ensure *Limit Enabled* is still checked before changing the *Min/Max* values to *–45* and *45*.

The spring settings allow the rope to expand and contract slightly, which automatically has the effect of distributing forces throughout the rope. A force applied to an individual rope segment will therefore spread throughout the entire rope. The smaller angle limit also causes any rope segment reaching the limit to pass on any further rotation to its connected segment. Again, this helps to give the impression that forces acting on individual rope segments affect the entire rope.

The resulting rope should look like the one in Figure 9-9. Notice that the ball was moved in front of all chain segments to ensure that chain segments are drawn in front of the ball.

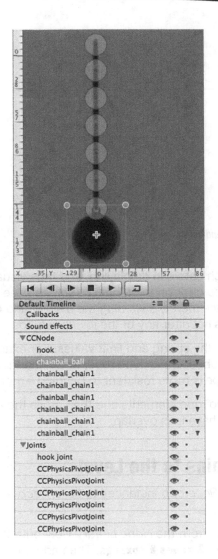

Figure 9-9. The chain is now a rope

You may have noticed that the rope's pivot joints now display two buttons underneath them, labeled *S* and *L* as shown in Figure 9-10.

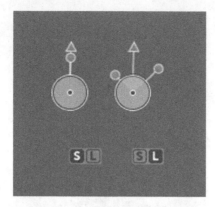

Figure 9-10. *Switching between spring and limit display*

These buttons allow you to switch between displaying, and thus visually editing, the spring's rest angle when *S* is highlighted. If you click on the *L* button, you can see and edit the joint's *Min/Max* angle limits. These two buttons are merely switching the display and edit modes of the joint. Changing the button states does not alter any of the joint's settings.

Feel free to later experiment with the spring and limit values. For example, try lowering stiffness and increasing damping to create a rubber-band-type rope, or try changing *Min/Max* angles to very low angles like –10/10 so that the rope is more resistant to bending—more like the stem of a young tree.

You may also want to remove two rope elements and then move the individual sprites and their joints apart so that the rope segments have less overlap.

Adding Ropes and Chains to the Level

You can now place one or more *Rope.ccb* instances to *Level1.ccb*—or any other level CCB, for that matter.

You should also drag a plain node from the *Node Library View* onto the level's *CCPhysicsNode* and rename it in the Timeline to **chains & ropes & springs**. Then add any chains, ropes, and (later) springs to this container node. You will mainly want to do so to ensure the proper draw order for these objects; they should be drawn behind the borders and in front of the gears and saws. (See Figure 9-11.)

▼CCPhysicsNode	👁 · ▼
level1_foreground_doughnut	👁 · ▼
exit	👁 · ▼
player	👁 · ▼
▶gears and saws	👁 · ▼
▶chains & ropes & springs	👁 · ▼
▶triggers	👁 · ▼
▶borders	👁 · ▼

Figure 9-11. *Chains, ropes, and springs draw order in the Level1.ccb Timeline*

You should definitely try to rotate the chain and rope instances so that they start out swinging due to gravity. Try to avoid placing chains and ropes within trigger areas or largely within borders for now. Positioning them in that way would cause incorrect collision behavior, which you'll see how to fix in the next section.

In SpriteBuilder, the placed chains and ropes will look rather stiff, like in Figure 9-12.

Figure 9-12. Chain and rope placed in the level

The result in-game will be nicely animated chains and ropes, as seen in Figure 9-13

Figure 9-13. Chain and rope in motion, bending and flexing nicely

Note   The rope's visual design using sprites works best if the rope can't bend too much. If you need a really elastic, flexible rope, you may need to resort to drawing the rope using Cocos2d's *CCRenderer*. Each node class can override the `-(void)draw:(CCRenderer *)renderer transform:(const GLKMatrix4 *) transform` method to perform custom drawing. You'll find an example in the next chapter.

Fixing Chain and Rope Collisions

The chain and rope may also appear wildly distorted, as shown in Figure 9-14, when they are partially stuck inside a collision or overlapping. This can lead to the entire chain or ball jittering, separating, or even leaving the screen. If the player character touches such an unresting chain or rope, it may be accelerated to a high velocity instantly.

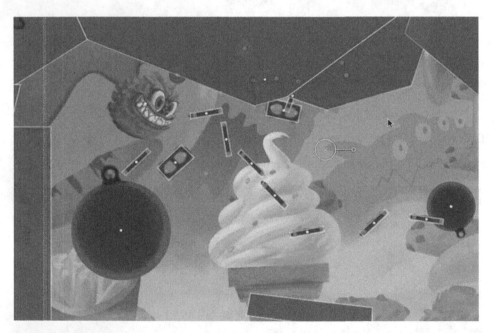

Figure 9-14. *The effect of a complex physics object "exploding." Physics debug drawing highlights the large distances between the chain and rope segments*

Figure 9-14 shows what can happen momentarily to the distorted chain and ball when they're placed so that they overlap each other. The _drawPhysicsShapes custom property on *GameScene. ccb* was enabled to highlight the physics objects and joints. This effect is typically referred to as an "exploding" physics object.

Minimizing the Risk of Physics Bodies "Exploding"

The number one cause you always have to watch out for but can never prevent entirely occurs when two complex physics bodies somehow get stuck inside each other. Both objects' constraints will frantically try to resolve their constraints, adding forces to the other body, which in turn fights back through its own constraints.

This can happen so quickly that the effect seems like everything is okay one moment and the objects are completely whacked, if not gone altogether, a moment later.

The effect isn't always this extreme, but it can be. Editing each joint's *Max force* setting will help reduce the probability of the complete and utter destruction of complex interacting physics objects. With a maximum force applied to all constraints, chains and ropes could still get stuck within each other, wiggling and fighting each other, but their joint connections will largely remain intact.

Of course, you should certainly avoid placing chains and ropes so that they start out overlapping in the first place.

The other cause of exploding complex physics objects is when the object is partially or entirely stuck in a static body's collision shape. In this instance, the most likely culprit will be the border elements, with which the chain and rope segments will currently collide. If you position a chain or rope in the level so that it partially overlaps a border sprite or even a trigger area, you will notice the chain or rope misbehaving.

You need to edit the affected body's collision categories and masks in order to fix this, and to allow the chain and ball to swing freely even when placed partially inside a border.

Defining the Collision Categories

Before I start to define collision categories, it really helps to take a moment to consider the goals for introducing collision categories. In this instance, the primary goal is to prevent the chains and ropes from colliding with triggers and borders. They should still be able to collide with other chains and ropes, and with the player.

The rest depends—chains and ropes may or may not need to collide with gears and saws. I'll assume you'll want them to collide with chains and ropes. Since gears and saws are static bodies, they will not collide with other static bodies anyway—this includes borders and triggers. Thus, gears and saws need not be in a specific category for now.

Of course, the player must still collide with everything, including chains, ropes, triggers, and borders. Obviously, the player needs to be included in editing the collision categories and masks.

Since chains and ropes should behave identically in terms of collisions, it makes sense to use a single collision category "obstacle" for both. This obstacle collision category also should be used for future objects whose exact collision behavior is the same, meaning collisions with everything but borders and triggers.

> **Tip**   It is important when creating categories to consider only the desired behavior rather than the types
> of objects. Otherwise, you'll quickly end up creating too many categories, which will make editing collision
> behaviors more time consuming, and you may even run out of categories. Remember that you can't create
> more than 32 unique categories. See the paragraph on collision categories and masks in Chapter 4.

This thought experiment helped to isolate the collision participants whose categories and masks
need to be edited: player, trigger, border, and obstacle. You'll later add the spring to the mixture
as well.

Coincidentally, you'll be naming the corresponding collision categories as follows: `player`, `trigger`,
`border`, and `obstacle`. The required collision categories and masks are outlined in Table 9-1.

*Table 9-1. Collision categories and masks needed to prevent chains and ropes from colliding with triggers and borders while
preserving existing collision behavior*

	Player.ccb	TriggerOnce.ccb	Border#.ccb	Chain.ccb, Rope.ccb
Categories	player	trigger	border	obstacle
Masks	trigger, border, obstacle	player	player	player, obstacle

Editing Collision Categories and Masks

Let's start the editing process with the player. Open *Player.ccb*, and select the root node (*CCSprite*).
On the *Item Physics* tab, enter player in the *Categories* field, and enter the following in the *Masks*
field: **trigger, border, obstacle**.

In order to create multiple independent category and mask labels, you have to separate them with a
comma. If you separate the tags with any other character—space, for instance—you'll get a single
combined label. You don't want a single "trigger border obstacle" label like you see on the left side
of Figure 9-15; you want three separate labels like on the right side of Figure 9-15.

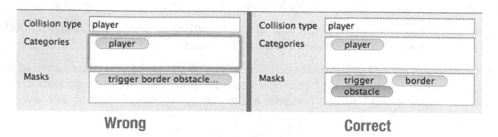

*Figure 9-15. Labels you type into the Categories and Masks fields must be comma-separated to create individual labels (like
those shown on the right side)*

The player is now set up to collide with triggers, borders, and obstacles.

Now open the *TriggerOnce.ccb*, and repeat the process for any additional triggers you may have created, such as the *TriggerForever.ccb*. Select the *CCNodeColor* node to edit its *Item Physics* properties.

Enter **trigger** in the *Categories* field and **player** in the *Masks* field. This ensures that the player can collide with triggers, since the player already has *trigger* in its collision mask and the trigger now has the player in its collision mask as well. Collisions occur only when both participants have each other's category in their *Masks* field, or when the *Masks* field is empty for at least one participant.

The borders are edited in the same way, except you'll find multiple border CCB files under *Prefabs/ Borders*, starting with *Border1.ccb*. You need to open each border CCB and in the its root node's *Categories* field enter *border* and in its *Masks* field enter *player*. This ensures that all border sprites continue to be impenetrable collisions for the player.

Finally, and this is where it gets tedious, you need to edit each physics-enabled node in both *Chain. ccb* and *Rope.ccb* to update their categories and masks. In each physics-enabled node's *Categories* field, enter **obstacle**, and in its *Masks* field enter **player, obstacle** to make the chain or rope collide with the player as well as other chains and ropes. Again, note that the items must be comma-separated to create separate labels, as you saw on the right side of Figure 9-15.

Tip   You may want to enter the *Masks* text once, ensure that it is correct, and then select the labels either by clicking in the field and pressing Cmd+A or by using text selection. To use text selection, drag the mouse from one end of the text to the other. The labels are drawn in a dark blue color when selected. You can then press Cmd+C to copy and Cmd+V to paste the labels in another node's *Masks* field. That way, you can reduce the risk of creating a typo.

If you forget to edit one chain or rope element's categories or masks, that element might still collide with the player. To ensure correctness, verify the categories and masks once you are done editing.

Select the first node in the Timeline; this will most likely be the static *hook* node. Look at its *Item Physics* tab, and confirm that the *Categories* and *Masks* are correct. Now press the down arrow key to select the next node in the Timeline. By repeatedly pressing the down arrow key, you can quickly verify the collision and other settings of a series of nodes. It definitely beats clicking each node with the mouse.

Good. Now that all the physics nodes in *Chain.ccb* and *Rope.ccb* have their categories and masks set, you can give this a try.

Publish the project in SpriteBuilder, and then build and run the project from Xcode. The chains and ropes should no longer collide with borders and triggers. To verify this, place or move a chain or rope in *Level1.ccb* so that it overlaps a border sprite or trigger area. Chains and ropes should also still collide with each other. The player's collisions should behave as they used to: being stopped by borders, being pushed by gears and killed by saws, and being able to trigger the level exit and other trigger areas.

If something is not quite as it is supposed to be, double-check and triple-check the collision categories and masks of the nodes involved in the collision. Note that some fringe cases have not been considered, which are most easily prevented by proper level design. For instance, chains and ropes will collide with the exit node.

Variations of Collision Behavior

As an exercise, consider the following cases:

1. What is necessary to allow chains and ropes to pass through each other?

2. What if you wanted chains and ropes to collide with borders, just not triggers?

3. What if you wanted ropes to collide with ropes and you wanted chains to collide with chains, but you also wanted to disallow ropes colliding with chains (and vice versa)?

Here are the solutions:

1. To allow chains and ropes to pass through each other, remove *obstacle* from each chain and rope node's mask so that only *player* is included in their collision mask. (See Table 9-2.)

Table 9-2. Settings to allow chains and ropes to pass through each other

	Player.ccb	TriggerOnce.ccb	Border#.ccb	Chain.ccb, Rope.ccb
Categories	player	trigger	border	obstacle
Masks	trigger, border, obstacle	player	player	player

2. To get chains and ropes to collide with borders (and not just triggers), add **obstacle** to each border's mask (player, obstacle) and add **border** to each chain and rope node's mask (player, obstacle, border). (See Table 9-3.)

Table 9-3. Settings to allow chains and ropes to collide with borders

	Player.ccb	TriggerOnce.ccb	Border#.ccb	Chain.ccb, Rope.ccb
Categories	player	trigger	border	obstacle
Masks	trigger, border, obstacle	player	player, obstacle	player, obstacle, border

3. The final scenario assumes you want ropes to collide only with ropes and chains to collide only with chains. This requires all chain and rope nodes to have unique categories, correspondingly named *chain* and *rope*, and include them in their collision mask (player, chain/player, rope). You would have to edit the masks of *player* (trigger, border, chain, rope) and, optionally, all border nodes (player, chain, rope) to include the *chain* and *rope* categories. The *obstacle* category can be removed from all masks. (See Table 9-4.)

Table 9-4. Settings to allow chains to collide with chains and ropes collide with ropes, but prevent chains from colliding with ropes. Player and borders collide with both chains and ropes

	Player.ccb	TriggerOnce.ccb	Border#.ccb	Chain.ccb	Rope.ccb
Categories	player	trigger	border	chain	rope
Masks	trigger, border, chain, rope	player	player, chain, rope	player, chain	player, rope

Creating a Springboard

Creating a springboard obviously involves using the spring joint. But you'll also need a distance joint to keep the spring locked until activated—just like an archer keeps the string pulled backward on her bow until she releases her grip on the string to fire the arrow.

All the Same: Springs, Slings, and Bows

First, let me clarify that the springboard object here will function no different than a slingshot or a bow. There's a spring trying to pull an object in a specific direction, though with varying degrees of force. I wager a bow will fire an arrow at a higher velocity than a slingshot fires a bird, angry or not.

There must also be an opposing force that pulls the spring backward and keeps it locked in place. Usually, the part of the opposing force is played by the archer's grip keeping the string pulled back while aiming. Only when the lock (grip) is released will the spring accelerate the object (arrow). The object will eventually leave the influence of the spring. Usually, this happens when the spring has passed its resting position and is slowing down.

In computer physics, the real problem is related to attaching the movable object while the spring is held back and while it is accelerating. Usually, you'll need some helper collisions—for instance, a bowl-shaped container that holds the object in place while the spring accelerates. Or in the case of bow and arrow, there could be two tiny, circular collision pins just above and below the arrow's head on the bow frame just to hold the arrow in place, and perhaps to ensure it is firing in the correct general direction.

You often have to implement such "cheats" to model real-world physics with computer physics—a common misunderstanding is that both types of physics work generally the same, but that's not true. Computer physics work with a lot of simplifications and gross exaggerations in order to process a decent quantity of physics objects in real time.

In the case of the springboard, you'll be most concerned with stopping the spring, to avoid the spring from shooting out and away from its base. Therefore, it has to have a stopper collision that stops the spring abruptly before it can leave the base's shaft.

That said, let's examine the springboard's constituent components, which are shown in Figure 9-16.

Figure 9-16. *The springboard consists of the following (from top to bottom): the board (springboard_spring.png), the spring (springboard_spring.png), and the base (springboard_metal.png)*

The board will be affixed to the spring, which poses an interesting question: how do you get two independent physics bodies to move together without their relative positions deviating at all?

Short answer: you can't do it. And you do not need to use two physics bodies.

No joint is "strong" enough to immovably affix one body to another. Two bodies connected with a joint can always deviate in their relative position to each other, no matter how stiff the connection is set up to be. You could also update the affixed body's position every frame after the physics simulation has run, but this may lead to undesirable physics collision behavior because the affixed body would snap rather than move into place.

The actual solution is to use just a single physics body that defines the collision properties and shape for the combined object. The affixed "bodies" are simply child sprites of the actual body, without physics. In this case, the spring will define the collision shape for both the spring and board, while the board has no physics body and is simply added as a child of the spring, thus following it at a fixed offset.

Another issue is how to keep the spring moving straight up, rather than rotating or moving sideways when it hits an object. This requires adding an invisible shaft to the base body and the aforementioned invisible "stopper" body that stops the spring at just the right moment.

Designing the Springboard

Right-click the *Prefabs* folder, and add a *New File*. Name it **Spring.ccb**, and set its type to *Node* before creating it.

From the *Tileless Editor View*, drag and drop the *springboard_spring* and *springboard_metal* images onto the stage. Make sure that *springboard_spring* is above *springboard_metal* in the Timeline. Then drag the *springboard_board* onto the *springboard_spring* in the Timeline so that the board becomes a child node of the spring. (See Figure 9-17.)

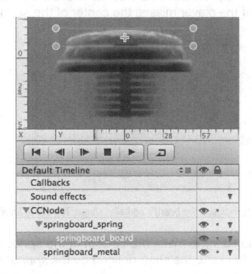

Figure 9-17. The visual setup of the springboard

Select the *springboard_metal*, and set its position to *0x0*. Select the *springboard_spring* and change its position to *0x-16*, which will sink it into the base. Finally, select the *springboard_board*, and change its position types to % and change its values to *50* and *105*.

> **Note** A 50% X offset combats the effect of having child sprites centered on their parent texture's lower left corner rather than on the parent's actual position. It's an unfortunate design decision of Cocos2D from its early days. This effect is best illustrated by adding several sprites, each a child of the previous sprite. You'll notice the positions are such that each new child is positioned below and to the left of its parent. Centering child sprites on their parent is best done by adding a 50% offset because even though changing anchor point would also work, it's best to avoid changing the anchor point whenever you can do so by altering the node's position.

Now select the *springboard_spring*, and switch to the *Item Physics* tab. Check *Enable physics*, and uncheck `Affected by gravity` and `Allows rotation`.

Unchecking *Affected by gravity* prevents gravity from influencing the spring. You deselect this check box because you may want to use the spring as an upside down or sideways spring, and gravity would only serve to decrease the force of an upward spring while increasing it for a downward-oriented spring. Disabling rotation will prevent the spring from rotating to the sides, especially when it hits an object. It's difficult enough to keep the spring aligned to the same outward-facing direction without resorting to programming.

And let's not forget to define the springboard's collision shape. Keep in mind that the spring's collision shape should encompass the shape of its child sprite, the board. Still, 10 points for the shape are plenty. (See Figure 9-18.) Two points are spent to allow the sides to give the player a slightly outward-oriented spin if the player misses the center of the springboard.

Figure 9-18. The shroom-shaped spring includes the board's collision shape. The zoom level is 8x, hence the blurred image

As seen in Figure 9-18, you should try to make the bottom of the spring as rectangular as possible. That's the "bolt" part that should fit into the shaft defined by the *springboard_metal* as closely as possible.

Speaking of which: select the *springboard_metal*, go to the *Item Physics* tab to *Enable physics*. Then change the body's type to *Static*. You can begin editing the shaft's collision shape right away.

Designing a shaft with a single body may be a little unusual at first because you have to trace both the inner and outer walls of the shaft. Here's a trick that makes this less confusing: from the initial rectangular polygon, drag the two bottom-most points down, several points past the bottom of the spring. Now you can carve out the shaft more easily. Again, 10 points should suffice. (See Figure 9-19 for reference.)

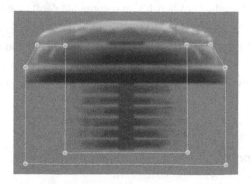

Figure 9-19. The springboard's shaft collision shape

The tricky part here is to design the shaft as straight as possible while making it just slightly larger than the springboard's bolt shape. After all, the spring is supposed to move unhindered up and down in the shaft, while its sideward movement should be restricted as much as possible by the shaft. Figure 9-20 shows both collision shapes overlaid, using advanced image-processing technology (an artist did it).

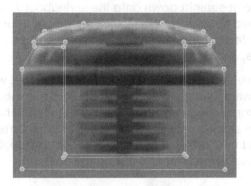

Figure 9-20. Shaft and bolt collision shapes rendered in the same image

> **Tip** If you want to test the overlap quickly, collapse the *springboard_spring* in the Timeline so that its child nodes are hidden. With either node selected in the Timeline, you can use the up and down arrows to quickly select the other node, which will change the collision shape on the stage, as long as the *Item Physics* tab is selected. Tap the up and down arrow repeatedly to quickly switch between the two shapes to verify that both shapes fit well, without any overlap.

Adding Joints to the Springboard

Now to the gist of it: making the springboard functional by using joints. This process will take several steps, and I will show you how each step improves the spring behavior.

Start by dragging a node from the *Node Library View* onto the stage. Rename the node in the Timeline to **springstopper**. On the *Item Physics* tab, check *Enable physics*, and then change the body type to *Static*. The position of the node and its collision shape don't matter for now.

Now drag a *Physics Spring Joint* from the *Node Library View* onto the stage and select it. Connect *Body A* of the joint with the *springstopper* node, and connect *Body B* with the *springboard_spring* node. Set *Anchor A* to *0x100* and *Anchor B* to *32x70*.

Select the *Enable* check box next to the *Rest length* field to enable the spring's desired resting length, and then enter **10** in the *Rest length* field. This will be the size the spring will want to expand or shrink to whenever it can. If enabled, the *Rest length* property adds a drag handle on the spring joint as in Figure 9-21. To make the spring pull harder toward the *Body A* anchor, increase *Stiffness* to *90*.

Figure 9-21. A spring joint with rest length enabled has a draggable length handle

Most likely, the joint will not point straight down onto the springboard, due to the springstopper's position. You generally have two options: edit the joint's anchor, or change the position of the node the joint is attached to. The latter option is always preferred whenever you are free to move the node. Select the *springstopper* node, and change its position to *0x64*.

Notice that whenever you move a node, the joint anchor attached to it will move along with it. This may or may not be what you want. It is generally advisable to move the nodes into their desired positions before adding and connecting joints. Also note that joint anchors need not be on or inside the connected node's collision shape or texture area. If the body is dynamic, it will "feel" the force at that point even if the point isn't near the shape or sprite—consider the joint's force acting more like magnetism than someone actually grabbing and pulling the object.

Testing the Springboard for the First Time

Naturally, you'll need to place an instance of the *Spring.ccb* onto *Level1.ccb*. Place it near the player's starting point so that you can immediately see it in the game. You should move the spring instance into the *chains & ropes & springs* node to ensure the spring's draw order is the same as the draw order of the chains and ropes.

You should place the spring so that the base seems to be glued onto a surface of a border sprite. No need to be perfect, though.

Publish, build, and run the project. You should find that the spring is pulled out and away from the shaft by an invisible spring. And this happens instantly when the level starts.

If the spring doesn't come out of the shaft easily or does not come out at all, verify that the shaft and bolt collision shapes don't touch or overlap, and that they are both almost parallel to each other. Refer to Figure 9-20 for a suitable example.

Blocking the Spring's Movement

Let's tackle the first problem: stopping the spring so that it won't leave the shaft. The springstopper will get that job.

Open *Spring.ccb*, and select the *springstopper* node. On the *Item Physics* tab, enter **springstopper** in the *Categories* field and enter **spring** in the *Masks* field.

Caution   Be sure to enter **springstopper**, not springboard, in *Categories* and *Masks*. For some reason, I kept mixing the two up. If the collisions in this section won't work, be sure to double-check the springstopper label.

You also need to edit the stopper's collision shape. The main problem right now is that it's only about half as wide as it ought to be. Drag the two leftmost points to the left and the two rightmost points to the right so that the collision shape spans the full width of the springboard base. The height of the springstopper's collision shape doesn't matter, but its lower horizontal collision segment should be almost parallel to the horizontal axis. (See Figure 9-22.)

Figure 9-22. The springstopper's collision shape

The springstopper is supposed to suddenly prevent the spring from expanding any further. It ought to keep the spring in its shaft so that it can't move to the side, and it gives the impression of a spring that is actually extending upward due to actual spring force rather than being pulled from the outside.

Before you can test this, you have to select the *springboard_spring*. On the *Item Physics* tab, enter **spring** in the *Categories* field and enter **springstopper, player, obstacle** in the *Masks* field. This will make the spring the only body that will collide with the springstopper.

To ensure collisions with the player continue to work, you also have to open *Player.ccb* and then add **spring** to the player sprite's *Masks* field so that it contains the following labels: **trigger, border, obstacle, spring**.

And if you want the spring to collide with the chains and ropes, you'll have to edit *Chain.ccb* and *Rope.ccb* in order to add **spring** to each physics body's *Masks* field.

> **Note**   The springboard's base (*springstopper_metal*) needs no specific *Category* or *Masks* settings. Because it's a static body, it won't collide with other static bodies anyway, and all other bodies should certainly collide with the springboard base.

If you run this now, you will notice that the spring is still passing through the *springstopper* node. There's one minor yet important detail I haven't mentioned yet. Select the *CCPhysicsSpringJoint* in *Spring.ccb*, and switch to the *Item Properties* tab. You'll see the *Collide bodies* check box isn't selected. This means that the two bodies connected to this joint will not collide, regardless of their collision categories and masks. In this case, you want the springboard to stop at the springstopper, so select the *Collide bodies* check box.

You can now publish and try this out. You may want to enable physics debug drawing to verify that the springboard is still slightly inside the shaft when it stops at the springstopper. If it isn't, simply increase or decrease the height of the bottom segment of the springstopper's collision shape. Also, verify that the player isn't blocked by the springstopper.

Adding a Spring Lock

A springboard that springs up the instant the level starts is pretty useless. You can easily turn this springboard into a touch-activated spring that can even reset itself to its locked position after a short time by using a distance joint.

In *Spring.ccb*, drag and drop a *Physics Distance Joint* onto the stage. Connect *Body A* with the springstopper. This will generate a static "world anchor" for this joint end, so it doesn't actually matter what the position of the connected static physics body is. In fact, you'll move that anchor far away shortly. Connect *Body B* with the *springboard_spring*. On the joint's *Item Properties* tab, change *Anchor A* to *0x-200*. This moves the world anchor far below the spring. Set *Anchor B* to *32x32*, which about centers that end of the joint on the spring.

The trick now is to enable both the *Minimum distance* and *Maximum distance* check boxes. By default, the distances encompass the full length of the joint as it is now. The joint will also draw two drag handles similar to the joint shown in Figure 9-21. Don't drag them. However, if you did drag them, you could click the *Enable* check box twice so that it is turned off and on. Doing this will reset the *Minimum distance* and *Maximum distance* fields.

This distance joint now allows absolutely no movement away from or toward its world anchor. Even without the spring joint pulling on the spring, it will rest in place now. Give it a try.

> **Caution**   You may be tempted to see how far you can take this. Try increasing the spring joint's stiffness from 90 to 900, and reduce damping to 0. Don't forget to reset these values after the test! You'll notice the spring board will not be entirely at rest, and if you touch it slightly, it will already and significantly push the player upward. This may give you ideas, and perhaps you can use it for a good effect, but really the point here is that very strongly opposing joints (and the forces they impose on the connected bodies) add unrest and inaccuracies to the physics simulation. Even potentially harmless-looking objects can suddenly infuse other objects with high velocities even though they aren't moving much by themselves.

Releasing the Spring Lock

With the lock in place, the spring is no longer usable. You'll need to create a SpringBoard class to release the lock and then also put the lock back in place to reset the springboard.

Select the *springboard_spring* node in *Spring.ccb*, and switch to the *Item Code Connections* tab. Enter **SpringBoard** as the custom class. Then switch to the *Item Physics* tab, and enter **spring** in the *Collision type* field. This allows the *GameScene* class to implement a collision method that calls a SpringBoard method when the player touches the springboard.

Now publish and open Xcode, but don't run the project just yet. First you have to create another Objective-C class (by right-clicking the *Source* folder and selecting *New File*). Name the class **SpringBoard**, and be sure to make it a subclass of *CCSprite* because the *springboard_spring* is a sprite.

Open the *SpringBoard.h* interface file. You only need to add a public method declaration with which other objects can instruct the spring to let go of its lock. Add the code in Listing 9-1 to *SpringBoard.h*.

Listing 9-1. The SpringBoard header declared the public letGo method

```
#import "CCSprite.h"

@interface SpringBoard : CCSprite

-(void) letGo;

@end
```

The goal is to temporarily disable the distance joint. Unfortunately, you can only invalidate (remove) a joint. So, to reset the springboard, you'll have to create a new distance joint instance in code and give it the same properties as the previously deleted joint. The easiest way to do so is to keep a reference to the joint even after it has been invalidated by simply not using the __weak keyword on the ivar. This makes _lockJoint a strong reference, meaning the joint assigned to the ivar will not deallocate until the SpringBoard instance itself deallocates.

Add the highlighted code of Listing 9-2 to *SpringBoard.m*. Note that the listing shows only the first half of the class, not the entire implementation. Most importantly, don't remove the @end.

Listing 9-2. Finding and assigning the _lockJoint distance joint

```
#import "SpringBoard.h"

@implementation SpringBoard
{
    CCPhysicsJoint* _lockJoint;  // Notice: not using __weak here!
}

-(void) didLoadFromCCB
{
    Class distanceJointClass = NSClassFromString(@"CCPhysicsSlideJoint");

    for (CCPhysicsJoint* joint in self.physicsBody.joints)
    {
        if ([joint isKindOfClass:distanceJointClass])
        {
            _lockJoint = joint;
            break;
        }
    }
}
```

Unfortunately, the Cocos2d engine exposes only the generic CCPhysicsJoint class publicly. All the other concrete joint classes, like CCPhysicsSpringJoint and CCPhysicsSlideJoint (the distance joint), are private. To avoid importing a private header or performing other trickery, the Class type of the CCPhysicsSlideJoint is obtained by its name. Of course, a class by that name still has to exist; otherwise, NSClassFromString would return nil.

In didLoadFromCCB, the list of self.physicsBody.joints is enumerated. Since the springboard contains only two joints, and they are of a different type, the search can be simplified to a simple isKindOfClass check. Once the first distance joint is found, it is assigned to the _lockJoint ivar and the loop ends with the break keyword.

Tip   The "find my joint" code in Listing 9-2 may cease to function when you add more distance joints to the *Spring.ccb*. Unfortunately, there's no name or tag for joints that helps you to identify them easily, neither in SpriteBuilder nor in code. However, you can give the joint's nodes a unique name to identify them. You can then access the joint's bodies and their nodes in code and compare the node names to find out if they are the nodes you are looking for. For example, this code snippet would work inside the for loop of Listing 9-2:

```
if ([joint.bodyA.node.name isEqualToString:@"node A"] &&
    [joint.bodyB.node.name isEqualToString:@"node B"]) {
        // do something
}
```

With the distance joint assigned to _lockJoint, implementing the letGo method is dead simple. Add the method in Listing 9-3 below the didLoadFromCCB method.

Listing 9-3. Invalidating the _lockJoint will remove it from the world

```
-(void) letGo
{
    if (_lockJoint.valid)
    {
        [_lockJoint invalidate];

        [self scheduleOnce:@selector(resetSpring) delay:0.5];
    }
}
```

Never mind the name of the method. It's named *invalidate*, but it could as well have been named *remove* because it does exactly that. Normally, if _lockJoint were a __weak ivar, the _lockJoint reference would be set to nil automatically after the call to invalidate. However, _lockJoint is a strong reference, so the CCPhysicsJoint instance remains in memory even though it no longer participates in the physics simulation.

After half a second, the resetSpring method is scheduled to run. Note that repeatedly calling the letGo method would reset the scheduled selector's timer. Because the player may continue to collide with the spring, it is first checked whether the _lockJoint is still valid. This guarantees that the spring will be reset 0.5 seconds after the initial collision with the player rather than after the most recent collision.

Now add the resetSpring method in Listing 9-4 below the letGo method.

Listing 9-4. Creating a new joint with the bodies from the previous _lockJoint

```
-(void) resetSpring
{
    _lockJoint = [CCPhysicsJoint
                    connectedDistanceJointWithBodyA:_lockJoint.bodyA
                                            bodyB:_lockJoint.bodyB
                                          anchorA:CGPointMake(0, -300.0)
                                          anchorB:CGPointMake(32.0, 32.0)
                                      minDistance:223.0
                                      maxDistance:223.0];
}
```

Unfortunately, you can't just re-add an invalidated joint to the physics world—you have to create a new one. This is the sole reason for keeping the invalidated CCPhysicsJoint instance in memory: to access its bodyA and bodyB properties so that you don't need to find the associated nodes every time you create the _lockJoint anew.

The anchor and distance properties have been entered as they were in SpriteBuilder. That, too, is a bit unfortunate because technically the _lockJoint instance still has all these properties internally. However, you'd have to go through a private Objective-C API (a private property named constraint) to gain access to another private ChipmunkConstraint class. In this case, the anchor and distance properties are unlikely to change, so you can just enter them in code.

The newly created joint is assigned directly to _lockJoint, replacing the previous one. Since the previous lock joint has no strong reference holding on to it, ARC will automatically release its memory. So you really just keep the most recently created _lockJoint in memory. And once the SpringBoard instance deallocates, the remaining _lockJoint instance will also deallocate.

The CCPhysicsJoint class allows you to create the same joints in code as the ones you can edit in SpriteBuilder (pivot, spring, and distance). However, variations exist that you can achieve only with SpriteBuilder. For instance, you can't create a pivot joint with both spring and limit enabled through the CCPhysicsJoint interface. See Listing 9-5 for a reference of available CCPhysicsJoint initializers.

Listing 9-5. Creating CCPhysicsJoint instances

```
// Creating a Spring Joint
+(CCPhysicsJoint*)connectedSpringJointWithBodyA:(CCPhysicsBody*)bodyA
                                          bodyB:(CCPhysicsBody*)bodyB
                                        anchorA:(CGPoint)anchorA
                                        anchorB:(CGPoint)anchorB
                                     restLength:(CGFloat)restLength
                                      stiffness:(CGFloat)stiffness
                                        damping:(CGFloat)damping;

// Creating a Distance Joint
+(CCPhysicsJoint*)connectedDistanceJointWithBodyA:(CCPhysicsBody*)bodyA
                                            bodyB:(CCPhysicsBody*)bodyB
                                          anchorA:(CGPoint)anchorA
                                          anchorB:(CGPoint)anchorB;

+(CCPhysicsJoint*)connectedDistanceJointWithBodyA:(CCPhysicsBody*)bodyA
                                            bodyB:(CCPhysicsBody*)bodyB
                                          anchorA:(CGPoint)anchorA
                                          anchorB:(CGPoint)anchorB
                                      minDistance:(CGFloat)min
                                      maxDistance:(CGFloat)max;

// Creating Pivot Joints
+(CCPhysicsJoint*)connectedPivotJointWithBodyA:(CCPhysicsBody*)bodyA
                                         bodyB:(CCPhysicsBody*)bodyB
                                       anchorA:(CGPoint)anchorA;

+(CCPhysicsJoint*)connectedRotarySpringJointWithBodyA:(CCPhysicsBody*)bodyA
                                                bodyB:(CCPhysicsBody*)bodyB
                                            restAngle:(CGFloat)restAngle
                                            stiffness:(CGFloat)stiffness
                                              damping:(CGFloat)damping;

+(CCPhysicsJoint*)connectedMotorJointWithBodyA:(CCPhysicsBody*)bodyA
                                         bodyB:(CCPhysicsBody*)bodyB
                                          rate:(CGFloat)rate;
```

```
+(CCPhysicsJoint*)connectedRotaryLimitJointWithBodyA:(CCPhysicsBody*)bodyA
                                            bodyB:(CCPhysicsBody*)bodyB
                                              min:(CGFloat)min
                                              max:(CGFloat)max;

// The only Pivot Joint properties not currently editable in SpriteBuilder
+(CCPhysicsJoint*)connectedRatchetJointWithBodyA:(CCPhysicsBody*)bodyA
                                           bodyB:(CCPhysicsBody*)bodyB
                                           phase:(CGFloat)phase
                                         ratchet:(CGFloat)ratchet;
```

What's still missing is to actually call the SpringBoard class' letGo method. This is done in the *GameScene* implementation file. Open *GameScene.m*, and add the header import highlighted in Listing 9-6.

Listing 9-6. Importing SpringBoard.h in GameScene.m

```
#import "GameScene.h"
#import "Trigger.h"
#import "GameMenuLayer.h"
#import "GameState.h"
#import "SpringBoard.h"
```

Then add the method in Listing 9-7 just below the other ccPhysicsCollisionBegin methods.

Listing 9-7. Responding to collisions between player and spring

```
-(BOOL) ccPhysicsCollisionBegin:(CCPhysicsCollisionPair*)pair
                         player:(CCNode*)player
                         spring:(SpringBoard*)spring
{
    [spring letGo];
    return YES;
}
```

Now when the player collides with a physics body whose *Collision* type is set to spring, it will run the method in Listing 9-7, which in turn calls the SpringBoard's letGo method. Here we can safely assume that all springs are instances of the SpringBoard class; therefore, it's safe to assume the spring parameter to be of type SpringBoard* rather than CCNode*.

Returning YES from the method ensures the player and spring do collide rather than passing through each other.

That's it for the spring. You can now place instances of *Spring.ccb* in the level. You should add them to the *chains & ropes & springs* node. When you run the game and touch a spring with the player, the spring should accelerate outward, pushing the player away. You can alter the spring joint's damping and stiffness parameters as well as the position of the spring's world hook (by editing *Anchor A*) to alter the spring force.

Breaking Joints and Motors

Thus far, I have neglected the properties related to breaking joints and adding torque. I know they can be very intriguing, so let's quickly try them on the chain and rope.

Breaking Force Example

Open *Chain.ccb*, and select the joint that connects the last chain segment with the ball. This is most likely the last `CCPhysicsPivotJoint` instance in the Timeline.

The *Breaking force* field on the *Item Properties* tab is set to a stress threshold that the joint is able to withstand. If the joint stress exceeds the arbitrary value entered in *Breaking force*, the joint will be removed. Change the radio button next to *Breaking force* so that you can enter a value in the text field next to it. As for the value, enter **1060**. If you ask me how I determined that value: trial and error. It should work if you change the joint properties as instructed; otherwise, you may find you need to use a higher or lower value—see the following discussion.

Caution   *Max force* must be either unlimited or set to a value equal to or higher than *Breaking force*.

Try this in the game with a chain instance whose rotation is 0 so that it does not swing. Swinging alone might cause the breaking force to be exceeded, because even just a slightly lower *Breaking force* value of *1050* would always sever the connection. If you get this right, merely touching the ball or chain with the player will cause the joint to disappear, and the ball will drop from the chain.

Now there's a problem here. The *Breaking force* setting is not very reliable and thus not suitable for triggered events that have to happen. For instance, if touching the ball should always drop it, you should implement a collision method rather than using collision types.

Breaking force is also tedious to determine, but it's not impossible to determine it if you follow this principle:

- Enter an arbitrary high value for *Breaking force*, say, *100*.
- Check if the joint in question breaks. Ideally, the joint bodies should be at rest.
- If the joint breaks, double the value and try again.
- Repeat doubling the value until the joint no longer breaks. You now know two upper and lower bounds between which the actual breaking point lies.
- Narrow down the breaking point by halving the difference. For instance, if at 5,000 the joint breaks but stops it breaking at 10,000, you should try 7,500 next.
- Keep narrowing down the value until you get close enough to the breaking point.

You don't have to know the exact breaking point value. For instance, if you determine that a joint (at rest) breaks at 1,100 but doesn't break at a 1,200 breaking force, you are within 10% of the breaking point (at rest) and can start experimenting actual gameplay behavior with the 1,200 value. If 1,200 causes the joint to break too easily when you apply just a minimal amount of force, you'll need to increase the breaking force, anyway.

Finding the breaking point is done only to show you the minimal base value where the joint breaks under minimal force, but you'll certainly have to consider that the joint is supposed to withhold some, but not too much, extra force.

You can disable the breaking force by simply setting the *Breaking force* field back to *unlimited*. You can alter a joint's `breakingForce` property in code as well. For instance, this code disables the breaking force by setting it to infinite programmatically:

```
joint.breakingForce = INFINITY;
```

Motor Example

Open *Rope.ccb*, and select the hook joint that connects the first rope segment with the *hook* node.

On the *Item Properties* tab, uncheck both *Spring Enabled* and *Limit Enabled* in case they are enabled for this joint. This allows the joint to rotate 360 degrees around itself; otherwise, a motor force that applies torque would be limited to within the angle limits.

Then select the *Motor enabled* check box and enter *–4* in the *Rate* field. The negative value will make the joint rotate counter-clockwise.

If you place a rope in the level and run the project, you'll see the rope is trying to swirl around its hook point. Try different rate values to see what happens if the rope spins faster or slower.

Programmatically altering a motor joint is very limited at the time of this writing. There is currently no public property to alter a motor joint's rate property in code. You also can't invalidate and create a new motor joint in order to change the rate property because this would reset the joint's existing momentum. You'd have to use the private Chipmunk classes and C functions to programmatically alter a motor joint.

Summary

In this chapter, you learned a lot about joints and how to make complex physics objects like chains and ropes. You also learned how to create mechanical, trigger-activated objects like the spring. You'll find the resulting project in the `10 - Chains Ropes and Springs` folder.

I hope you also take away the many potential problems associated with joints. They can cause very odd behavior if used incorrectly or allowed to accumulate too much force. It takes time to get a good feel for both values and how to model complex physics bodies with joints.

In the next chapter, you'll raise the complexity level as you implement a soft-body physics player with custom rendering to deform the player's texture.

Chapter 10

Soft-Body Physics

In this chapter, you will change the player character from a rigid object to a soft-body physics object. A *soft body* is an object whose predetermined shape can bend and flex under the forces applied to it. If the body is also trying to relax back into its predetermined shape, it is often referred to as "jelly" physics—especially if the shape is easily deforming and altogether wobbly. That's the kind of soft body you'll create in this chapter.

Since a deformable body changes its shape, the texture (sprite) used to display the body needs to be deformed also. A regular CCSprite won't do that, as skewing and scaling the texture alone won't suffice. So in the second half of this chapter you'll dive into Cocos2D's rendering API, which is based on OpenGL. You'll use it to wrap all OpenGL commands for the renderer in such a way that even custom drawing code can be accelerated by benefitting from Cocos2D's internal-rendering optimizations.

Rigid Bodies vs. Soft Bodies

A rigid body has a shape that simply will not budge. The shape remains the same no matter how much force is applied to the rigid body. The main reasons why this kind of physics is predominant is that it's a lot easier to program, it can utilize faster algorithms, and the resulting physics simulation produces coherent, reliable results.

The disadvantage of rigid bodies is that it only coarsely simulates real-world physics. As long as bodies aren't contacting one another, everything works, feels and behaves like in the real world. But once two rigid bodies collide, their collision response is only a rough approximation of what would happen in the real world. The absorption of collision force into heat and dissipation of force due to deformation is approximated with only a single parameter: *elasticity* (sometimes called *bounciness* or *restitution*).

In other words, even rigid bodies that are supposed to model light objects such as balloons or leaves will stack on top of one another as if they were strong, solid bodies.

Soft-body physics tries to solve this problem by allowing each body's shape to be deformable to varying degrees. The application of soft-body physics in games is currently limited to modeling vehicle damage (most notably `BeamNG.drive`) and so-called "jelly physics," where the shape of bodies is easily deformable but the shape itself tries to revert back to its designed shape.

> **Note**   You may have heard of other applications for soft-body physics—for instance, cloth and hair simulation and modeling facial expressions by simulating muscles. However, these are almost exclusively used as visual effects and do not affect the physics world as a whole. That's the kind of physics that can be GPU-accelerated on current desktop computers. It looks impressive, but it is purely a visual effect and likely to remain that way—unlike fluid simulation, which has been used by games like "Where's My Water" and "Feed Me Oil" to great effect. In games, fluid simulation is achieved by using a large number of tiny rigid bodies with a circle shape and a custom renderer that traces the outer bodies to draw blobs formed by a group of bodies. To prevent individual bodies from simply becoming tiny droplets, the bodies attract each other to form bonds—most likely programmatically, but spring joints could also be used.

Soft-body physics does not require a specialized physics engine. It can be simulated using rigid bodies and joints. The basic underlying principle to make a body "soft" is to model the body in question using several rigid bodies that form the outer shape and joining the bodies together by using a combination of spring joints, often combined with a distance joint to define the minimum and maximum distances the connected bodies can be apart. Normally, the inside of the body consists of one or more shapes that hold the outer form more or less in shape. They act as the bones for the soft part.

By far the easiest shape to model as a soft body is the circle, since every two opposing bodies on the circle's circumference can be connected with joints, while more joints connect the circumference bodies together to hold the shape in circle form. The joint connections naturally balance each other out.

Unless the body is meant to be heavily deformable, it helps to have a center body that connects to the circumference bodies with distance joints to prevent the shape from folding in on itself. And many, if not all, the connected bodies need to collide with one another to distribute the forces properly and again to reduce the risk of the body folding in on itself. Figure 10-1 shows the finished setup of the soft-body player object you're going to create in this chapter.

Figure 10-1. The final setup of the soft-body player

By far the easiest shape to model as a soft-body is the circle, since every two opposing bodies on the circle's circumference can be connected with joints, while more joints connect the circumference bodies together to hold the shape in circle form. The joint connections naturally balance each other out.

Unless the body is meant to be heavily deformable it helps to have a center body which connects to the circumference bodies with distance joints to prevent the shape from folding in on itself. And many, if not all of the connected bodies need to collide with one another to distribute the forces properly and again to reduce the risk of the body folding in on itself. Figure 10-1 shows the finished setup of the soft-body player object you're going to create in this chapter.

Configuring the Soft-Body Player

You'll create this body in discrete steps so that you can see the effect each step adds. I hope this gives you a good feel of how the joint connections interact and ultimately create a soft and wobbly body.

Creating the New Player CCB

Let's start with the basics. Right-click the *Prefabs* folder in SpriteBuilder to add a new file. Name the document ***PlayerSoftBody.ccb***, and change its type to *Sprite* before creating it.

In the new *PlayerSoftBody.ccb*, select the root node, and on the *Item Properties* tab change the Sprite frame to *SpriteSheets/Global/player.png*. Then switch to the *Item Code Connections* tab and enter **SoftBodyDrawNode** as the custom class of the root node.

For this and the following steps, it's best to have physics debug drawing enabled. This will be very educational because you can observe the behavior of the otherwise invisible parts of the soft body—both circumference bodies and the joint connections. Open *GameScene.ccb*, and select its root node. On the *Item Properties* tab, you'll find the familiar _drawPhysicsShapes setting. Set its value to 1 to enable physics debug drawing.

Now open *Level1.ccb*, and repeat the following steps for any other Level CCB file you want to play with the new soft-body player:

1. Locate the player object in the level and select it. Use the Timeline in case selection on the stage proves difficult. On the player's *Item Properties* tab, change the *CCB File* property from *Prefabs/Player.ccb* to *Prefabs/ PlayerSoftBody.ccb*. This level will then use the new soft-body player.

2. In Xcode, right-click the *Source* group and select *New File*. Create yet another Objective-C class, and name it **SoftBodyDrawNode**. Be sure to set the subclass to CCSprite, since the *SoftBodyPlayer.ccb* is a CCB file of type *Sprite*. For now, leave the class empty as is—you only need the class right now to avoid CCBReader errors when testing the app.

You can test it out by publishing and running the app. If the player in the specified level appears frozen in place, you've correctly replaced it. The player won't move at the moment because it doesn't have physics enabled.

Adding Center and Circumference Bodies

This new player needs a soft outer shell, so to speak. Instead of using one large circle shape, you now have to approximate the circular shape using several smaller bodies, also with a circle shape. I call these the *circumference bodies*. For the size of this player, a total of eight circumference bodies are needed, plus an additional body at the center.

The center body is easy. Drag and drop a node from the *Node Library View* onto the stage. Edit the node's position to 32x32 so that it is centered on the player image. Then switch to the *Item Physics* tab, and check the *Enable Physics* check box. Change the shape type to *Circle*, and set the *Corner radius* to *10*. Also, uncheck *Allows rotation*.

> **Note**   Individual bodies of the soft body needn't and shouldn't rotate around their own axis. Any rotation will come from the combined force applied to the body as a whole, distributed through body-to-body collisions and, of course, the joints.

Now edit the callback and collision properties. The *Collision* type should be set to *player*, and likewise enter **player** in the *Categories* field, too. In the *Masks* field, enter (without quotes): "**trigger, border, obstacle, spring, player**". Notice that player is now part of the mask because the individual bodies making up the player's new soft body should also collide with each other, both to distribute force to one another as well as prevent circumference bodies from being pushed into or past the center body.

With the center node selected, copy (Cmd+C) and paste (Cmd+V) the node eight times so that you get a total of nine nodes, each with physics enabled and the same properties as the initial node. You may want to rename the first node in the Timeline to **center** so that you know which one the center node is. This is crucial because the code you're about to write assumes that the center node is the first of the root node's children. If that isn't the case, you can drag the node in the Timeline to reorder it.

You should also rename the other nodes in the Timeline as well, to highlight their position on the circle. The following description assumes the first node is on the right and the nodes will be arranged in clockwise direction. Therefore, the node names ought to be: *right, bottom-right, bottom, bottom-left, left, top-left, top, top-right*. See Figure 10-2 to see what the *SoftBodyPlayer.ccb*'s Timeline should look like now.

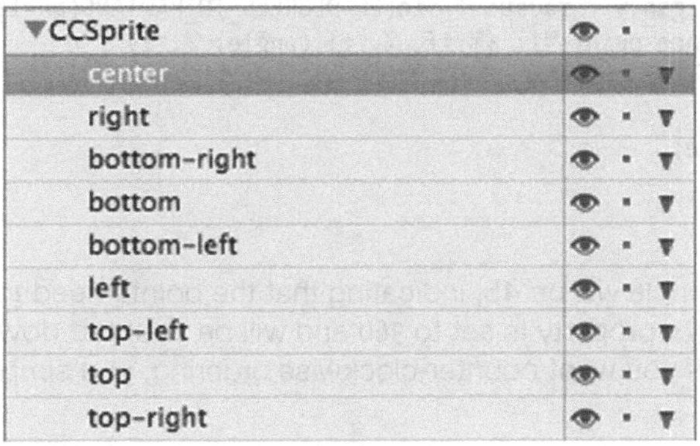

Figure 10-2. The player's center and circumference nodes

Finding Points on the Circumference of a Circle

Now here's the first problem: positioning the nodes on a circle. The right, left, top, and bottom nodes are fairly easy, but what about the other ones? An approximation may suffice, but the positions of the nodes should be equally spaced; otherwise, the body won't roll and rotate evenly. Especially if you want to create a larger body, you may even need more than eight bodies to form the circumference. So how would you go about determining the position of bodies (or points) on a circle's circumference?

It turns out that it just involves applying sin and cos to a specific angle, multiplied by the circle's radius to get the x,y coordinates of a point on the circle. You are going to write a simple method that prints out the position of a given number of points on a circle, distributed evenly.

Open *SoftBodyDrawNode.m* in Xcode. Add the code in Listing 10-1 between the @implementation and @end lines.

Listing 10-1. Printing positions of points on a circle to the Xcode console

```
-(void) didLoadFromCCB
{
    [self logPointsOnCircleWithRadius:30
                              origin:CGPointMake(32, 32)
                           numPoints:8];
}

-(void) logPointsOnCircleWithRadius:(CGFloat)radius
                             origin:(CGPoint)origin
                          numPoints:(int)numPoints
{
    CGFloat deltaAngle = 360.0 / numPoints;
    CGFloat angle = 360.0;

    for (int i = 1; i <= numPoints; i++)
    {
        CGPoint pos = CGPointMake(
                        origin.x + radius * cos(CC_DEGREES_TO_RADIANS(angle)),
                        origin.y + radius * sin(CC_DEGREES_TO_RADIANS(angle)));
        NSLog(@"circumference point %i: {%.1f, %.1f} (angle: %.1f)",
              i, pos.x, pos.y, angle);

        angle -= deltaAngle;
    }
}
```

The `deltaAngle` in this example will be 45, indicating that the points need to be distributed on 45-degree angles. The `angle` property is set to 360 and will be counted down to 0. This will print the points in clockwise order. If you want counter-clockwise ordering, you simply count up the angle variable from 0.

The `for` loop enumerates each point. The loop counter "i" is used only to print out the point's number in the log. The actual calculation for determining a point on a circle's circumference is written in pseudo-code as shown in Listing 10-2.

Listing 10-2. Algorithm to determine a point on a circle with a given radius and angle in radians

```
x = radius * cos(angle);
y = radius * sin(angle);
```

This calculation requires that angle is expressed in radians, not degrees. Hence, you perform the conversion using the Cocos2D built-in macro `CC_DEGREES_TO_RADIANS(angle)`, which takes an angle in degrees and returns the angle in radians. Of course, a companion macro to do the same in reverse also exists: `CC_RADIANS_TO_DEGREES(angle)`.

The result of the code in Listing 10-2 returns a position relative to the circle's origin. In other words, the circle is assumed to have its center at position 0x0. Since, in the case of the player, the circle is centered on the player image at position 32x32, the final *x/y* coordinates need to be offset by the circle's actual origin position. The `NSLog` line in Listing 10-1 prints only one digit after the comma, as indicated by the `%.1f` format string. This is sufficiently accurate for our purposes.

If you run the project now, the desired locations of the points on the circle will be printed to the Xcode console. See Listing 10-3.

Listing 10-3. Output of the code in Listing 10-1. Points on a circle with radius 30 and center at 32x32

```
circumference point 1: {62.0, 32.0} (angle: 360.0)
circumference point 2: {53.2, 10.8} (angle: 315.0)
circumference point 3: {32.0, 2.0} (angle: 270.0)
circumference point 4: {10.8, 10.8} (angle: 225.0)
circumference point 5: {2.0, 32.0} (angle: 180.0)
circumference point 6: {10.8, 53.2} (angle: 135.0)
circumference point 7: {32.0, 62.0} (angle: 90.0)
circumference point 8: {53.2, 53.2} (angle: 45.0)
```

> **Note**   You may be wondering why the radius is 30 rather than 32. It's the same collision radius as for the rigid player. But, bearing in mind that each circumference body represents a circle shape of its own, this will actually increase the collision radius of the player. If anything, the radius for the positions of the circumference nodes ought to be less than the previous collision radius. But it turned out that it's better to compromise. Allowing the player's total size to grow compared to the previous rigid-body version serves to better illustrate the design and resulting effects of soft-body physics. The smaller an object is, the harder it becomes to make it soft *and* stable.

Positioning Nodes on the Circle's Circumference

Now you can take the positions of Listing 10-3 and apply them to the nodes from right to top-right in clockwise fashion. The position of the node named *right* should be 62x32, the node *bottom-right* should be at position 53.2x10.8, the node *bottom* should be at position 32x2, and so on. Verify that you updated the node positions correctly by selecting all nodes from center down to top-right. This should give you the same circular layout as shown in Figure 10-3. Zoom in (Cmd +/–) to better see the positions of the nodes relative to each other.

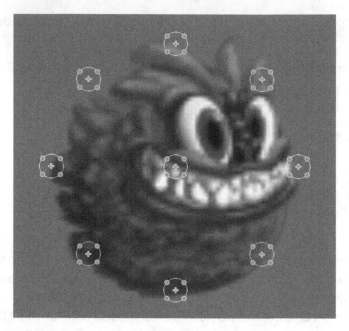

Figure 10-3. *The eight circumference nodes are positioned and distributed evenly in a circle*

Notice that you now have a total of nine child nodes, each with physics enabled, distributed evenly on the player's sprite. Also, note that the player sprite itself (the root node) does not have physics enabled.

One more thing to take note of: if you switch to the *Item Physics* tab, select a circumference node, and then keep selecting the currently selected node and a neighboring circumference node, you'll see the collision radius of the neighbors do not overlap. Instead, there's a tiny gap in between them, as shown in Figure 10-4. This gap is crucial!

Figure 10-4. *The circumference physics bodies and their circle shapes highlighted through physics debug drawing*

If any two circumference bodies in a soft-body physics object overlap or touch, the entire soft-body will be in constant unrest. If the gap is too wide, however, other bodies (both those on the soft-body object itself and external bodies such as the chain and rope elements) may too easily pass in between the soft-body's outer bodies, thus causing the soft body to become stuck.

Figure 10-4 also illustrates how the circumference bodies enlarge the player's actual collision radius. You'll later accommodate this by simply drawing the player's texture using the larger radius, effectively scaling it up.

Moving and Drawing the Soft-Body Player

If you run the current state of the project with physics debug drawing enabled, you'll notice the player's circle bodies falling down, and no more. The player sprite itself remains at its original location, and you can't move the player either because the sprite itself no longer has a physics body. You will have to apply the movement force to all bodies equally, and you'll have to use the center node as the new player node.

Moving the Soft-Body Player

The movement changes are quickly implemented. In Xcode, open *GameScene.m* to add a new BOOL ivar named _softBodyPlayer that allows you to make the code backward-compatible for those levels where you haven't replaced the player with the new soft-body player. Add the line highlighted in Listing 10-4.

Listing 10-4. An ivar that is set when the player node is the soft-body version

```
@implementation GameScene
{
    __weak CCNode* _levelNode;
    __weak CCPhysicsNode* _physicsNode;
    __weak CCNode* _playerNode;
    __weak CCNode* _backgroundNode;
    __weak GameMenuLayer* _gameMenuLayer;
    __weak GameMenuLayer* _popoverMenuLayer;

    CGFloat _playerNudgeRightVelocity;
    CGFloat _playerNudgeUpVelocity;
    CGFloat _playerMaxVelocity;
    BOOL _acceleratePlayer;

    BOOL _drawPhysicsShapes;
    BOOL _softBodyPlayer;
}
```

Then locate the loadLevelNamed: method. Replace the code at the end of loadLevelNamed: so that the end of the method looks like Listing 10-5. To be precise, the if condition needs to be added while the scrollToTarget: method is replaced by the one in Listing 10-5.

Listing 10-5. Determining the soft-body player and updating _playerNode accordingly

```
-(void) loadLevelNamed:(NSString*)levelCCB
{
    // ... previous code omitted

    _playerNode = [_physicsNode getChildByName:@"player" recursively:YES];

    // Soft-body player's first child node is the actual player sprite
    if (_playerNode.children.count > 0)
    {
        CCNode* center = _playerNode.children.firstObject;
        _playerNode = center;
        _softBodyPlayer = YES;
    }

    CGPoint offset = (_softBodyPlayer ?
                      _playerNode.parent.positionInPoints : CGPointZero);
    [self scrollToTarget:_playerNode withOffset:offset];
}
```

If the _playerNode has children, which is only the case for the new soft-body player object, the first object replaces the _playerNode reference. This makes the soft-body player's center node the new _playerNode. The _softBodyPlayer ivar is set to YES to indicate that this level is using the soft-body player.

The scrollToTarget: method will be updated shortly. Here in Listing 10-5, the new version is already being called. The new version takes an offset parameter to account for the fact that the center node's position is an offset to its parent position rather than being in-scene coordinates.

Locate the update: method in *GameScene.m*. It also needs to be updated with the changes highlighted in Listing 10-6.

Listing 10-6. Accelerating all bodies and scrolling with offset

```
-(void) update:(CCTime)delta
{
    if (_acceleratePlayer)
    {
        if (_softBodyPlayer)
        {
            for (CCNode* node in _playerNode.parent.children)
            {
                [self accelerateTarget:node];
            }
        }
        else
        {
            [self accelerateTarget:_playerNode];
        }
    }
```

```
    CGPoint offset = (_softBodyPlayer ?
                        _playerNode.parent.positionInPoints : CGPointZero);
    [self scrollToTarget:_playerNode withOffset:offset];
}
```

If the _softBodyPlayer flag is set, instead of the force being applied to the _playerNode, it is applied to all nodes. Remember that _playerNode is the center node in the *PlayerSoftBody.ccb*, so its children are the soft-body player's physics-enabled nodes. And each one is now accelerated instead of the _playerNode.

> **Note** It may be worth a try at a later time to apply the force only on the _playerNode (center node) or to spread the force unevenly—for instance, applying the force only on the circumference bodies and not on the center body. Each approach will result in different movement behavior, and you are welcome to experiment.

The scrollToTarget: method is called with the _playerNode's parent position as offset, just like in Listing 10-5 before.

Before you can compile this code without errors, you'll have to update the scrollToTarget: method. Apply the changes highlighted in Listing 10-7. It's not much, you just need to add the withOffset:(CGPoint)offset parameter and add the offset to target.positionInPoints in the line where viewPos is assigned. The rest of the method is omitted for brevity. You should not remove the remainder of the method; rather, leave it unchanged.

Listing 10-7. Adding the offset parameter to the scrollToTarget: method

```
-(void) scrollToTarget:(CCNode*)target withOffset:(CGPoint)offset
{
    CGSize viewSize = [CCDirector sharedDirector].viewSize;
    CGPoint viewCenter = CGPointMake(viewSize.width / 2.0,
                                     viewSize.height / 2.0);

    CGPoint viewPos = ccpSub(ccpAdd(target.positionInPoints, offset),
                             viewCenter);

    // ... remaining code omitted
}
```

With this code in place, you are almost ready to try. Before you do so, open *GameScene.ccb* in SpriteBuilder and select the root node. Remember there are custom properties that control some of the player behavior. With nine smaller, and thus less massive, bodies instead of one large body and with the physics forces applied to all nine bodies equally, the bodies will move far too quickly if you do not change the design parameters. For _playerNudgeRightVelocity, enter **4**, and a good value to enter for _playerNudgeUpVelocity is **12**. Check again that _drawPhysicsShapes is set to 1.

Save and publish. Build and run. You now have. . . well, nine smaller bodies (drawn by physics debug drawing) bouncing around the level, with the supposed camera following one of them (the center node). Each body behaves like a player of its own. If any one of the bodies collides with a saw, it's game over.

Setting Up Vertices and Texture Coordinates

You surely noticed that the player's friendly face is stuck to its original location. It won't move at all with the bodies. In fact, with the custom draw code you're going to implement, the sprite position will never change. Instead, you'll simply draw the sprite's texture at a location determined by the center node and use a shape determined by the circumference nodes.

Even though the soft body is anything but a coherent body, that's exactly what will allow you to see how the drawing code works. It also allows you to see what happens if the soft-body setup is somehow askew, be it because of an editing mistake or because the soft-body object has folded in on itself.

Let's start with the unspectacular part first: declaring variables, calling the setup code, and taking care of deallocation. Update *SoftBodyDrawNode.m* to the code in Listing 10-8.

Listing 10-8. Variables, setup and dealloc of the SoftBodyDrawNode class

```
#import "SoftBodyDrawNode.h"

@implementation SoftBodyDrawNode
{
@private
    int _numVertices;
    CCVertex* _vertices;
    CGPoint* _initialBodyPositions;

    CGFloat _enlargeTextureRadius;
    CGFloat _enlargeDrawRadius;
}

-(void) dealloc
{
    [self freeAllocatedMemory];
}

-(void) freeAllocatedMemory
{
    free(_vertices);
    _vertices = nil;

    free(_initialBodyPositions);
    _initialBodyPositions = nil;
}

-(void) didLoadFromCCB
{
    [self setup];
}

@end
```

For the drawing code, you'll make use of the allocated memory buffer. This is classic C-programming memory management. Since CGPoint and CCVertex are struct data types, they cannot be added to regular Cocoa collection classes like NSArray without wrapping (boxing) them first with NSValue objects. Since wrapping and unwrapping creates unnecessary overhead, something you'll want to avoid in tight render loops, and since C-style memory buffers really aren't that complex, they are arguably the best choice.

In this case, _vertices and _initialBodyPositions are pointers to a block of memory that will be allocated to hold exactly _numVertices CCVertex and CGPoint types. The vertices are used to draw the texture, while _initialBodyPositions gives you access to the positions of the bodies as they were designed in SpriteBuilder. They are needed to compute the texture coordinates from the nondeformed player, but theoretically you could also use them to determine the degree of deformation (the deviation from its original position) each body is currently experiencing.

The freeAllocatedMemory method called by dealloc takes care of releasing the memory allocated to these pointers by calling free on them. The variables are also set to nil simply because it's good style never to leave a pointer dangling. (A *dangling pointer* is a pointer that points to a deallocated block of memory.) Since both _vertices and _initialBodyPositions will be allocated manually using the C programming language's standard library functions (malloc, calloc, realloc), their memory must also be deallocated manually using the free function.

> **Caution**   ARC frees you only from manually managing the memory of Objective-C class instances, but not memory allocated with C functions or the C language variant and the predecessor of Cocoa, named Core Foundation.

CCVertex is a struct type exposed by the Cocos2D rendering API. See Listing 10-9 for reference, with the fields shown in brackets.

Listing 10-9. The CCVertex type defines the vertex position, two texture coordinates,and a color property

```
typedef struct CCVertex {
    GLKVector4 position;  // position (x, y, z, w)
    GLKVector2 texCoord1, texCoord2;  // texture coordinates (x, y)
    GLKVector4 color;  // color (r, g, b, a)
} CCVertex;
```

The GLKVector2 and GLKVector4 types are defined by Apple's GLKit and are also structs containing two four-float (not CGFloat) values. The position, unlike most low-level OpenGL commands, is in points. That's one benefit of the new Cocos2D rendering API—you no longer have to consider point-to-pixel conversion when writing rendering code. Of the two texture-coordinate fields, only texCoord1 is used in this example. It defines the coordinate within the texture that maps to this vertex. Texture coordinates are expressed as a percentage of the texture's size in the range 0.0 to 1.0. Finally, the colors are RGB values with an alpha value, also in the range of 0.0 to 1.0.

The _enlargeTextureRadius ivar will be used to increase the radius for the texture coordinates. This ensures that the player image isn't cut off. The _enlargeDrawRadius is used to enlarge the player as a whole, effectively scaling it up. I'll say more about this shortly.

Now add the missing `setup` method in Listing 10-10 just below `didLoadFromCCB`.

Listing 10-10. Initial setup of memory buffers and storing the bodies' initial positions

```
-(void) setup
{
    [self freeAllocatedMemory];

    _numVertices = (int)_children.count + 1;
    _vertices = calloc(_numVertices, sizeof(CCVertex));
    _initialBodyPositions = calloc(_numVertices, sizeof(CGPoint));

    int i = 0;
    CGPoint centerPos = ((CCNode*)_children[0]).positionInPoints;

    for (CCNode* child in _children)
    {
        if (child.physicsBody)
        {
            if (i == 0)
            {
                _initialBodyPositions[i] = centerPos;
            }
            else
            {
                CGPoint centerToChild = ccpSub(child.positionInPoints,
                                               centerPos);
                CGFloat newRadius = ccpLength(centerToChild) +
                                    _enlargeTextureRadius;
                CGPoint newPos = ccpMult(ccpNormalize(centerToChild),
                                         newRadius);
                _initialBodyPositions[i] = ccpAdd(newPos, centerPos);
            }

            i++;
        }
    }

    [self updateTextureCoordinates];
}
```

The `setup` method first calls `freeAllocatedMemory`. This is just in case the method runs more than once. If the previously allocated memory isn't freed, it will be lost (leaked), because the memory will still be allocated but you won't have any access to it anymore. This is because the setup method allocates new chunks of memory and assigns the pointers to the `_vertices` and `_initialBodyPositions`.

The `_numVertices` ivar is set to the number of child nodes plus one. With nine child nodes (one center plus eight circumference nodes), that makes 10 vertices. Why 10? The tenth vertex is the one that closes the loop. The center vertex is the first, then comes the right one, then the other ones, up to the top-right vertex. And that's where you need to duplicate the right vertex once more so that the triangle formed by the vertices center (1), top-right (9), and right (2) can be drawn. See Figure 10-5 for visual clarification.

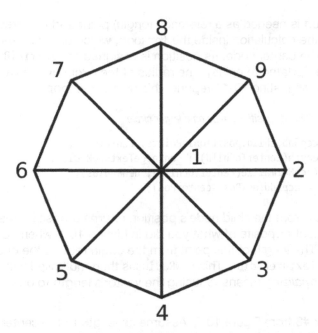

Figure 10-5. This triangle fan (with vertex numbers) is used to draw the textured soft-body player

Essentially, the soft-body circle must be divided into triangles to be drawable by the Cocos2D renderer. The first triangle is 1-2-3, and subsequent triangles can be added by simply adding one more vertex each. After 1-2-3, the next triangle is 1-3-4 followed by 1-4-5 and so on. This is called a *triangle fan*, which is a drawing mode where each subsequent vertex is assumed to form another triangle with the originating vertex and the last vertex.

In Listing 10-10, both `_vertices` and `_initialBodyPositions` are allocated. The amount of memory allocated is `_numVertices` multiplied by the size of the corresponding type. For instance, `_vertices` will allocate 10 * 48 bytes of memory, a total of 480 bytes. So it's really not much, especially in relation to the sprite's texture memory. Both pointers point to an allocated chunk of memory, and both can be accessed like an Objective-C array using the same subscripting operator as in C. See, for instance, the assignment in the last line in Listing 10-11.

> **Tip** Texture memory size is a multiple of the texture size times color depth. The file size of the corresponding image will typically be far smaller. A common beginner's mistake is to assume texture memory usage is identical to the image file size. Alas, texture memory (for uncompressed formats) can be calculated with the following pseudo-code: `pixelWidth * pixelHeight * (colorBitDepth / 8)`. For instance, a 4096x4096 image with 32-bit colors will use this much memory as an uncompressed texture: `4096 * 4096 * (32 / 8) = 67,108,864` bytes (equals 64 megabytes).

The center node's position is needed as a reference (origin) point and is stored in the centerPos variable. You need it for the calculation inside the for loop, which enumerates over all child nodes. The first node is the center node. Its position is assigned to _initialBodyPositions as is. The remaining points are updated to enlarge the radius of the circle by the value specified in the _enlargeTextureRadius ivar. Listing 10-11 reprints this part of the loop.

Listing 10-11. Assuming the initial body positions to be on a larger circle

```
CGPoint centerToChild = ccpSub(child.positionInPoints, centerPos);
CGFloat newRadius = ccpLength(centerToChild) + _enlargeTextureRadius;
CGPoint newPos = ccpMult(ccpNormalize(centerToChild), newRadius);
_initialBodyPositions[i] = ccpAdd(newPos, centerPos);
```

Subtracting the centerPos from the child node's position returns a position that is relative to the origin (0x0). That's the exact opposite of what you did in Listing 10-1 when adding the origin to each point on the circle. The length of this point from the origin returns the circle's radius, which is increased by _enlargeTextureRadius. This newRadius is then multiplied with the normalized centerToChild point. *Normalizing* means reducing the vector's length to one unit while retaining its relative orientation.

Take, for instance, vertex #3 from Figure 10-5. Assume its length to the center (vertex #1) is 25 points, which is equal to the circle's radius. Now if you multiply the normalized vector between vertices 1 and 3 by 33, you'll get a point *3b* that extends further outward on the line defined by vertices 1 to 3. Do this to all the points and the circle ends up being larger.

Since the _initialBodyPositions are used to calculate the texture coordinates, let me illustrate why exactly you may need to do so. Figure 10-3 already illustrates that some of the nodes are positioned still within the image, resulting in the suboptimal texture coordinates shown in Figure 10-6. To avoid cutting off parts of the texture, the texture coordinates need to assume a circle with a slightly larger radius. Otherwise, some of the hair, belly, and mouth of the player may be missing. On the other hand, this added radius must not be too large. If it is, parts of other images in the *Global* Sprite Sheet may be drawn as well.

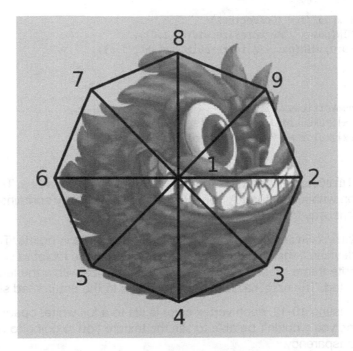

Figure 10-6. Texture coordinates need to be large enough to encompass the entire image, but so large that they draw parts of neighboring images in the Sprite Sheet

Calculating the texture coordinates is done in the updateTextureCoordinates method. Add the code in Listing 10-12 below the setup method. The method was separated because if you want to run a sprite frame animation in the soft-body player, you have to call this method every time the spriteFrame property changes in order to update the texture coordinates to the new sprite frame's coordinates.

Listing 10-12. Updating texture coordinates

```
-(void) updateTextureCoordinates
{
    CCSpriteFrame* spriteFrame = self.spriteFrame;
    CGSize textureSize = spriteFrame.texture.contentSize;
    CGRect frameRect = spriteFrame.rect;
    CGSize frameSize = spriteFrame.originalSize;

    for (int i = 0; i < _numVertices; i++)
    {
        _vertices[i].color = GLKVector4Make(1.0, 1.0, 1.0, 1.0);

        CGPoint pos = _initialBodyPositions[i];
        pos.x += frameRect.origin.x;
        pos.y = (frameRect.origin.y + frameSize.height) - pos.y;
```

```
        _vertices[i].texCoord1 = (GLKVector2){
            MAX(0.0, MIN(pos.x / textureSize.width, 1.0)),
            1.0 - MAX(0.0, MIN(pos.y / textureSize.height, 1.0)),
        };
    }

    int lastIndex = _numVertices - 1;
    _vertices[lastIndex].texCoord1 = _vertices[1].texCoord1;
    _vertices[lastIndex].color = _vertices[1].color;
}
```

At first, the updateTextureCoordinates creates local copies of some variables. The CCSpriteFrame class defines the region within a texture. A Sprite Sheet texture typically contains multiple images, and sprite frames are the way to access these images.

The spriteFrame.texture.contentSize is the total size of the texture in points. This size will be consistent across all devices, regardless of whether the texture is the *tablethd* version or the regular phone version. The sprite frame's *rect* defines the position and size within the texture where this particular image is located. The originalSize property refers to the untrimmed size.

Within the for loop in Listing 10-12, each vertex color is set to a full white, opaque color. If they weren't set to this color, you wouldn't be able to see the texture you're going to draw. Feel free to try different colors and transparency.

Each body's position is first offset by the sprite frame's origin. Since OpenGL draws textures upside down, and internally Cocos2D maps most commands directly to OpenGL (or Metal) commands, the *y* coordinate needs to be subtracted from the sprite frame's origin plus its height. Otherwise, the player would be drawn upside down.

The resulting position is assigned to the texCoord1 field of the vertex. But first, it is converted from absolute coordinates in points to percentage values in the range of 0.0 to 1.0. The MIN/MAX macros ensure the values aren't outside of this range, which would likely provoke a crash. Once more, the *y* coordinate needs to be upside down—subtracting the result from 1.0 inverses the texture coordinate.

After all nine _numVertices have been processed, there's but one last vertex. The values are simply copied from the second vertex (at index 1), thus creating a duplicate of vertex #2, which was shown in Figure 10-6 as the last vertex in the _vertices array.

This concludes the setup of vertices and texture coordinates.

Not Trimming Sprite Sheet Sprites

While we're on the topic of sprite frames, you should uncheck the *Trim sprites* check box for the *Global* Sprite Sheet in SpriteBuilder, as shown in Figure 10-7.

Figure 10-7. Uncheck the "Trim sprites" check box to prevent the images from being rotated

Unchecking *Trim sprites* prevents the player image from possibly being rotated. The custom drawing code does not account for the sprite frame possibly being rotated within the Sprite Sheet.

Drawing the Texture with CCRenderer

What's left is to actually draw the texture based on each body's current position. In Cocos2D, all custom drawing has to be done within the draw:transform: method, using the supplied CCRenderer object. Add the code in Listing 10-13 below the updateTextureCoordinates method in *SoftBodyDrawNode.m*.

Listing 10-13. Drawing the soft-body texture

```
-(void) draw:(CCRenderer *)renderer transform:(const GLKMatrix4 *)transform
{
    int numTriangles = _numVertices - 2;
    CCRenderBuffer buffer = [renderer enqueueTriangles:numTriangles
                                        andVertexes:_numVertices
                                          withState:self.renderState
                                    globalSortOrder:0];

    int i = 0;
    CGPoint centerPos = ((CCNode*)_children[0]).position;
```

```
    for (CCNode* child in _children)
    {
        CGPoint vertexPos = child.position;
        if (i > 0)
        {
            CGPoint vectorToCenter = ccpSub(child.position, centerPos);
            CGFloat length = ccpLength(vectorToCenter);
            CGPoint normalVector = ccpMult(vectorToCenter, 1.0 / length);
            vectorToCenter = ccpMult(normalVector, length +
                                        _enlargeDrawRadius);
            vertexPos = ccpAdd(vectorToCenter, centerPos);
        }

        _vertices[i].position = GLKVector4Make(vertexPos.x, vertexPos.y,
                                        0.0, 1.0);

        CCVertex v = CCVertexApplyTransform(_vertices[i], transform);
        CCRenderBufferSetVertex(buffer, i, v);
        i++;
    }

    int lastIndex = _numVertices - 1;
    _vertices[lastIndex].position = GLKVector4Make(
                                    _vertices[1].position.x,
                                    _vertices[1].position.y,
                                    0.0, 1.0);
    CCVertex v = CCVertexApplyTransform(_vertices[lastIndex],
                                    transform);
    CCRenderBufferSetVertex(buffer, lastIndex, v);

    for (int i = 0; i < numTriangles; i++)
    {
        CCRenderBufferSetTriangle(buffer, i, 0, i+1, i+2);
    }
}
```

First, the number of triangles is determined. Since the first three vertices form one triangle and each subsequent triangle forms another triangle in a triangle fan, the number of triangles is the number of vertices minus two. The CCRenderer object is then queried for a CCRenderBuffer struct type. The buffer is allocated by CCRenderer to hold the given number of triangles and vertices.

The render state to draw textured triangles is already set up for you by the CCSprite base class, so you can simply pass in self.renderState. The render state is simply the combination of the blend mode, shader, and texture. Already and implicitly set up by CCSprite are the blend mode and shader program, whereas the texture is assigned by CCBReader via the spriteFrame property. In case you want to know, the default blend mode and shader for a CCSprite are set as follows:

```
self.blendMode = [CCBlendMode premultipliedAlphaMode];
self.shader = [CCShader positionTextureColorShader];
```

Tip   If you want to do custom drawing with textures, it'll be easiest to do so in a CCSprite subclass. Otherwise, you'll have to create a CCRenderState object yourself in order to pass the blend mode, shader program and a (optional) texture to CCRenderer. You may also want to make use of the CCRenderCheckVisibility method that prevents anything from being drawn outside the region defined by this method. It's not used in this example because the player is always visible. And if you have to or want to use OpenGL commands directly, you should do so by writing the code in a block or method enqueued by CCRenderer's enqueueBlock: or enqueueMethod: method. Bypassing CCRenderer for custom drawing code may lead to unexpected side effects, and you won't benefit from Cocos2D's new Metal renderer (not to be confused with Nu Metal).

A for loop is used to enumerate over every child node in order to create the vertex positions for the current frame. The first node is the center node, and its position is simply taken as is. For all remaining child nodes, the position is extended outward from the center by _enlargeDrawRadius. The principle and algorithm are the same as in Listing 10-11.

The resulting vertexPos is converted to a GLKVector4 type by using the GLKVector4Make function and assigned as the position of the vertex at the index that corresponds to the child node being enumerated. The third coordinate is the z coordinate, with which you can influence the draw order of the vertex. In this case, it is zero, so it will use the same draw order as designed by SpriteBuilder. The last coordinate (w) has to be 1.0 for all vertices.

Updating the render buffer with the new vertex is done by CCRenderBufferSetVertex, which essentially copies _vertices[i] to the render buffer at index i. Since the vertex position is expressed in coordinates relative to the sprite's parent, CCVertexApplyTransform is used to apply the transform passed into the draw method. This has the effect of moving the vertex position to world (scene) coordinates.

After the for loop, the last vertex is set to become a copy of the second vertex. This closes the last triangle 1-9-10, which is the same as 1-9-2 in Figure 10-6.

Finally, the CCRenderBufferSetTriangle creates all the triangles from the vertices already set before with CCRenderBufferSetVertex, in the order 0-1-2, 0-2-3, 0-3-4 and so on. Keep in mind that index i is zero-based, so index 0 is the center vertex, unlike in Figure 10-6 where the center node is labeled as *vertex #1*.

You can have some fun now by running the game in its current state with the new renderer. Since the player's bodies aren't held together by joints, they are free to go, while the new renderer draws the texture between the individual bodies. This leads to some heavy distortion and some hilarious results, one can be seen in Figure 10-8. But it does prove that drawing the texture works in general, and it also gives you an example of what things may look like if all the bodies together don't form a coherent body. The texture can sometimes stretch far and thin, or it can become flipped as bodies travel in opposite directions.

Figure 10-8. Zooming in on the newly textured player shows its lack of coherence

Playing Me Softly. . .

Let's add some coherence to the player body to make it truly "soft." It's important to understand (and thus I repeat it) how each joint adds to the mix.

A *distance joint* keeps two bodies a fixed distance apart, no more and no less. If neither the *Minimum distance* nor *Maximum distance* check box is enabled, you can remove the distance joint. If either or both the *Minimum distance* and *Maximum distance* check boxes are enabled and set to different values, you can add a *spring joint* to the same two bodies to make the connection springy.

But without the proper stiffness of the spring joint or a very small difference between minimum and maximum distance, the spring joint will not contribute much to the mix. A spring joint alone should have its rest length enabled; otherwise, it will not be able to keep the bodies at the desired distance, much like a distance joint without the minimum and/or maximum distance enabled.

Connecting the Circumference Bodies

The first thing to try is to connect the circumference bodies. It's best to start simple with a distance joint—you can always add more joints at a later time. Open *PlayerSoftBody.ccb* in SpriteBuilder. From the *Node Library View*, drag and drop a *Physics Distance Joint* onto the stage. Drag the left circle of the two small circles onto the node labeled *right* so that it becomes *Body A*, and then drag the right circle onto the node labeled *bottom-right* so that it becomes *Body B*.

On the joint's *Item Properties* tab, check the *Collide bodies* check box. If you don't do this, when connecting two bodies that were previously able to collide, they would no longer collide, even if their Categories and Masks matched. Set all Anchor values to 0 so that the joint anchors exactly on the positions of the two nodes. Then enable both the *Minimum distance* and *Maximum distance* check boxes. This will automatically fill the distance fields with the current distance (22.95) between the joint's bodies.

> **Tip**   Be sure to enable the *Minimum distance* and *Maximum distance* check boxes after you've edited the anchor points. Editing the anchor point will change the joint's length (the distance between two bodies), so the *Minimum distance* and *Maximum distance* values may no longer represent the joint's actual length and instead represent the length it formerly had. If you need to update the distance values, simply uncheck and check the *Enable* check box to update the value.

For reference, the distance joint's properties are shown in Figure 10-9.

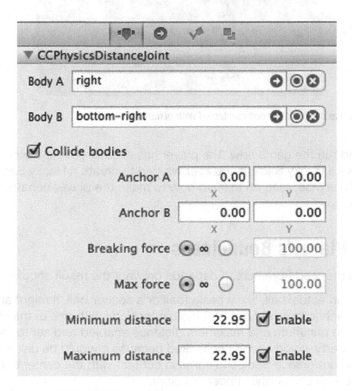

Figure 10-9. The first circumference distance joint's properties

Now continue to add seven more distance joints in the same way. Start by connecting the bottom-right node with the bottom node, and continue to connect the neighboring nodes in clockwise order. Once you have added eight distance joints that form a circle as shown in Figure 10-10, be sure to verify that all of the joint's properties are identical. Tiny variations in minimum/maximum distance are acceptable.

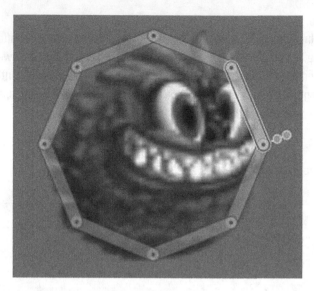

Figure 10-10. All circumference nodes have been connected with distance joints

You should publish and run the game now. The player has already gained the necessary coherence, yet it behaves more like a Hacky Sack. If you ever wanted to create a Hacky Sack game, now you know how to do so. Otherwise, read on to learn how to make the player behave more like a squishy ball.

Increasing the Player's Bounciness

There are two ways to proceed from here. It depends on what the result should feel like.

If you wanted to make an actual ball, like a basketball or a soccer ball, it might suffice to add eight more distance joints. Each joint would connect the center body with one of the circumference bodies and would have both the minimum and maximum distance enabled and set to the same value. The *Collide bodies* property would be left unchecked because it would be unlikely the ball would contract enough for circumference bodies to come in contact with the center body. The result would be a bouncy ball that compresses while under pressure.

However, you couldn't control the ball's bounciness when using only distance joints. The fact that the distance joints even allow being compressed despite the minimum and maximum distance settings means you would be relying on a side effect of the physics engine's implementation of the distance joint. That's never a good thing to do, as it can change in future updates.

The solution you should be more interested in uses spring joints. Again, you have two choices. One is to connect the center body with each circumference body as explained in the previous paragraph. However, despite using eight spring joints, this creates a rather wobbly structure that is prone to collapse in on itself if a strong force is applied to the body at one point. Increasing spring stiffness doesn't really help. Though there are certainly uses for this kind of wobbly, bouncing, pudding-like blob.

The other solution is to use just four spring joints that connect one circumference body with the body directly opposite to it. That's what you should be doing. With the *PlayerSoftBody.ccb* open, drag and drop four spring joints onto the stage. Connect a joint with the right node and the left node. Connect the next joint with the bottom-right and top-left nodes, and then bottom and top nodes as well as bottom-left and top-right nodes.

Then select each spring joint in turn to edit the joint properties. The *Collide bodies* property can be left unchecked, while opposing bodies are unlikely to get close enough to ever get in contact with each other. The anchor-point values should all be set to 0 to align the joint anchors with the node positions. Afterward, you should enable *Rest length*, which will show *60* as the length value, give or take a tiny fraction for the two diagonal spring joints. Leave damping set to *1*, but change stiffness to *100*. Confirm that you've applied all these settings to all four spring joints correctly. The result should be a ball-grid that looks like the one in Figure 10-11.

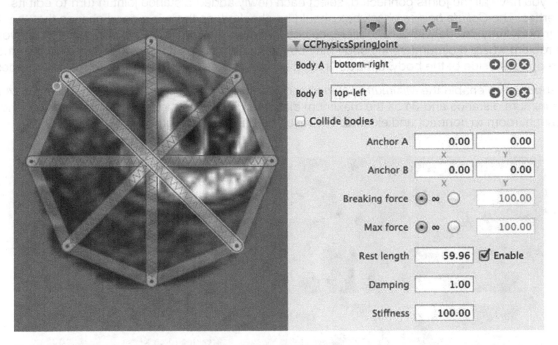

Figure 10-11. Four spring joints connect opposing circumference bodies

You should try this version in the game to see how this design has improved the previous version. The Hacky Sack has become a jelly blob. It works well, but the center node isn't attached to the body yet, and the body is perhaps too easily deformed.

Connecting the Center Node

One problem of the current setup is that it does not prevent the springs from expanding or contracting too much. And, of course, the center node ought to be affixed to the entire construct; otherwise, it may be squeezed outside the player.

You could use spring joints to connect the center with the circumference bodies, but you already have springs set up with opposing circumference bodies. Additional spring joints to the center won't affect the body much. In fact, either the opposing spring joints or the ones connecting with the center would take precedence, making the others mostly useless.

It makes more sense to add distance joints to the center. That way, you can control the minimum and maximum contraction of each circumference body from the center. This allows you to take control of the overall deformability of the shape.

From the *Node Library View*, drag and drop eight distance joints onto the *PlayerSoftBody.ccb* stage. Connect the first joint with the center node and the right node. Continue connecting the other joints so that all connect with the center node as *Body A* and with a circumference node as *Body B*—just like the spokes of a wheel.

Once you have all the joints connected, select each newly added distance joint in turn to edit its properties. The *Collide bodies* check box should be checked, as there is a good chance that the center body may collide with a circumference body. Allowing this collision to happen helps to avoid the problem where a circumference body may be pushed inward past the center and then get stuck at the opposite side of the body. It may still happen, but it takes a lot more force to make it happen.

You should also enable the *Minimum distance* and *Maximum distance* check boxes, and enter **24** as the minimum distance and **34** as the maximum distance. This gives the spring joints some, but not too much, room to contract and expand. The result can be seen in Figure 10-12.

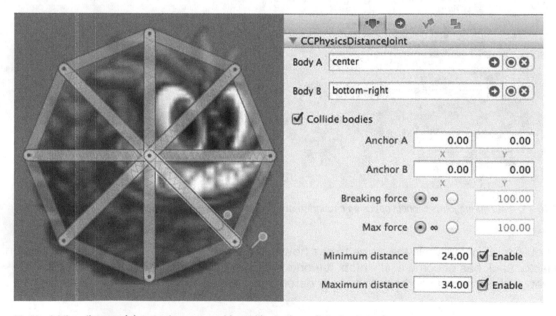

Figure 10-12. Adding distance joints to the center add stability to the soft-body player

Try this version in the game. It feels almost complete, depending on what you imagine a good soft-body player should feel like.

Improving the Soft-Body Player

There are numerous ways to create a soft-body object, but many follow the same guiding principles outlined so far. There are also many ways to tweak the behavior of the soft-body player without changing the setup by much.

I'd like to suggest some changes that you may want to experiment with at a later point:

- Center Body:

    - Increase or decrease its circle shape radius.

    - Increase or decrease the body's density (and thus its mass).

    - Remove "player" from its mask to prevent circumference bodies from colliding with it.

- Circumference Bodies:

    - Change the friction and elasticity to alter the collision behavior with borders and other objects.

    - Double the number of circumference bodies while decreasing their circle shape radius.

- Circumference Distance Joints:

    - Alter the *Minimum distance* and *Maximum distance* values to allow more room between circumference bodies.

    - Replace them with spring joints with rest enabled.

    - Uncheck *Collide bodies*.

- Center Distance Joints:

    - Alter the *Minimum distance* and *Maximum distance* values.

    - Uncheck *Collide bodies*.

- Opposing Spring Joints:

    - Increase or decrease *Stiffness*.

    - Replace them with distance joints with distance limit enabled.

- Any Joint:

    - Enable *Max Force*, and experiment with force values.

Depending on the design of your game, one of those solutions may work better than the one I present in the book. Factors to consider are the overall bounciness of the object, how much it can be deformed, how stable it is in general, and how prone it is to warp in on itself if put under enormous pressure.

In particular, if you can't allow your object to permanently deform in an unfortunate way, you may need to resort to programming. For instance, you could have a check in place that determines opposing nodes' positions, perhaps in relation to the center node. If the opposing bodies are determined to be too close (for too long), you may want to manually set their positions to the initial positions.

One more thing to keep in mind: if you move body positions or change joint anchors, be sure to check all connecting joints. They may need to have their *Minimum distance*, *Maximum distance*, and *Rest Length* properties updated.

And finally, apply only one change at a time! This makes it easier to learn the effect of individual changes. Two or more changes combined can create quite a different result, and it's very hard to determine which changes contribute what to the newly observed behavior.

Improving Texture Rendering

There are two remaining problems with the player as of now. Thanks to the circumference bodies, the actual collision shape of the player has become larger—by about the radius of the circumference body's circle shape. The other problem relates to the texture. As of now, the positions of the circumference nodes determine the texture coordinates. Since the circumference nodes are somewhat inside the player, the player's outer shape seems cut off.

Both issues are visible in Figure 10-13. For one, you'll notice the rather large distance between the player and the gear spokes, despite the player being squeezed in between two spokes. The other problem is that some of the player's curly hair is cut off, as is its round belly shape. Compare it with Figure 10-3.

Figure 10-13. The player is drawn too small for its collision shape, and its curly hair is cut off

Let's fix these problems. Open *PlayerSoftBody.ccb*, and select the root node. On the *Item Properties* tab, click the *Edit Custom Properties* button at the bottom. Add two custom properties of type float, named _enlargeDrawRadius and _enlargeTextureRadius. Both are already declared and in use by the SoftBodyDrawNode class. Leave both values at 0 for the moment.

Now disable physics debug drawing for a second. Open *GameScene.ccb*, select the root node, and set the _drawPhysicsShapes property to 0. Then run the game, and try to focus on the player's texture. If you look closely enough in the game, you'll notice the player's texture has a noticeable octagonal shape with parts of it cut off, as in Figure 10-14.

Figure 10-14. The player's texture is clearly cut off (4x scale)

In order to improve this, the texture coordinates need to be moved outward, away from the center. Effectively, this increases the radius for the player's texture coordinates. This is what the _enlargeTextureRadius value does. You should set it to 6, and try it out again in the game. The result should be what you see in Figure 10-15.

Figure 10-15. Moving the player's texture coordinates outward ensures all of the texture is drawn (4x scale)

I determined the value 6 for _enlargeTextureRadius merely by increasing it until no parts of the texture were noticeably cut off. Notice that you can set the value much higher, though with increasing values the texture may become distorted, the player becomes smaller, and the player will eventually start to draw parts of other nearby images within the Sprite Sheet. Therefore, you should opt to use the lowest possible value that draws the texture without glitches.

The player is still too small compared to its overall collision shape. Therefore, SoftBodyDrawNode allows you to draw the player larger than its body positions indicate, by moving the actual vertex positions away from the center. This will stretch the texture and has a similar effect as increasing the scale property.

> **Note**   So why not just increase the scale property? Because the SoftBodyDrawNode does not incorporate scale, rotation, or even the sprite's position into its drawing code. Once you start to use custom drawing code for a sprite, it's all yours and each convenience feature Cocos2D provides no longer works unless you re-implement it yourself.

Open *GameScene.ccb*, select the root node, and change the _drawPhysicsShapes property back to 1. Then run the game to observe the player's collision shape. You'll notice the player will be drawn noticeably smaller than the collision shapes. This is true now more so than before, because you already increased the radius for the texture coordinates, which has the effect of decreasing the player's size. See Figure 10-16 for the current state.

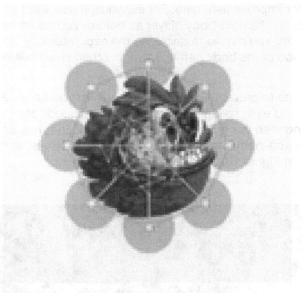

Figure 10-16. *The player's texture is drawn well within the collision shape (4x scale)*

In SpriteBuilder, open *PlayerSoftBody.ccb* and select the root node. Change the *_enlargeDrawRadius* property to *14*. Again, this value is determined by experimentation and should be as large as it needs to be to stretch the texture so that it aligns well with the circumference bodies' circle shapes. If you run this in the game, the result will be more like in Figure 10-17. The player is now noticeably larger than before. You may want to disable physics shape drawing to better experience the final soft-body player.

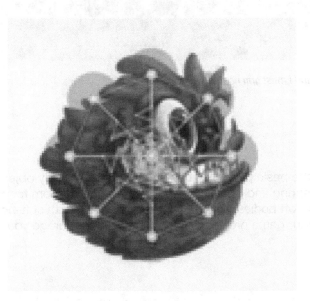

Figure 10-17. *The player's texture is stretched to encompass the entire collision shape (4x scale)*

There's, of course, room for improvement here. For instance, if you want to make the soft-body player about the same size as the rigid-body player as before, you could try to do so. This won't be as easy as it sounds, though. You'd have to decrease the circumference bodies' radius, which in turn would increase the likelihood of the body getting stuck in other, small collision shapes, such as chain and rope segments.

Nevertheless, don't allow me to prevent you from doing so. Just be prepared for lots and lots of tweaking, experimenting, and even failing every so often. It's a good idea to make backup copies of the player every now and then using Finder (or once SpriteBuilder has a "duplicate CCB" feature, use that). Creating reliable soft-body physics takes time, sweat, nerves, and everything else you can spare. The results (shown in Figure 10-18) are well worth the effort!

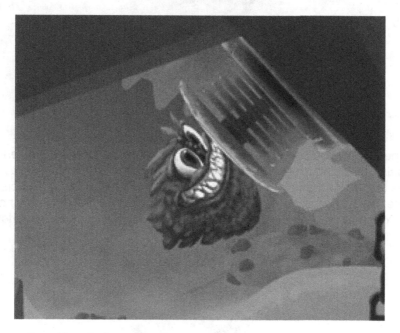

Figure 10-18. I have a mouth, and I must grin no matter how much it hurts

Summary

This chapter taught you the basic principles behind creating soft-body objects. It's essentially just the right combination of spring and distance joints. There's lots of room for experimentation to achieve different kinds of soft bodies. It's also fun to experiment with soft-body physics in general, whether you need it for your game project or not, so I would encourage you to try out different variations.

You've also learned about custom drawing using Cocos2D's own renderer. I hope I was able to convey how it's easier to use than pure OpenGL. Custom drawing a texture with a varying number of vertices has many applications beyond soft-body physics. For instance, you could animate a flag waving in the wind with manageable effort and without having to resort to shader programming, a completely different beast well beyond the scope of this book. You may want to look into Pro OpenGL ES for iOS from Apress if you want to learn more about low-level graphics programming for iOS.

The soft-body player concludes the changes to how the game is played. You'll find the resulting project in the *11 - Soft-Body Player* folder. In the next two chapters, you'll add music, sound, and visual effects.

Now You're a SpriteBuilder Pro!

Chapter **11**

Audio and Labels

In this chapter, you will learn how to play audio, both sound effects and music. Sound effects can be played via the Timeline, but most of it will have to be programmed using ObjectAL, the audio engine used by Cocos2D and SpriteBuilder.

The second half of the chapter is dedicated to labels—specifically, TrueType font effects as well as why and how to use bitmap font labels. You will also find an introduction on localizing label texts, and how to ensure a localized label can be changed to embed numeric information at runtime, such as score and other counters.

Introducing ObjectAL

Cocos2D includes the ObjectAL audio framework to play back sound effects and music. ObjectAL is a framework built around the low-level OpenAL API, which is best used for short sound effects (.wav, .caf, .aiff), and Apple's AVAudioPlayer, which is best used to decode and stream long-running audio (mp3, m4a, mp4, ac3). The architecture is depicted in Figure 11-1.

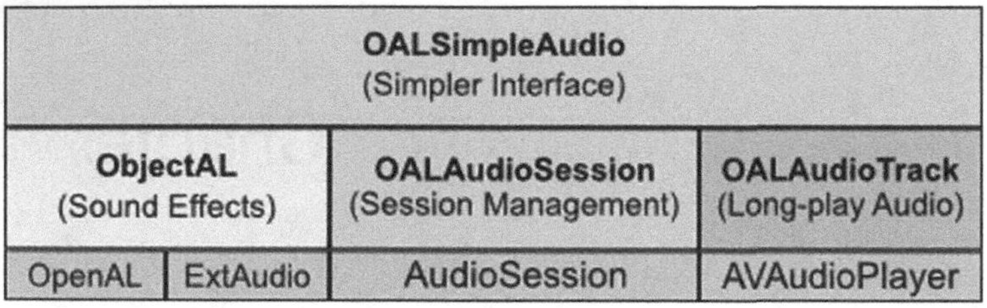

Figure 11-1. The architecture of ObjectAL encapsulates both OpenAL and AVAudioPlayer frameworks

The OALSimpleAudio singleton provides a simple-to-use programming interface for all essential audio needs. It generally knows of two types of audio: *effects* for short, memory-buffered sound effects, and *bg* (background) for long-running audio like music and speech. The effects commands will play audio through OpenAL, while the background commands will be played back by AVAudioPlayer.

It's crucial to know the difference between the two types of audio files and corresponding formats. Table 11-1 summarizes the important details.

Table 11-1. Differences between short sound effects played through OpenAL and long audio played through AVAudioPlayer

	Short Sound-Effects/OpenAL	Long-Running Audio/AVAudioPlayer
Playback Delay	None or small delay, depending on file size and format	Small delay if not preloaded
Format on Disk	Any software-decodable format	Any software-decodable format, or any hardware format if using hardware
Decoding	During load	During playback
Memory Use	Entire file loaded and decompressed into memory	File streamed in real time (very low memory usage)
Simultaneous Playback	32 simultaneous effects	Limited only by CPU
Playback Performance	Good	Excellent with 1 track (hardware decoding). Still good with 2 or a few tracks, but additional tracks tax the CPU significantly.
Looped Playback	Yes (on or off)	Yes (specific number of loops, unlimited loops, or off)
Panning	Yes (mono files only)	Yes
Positional Audio	Yes (mono files only)	No
Modify Pitch	Yes	No
Audio Power Metering	No	Yes
Recommended Formats	44 or 22 kHz sample rate with 16 bits per sample. Uncompressed PCM. Prefer mono. Containers: .caf, .aiff or .wav. Duration: a fraction of a second to a few seconds.	MP3 or AAC encoding, variable or constant bitrate between 80 kbps to 192 kbps. Mono or stereo. Containers: mp3, m4a, mp4. Duration: a few seconds to several minutes.

> **Caution**   Not all audio formats are supported by mobile devices. For instance, OGG and FLAC files cannot be played on iOS. It's best to stick to the most common formats: .caf and .wav for sound effects, and for long-running audio use either mp3 or m4a. If you have an audio file in a different format, use an audio converter like SoundConverter or an audio editor like Audacity to convert the files. And if you have an audio file in the correct format but it won't play, it may have been created/modified by an audio program that writes nonstandard extensions or adds metadata that will trip up OpenAL or AVAudioPlayer. In that case, open the audio file in Audacity, re-export it to the same format, and then try again.

You'll learn more about OALSimpleAudio's programming interface shortly in this chapter. Suffice it to say that ObjectAL covers all of your audio needs. If you need more functionality than offered by OALSimpleAudio but don't know where to start (besides the documentation and ObjectAL demos, obviously), I recommend you take a look at how the OALSimpleAudio class uses the ObjectAL, OALAudioTrack, and OALAudioSession classes.

You can dig deeper into ObjectAL on its homepage at http://kstenerud.github.io/ObjectAL-for-iPhone, where you'll find the documentation and class reference as well as the download archive, which contains additional demo projects.

Using Audio Files in SpriteBuilder

Although you can add audio files directly to the Xcode project, bypassing SpriteBuilder, it is recommended that you allow SpriteBuilder to manage all audio files, whether they'll be used in Timelines or not.

Importing Audio into SpriteBuilder

If you use SpriteBuilder to manage your audio files, you needn't worry too much about the audio format details. It's best if your input files are uncompressed audio files like WAV files.

In the book's downloadable archive is an Audio folder that contains the audio files. If you want to use your own audio files, you can use any other audio files instead, but they should be in .wav or .caf format. You should visit http://opengameart.org if you are looking for free sound effects and music, but keep in mind that "free to download" doesn't necessarily mean "free to use in a commercial app." Always check the licenses for OpenGameArt resources to see if re-use in commercial applications is allowed. (The commercial apps category includes free apps showing commercial ads.)

I assume you have either located or created an *Audio* folder that contains two music files, named *game-music.wav* and *menu-music.wav*, and short sound effects named *menu-sfx.wav*, *splat1.wav*, *splat2.wav*, and *splat3.wav*. You should drag and drop the *Audio* folder onto SpriteBuilder's *File View* so that the *Audio* folder appears in the *File View*. If you select one of the .wav files in the *Audio* folder, you'll see a preview image with settings as shown in Figure 11-2.

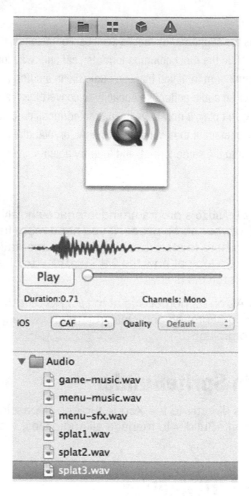

Figure 11-2. Audio file preview and settings

You can play back the audio within SpriteBuilder using the *Play* button. Underneath, you see the duration expressed in seconds and an indication of whether the audio file is mono or stereo. Below that are the publishing settings, where you can choose between CAF format (uncompressed) for short sound effects and MP4 format (compressed) for long-running audio. The MP4 format also allows you to change the quality setting. The lower the quality setting is, the smaller the resulting file will be. The default audio quality settings are editable in the *File ➤ Project Settings* dialog.

SpriteBuilder will automatically assume an imported audio file shorter than 15 seconds is a sound effect and will thus select the corresponding CAF format. Otherwise, it will have MP4 preselected for you. Also note, at the time of this writing, only audio files with the .caf and .wav extensions could be imported. If you already have files in the .mp3 or .m4a format, you can either add them to Xcode directly or, preferably, convert them to .wav or .caf to be able to manage them with SpriteBuilder.

Playing Sound Effects via the Timeline

In SpriteBuilder, you can add sound-effects keyframes to any Timeline. This is most useful if you need to synchronize audio playback with other Timeline animations, such as the appearance of an object or matching the moment when the moving object starts to slow down. Timeline sound effects will be played through OALSimpleAudio's effects channel, thus using OpenAL for playback regardless of the file format.

> **Caution**   If the node owning a Timeline's CCBAnimationManager deallocates, any sound effect played through that Timeline will be cut short (stopped) or won't even get to play at all. This typically affects the playback of audio files with a duration longer than the Timeline whose end has the node removed from the scene—for instance, via a *Callbacks* keyframe.

In SpriteBuilder, open *MainMenuButtons.ccb* in the *UserInterface* folder. The goal is to synchronize the sound-effects playback with the appearance of the logo and buttons.

You can add *Sound effects* keyframes just like *Callbacks* keyframes by holding down the Option key, and then left-clicking to add a keyframe. You should add a total of three *Sound effects* keyframes. Place the first one near the start of the Timeline, and place the other two close to when the *Play* and *Settings* buttons start to appear. Refer to Figure 11-4 for the final result.

To actually have the keyframes play back a sound effect, you have to double-click each one to edit the keyframe's properties. The popover menu is shown in Figure 11-3. From the popover menu, select an audio file. The leftmost keyframe should use the *Audio/splat2.wav* file, while the other two keyframes should use *Audio/splat3.wav*.

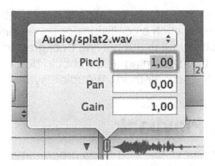

Figure 11-3. Assigning an audio file to a Sound effects keyframe

Feel free to play with the *Pitch*, *Pan*, and *Gain* settings. A pitch of 1.0 means the audio file will be played back at its original pitch (frequency). Choose a value between 0.01 and 1.0 to lower the sound's pitch, which will also increase its duration. Use a value above 1.0 to increase the pitch and shorten its duration. A pitch of 2.0 will play back the effect at twice its original speed.

Pan is in the range of −1.0 and 1.0, where −1.0 plays the sound effect entirely on the left speaker and 1.0 plays it only on the right speaker. The default panning value of 0.0 plays the sound equally on both speakers. Panning has no effect on stereo files; only mono audio files can be panned.

The *Gain* setting increases the sound's volume. It's not quite the same as volume though. If you increase *Gain* by too much, it will add distortion to the sound. But, generally, it can be used to level out some sounds that would otherwise be 10 to 20% quieter or louder than other sounds. A value of 1.0 means the volume is unchanged. Lower values reduce the volume, while higher values increase it.

Once you've moved the keyframes to the desired locations and assigned the audio files, the result will resemble Figure 11-4. Notice that the audio file waveforms may run past the end of the Timeline, indicating that the audio plays longer than the Timeline. Whether this is or isn't a problem depends on the situation. Here it doesn't matter.

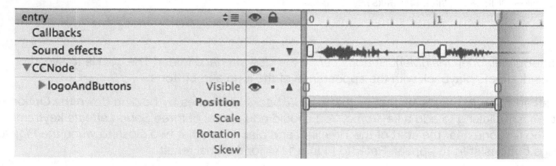

Figure 11-4.   Three Sound effects keyframes with assigned audio files

If you publish and run the game, the menu logo and buttons should appear together with the sound effects. This will be repeated if you exit the game and return to the main menu.

While this is neat and dandy, the sound-effects Timeline is not suitable for playing sounds that need to be synchronized with game events, such as collisions or acceleration. It also can't be used to play back looping sounds, which effectively rules out playing background music through the Timeline— even when you put aside the fact that streaming audio should be played back through ObjectAL's "long audio" background audio-playback method (AVAudioPlayer).

Programming Audio Playback

Streaming audio and audio for game events need to be programmed, but that's rather easy with ObjectAL's simplified interface provided by the OALSimpleAudio class. You'll find the class reference here: `http://kstenerud.github.io/ObjectAL-for-iPhone/documentation/interface_o_a_l_simple_audio.html`.

Playing Long/Streaming Audio

You generally have two ways of playing streaming audio. ObjectAL refers to streaming audio as "background" music, usually abbreviated as "bg." One way to play it is to preload a piece of streaming audio and then play it. Or you can play a piece of music without preloading it.

Preloading background tracks is only required if you need to start the playback at a very specific point in time (in seconds) by using by the seekTime parameter. Or when you need to be sure that the background track starts playing with no delay whatsoever—for example, if it's a speech audio that needs to be lip-synched. Listing 11-1 shows an example of playing a preloaded background track.

Listing 11-1. Preloading a background track and playing it at a later time

```
OALSimpleAudio* audio = [OALSimpleAudio sharedInstance];
[audio preloadBg:@"Audio/menu-music.m4a" seekTime:0.0];

// later you can play back the most recently preloaded track:
[audio playBgWithLoop:YES];
```

In the OALSimpleAudio interface, there is no delegate mechanism or notification that tells you when preloading has finished, nor is there a need to have one. Preloading is not multithreaded. In the preceding example, execution will not continue to the playBgWithLoop method unless preloadBg has done its job and already preloaded the file.

Caution   As with other resource files, the audio file is in a subfolder in the SpriteBuilder project. Thus, the Audio folder needs to be specified in the path. And if the audio file's output type is set to MP4, its file extension will be .m4a (audio-only MPEG-4) and not .mp4 (regular audio/video MPEG-4).

In addition to that, specifying the published file extensions (.m4a and .caf) as in these examples is not recommended if you plan to port to Android. All Audio files for Android will be published in the OGG format with the .ogg extension. By the time you read this, Cocos2D respectively ObjectAL will allow you to omit the audio file extension altogether or you can use the audio file's original extension (.wav).

In most cases, it's simpler and fast enough to just play the background music directly. Open the *MainScene.m* file in Xcode, and locate the didLoadFromCCB method. Add the lines highlighted in Listing 11-2 to the end of the method.

Listing 11-2. Adding music playback to MainScene.m

```
-(void) didLoadFromCCB
{
    // existing code omitted for brevity ...

    OALSimpleAudio* audio = [OALSimpleAudio sharedInstance];
    [audio playBg:@"Audio/menu-music.m4a" loop:YES];
}
```

The playBg method internally preloads the audio file before playing it. With looping enabled, the audio track will loop indefinitely. The drawback of playing audio this way is that you can't specify a seekTime.

Let's complete the music playback by opening *SceneManager.m* and locating its presentGameScene method. In order to play the game music, add the code highlighted in Listing 11-3 to the end of the method.

Listing 11-3. Playing game music when presenting the game scene

```
-(void) presentGameScene
{
    // existing code omitted for brevity ...

    OALSimpleAudio* audio = [OALSimpleAudio sharedInstance];
    [audio playBg:@"Audio/game-music.m4a" loop:YES];
}
```

If you play the game now, you should hear music playing in the menu and different music when you play the game.

You may want to improve this behavior—for instance, to have the game music track start over if you advance from one level to another or restart the level. One way to fix that is to extend the presentGameScene method in SceneManager with an additional parameter of type BOOL—for instance, presentGameSceneWithMusic:(BOOL)playMusic. You would only pass in YES for playMusic when presenting the game scene from the main menu; otherwise, you would pass NO to that parameter. Inside the method, add a condition to play the music only when playMusic is YES.

Playing Sound Effects

Assuming you'll want to play a sound effect every time a popover layer is closed, you can do so easily by adding the code highlighted in Listing 11-4 at the end of the shouldClose method found in *CloseButton.m*.

Listing 11-4. Playing a sound effect when closing popovers

```
-(void) shouldClose
{
    // existing code omitted for brevity ...

    [[OALSimpleAudio sharedInstance] playEffect:@"Audio/menu-sfx.caf"];
}
```

The menu sound effect is small and not time-critical, so it's not a problem to play it without preloading. But unlike background tracks, sound effects played during gameplay should always be preloaded. Otherwise, the first time a specific sound effect plays, there may be a small but possibly noticeable hiccup. Imagine if the player jumps, shoots, or gets hit and the game freezes for a tenth of a second the first time this happens because the sound effect needed to be loaded from relatively slow flash memory. You'll want to avoid that scenario even if the sound effects used in this particular project will most likely load quickly enough that you will not notice a delay.

Unfortunately, there's no way to assign audio files to a given scene and then tell it to preload all associated audio files. You essentially have to keep a list of sound effects used by a given scene, or by the game overall, and then preload those sound effects one after another. Fortunately, in this project you're using only three gameplay sound effects, and they're consistently named. (See Figure 11-2.)

Add the code highlighted in Listing 11-5 at the end of the presentGameScene method in *SceneManager.m*.

Listing 11-5. Preloading all splat sound effects

```
+(void) presentGameScene
{
    // existing code omitted for brevity ...

    OALSimpleAudio* audio = [OALSimpleAudio sharedInstance];
    for (int i = 1; i <= 3; i++)
    {
        NSString* path = [NSString stringWithFormat:@"Audio/splat%i.caf", i];
        [audio preloadEffect:path];
    }
}
```

Here the path string for every audio file is generated within the for loop. It helps to have similar audio files numbered in the same way so that if you were to add a dozen more, you would need to increase only the loop's upper bound—even though there's nothing speaking against preloading the three existing audio files without a loop. For example, the following will do the job just as well:

```
[audio preloadEffect:@"Audio/splat1.caf"];
[audio preloadEffect:@"Audio/splat2.caf"];
[audio preloadEffect:@"Audio/splat3.caf"];
```

To play back a preloaded sound effect, you would simply play it with the exact same path you've used to preload it—for instance:

```
[[OALSimpleAudio sharedInstance] playEffect:@"Audio/splat3.caf"];
```

Be sure to watch the Xcode Debug Console (*View ➤ Debug Area ➤ Activate Console*) for any ObjectAL errors. For instance, if you try to preload or play an audio file that isn't in the bundle or where you made a mistake in the path, you'll see it logged in the console:

```
OAL Error: +[OALTools urlForPath:bundle:]: Could not find full path of file Audio/splash3.caf
```

When and where to play sound effects is a good design question. In this project, you'll play the splat sounds whenever the player impacts the gears, springs, chains, and ropes, but only if the impact was significant. One way to decide that is to look at the CCPhysicsCollisionPair object passed into every physics-collision delegate method.

The CCPhysicsCollisionPair method contains two properties, totalImpulse and totalKineticEnergy, that reveal both the impulse vector (that is, the direction of impact force) and the total energy dissipated by the impact. The latter may seem odd for physics buffs: energy doesn't dissipate; it only changes form. However, in computer-game physics simulations, there is no concept of heat, which is the most common form of how impact energy is transformed. Therefore, it is simply said that *energy dissipates*, or is lost, when there is a forceful impact. Otherwise, the physics simulation couldn't get rid of the colliding body's velocities, effectively making all collisions "perfect" in the sense that the sum of the velocities of both impacting bodies would remain the same.

The totalKineticEnergy is only non-zero for significant impacts. We can use that to simply assume a splat sound needs to be played if the totalKineticEnergy is non-zero. Add the method in Listing 11-6 to *GameScene.m*, preferably just below the ccPhysicsCollisionBegin methods.

Listing 11-6. Playing impact sounds

```
-(void) playCollisionSoundWithPair:(CCPhysicsCollisionPair*)pair
{
    if (pair.totalKineticEnergy > 0.0)
    {
        NSString* splat = [NSString stringWithFormat:@"Audio/splat%i.caf",
                            arc4random_uniform(3) + 1];

        CGFloat pitch = 0.8 + (arc4random_uniform(50) / 100.0);
        [[OALSimpleAudio sharedInstance] playEffect:splat
                                    volume:1.0
                                     pitch:pitch
                                       pan:0.0
                                      loop:NO];
    }
}
```

If totalKineticEnergy is greater than zero, the impact dissipated energy and therefore must have been significant. In this case, one of three splat sound effects is chosen randomly. The arc4random_uniform(3) method returns an integer number less than 3—in other words, a number in the range of 0 to 2. By adding 1, you get a number in the range of 1 to 3.

> **Tip**   There are many ways to generate random numbers, but only arc4random methods come closest to generating "truly random" numbers. The arc4random_uniform variant specifically generates uniformly distributed random numbers without (modulo) bias. An explanation would go too far, so I'll just say it's generally recommended to favor arc4random_uniform() over rand() and other random-number methods.

The effect is played using OALSimpleAudio's playEffect variant with the most parameters. Next to the audio file itself, you can specify a volume to play the effect at. This volume is not an absolute volume but relative to the effectsVolume property that we'll be getting at next. A playEffect volume of 1.0 means the audio file is played at the same volume as effectsVolume.

The pitch is randomized between 0.8 and 1.3 to create greater sound variety without having to use multiple effects. This also shows an example of how to generate floating-point numbers with arc4random_uniform. If you divide a value in the range of 0 to 49 and divide it by 100.0, you get a value in the range of 0.0 to 0.49. Note that it's important to write *100.0* with the dot or casting the value: (CGFloat)100. If the divisor is simply written as *100*, it is an integer division that always results in *0*.

To quickly test this sound effect playback, add the highlighted line in Listing 11-7 to the ccPhysicsCollisionBegin: method that is called when the player collides with a spring object.

Listing 11-7. Playing a sound effect when colliding with springs

```
-(BOOL) ccPhysicsCollisionBegin:(CCPhysicsCollisionPair *)pair
                         player:(CCNode *)player
                         spring:(SpringBoard *)spring
{
    [spring letGo];
    [self playCollisionSoundWithPair:pair];
    return YES;
}
```

You should also add two more ccPhysicsCollisionBegin methods, pairing the player with obstacles and gears. Add the code in Listing 11-8 below the other ccPhysicsCollisionBegin methods.

Listing 11-8. Playing sound effects when colliding with obstacles and gears

```
-(BOOL) ccPhysicsCollisionBegin:(CCPhysicsCollisionPair *)pair
                         player:(CCNode *)player
                       obstacle:(CCNode*)obstacle
{
    [self playCollisionSoundWithPair:pair];
    return YES;
}

-(BOOL) ccPhysicsCollisionBegin:(CCPhysicsCollisionPair *)pair
                         player:(CCNode *)player
                           gear:(CCNode*)gear
{
    [self playCollisionSoundWithPair:pair];
    return YES;
}
```

In order for the latter two collision methods to be called, you will have to open *Chain.ccb*, *Rope.ccb*, and *Gear1.ccb* in SpriteBuilder. Then edit the corresponding physics *Collision* type for the chain and rope elements and for the gear's physics body. The *Collision* type for *Chain* and *Rope* should be *obstacle*, and the collision type for *Gear* should be *gear*.

If you play the game now, you should at least hear the occasional sound effect playing, in particular when touching springs. The current setup isn't great sound design, but it shows the basic principle of playing sound and determining the force of an impact.

Not Playing Sound Effects for a Short While

A common problem when playing sound effects for game events—specifically, if there are physics collisions involved—is that sound effects may play repeatedly in a short time frame. Either the new sound always cuts off the previous one or the new sounds add to the already-playing sounds, increasing the volume and general noisiness of the effect. Both are generally undesirable.

With OALSimpleAudio, there is no way to determine whether a given sound effect is still playing or to be notified of its completion. Instead, you have to add a BOOL ivar that you flip on when playing the sound and flip off after a short time period.

Add the ivar shown in Listing 11-9 to *GameScene.m*.

Listing 11-9. Adding the play sound flag

```
@implementation GameScene
{
    // existing ivars omitted ...

    BOOL _playingCollisionSound;
}
```

Then improve the playCollisionSoundWithPair: method in Listing 11-6 with the lines highlighted in Listing 11-10.

Listing 11-10. Don't play a new sound effect for a short time after a sound effect has started playing

```
-(void) playCollisionSoundWithPair:(CCPhysicsCollisionPair*)pair
{
    if (_playingCollisionSound == NO)
    {
        NSString* splat = [NSString stringWithFormat:@"Audio/splat%i.caf",
                            arc4random_uniform(3) + 1];

        CGFloat pitch = 0.8 + (arc4random_uniform(50) / 100.0);
        [[OALSimpleAudio sharedInstance] playEffect:splat
                                        volume:1.0
                                        pitch:pitch
                                        pan:0.0
                                        loop:NO];

        _playingCollisionSound = YES;
        [self scheduleBlock:^(CCTimer *timer) {
            _playingCollisionSound = NO;
        } delay:0.4];
    }
}
```

Now the sound effect is no longer tied to totalKineticEnergy but plays on every collision. Without the _playingCollisionSound flag, this will likely cause the sound to be played repeatedly in a short time frame. Therefore, it is set to YES when playing the sound, and a block is scheduled with a 0.4-second delay to reset the _playingCollisionSound ivar to NO so that the next collision will play another sound effect.

You should apply this principle to all sounds that must not be played again for a short time after a sound effect of the same type has begun playing.

Adjusting Audio Volumes

You probably remember that you've already created a Settings popover with volume sliders. Now would be a good time to make them functional.

Open *SettingsLayer.m* in Xcode, and add the _playingEffectSliderAudio ivar highlighted in Listing 11-11.

Listing 11-11. Adding another playback timing variable

```
@implementation SettingsLayer
{
    __weak CCSlider* _musicSlider;
    __weak CCSlider* _effectsSlider;

    BOOL _playingEffectSliderAudio;
}
```

Then add the highlighted lines of Listing 11-12 to the volumeDidChange: method in *SettingsLayer.m*.

Listing 11-12. Playing a sound effect when moving the sound-effect slider

```
-(void) volumeDidChange:(CCSlider*)sender
{
    if (sender == _musicSlider)
    {
        [GameState sharedGameState].musicVolume = _musicSlider.sliderValue;
    }
    else if (sender == _effectsSlider)
    {
        [GameState sharedGameState].effectsVolume = _effectsSlider.sliderValue;

        if (_playingEffectSliderAudio == NO)
        {
            [[OALSimpleAudio sharedInstance] playEffect:@"Audio/menu-sfx.caf"];

            _playingEffectSliderAudio = YES;
            [self scheduleBlock:^(CCTimer *timer) {
                _playingEffectSliderAudio = NO;
            } delay:0.2f];
        }
    }
}
```

This will play a sound effect as an audio cue when moving the sound-effects volume slider. The sound is prevented from repeating for 0.2 seconds to make it a little more pleasing to the ears.

Without playing the sound effect, when dragging the sound-effects volume slider the player wouldn't know how loud a given volume actually is. You don't have this problem with music since the menu music is already playing and will adjust its volume when you drag the music volume slider.

To actually change the volumes used by OALSimpleAudio's effects and background channels, you'll have to edit the *GameState.m* file. Locate the setMusicVolume and setEffectsVolume methods, and add the highlighted lines of Listing 11-13.

Listing 11-13. Changing volumes

```
-(void) setMusicVolume:(CGFloat)volume
{
    [OALSimpleAudio sharedInstance].bgVolume = volume;
    [[NSUserDefaults standardUserDefaults] setDouble:volume
                                        forKey:KeyForMusicVolume];
}

-(void) setEffectsVolume:(CGFloat)volume
{
    [OALSimpleAudio sharedInstance].effectsVolume = volume;
    [[NSUserDefaults standardUserDefaults] setDouble:volume
                                        forKey:KeyForEffectsVolume];
}
```

The sound volume sliders are now functional. Feel free to try them out. Notice that the volumes are not respected when starting the app, however. To fix that, add the highlighted lines of Listing 11-14 to the sharedGameState method in *GameState.m*.

Listing 11-14. Initializing volumes upon launching the app

```
+(GameState*) sharedGameState
{
    static GameState* sharedInstance;
    static dispatch_once_t onceToken;
    dispatch_once(&onceToken, ^{
        sharedInstance = [[GameState alloc] init];
        OALSimpleAudio audio = [OALSimpleAudio sharedInstance];
        audio.effectsVolume = sharedInstance.effectsVolume;
        audio.bgVolume = sharedInstance.musicVolume;
    });
    return sharedInstance;
}
```

This sets the volumes of OALSimpleAudio to the volumes restored from the GameState sharedInstance, which ensures the volumes are loaded from NSUserDefaults the first time the class GameState is used. This is guaranteed to happen very early in the game, but it could be forced by adding a seemingly nonsensical line like the following:

```
[GameState sharedGameState];
```

This would just initialize the singleton (if it isn't already), discarding the returned instance.

Working with Labels

Thus far, I haven't provided a thorough introduction to label-specific properties. And I haven't mentioned the fact that you can localize them or explained why there are two types of labels: TTF (TrueType font) and BM-Font (bitmap font).

Importing a Custom TrueType Font

In principle, adding a custom TrueType font to SpriteBuilder is as simple as dragging and dropping it onto the project. In the book's *Graphics* archive, you'll find a *Fonts* folder that you should drag and drop onto SpriteBuilder's *File View*. Alternatively, create a *Fonts* folder and drag and drop a custom .ttf file into it. You can easily find TrueType fonts on the web—just be careful that the font is distributed under a permissive license or is in the public domain.

You can then select the font on the *Item Properties* tab of a *Label TTF* node. Click on the *Font name* drop-down list in the *CCLabelTTF* section, select the *User Fonts* section, and browse into the *Fonts* folder. The *System Fonts* are the fonts that are built into iOS and always available.

In practice, there are several hurdles that may prevent you from using the custom TrueType font. First of all, it needs to be a valid file. Double-clicking the .ttf file in Finder should open the Font Book app, displaying an alphabet of glyphs. If that doesn't happen or you get an error, the font is most likely corrupt or not in the correct format.

Next you have to consider that the font name does not necessarily refer to the font's file name. There are three names for a font: its file name, its family name, and its font name. For use in SpriteBuilder, the font name and file name (excluding the file extension) should match; otherwise, the font will not work.

Once you have added a TrueType font to SpriteBuilder, publish and add the code fragment in Listing 11-15 to any method that runs when the app launches—for instance, the `didLoadFromCCB` method in *MainScene.m*.

Listing 11-15. Logging a font family and names

```
for (NSString* family in [UIFont familyNames])
{
    NSLog(@"%@ (family)", family);
    for (NSString* name in [UIFont fontNamesForFamilyName:family])
    {
        NSLog(@"   %@ (name)", name);
    }
}
```

Check the Debug Console in Xcode. If you added the PARPG.ttf font file from the Graphics archive, the log will print something like this amidst many other fonts:

```
2014-09-09 16:36:25.433 LearnSpriteBuilder[91808:60b] Fixed (family)
2014-09-09 16:36:25.434 LearnSpriteBuilder[91808:60b]    PARPG (name)
```

It shows that the font family is oddly named "Fixed," while the font name is identical to the font's file name. In cases where you have a font file whose file name doesn't match the font name, you should simply rename the font, re-import it in SpriteBuilder, and update any labels in question to use the font with the new name.

Note   Using a custom TrueType font with SpriteBuilder does not require editing the *Info.plist* file. You would only have to if you wanted to add a custom TrueType font but aren't using SpriteBuilder to do so.

Whether the importing of the TrueType font was successful can only be determined by running the app. SpriteBuilder will use and display the font correctly. However, when you run the game and there's a mismatch between the font name and the font's file name, the font will be replaced with a font of a closely related (or wild guess) font family. More often than not, this means that Arial will be used in place of the custom font. It shouldn't be too hard to notice, but a safe indicator is when the label's dimensions aren't the same as in SpriteBuilder.

Editing Label Properties

The *CCLabelTTF* properties were partially covered in Figure 6-4 where the label is edited as part of a *Button* node. Now let's look at the label properties as shown by an actual *Label TTF* node. See Figure 11-5 for reference.

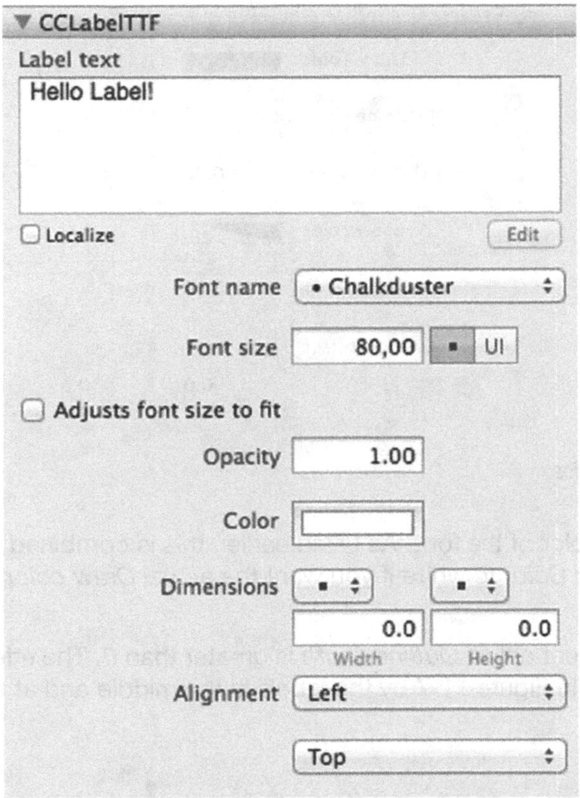

Figure 11-5. Label TTF properties

The *Label text* field obviously allows text entry. Underneath it is the *Localize* check box, and to the right of it the localization *Edit* button. The *Label text* field and the *Localize* check box also exist for *Label BM-Font* nodes. I'll explain how localization works shortly.

Font name and *Font size* should be pretty clear by now. The *Opacity* is the same as for sprites and tells how transparent the label is—in the range of 0 (fully transparent) to 1 (opaque). The *Color* property affects the label's texture but has the same effect as setting the draw color. Interestingly, you can set both *Color* and *Draw Color* under the *Font Effects* section to create a sort of combined color. To avoid that side-effect, make sure that either *Color* or *Draw Color* is set to white.

The *Adjusts font size to fit* check box is slightly misplaced—it actually belongs to the *Dimensions* property further down. If you set a non-zero dimension and check *Adjusts font size to fit*, the font will use the largest possible font size to fit all the text on a single line into the given dimensions. Naturally, this means that *Adjusts font size to fit* also disables line wrapping. *Alignment* defines how the label is aligned within its dimensions.

Label TTF nodes have a special section labeled *Font Effects*, where you can edit outlines and shadows. See Figure 11-6 for reference.

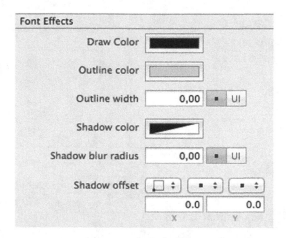

Figure 11-6. Font Effects properties

The draw color is the fill color of the font. As I said earlier, this is combined with the node's *Color* property. So be sure to set *Color* to white if you want the actual *Draw color* being used to be unchanged.

The *Outline color* takes effect only if *Outline width* is greater than *0*. The effect of setting *Outline width* to *2* and *8* is shown in Figure 11-7 by the labels in the middle and at the bottom.

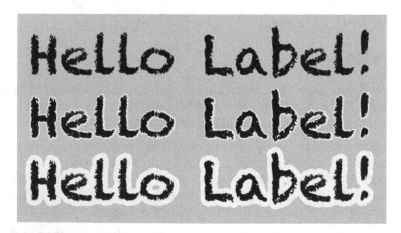

Figure 11-7. Label TTF outline widths from top to bottom: no outline, 2 points, and 8 points

Shadow color also takes effect only if the *Shadow blur* radius is greater than *0*. With *Shadow offset*, you can alter the position of the shadow underneath the label. Figure 11-8 shows example shadows with a blur radius of *8* and *24*, offset slightly to the right and down.

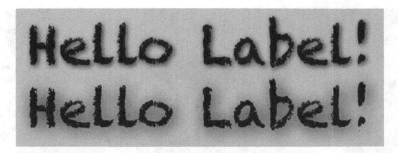

Figure 11-8. Label TTF with shadows that have a blur radius of 8 (top) and 24 (bottom)

You can create rather interesting effects by combining outlines and shadows with a little experimentation.

Adding a Credits String

Let's try adding a neat-looking credits label that you can then use to test the translation feature. Open *MainScene.ccb*, and drag and drop a *Label TTF* node onto the stage. Change the label's position types to % and values to 50x7 on the *Item Properties* tab.

As *Label text*, enter the following without the quotes: "Made with SpriteBuilder & Cocos2D". As *Font name*, use the Fonts/PARPG.ttf font that you'll find by browsing into the *User Fonts* section of the drop-down menu. Use a *Font size* of *23*. You may later want to decrease the font size, but for now let's assume you want to optimize the label size for the English language to see what can happen when you switch to a different localization setting.

Under the *Font Effects* section, change the *Draw Color*. The actual colors aren't that important, but I'll tell you which ones I used. In the color-picker dialog, click the middle tab of the five tabs at the top, and select *Web Safe Colors* from the *Palette* drop-down menu. Then find the brownish color labeled *CC6633*. Repeat the same for the *Outline Color*, which should be set to *330033*, and set the *Shadow Color* to *FF9966*. The *Outline width* should be set to *2*, and set the *Shadow blur radius* to *12*.

This should make a neat-looking label with an outline and shadow that sort of blends in with the background. See Figure 11-9.

Figure 11-9. Main menu with a credits label

Localizing the Credits Label

Localization of text is done by providing multiple-language versions of the same text under the same key. A *key* is any text string (usually the original English text) used to identify a set of localized strings.

In *MainScene.ccb*, select the *CCLabelTTF with the credits* text, which is the one that you've added most recently. Under the *Label text* field, check the *Localize* check box. This enables the *Edit* button to the right of the check box. Click the *Edit* button. This brings up the string localization dialog shown in Figure 11-10.

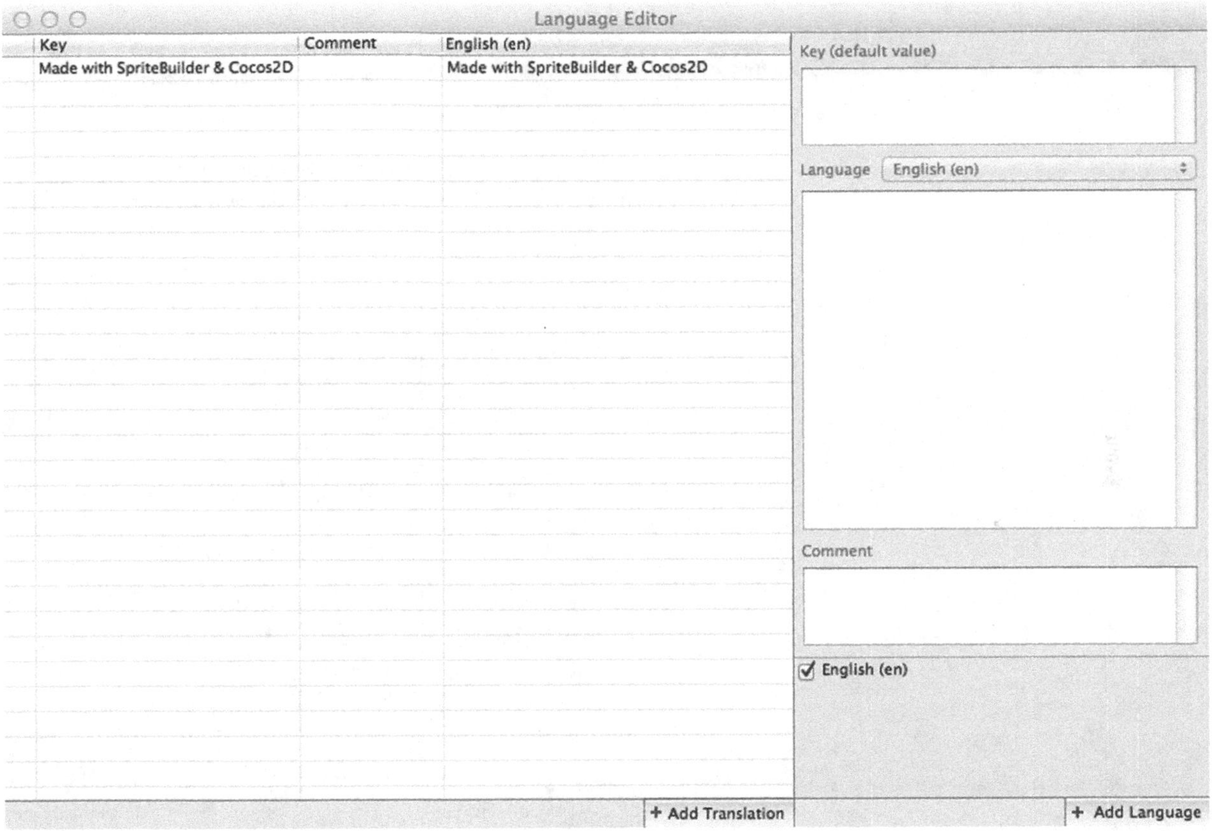

Figure 11-10. The initial localization dialog with just one string and one language

The very first thing you need to do when adding localized strings is add one or more languages. Click the *+Add Language* button to bring up a drop-down list of possible languages. You can use any language you like. I went with German because that's what I grew up with. After adding a language, it will appear in the list at the bottom right. But adding a language also adds another column to the text grid view on the left. And it places a yellow exclamation mark icon to the left of the *Key* column, because for the given *Key*, there is no German translation yet. See Figure 11-11.

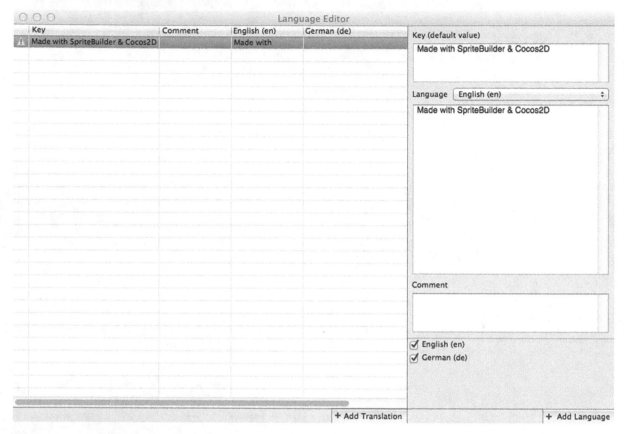

Figure 11-11. After adding German as a language, the columns are updated and the warning icon indicates missing translation text

Now all you have to do is to enter text in the *German (de)* column for the only string that's currently in the localization dialog. Enter the following as a possible German translation (without quotes): "Entwickelt mit SpriteBuilder & Cocos2D". Be sure to enter the string in the *German (de)* column. If you've done this correctly, the warning icon should be gone.

You can leave the *Comment* field empty. It can be used to leave notes for the translators, perhaps to mention the maximum number of characters this string must not exceed in any language.

Note that you can and should change the entry in the *Key* column, mainly to prevent you from accidentally editing the key where you meant to enter an actual language string. I prefer to use all uppercase characters for keys to highlight the fact that it is a key, not an actual string used by labels. Enter **CREDITS_LABEL** as the key.

When you are done editing, just close the window via the red X button in the upper left corner.

Depending on whether your SpriteBuilder version automatically synchronizes the key from the localization dialog with the label's text field, you may or may not have to edit the *Label text* field. Enter **CREDITS_LABEL** in the *Label text* field if it contains any other text. You'll notice that the label no longer changes to the text in the *Label text* field. That's because the meaning of the *Label text* field changes when *Localize* is enabled. It becomes the localized string's key.

You can quickly try out your localized string within SpriteBuilder. From the menu, select *Document* ➤ *View in Language* ➤ *German (de)* to see the German version of this screen. All localized labels with a corresponding German string will show up in German. Those labels that have missing strings for the selected language will show the key instead. This is another good reason to use all-caps text for keys or any other style to clearly differentiate keys from actual strings. Figure 11-12 shows the menu screen with labels translated into German.

Figure 11-12. The main menu with labels translated into German

As you can see in Figure 11-12, two labels no longer fit because they run longer with German text. This is just scratching the surface of why localization is difficult and time consuming, especially if it wasn't considered from the get-go. Although you can reduce the credit label's font size in the German version, you'd have to do so in code. And that option is not suitable for the *Settings* button—if you made that label any smaller, you could barely read the text anymore, if at all.

Last, the logo remains in English. Localization of resource files is planned for a future SpriteBuilder update, but there's no estimated time of arrival for that at the time of this writing. You have to localize any audio (speech) and image files using the regular iOS app internationalization techniques for now.

Localization Considerations

If you want to properly localize your app, you have to consider the following problem areas:

- **String length**   Some languages are more verbose than others. That doesn't mean that the verbose language doesn't have a very short word for a rather long word in the original language.

- **Foreign characters**   These require proper string handling. All strings should be Unicode and properly encoded. A user will want to save documents using all language characters, and your app should allow it and not crash when the name of a file contains an umlaut, acute or grave character—let alone Arabian, Russian, or Asian characters.

- **Date, time, and number formats**   These may be different. For instance, in the USA the value 1,001 is a thousand and one, but for us Germans it's just barely more than 1. Also, consider that we format our dates with the least significant number first: 16/12/14 is the sixteenth of December in the year 2014. For you, this date may not make any sense. For us Germans, the slashes are unusual date separators; we use dots.

- **Localization**   This must not affect your app's storage format, such as savegames. A common problem is saving a number like 1,234 to a file on a device with an English locale. With the locale changed to German, the app is relaunched and reads the value back as 1.234 or raises a runtime error because the app doesn't (correctly) interpret the dot.

- **Currency**   The currency may be different for the language you switch to. It could be USD, Euros, Pound, Yen—you name it.

- **Units of measure**   These also may be different. How many elbows is a yard, anyway? How many inches are in a yard, and do I really need to know? In Europe and other countries, lengths are measured in meters and centimeters. Who knows, maybe some country even measures weight in potatoes and toes. And the German shoe sizes for typical adults are mostly in the range of 36 to 46, not 6 to 12 and a shirt size of 52-54 translates to the abbreviation XXL in the UK/US. So you can't even rely on sizes being numbers or letters everywhere.

- **Onscreen vs. offscreen keyboards**   These have different layouts. Especially OS X apps should react to a key's keycode rather than the letter it prints—for instance, the WASD keys are scattered across a Dvorak keyboard. But generally, you need to consider that nonalphabet and nondigit characters may be harder to write in some languages, requiring the use of Shift and Control keys or switching the onscreen keyboard to a different page.

- **Word order**   The order of adjectives, nouns, and verbs in a sentence may be different or understood differently. This can be crucial for name generators. For instance, in an RPG that generates "Plentiful Sword of Hurting," the direct translation in the same order of words might read more like "Hurting Sword of Plenty" to a French speaker, somewhat or even completely altering its meaning.

- **Proper nouns**   These needn't be translated. The most obvious case is the app's name. Should the book's app be called "Hüpfende Bestie" in German, or would you rather leave it as "Bouncy Beast" internationally? Of course, the translator needs to be aware of any proper nouns, including character and location names.

- **Cultural differences**   It's customary in one country to greet with "How are you?" which may be seen as disingenuous politeness and generally unfitting in other regions of this world. Likewise, gestures can also be a problem. Probably the best known offender is the thumbs up, which is considered rude and offensive in Islamic and Asian countries. In Australia, it is so-so—by moving the gesture up and down, it becomes a grave insult.

- **Context**   The same words can mean different things depending on context in some languages. In one context, it's a confirmation; in another context, it's an insult.

- **Pronunciation**   Some languages have subtle variations in pronunciation for the same word that can make all the difference between two completely different meanings.

- **Embedded text**   Avoid embedding text in images that need to be translated. This will increase the app size for everyone, and you'll have to re-create each image with the translated text. Translation services will not translate images for you, only text.

- **Auto-translation services**   These don't work well enough. Forget Babelfish or Google Translate unless you want your users to laugh and cry at your app and generally consider your attempt at translation a cheap effort. It significantly decreases the app's subjective value in the eyes of the user if it was clearly translated by a computer.

I used to work on game-translation tools and processes. If the preceding list sounds like a lot to consider, I can tell you it's just the tip of the iceberg. And I'm merely recalling these issues from memory; I probably neglected to mention a few more things to consider.

Fortunately, you don't have to consider all cases, as they won't all apply to your app. And as an independent developer, you're more easily forgiven if your app is English-only or provides great fun for players despite the occasional localization oddity. Yet there's a real risk for ridicule if you try to translate cheaply or automatically. In that case, it's probably better not to translate at all.

Also, iOS provides ways to format strings in a localized manner, based on the device's locale. For example, you can format dates in the current locale by passing an `NSDate` through a `NSDateFormatter`.

> **Tip**   You'll find a plethora of helpful information on Apple's Internationalization website: `https://developer.apple.com/internationalization/`.

TrueType vs. Bitmap Fonts

On modern GUI operating systems, TrueType fonts with the .ttf or similar extension are used almost exclusively. Their main benefit is that they scale to any dimension without losing quality, because TrueType fonts describe the characters (also called *glyphs*) as outlines. A glyph's outlines are either straight lines or Bezier curves. With a purely mathematical description of the glyphs in a font, it is possible to render them at various point sizes with clearly defined, sharp outlines. A glyph can also be expressed with a relatively small dataset, thus TrueType fonts are typically smaller in file size than a bitmap font.

Bitmap fonts are relatively common in games. They don't scale without losing image quality, but they render faster because glyphs in a bitmap font are just sprites that need to be drawn at the right position, rather than each outline and curve having to be calculated by the CPU and then drawn onto the frame buffer. With the font being sprites, you can also use any image as a glyph. The screenshot of Glyph Designer in Figure 11-13 illustrates this perfectly.

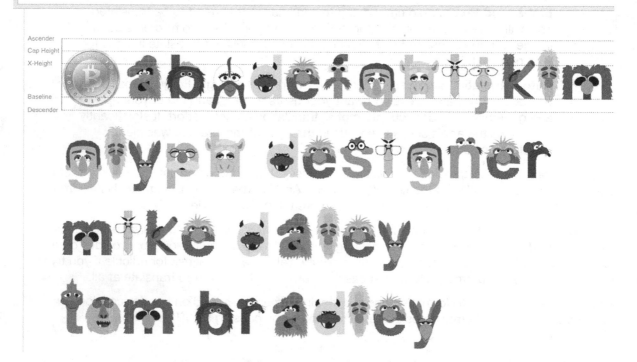

Figure 11-13. Any image can be used as a glyph in a bitmap font

As long as a label's text doesn't change at all, the rendering performance of TrueType and bitmap fonts in Cocos2D is the same. Both are drawn just like sprites. If you are considering having multiple labels using the same font, bitmap fonts will be faster because the bitmap font can draw all glyphs from the same texture, whereas the TrueType label uses a unique texture for each label. This also affects memory usage—with few labels, TrueType fonts may require less memory, but each additional TrueType font label eats up significantly more memory than additional bitmap font labels using the same font.

Also, if the text of a TrueType font changes, a new texture needs to be created with the new text rendering. It's the throwing away the old texture and replacing it with a new one part that makes TrueType labels particularly unfitting for text that frequently changes. The larger the area occupied by the label, the longer it takes to update its text.

So while you can make decent menus with TrueType fonts and get to choose from a great variety of fonts, for any in-game UI text that changes frequently (scores, lives, timers, unit names, etc.), you should consider using bitmap fonts. In fact, the performance hit of a TrueType font label can be so severe that updating even a single timer label every second can cause the game to hiccup slightly when the label is updated.

But the usual premature-optimization caveat applies: if you don't experience any performance or memory issues, choose whatever type of font works well enough to do the job.

Creating and Importing a Bitmap Font

To create a bitmap font, you'll typically use a tool made for the job. The most popular tools on OS X are Glyph Designer and bmGlyph, which cost in the range of $10 to $30. Both tools can export the format supported by Cocos2D, which is an .fnt file alongside a .png file of the same name. If your tool allows you to choose the encoding for the .fnt file, choose text and not XML.

The .fnt format is a plain-text format; you can open it with any text editor. Unfortunately, the extension *.fnt* is used by a number of different formats. To verify that an .fnt file you created or downloaded is in the correct format, the first couple lines should look very similar to the ones in Listing 11-16. If your file looks very different from this, it's probably not in a format that Cocos2D understands. You may need to re-export the file or use a different glyph tool.

Listing 11-16. An excerpt of an .fnt file when viewed in a text editor (indentation is not representative)

```
info face="Fixed" size=64 bold=0 italic=0 charset="" unicode=0
     stretchH=100 smooth=1 aa=1 spacing=2,2
common lineHeight=84 base=82 scaleW=1024 scaleH=512 pages=1 packed=0
page id=0 file="gd.png"
chars count=95
char id=32 x=424 y=277 width=0 height=0 xoffset=0 yoffset=80
     xadvance=38 page=0 chnl=0 letter="space"
char id=33 x=268 y=214 width=21 height=58 xoffset=26 yoffset=11
     xadvance=46 page=0 chnl=0 letter="!"
...
```

While all tools can export in the .fnt format that Cocos2D understands, SpriteBuilder has additional requirements that some glyph tools may not adhere to. SpriteBuilder requires the bitmap font to be supplied in four resolutions, which typically implies different scaling for each font.

Assuming you created a single font named *gd.fnt* with an accompanying *gd.png*, you can make this font compatible with SpriteBuilder by creating a folder named **gd.bmfont**. Inside that folder, create four additional subfolders named **resources-phone**, **resources-phonehd**, **resources-tablet**, and **resources-tablethd**. Then add a copy of the *gd.fnt* and *gd.png* files to each resources subfolder. The resulting structure should be like the one in Figure 11-14.

Figure 11-14. SpriteBuilder requires bitmap fonts to be in a .bmfont folder with additional subfolders

> **Caution**   Be sure to use the same name (excluding the extension) for the *.bmfont* folder and the actual font files. If you were to rename *gd.bmfont* to *myfont.bmfont*, the font would no longer work because SpriteBuilder would be looking for *myfont.fnt* and *myfont.png* files.

However, you'll probably want the bitmap font to have a different scaling for each resolution. There are two variants that will work well for SpriteBuilder that resemble the two scaling options available in SpriteBuilder: absolute scaling (iPad screen is assumed to be 512x384 points) and UI scaling (iPad screen is assumed to be the original size of 1024x768 points). The default option should be absolute scaling unless you designed your game to use UI scaling throughout. Table 11-2 shows the bitmap font scaling factors for each folder and an example of what this means specifically for a given font size of 48 at 100% scaling.

Table 11-2. Bitmap font scaling for each resources folder

	Absolute (iPad screen is 512x384)	UI Scale (iPad screen is 1024x768)
resources-phone	25% (i.e., Font size: 12)	50% (i.e., Font size: 24)
resources-phonehd	50% (i.e., Font size: 24)	100% (i.e., Font size: 48)
resources-tablet	50% (i.e., Font size: 24)	50% (i.e., Font size: 24)
resources-tablethd	100% (i.e., Font size: 48)	100% (i.e., Font size: 48)

Basically, what you need to do when your glyph tool doesn't natively create a SpriteBuilder-compatible bitmap font with the four resource folders is create the folder structure like in Figure 11-14. Just the folders—no files yet. Then open your glyph tool, and export the font at its original font size (I'm assuming 48) to the *resources-tablethd* folder. Then change the font size in the glyph tool to 24, and re-export the font to the *resources-tablet* folder and once more to the *resources-phonehd* folder to create the 50% downscaled version. And finally, set the font size to 12 and re-export the font to the *resources-phone* folder.

The result should be like the one shown in Figure 11-14, with "gd" being whatever name you chose for your font. And no matter what scaling you choose for each resources folder, they all have to be there. You should not omit a folder and font, but rather leave it to SpriteBuilder to publish only what's necessary. If this process proves tedious and error prone, I highly recommend switching to a glyph tool that natively supports the format required by SpriteBuilder—like Glyph Designer and bmGlyph.

Finally, to import a bitmap font into SpriteBuilder, you simply drag and drop the *.bmfont* folder onto SpriteBuilder's *File View*. Since you've already added the *Fonts* folder from the Graphics archive onto SpriteBuilder, there should already be a *gd.bmfont* added to SpriteBuilder. But if not, you should add it now or create a custom bitmap font and add that to the *Fonts* folder in SpriteBuilder. Once added, you should see a single item with the *.bmfont* extension in SpriteBuilder's *File View*, like in Figure 11-15.

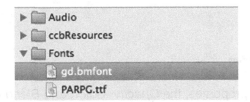

Figure 11-15. A bitmap font's .bmfont folder is listed as a single item in SpriteBuilder's File View

Note   In the SpriteBuilder version that I used, dragging and dropping a *.bmfont* onto a stage did not create a *Label BM-Font.* If this occurs to you too, it doesn't indicate a problem with the font. Bitmap fonts simply have no drag and drop support yet.

Using the Bitmap Font

There's not a really good use for a score label in this game, but we could count the number of high-impact hits the player has experienced. Just because. And to demonstrate how you can alter a localized label at runtime.

The first order of business is to open *GameMenuLayer.ccb* in SpriteBuilder. You'll find it in the *UserInterface* folder. From the *Node Library View*, drag and drop a *Label BM-Font* node onto the stage.

Edit the label's properties—specifically, you should set the position type to % and the values to 99x99 so that the label is somewhere in the top right corner. To easily align the label with the screen border, change both *Anchor point* values to 1. This will move the label from partially outside the screen to fully inside the screen. The *Anchor point* is quite effective when it comes to aligning bitmap font labels. You may have noticed that the *CCLabelBMFont* properties do not offer any kind of text-alignment properties, as you can see in Figure 11-16.

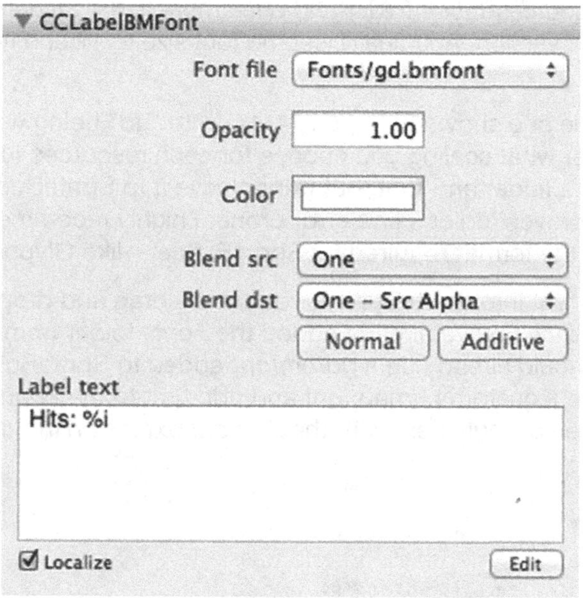

Figure 11-16. Bitmap font label properties

Speaking of bitmap font label properties, the *Opacity*, *Color*, and *Blend* mode properties are borrowed from the sprite properties and have the same effect. The *Label text* and *Localize* properties are the same as for TTF labels. Only the *Font file* property is new, but it's nothing special.

Use the *Font file* property to browse and select the *gd.bmfont* file in the *Fonts* folder. If you are using your own bitmap font, just select that. The type of font doesn't actually matter as long as the font is working.

Then enter **Hits: %i** in the *Label text* field as seen in Figure 11-16. You can use any string format specifiers, like *%i*, *%@*, *%.1f*, and so on in a label's text field. This allows you to fill in the missing parts at runtime with little effort. Click the *Localize* check box to make the initial string the key for the localized string and to enable the *Edit* button. Click the *Edit* button to bring up the localization dialog.

In the localization dialog, enter **Hits: %i** in the column labeled *English (en)* and enter **Treffer: %i** in the column labeled *German (de)*, or use whatever language you initially added and enter the corresponding language string instead of the German text. Just make sure all language strings contain the same number and types of string format specifiers. In this case, there ought to be a *%i* in every translated language string. Figure 11-17 shows the result of editing the localized strings.

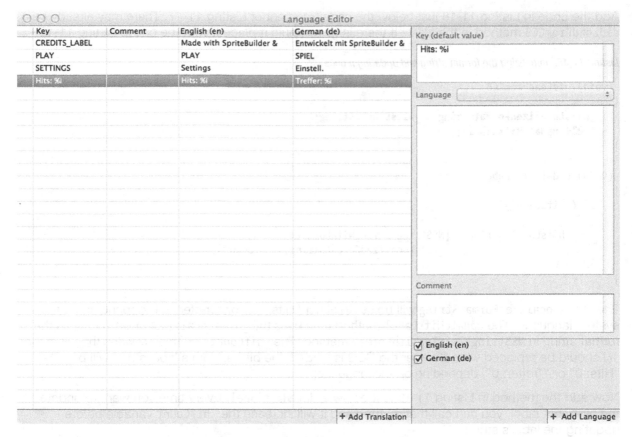

Figure 11-17. Editing localized strings, each containing the %i string format specifier

Finally, with the bitmap font label still selected, switch to the *Item Code Connections* tab. Enter **_hitsLabel** as the doc root var for the label. Now you can switch to Xcode. Open the *GameMenuLayer.m* file, and append the ivars highlighted in Listing 11-17.

Listing 11-17. The ivars needed to format the localized string

```
@implementation GameMenuLayer
{
    __weak CCLabelBMFont* _hitsLabel;
    NSString* _hitsLocalizedFormatString;
    int _hitCount;
}
```

Next to the expected _hitsLabel, you'll need the _hitsLocalizedFormatString as a reference to the label's original localized string. That's one of the localized strings with the *%i* format string specifier that was shown in Figure 11-17. You need to keep a copy of the original string simply because the string needs to be formatted and then set to the label to show an actual value in place of the *%i* format specifier. But once you've done so, that format specifier will be replaced by the _hitCount number.

Add the code in Listing 11-18 just below the code fragment of Listing 11-17. There may already be a didLoadFromCCB method in the class. If there is, you should replace it with the one in Listing 11-18.

Listing 11-18. Initializing the format string and updating it once

```
-(void) didLoadFromCCB
{
    _hitsLocalizedFormatString = _hitsLabel.string;
    [self updateHitsLabel];
}

-(void) updateHitsLabel
{
    if (_hitsLabel)
    {
        _hitsLabel.string = [NSString stringWithFormat:
                             _hitsLocalizedFormatString, _hitCount];
    }
}
```

The _hitsLocalizedFormatString will be set to either "Hits: %i" or "Treffer: %i" depending on the system language. The updateHitsLabel method then uses the _hitsLocalizedFormatString as the format string in NSString's stringWithFormat method. The _hitCount variable provides the value that %i should be replaced with. So after the CCB is loaded, the bitmap font's label string will be either "Hits: 0" or "Treffer: 0", depending on the language.

Now add the method in Listing 11-19 just below updateHitsLabel. Every time you want to update the hit-count label, you can call that method and it will increase the _hitCount variable before updating the label's string.

Listing 11-19. Increasing the hit-count label

```
-(void) increaseHitCount
{
    _hitCount++;
    [self updateHitsLabel];
}
```

To make the method publicly available to other classes, you'll have to declare it in the GameMenuLayer interface. Add the line highlighted in Listing 11-20 to *GameMenuLayer.h*.

Listing 11-20. Declaring the increaseHitCount method as public

```
#import "CCNode.h"

@class GameScene;

@interface GameMenuLayer : CCNode

@property (weak) GameScene* gameScene;
-(void) increaseHitCount;

@end
```

Just to make this easy, you'll call the increaseHitCount method from the GameScene method responsible for playing the collision sound. Open *GameScene.m*, and locate the playCollisionSoundWithPair: method. Add the lines highlighted in Listing 11-21 to the beginning of the method, and leave the existing code unchanged.

Listing 11-21. Increasing the hit counter when a massive force impacts the player

```
-(void) playCollisionSoundWithPair:(CCPhysicsCollisionPair*)pair
{
    if (pair.totalKineticEnergy > 0.0)
    {
        [_gameMenuLayer increaseHitCount];
    }

    // existing code omitted for brevity ...
}
```

Whenever there's a decent force acting upon the player, the hit counter will be increased and the label changes the value it displays. Figure 11-18 shows the German version of the game.

Figure 11-18. German version of the game with the hit-count bitmap font label in the upper right corner

Summary

In this chapter, you learned how to play sound effects through the Timeline as well as programming audio playback with ObjectAL. You learned the difference between short (.caf/.wav) and streaming (mp3, m4a) audio playback.

You also should have a firm grasp on the differences between TrueType (TTF) and bitmap font labels. You also know how to localize text strings, including how you can use format strings to update the localized string with numbers, or possibly other strings.

The results can be seen in the book project in the folder *12 - Audio Labels and Localization*.

Chapter 12

Visual Effects and Animations

In this chapter, you'll learn how to create sprite frame animations, how to design particle effects, and how to apply shader effects via the *Effect* node, which is essentially a sprite's effects list.

Sprite Frame Animations

A common way to animate sprites is by cycling through a series of images. This is called a *sprite frame animation*. In essence, it's the same as changing a sprite's texture every so often.

The term *sprite frame* refers to an extra class, CCSpriteFrame, provided by Cocos2D, which has a reference to the texture plus extra information to address the sprite as an area within the texture. Often, the texture is in fact a Sprite Sheet texture, and the CCSpriteFrame class contains information where a specific image can be found within the texture.

Creating a Sprite Frame Animation

In the SpriteSheets/Global Sprite Sheet, you should find images named *player-anim1.png* through *player-anim3.png*.

If they aren't there, check the Graphics archive that came with the book. Inside the Global folder, you will find those images, drag and drop them from Finder onto the SpriteSheets/Global Sprite Sheet to add them. You can also use your own series of images as long as they have the same dimensions as the existing *player.png*.

Now when you select all three *player-anim#.png* images in the SpriteSheets/Global Sprite Sheet and right-click to bring up the context menu, you'll see the same menu item highlighted in Figure 12-1. But don't click on this menu item just yet.

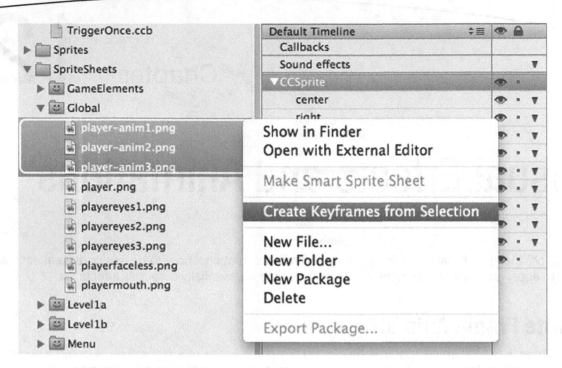

Figure 12-1. *"Create Keyframes from Selection" creates Sprite Frame animation keyframes on the currently selected sprite node*

Because *Create Keyframes from Selection* is a context menu item, you'd expect it to apply at any time—but apply to what?

In fact, this menu item works only if you have an open CCB file and have selected a sprite node. The menu item will do nothing if the selected node isn't a sprite node, or if you have multiple sprite nodes or no sprite nodes selected. There's no feedback in those cases whatsoever. You'll just notice that the command didn't add any keyframes.

So open the *PlayerSoftBody.ccb* in the *Prefabs* folder, and then select the root node labeled *CCSprite* as seen in Figure 12-1.

Make sure the Timeline Cursor is moved to the far left. Then select the three *player-anim#.png* images, right-click to bring up the context menu, and select *Create Keyframes from Selection*.

You'll notice that three sprite frame keyframes have been added to the Timeline. If you play this animation, you should see the player close his eye lids.

Caution   At the time of this writing, SpriteBuilder had an issue with keyframes on a CCB's root node: A root node's sprite frame keyframes could not be selected. I had to manually add each sprite frame animation keyframe one by one, moving the Timeline Cursor into the desired keyframe position before issuing the *Create Keyframes from Selection* command on an individual *player-anim#.png* image. I assume the issue will be fixed by the time you read this book; but if it is not, at least now you know how to work around it.

Since the *Create Keyframes from Selection* command creates a very fast sequence of keyframes and will almost never match the desired animation speed, SpriteBuilder provides a way to evenly space a selection of keyframes.

In order to select multiple keyframes, you can either click on them with the Shift key held down or simply click with your mouse on an empty area on the Timeline (where the keyframes are) and start dragging. This will draw a selection rectangle that will select all keyframes inside the rectangle when you let go of the mouse button.

With the three sprite frame animation keyframes selected, select the *Animation* ➤ *Stretch Selected Keyframes* menu item as seen in Figure 12-2.

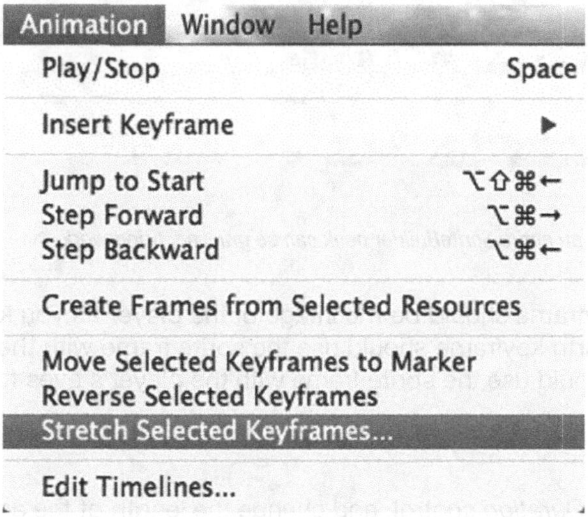

Figure 12-2. Spacing keyframes equally can be done via the Stretch Selected Keyframes command

This will bring up a small dialog where you can enter a *Stretch Factor* value. Enter *3.0* as the value and click *Done*. The keyframes should now be further apart.

Since the player is closing his eye lids in the animation, it should also open them again a short while later. Move the Timeline Cursor to the position where the player should open its eyes again, perhaps half a second after the last sprite frame keyframe.

With the *CCSprite* root node still selected, select *player-anim1.png* and *player-anim2.png* in the SpriteSheets/Global Sprite Sheet. Or if you still have all three selected, you can also just deselect *player-anim3.png* by clicking on it with the Cmd key held down. Either way, *player-anim1.png* and *player-anim2.png* should be selected. Then right-click one of the selected images and run the *Create Keyframes from Selection* command once more.

Now those two keyframes are in the wrong order. Select them both, and then run *Animation* ➤ *Reverse Selected Keyframes* (as shown in Figure 12-2) to reverse their order.

Running this animation will now have the player close its eye lids and open its eyes shortly thereafter. For reference, Figure 12-3 shows the approximate result for this sprite frame animation with a total of five sprite frame keyframes.

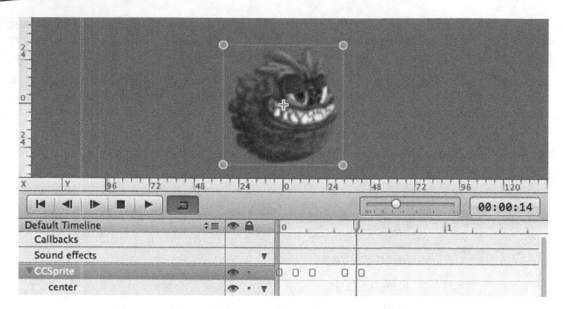

Figure 12-3. Being the model for an entire SpriteBuilder book can be grueling, tiring work

The first and fifth (last) keyframe should be the image of the player as you know it, with eyes wide open. The second and fourth keyframe should use the sprite frame with the eyes half closed. The third (middle) keyframe should use the sprite frame with the player's eyes fully closed.

Played together, this will make the player blink, and the entire animation runs for just about half a second.

Now click on the *Timeline Duration* control, and change the length of the animation to about 3 seconds. This affects how often the player will blink. If you let the Timeline run for 10 seconds, the player will blink only every 10 seconds. If you change it down to just a second, the player will blink very frequently.

> **Caution**   After changing the *Timeline Duration,* verify that none of the sprite frame keyframes have been cut off. The blinking animation shouldn't run much longer than half a second. If you change the *Timeline Duration* to less than half a second, this may irreversibly remove excess keyframes—namely, those whose timestamp would now be greater than the Timeline's duration.

Finally, click on the *Timeline Chain* drop-down menu, and select *Default Timeline*. This will have the Timeline loop indefinitely in the game.

Now if you try this out in the game. . . there won't be an animation playing. The sprite frame keyframes don't have any effect yet because the *SoftBodyPlayer.ccb* uses a custom class to perform custom rendering.

Adding Sprite Frame Animations to SoftBodyDrawNode

SoftBodyPlayer.ccb uses a custom class called SoftBodyDrawNode. This CCSprite subclass uses the initially assigned spriteFrame property of CCSprite to initialize the vertex and texture coordinates for the sprites.

However, it doesn't currently update the texture coordinates when the spriteFrame property changes. Thus, the sprite frame animation currently has no effect.

To fix this, you'll first have to add an ivar that marks the point in time at which the player has been initialized. This _didLoad flag is important because initially CCBReader will assign at least one CCSpriteFrame to the sprite's spriteFrame property, whose setter you're going to override in order to call the updateTextureCoordinates method every time the sprite frames change.

But the initial spriteFrame assignments should not trigger the updateTextureCoordinates method, as its values may not be set up and initialized yet.

Add the ivar highlighted in Listing 12-1 to the SoftBodyDrawNode implementation in *SoftBodyDrawNode.m*.

Listing 12-1. The _didLoad flag is used to determine whether the node has been fully initialized

```
@implementation SoftBodyDrawNode
{
    // existing ivars omitted for brevity ...

    BOOL _didLoad;
}
```

Then update the didLoadFromCCB method. Add the highlighted line in Listing 12-2 to the end of the method. This will mark the node as being fully set up for our intents and purposes.

Listing 12-2. The node is considered initialized by the time the didLoadFromCCB method returns

```
-(void) didLoadFromCCB
{
    [self setup];
    _didLoad = YES;
}
```

The key change here is to override the spriteFrame property setter method, which is aptly named setSpriteFrame:. It follows the common naming scheme for property setters (*set* with an uppercase first letter of property name, receiving a parameter of property type) and getters (same as the property name, taking no parameters and returning the property type).

Every time the Timeline animation changes the spriteFrame property, you'll need to run the updateTextureCoordinates method in order to point it to the new area within the Sprite Sheet texture to draw from. If that isn't done, it will simply keep on drawing the sprite frame that was set initially.

Add the setSpriteFrame: method of Listing 12-3 to *SoftBodyDrawNode.m*, preferably at the very bottom just above the @end line.

Listing 12-3. Overriding the spriteFrame property setter to update texture coordinates

```
-(void) setSpriteFrame:(CCSpriteFrame *)spriteFrame
{
    [super setSpriteFrame:spriteFrame];

    if (_didLoad)
    {
        [self updateTextureCoordinates];
    }
}
```

The _didLoad flag prevents the updateTextureCoordinates method from being run before didLoadFromCCB. This is important because the setup method called in Listing 12-2 needs to run before any call to updateTextureCoordinates; otherwise, the _vertices pointer's memory would not have been allocated, resulting in a crash.

Of course, setSpriteFrame: does get called at least once before didLoadFromCCB, by CCBReader. At some point, CCBReader has to assign the sprite's initial spriteFrame as set up in SpriteBuilder, and any assignments issued by CCBReader itself need not update the texture coordinates.

Now you can build and run the game, and you'll see the player blink its eyes about every three seconds, or whatever duration you set for the default Timeline in SoftBodyPlayer.ccb.

Comparing Sprite Frames

You may also want to override the setSpriteFrame: method in other CCSprite subclasses if you want to run code when specific frames are being displayed but you don't want to (or can't) use the *Callbacks* keyframes to do so.

You can get and store sprite frames in ivars (or arrays or dictionaries) which, when passed into the setSpriteFrame: method, should run specific selectors. For instance, this can be used to synchronize sound effects or speech to start with a specific sprite frame.

> **Note**   This is a theoretical example. You needn't add the following code to the project.

Assuming that _triggerFrame is a CCSpriteFrame* ivar (it must be declared without the __weak keyword), you can assign it in didLoadFromCCB of the CCSprite subclass in which you want to monitor an animation to play a sound effect when a specific sprite frame is set. Listing 12-4 shows you how it's done. Take note that, as with all resources, you have to specify the relative path to the file.

Listing 12-4. Obtaining a sprite frame reference for a given animation image

```
-(void) didLoadFromCCB
{
    _triggerFrame = [CCSpriteFrame frameWithImageNamed:
                     @"SpriteSheets/Anims/facepalm42.png"];
}
```

The frameWithImageNamed: method will return the cached image if it has already been loaded. This will be the case if the image is in the same Sprite Sheet as the sprite frame that the sprite initially uses. That would be the sprite frame that's assigned to the sprite in SpriteBuilder.

The frameWithImageNamed: method and similar "look up by name" methods perform at least a string comparison. More likely, they'll also run some name-mangling code in order to locate the image resource, which could theoretically be found in a number of different locations.

Therefore, it's recommended to avoid running frameWithImageNamed: and similar methods while the gameplay is underway. Loading resources at runtime is a common source of short, intermittent drops in frame rate (appropriately nicknamed *hiccups*).

With a strong reference to the sprite frame in question assigned to _triggerFrame, you can now override setSpriteFrame: and compare the incoming spriteFrame parameter with the one referenced by _triggerFrame.

If both are equal, that's when you can fire a method to run any code that's supposed to be synchronized with specific sprite frames. In Listing 12-5, that would play a sound effect specific to the animation.

Listing 12-5. Running a method when the new spriteFrame matches a specific sprite frame

```
-(void) setSpriteFrame:(CCSpriteFrame *)spriteFrame
{
    [super setSpriteFrame:spriteFrame];

    if ([_triggerFrame isEqual:spriteFrame])
    {
        [self playFacepalmSoundEffect];
    }
}
```

To compare the two sprite frames, the isEqual: method is used. While in this case a direct pointer comparison _triggerFrame == spriteFrame would have worked too, it is better style to use isEqual: because many Objective-C objects can't be compared through their pointer values alone.

This potential pitfall is best explained by example: you can create two instances of CCColor, both using the same init method and parameters (initWithWhite:1.0 alpha:1.0), yet you'll have two different objects occupying two different memory addresses.

The pointer equality test using the equality operator == will evaluate to NO (false), but using isEqual: gives CCColor the chance to compare its properties. Assuming the isEqual: method is properly implemented, it will determine that all of its properties are identical—in which case, isEqual: returns YES (true) even though both may be two separate objects.

Particle Effects

Particle effects are possibly the best known type of visual effect, at least in 2D games. In SpriteBuilder and Cocos2D, they're referred to as a *particle system*, which is the equivalent of the better known and more descriptive term *particle emitter*.

The *CCParticleSystem* node is a node that emits particles. Henceforth, I shall use *emitter* when I refer to a particle system. It better describes what the node does.

Limitations of Particle Effects

The thing with particles is that they can be rendered more efficiently than if you were to use the same number of sprites with the same behavior. The downside to that is that you have absolutely no access or control over individual particles except for the parameters provided by the emitter.

For instance, you can't access, remove, or otherwise modify specific particles. You can't even identify or obtain references to individual particles, nor can you run actions on them.

While the particle system node itself can have physics enabled, there's little use in that: individual particles will not collide with other physics bodies or other particles. Only the emitter node as a whole can have a collision shape and can be moved about by the physics engine. Unless the particle effect is designed to (roughly) contain all emitted particles within the physics shape, this probably won't be too useful. A ring of particles with a circle physics shape is likely the best possible use case.

Particle effects are also a major source of performance issues. Particle emitters with a total particles count of over 100 are likely using far too many particles. A three-digit particle count should definitely ring an alarm bell and be put under tight scrutiny.

A large particle count may be justifiable for a special effect designed to be used in a specific scene, perhaps as the only particle effect or where the scene isn't performance critical. Also, using a lot of very small particles with a small particle texture can still work well.

A common mistake is to design particle effects with hundreds of allowed particles only to realize that this emitter will sink the frame rate to rock bottom even on high-end devices. Another common mistake is having a particle effect that runs (mostly) fine except for specific older devices, with the iPhone 4 being a particularly common candidate due to its underpowered graphics hardware. Always be prepared to remove an effect, or have a backup effect with fewer particles for such cases. Test your particle effects early on a device, and if you can, test them specifically on the slowest device you have access to.

Particle textures have to be square images. Any nonsquare texture will be scaled and therefore stretched to match the nearest square size. In general, particle textures should be rather nondescript, like a cloud or gradient pattern. Particle effects typically look best if the particle texture has little discernible detail. Exceptions are very specific particle effects with few individual particles, like dropping leaves or cartoon stars circling around a knocked-out character's head.

Each particle emitter can only emit particles using a single texture. If you need to combine multiple textures into the same particle effect, you'll have to create multiple emitter nodes and decide whose particles should be drawn over or under the other emitter's particles.

The same goes for effects that should have more complex behavior, such as an effect where most particles should orbit the emitter's position but occasionally some of them should shoot out and away from the center. This requires two emitters.

Editing Particle System Parameters

For the particle-emitter example, you'll be adding a fire glow to the menu background.

Open *MainMenuBackground.ccb* in the *UserInterface* folder. From the *Node Library View*, drag and drop a *Particle System (emitter)* node onto the stage. Then drag and move it in the Timeline so that it is between the *M_monsters* and *M_frontsmoke* nodes. (See Figure 12-4.)

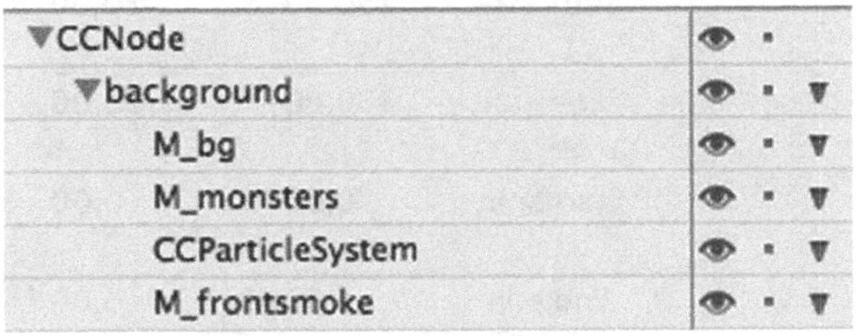

Figure 12-4. The CCParticleSystem node should be above the M_frontsmoke image

With the *CCParticleSystem* node selected, switch to the *Item Properties* tab and set the position of the emitter node to 0x-200. New particles should appear close to the bottom of the background images.

I will explain each particle-emitter property. As you go over each particle-emitter property, you should apply the values shown in Figure 12-5 and Figure 12-6 to the newly added *Particle System* node.

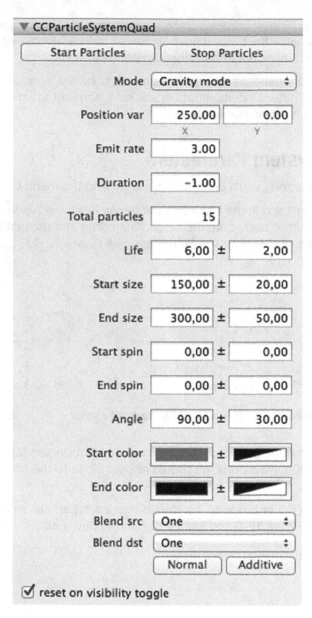

Figure 12-5. *Particle System values common to both radial and gravity particle emitters*

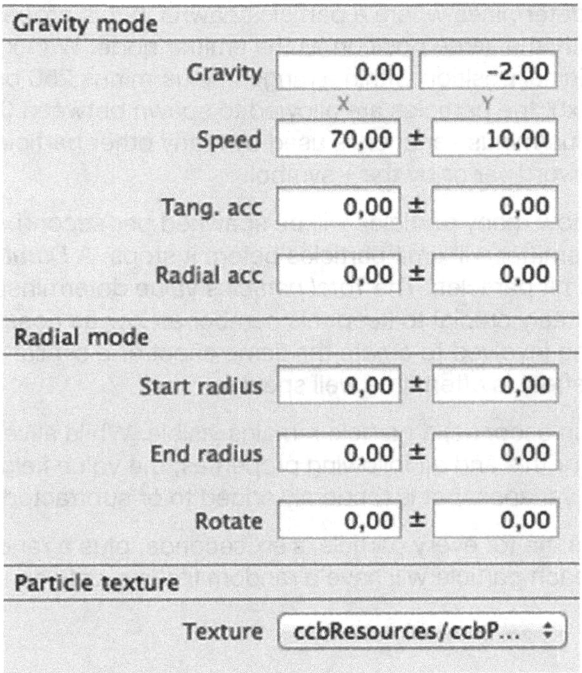

Figure 12-6. Mode-specific properties and the particle texture

Feel free to use other values as you see fit if you don't care much about the end result, which is supposed to look like hot plasma moving upward, generating a nice lighting effect on the monsters and in the clouds at the top.

If the effect is done right, you'll find that the final effect is very hard to discern as an actual particle effect. It could almost be mistaken for a much more complex shader effect.

The only control you have over a particle emitter is the particle spawn parameters. And there are plenty of them. Figure 12-5 contains just the functions and parameters common to both radial and gravity particle emitters.

The *Start Particles* and *Stop Particles* buttons allow you to start and stop emitting particles within SpriteBuilder. These buttons do not alter the emitter's behavior in the game; they exist only to stop emitters from emitting particles in the editor.

A particle emitter can be in one of two modes, radial or gravity. The radial mode enables you to create an effect where the particles swirl around the position of the emitter, while the gravity mode enables you to let particles fly away in any direction, curved or straight, with or without gravity.

Note that this gravity is set per emitter and is completely independent from the physics world's gravity. Changing the emitter mode will drastically alter the behavior of the particles and allow you to use one of the two sets of mode properties shown in Figure 12-6.

The *Position var* property determines where a particle spawns. If this property is set to 0x0, the particle will spawn at exactly the same position as the emitter node. With x set to 250, each new particle will randomize its initial position within a range of plus/minus 250 points. If the particle emitter's position is at 250x0, the particles are allowed to spawn between 0 to 500 along the *x* axis. This type of randomized plus/minus variation is used by many other particle-emitter properties, indicated either by the keyword var or by the ± symbol.

The *Emit rate* determines how many particles will be spawned per second. The *Duration* determines how long (in seconds) the emitter will emit particles before it stops. A *Duration* of –1 means the emitter will never stop to emit particles. The *Total particles* value determines how many particles can be alive at most. It is absolutely crucial to keep this number as low as possible to still achieve the desired effect. The tweaking involved to create the same effect or a similar effect that uses fewer particles than the original effect is often time well spent.

Life refers to the duration (in seconds) a particle remains visible. While alive, a particle counts toward the *Total particles* count. For this and all following properties, the value field to the right of the plus/minus sign refers to a variance that is randomly added to or subtracted from the value to the left.

In this case, the default lifetime for every particle is six seconds, plus a random value in the range of –2.0 and 2.0. This means each particle will have a random lifetime between four to eight seconds.

Tip   Life, emit rate, and total particles influence each other. If you want an emitter that shoots out a stream of particles and then pauses, you'll simply have to ensure that the lifetime and emit rate are such that the emitted particles reach the total particle count before some of the particles' lives end.

With an emit rate of 10 particles per second and a lifetime of 3 seconds, you'll have 30 particles living within 3 seconds. Now if you set the total particle count to 15, the emitter will emit particles for 1.5 seconds and then stop emitting new particles for another 1.5 seconds. After 3 seconds, it will emit new particles for another 1.5 seconds and then pause another 1.5 seconds.

Accordingly, if you want the particle effect to emit a continuous, uninterrupted stream of particles, the total particle count must be large enough and the lifetime and/or emit rate may need to be reduced.

Start size and *End size* refer to the size of particles when they are spawned and when their lifetime ends, respectively. The values are linearly interpolated during the lifetime of the particle. Given that particle textures are square, the dimensions refer to both particle width and height.

In this example, ignoring the variation values for a moment, the particles start out at 150x150 and after 6 seconds, the moment they disappear, their size will be 300x300. That's pretty big for particle effects, but that size can be effective for creating large-scale effects using relatively few individual particles.

Start spin and *End spin* determine both the rotation of the particles at the start and end of their lifetime as well as the speed of rotation. The rotation speed is determined by the difference between *Start spin* and *End spin*, which is linearly interpolated over the particle's lifetime. If *Start spin* was 0 and *End spin* was *360*, the particles would rotate one revolution over their lifetime. Naturally, this rotation will be faster if the lifetime is 1 second rather than 10 seconds.

The *Angle* sets the initial direction the particles take, in degrees and in counter-clockwise direction. An angle of 0 degrees means the particles move to the right; an angle of 90 degrees means the particles move upward.

Start color and *End color* determine the color and transparency that particles begin and end their lives with. The colors are interpolated linearly over the lifetime of a particle.

If you want the particles to fade out smoothly toward the end, make sure to set the *Opacity* in the color wheel dialog to *0%* for the *End color*. If you want to avoid the particle having to change its initial color over its lifetime, use black as the *End color*. Most commonly, particles are set up to end with the color black at *0%* opacity to create a nice and smooth fade-out effect.

Blend src and *Blend dst* are the same settings as for *Sprite* nodes. They affect how the particles blend with the background. Unlike most other nodes that support blending, particles default to additive blending. Basically, this means that particles brighten the already existing background colors.

Most combinations of *src* and *dst* blend values just create more or less black rectangles. Besides the two basic modes—*Normal* and *Additive*—I found that *Dst Color* for *src* with *Dst Alpha* for *dst* create a very subtle blending effect that is well suited to enhancing a scene's lighting as particles move about.

The *reset on visibility toggle* check box, if enabled, means that the particle emitter will remove all existing particles when its visible state is changed by code. If the box is unchecked, the emitter will keep spawning but not render particles while its visible state is set to NO.

> **Tip**   You can create a particle emitter, uncheck the *reset on visibility toggle* check box, and keep the particle emitter running for a few seconds to allow it to spawn some of the initial particles. You can then use a fade action or play a Timeline that changes the opacity of the emitter node from 0 to 1, fading it into view. This is commonly needed where the particle emitter should not be seen building up its particles but instead should start out "fully developed."

Figure 12-6 shows the mode-specific properties of the *CCParticleSystem* node. The *Gravity mode* properties are applied only when the particle emitter is in *Gravity mode*, and the *Radial mode* properties are effective only when the particle emitter is in *Radial mode*.

Gravity affects each particle. You can use this, for example, to accelerate particles upward by setting a positive Y value or to create a spring where particles start moving upward but eventually turn around and fall back down. Gravity is specified in points, and it is simply added to the particle's position every frame.

Again, this gravity is applied only to that particular *Particle System* node's particles, and it has no correlation with the gravity of the CCPhysicsNode.

Speed determines the speed of motion of particles, in points per second. *Speed* is initially in the direction given by the *Angle* property, but it can change over the lifetime of a particle due to gravity, tangential acceleration, and radial acceleration.

The property labeled *Tang. acc* refers to *tangential acceleration*, while *Radial acc* stands for *radial acceleration*. Both contribute to rotational spin for particles.

By increasing the radial acceleration value alone, you'll notice that particles will speed up and move away from the emitter's position the longer they live. Add tangential acceleration to the mix and particles will spiral outward from the emitter's position. With tangential acceleration, you can make emitters look like the ones in radial mode except that you can't prevent the particles from speeding up. Thus, inevitably, they'll be moving away from the emitter position.

To create truly orbiting particles, you have to set the particle emitter to radial mode. Then you can edit the *Start radius* and *End radius* to determine the radius of the orbit of the particles, either moving outward or inward. Or set both *Start radius* and *End radius* to the same radius, only adjusting the variance, to create a ringlike effect.

The *Rotate* property is the angle (in degrees) that the particles will move around the emitter's position every second. You will see the particles orbiting from *Start radius* to *End radius* only if you specify a decent *Rotate* value and the particle lifetime is long enough.

> **Tip**   You may find it easier to design certain effects by leaving all variation values at zero initially. The variation values are the property fields to the right of the plus/minus sign. Also, try to focus on editing one aspect of the particle effect at a time. And do edit particle effects in a stage that at least resembles a possible use case. If you test a particle effect against a simple color (or gradient) background, you can't really judge what the effect looks like in the game. Particle effects can look very different depending on the background they blend with.
>
> You may want to design the particle effect in a Node CCB and then (temporarily) add various test-scene CCBs as the background node for the particle CCB. This allows you to quickly toggle through possible particle emitter backgrounds by using the visibility property. The test scenes would be specifically made to look like a typical use case in the game.

Finally, the *Texture* property is just like the *Sprite frame* property of sprite nodes. SpriteBuilder comes with five built-in particle textures that you'll find in the *ccbResources* folder with names starting with *ccbParticle*. They are sufficient for many uses, but of course you can use your own particle textures. Be sure to design the particle textures as square images.

Though particles can use any texture size allowed by a device, it is strongly recommended that you use the smallest possible texture. The size of a particle texture can significantly affect the effect's performance. In most cases, particles blend really well even when using a very low resolution texture.

Figure 12-7 shows what the result of the particle effect might look like if you applied the same values or similar values as in Figure 12-5 and Figure 12-6 to the *Particle System* node.

Figure 12-7. The monsters are glowing red hot thanks to the particle effect

The effect is most visible on the monsters, which seem to be glowing hot. Yet you can't make out individual particles and they blend perfectly with the background, which makes this effect worth seeing in the game. Preferably you'll check this out on a device since the Simulator now renders this scene with maybe 15 frames per second (fps) at most.

Shader Effects

Cocos2D's latest feature is shader effects, typically in the form of the *Effect* node, which applies a given shader effect to all of its children.

Sprites can also have one or more shader effects applied to them without the need for a separate *Effect* node. The user interface and available shaders and their parameters are the same for both.

Adding an Effect Node

To try out the *Effect* node, open *MainScene.ccb* and then drag and drop an *Effect* node from the *Node Library View* onto the stage. The *Effect* node, much like the *Color* node, has an implied size of 100x100 points.

Since the *Effect* node applies its effect to its children, this also means that it will draw only the children within its frame, determined by the *Effect* node's *Content size* property.

> **Tip** An *Effect* node without any effects can be used like a clipping node, where any content outside the *Effect* node's rectangle will simply not be drawn (clipped). You could make use of that for a split-screen view by dividing the screen into two *Effect* nodes, appropriately positioned and sized. Then whatever you draw in one *Effect* node will not overlap into the area of the other *Effect* node.
>
> There are many uses for this. For instance, a minimap overlay could use a large image for the entire map, but it's added to an *Effect* node so that it will draw only a small portion of the map in a corner of the screen.

In this case, the *Effect* node should be a full-screen effect. Select the *CCEffectNode* in the Timeline, and change its position to *0x0*. Then change the *Content size* types to %, with both values set to *100*. This stretches the size of the effect to the size of the screen.

Next, drag and drop the *CCEffectNode* in the Timeline so that it becomes the topmost node in the list. Then drag the existing background node onto the *CCEffectNode* so that the background node becomes a child node of the *CCEffectNode*. See the Timeline in Figure 12-8 for reference.

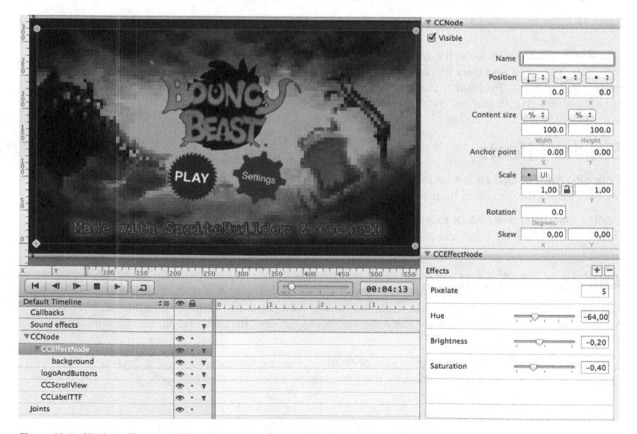

Figure 12-8. Multiple effects applied to the menu background give it an entirely different look

Now any effect added to the *CCEffectNode* will be applied to the entire background node. In this case, the entire *MainMenuBackground.ccb* will have the shader effects applied to it, including the recently added particle effect.

The results will look something like in Figure 12-8. A darker, scarier, and pixellated version of the background.

To create this effect, select the *CCEffectNode* in the Timeline and switch to the *Item Properties* tab.

You'll notice the *CCEffectNode* section at the bottom of the *Item Properties* tab shown in Figure 12-8. With the [+] button, you will open a context menu from which you can choose one effect to add to the list. At the time of this writing, there are a total of 10 effects, as seen in Figure 12-9.

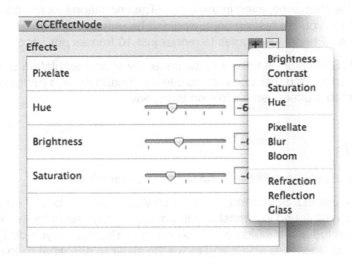

Figure 12-9. Adding an effect

To create the effect seen in Figure 12-8, add *Pixellate*, *Hue*, *Brightness*, and *Saturation* effects. The order in which you add these effects doesn't matter, although it may make a difference for other effect combinations.

The *Pixellate* effect should have a value of *5*, *Hue* a value of –64, *Brightness* a value of –0.2, and *Saturation* a value of –0.4. Feel free to alter the values as you see fit. You can also add additional effects if you want.

> **Note** In the SpriteBuilder version I used, you can add the same effect multiple times. This does not make sense for most effects. For instance, using *Pixellate* multiple times will make a difference only if each effect uses a different pixellation value (say: 3, 5, and 8), and the result will look barely any different from using a single *Pixellate* effect with a value of *8* in this example.
>
> There may be some use for applying the same effect multiple times, but no matter how hard I tried, I couldn't find or even imagine a possible use case. This may change once more effects are added in the future.

If you want to remove an effect, you have to select it in the list by clicking on its name or an empty area not used by any controls. Once the effect is highlighted, click the [–] button to remove it.

Caution   I found myself frequently hitting Backspace to remove a selected effect. Alas, this will in fact remove the CCEffectNode and all of its children. Fortunately, you just need to issue *Edit* ➤ *Undo (Cmd+Z)* to bring back the *Effect* node and its children.

You should publish, build, and run the game. You may see that the effects have a noticeable, negative effect on the performance, even in the menu. The animations won't look smooth. Of course, this varies with the device you are testing on. It wouldn't be unheard of if an iPhone 6 runs these effects at 60 fps while an iPhone 4 struggles to render just 10 frames per second.

Not to mention the iOS Simulator—it uses a software renderer, and emulating shader effects is particularly slow. Therefore, it's rather common to see a dramatic drop in performance on the Simulator once one or more effects are visible on the scene.

Available Effects

The currently available effects are roughly divided into three groups:

- *Brightness, Contrast, Saturation, and Hue* only change the color of individual pixels and can be found in almost any imaging program. All of these effects use just a single value and should be self-explanatory. But even if you don't know what the effect does, just add it and move the slider to see what it does.

- *Pixellate, Blur, and Bloom* alter the look of the rendered content. You've already seen *Pixellate*, which basically scales down its content, turning it into pixel art. The *Blur* effect smooths the content, making it look less sharp. *Bloom* is an effect where bright areas bleed into surrounding darker areas, making them appear to glow. You can alter its *Blur Radius* and the *Intensity*, while the *Luminance Threshold* determines how bright an area needs to be before the bloom effect is applied.

- *Refraction, Reflection, and Glass* are complex effects requiring a Normal Map, which is an image where each pixel's RGB values are considered the normal vectors. In layman's terms, the Normal Map image alters how light is supposed to refract or reflect from the surface. All three effects also use an Environment reference, which is one or more nodes that should be seen reflected in the *Effect* node. (See Figure 12-10.)

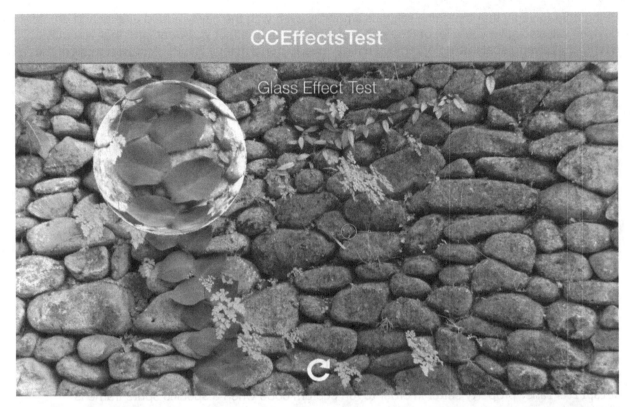

Figure 12-10. The glass effect distorts the background like a lens while slightly reflecting the Environment node on its surface

The *Effect* node is very powerful, but the more complex effects require some understanding of graphics and shader programming to grasp the meaning and to imagine the resulting effects of the various parameters.

The programming interface of CCEffectNode and CCEffect and related classes hasn't been made available to the public while I'm writing this and is still a work in progress. Of course, you'll eventually find these classes documented in the Cocos2D Developer Library Reference (also known as a *class reference*), and you can always peek into the header files *CCEffect.h* and *CCEffectNode.h*.

Shader-Effects Best Practices

As with any effect, creating good shader effects is mostly a matter of using images that work well with the effect. I had it easy with a well-designed menu screen that works well with both particle and shader effects. Imagine if you had only flat-colored dummy graphics—it wouldn't look nearly as good. Effects in themselves can't work magic. You have to provide good input for shaders and particle effects to generate good output.

While it's tempting to start designing effects early, the development of effects should really be deferred until the project has all of the features and most of the artwork. By that time, you have established that the game runs well and there's spare performance to be taken up by effects.

Being able to verify that the game still runs smoothly even with the newly added effects and on older devices will also save you a lot of time **not** designing the uber-effect you want, and that you may eventually have to scale down or remove entirely due to performance issues. And with most of the artwork finalized, it'll be a lot easier to design great-looking effects, too.

Keep in mind that even simple effects like *Brightness* and *Contrast* can have a significant impact on performance, depending on which device you test them on. And do test effects on the device, because the Simulator is very slow to begin with.

That's also another reason to defer implementing effects until late in the project: adding effects can easily make the Simulator unusable even for simple tests, let alone actually playing the game.

> **Tip**   Remember that you don't have to use the *Effect* node if you want to apply an effect to a specific sprite. Just select the sprite in question, and switch to the *Item Properties* tab to find the effects user interface at the bottom of the *CCSprite* properties, just below the blend modes. Unlike the *Effect* node, effects applied directly to a sprite will not affect the sprite's child nodes.

Summary

You've learned how to create sprite frame keyframe animations, and you've enhanced the SoftBodyDrawNode to work with sprite frame animations. You also know how to override the setSpriteFrame: property setter in order to run custom code when a specific sprite frame is displayed.

On the particle and shader effects front, you've learned how to implement them technically, although designing great effects takes a lot of experimenting and experience. Fortunately, it's fun to spend time tweaking and experimenting with effects—so much so that I should warn you not to spend too much time tweaking effects too early in the project if your goal is to complete a game and create one that performs well across most devices.

You'll find the version of the project with sprite frame animations, particle effects, and shader effects in the *13 - Animations and Effects* folder in the book's download archive.

Chapter 13

Porting to Android

How cool would it be if you could build and run your SpriteBuilder app on Android devices?

You can!

There's no Java or C++ programming needed to do so. SpriteBuilder provides the necessary plugins for Xcode to cross-compile your Objective-C code to Android. In fact, all the libraries used by SpriteBuilder apps—most notably Cocos2D-Swift, Chipmunk2D and ObjectAL—are fully compatible.

How Does Android Support Work?

The development of SpriteBuilder and Cocos2D since version 3 (Cocos2D-Swift to be precise) is done by Apportable developers. Apportable is a company that specializes in cross-compiling Objective-C code for the Android platform.

Originally, Apportable was a command-line tool for expert programmers and game-development studios. The company has since created Xcode plugins and integrated them into SpriteBuilder, beginning with version 1.3. You'll know them as SpriteBuilder Android plugins.

You will also often hear of a framework called *BridgeKit*. This is the framework that Apportable created to give Objective-C developers access to Android, Java, and Verde features and functionality. Verde is a lightweight equivalent of UIKit. You'll find the BridgeKit reference here: http://static.apportable.com/documentation/BridgeKit/html/.

The SpriteBuilder Android plugins work by cross-compiling Objective-C code to native ARM and x86 code that runs on Android devices. There are no emulation layers, virtual machines, or Java translations done. The resulting executable will typically run faster than if the same code were written in Java using Google's Android SDK.

Like any other cross-platform development, porting to Android with the goal of publishing a nontrivial app on the Android store(s) does require extra work compared to targeting a single platform. There's no such thing as free ports. Each ecosystem has its own unique programming interfaces, device capabilities, design requirements, user expectations, developer guidelines, publishing policies, and processes.

Most notably, on Android there's a much wider variety of devices, which poses challenges regarding how to scale the app to a great variety of screen resolutions but also varying CPU and GPU performance specs, different OS versions, and so on.

Fortunately, SpriteBuilder does make it easier to adapt to varying screen resolutions, while the Android Xcode plugins allows you to use any Cocos2D feature and continue to use many iOS frameworks. BridgeKit then gives you access to all the important Android features without having to revert to writing C++ or Java code.

Yet it's not possible to map all iOS frameworks and functionality to some Android equivalent. For instance, to store leaderboards and achievements, you use Game Center on iOS whose equivalent on Android is Google Play Games. Both have to be integrated separately. Game Center won't work on Android, and Google Play Games won't work on iOS. In addition, both are technically too different (with different requirements and feature sets), so it isn't feasible to have equivalents to a simple translation layer that maps Game Center methods and callbacks to Google Play Games.

All this means you might have to do some extra work manually. You also might have to write against the Android SDK interfaces directly with C++ or Java, but it's getting less and less complicated every day, as Apportable is constantly adding features to the SpriteBuilder Android plugins.

SpriteBuilder Android Documentation

You'll find more details than I can possibly cover on the SpriteBuilder Android documentation page: `http://android.spritebuilder.com`.

If you plan on taking the cross-platform route, you should definitely take the half hour or so to read through the entire documentation. You'll learn a great number of things, including what's possible, what the known issues are, and anything else you may have to consider **before** starting with your project. Some things may affect design and technical decisions, while others simply haven't been decided at the time of this writing, such as the lowest supported Android version.

You should also refer to the documentation if you have a project that was created with SpriteBuilder v1.2 or earlier (like the book's projects in earlier chapters). These projects have to undergo a conversion process.

The recommended way is to create a new SpriteBuilder project with the latest SpriteBuilder version, and then restore your original CCB, resource, and source code files into both SpriteBuilder and Xcode. Again, for details refer to the SpriteBuilder Android documentation because the process is a bit more involved, though not too difficult to follow.

Installing Android Xcode Plugins

If you run SpriteBuilder v1.3 beta for the first time or whenever there's an update, you'll see a message stating that Android Xcode plugins are being installed, as shown in Figure 13-1.

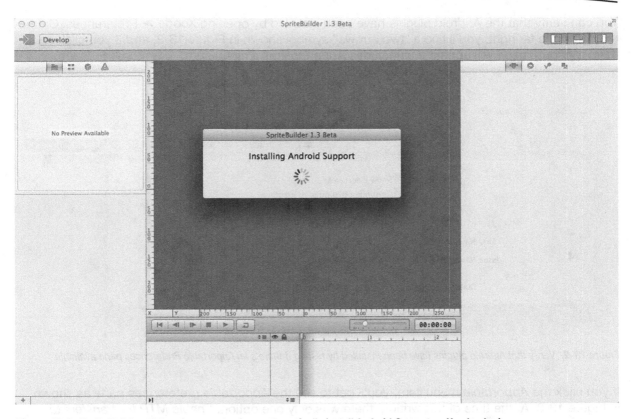

Figure 13-1. SpriteBuilder v1.3 and newer versions automatically install Android Support as Xcode plugins

Caution   Whenever you see the message in Figure 13-1, you should close and restart Xcode so that Xcode will load and use the latest versions of the plugins.

If you need to uninstall or re-install the Android Xcode plugins, you can find the instructions on how to remove the plugins here: `http://android.spritebuilder.com/#uninstalling-the-spritebuilder-android-plugin`. Once you've removed all of the plugin files, they will automatically be re-installed the next time you launch SpriteBuilder.

Note   The Android plugins are bundled with SpriteBuilder v1.3 beta, but in the future they will have to be installed separately. You can find out whether this is already the case by visiting `http://android.spritebuilder.com`, where you'll also find up-to-date installation instructions.

You can verify that the Android plugins have been installed by opening Xcode ➤ Preferences. On the toolbar at the far right, you'll find a "two arrows" symbol shown in Figure 13-2, and if you click on them a popup menu will appear that includes *Apportable* as a menu item.

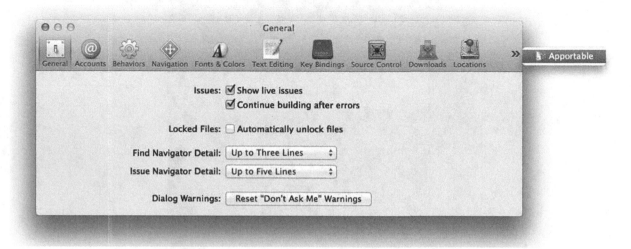

Figure 13-2. Verify that Android plugins have been installed by testing if there's an Apportable Preferences pane available

If you click the *Apportable* menu item, you'll get to see the *Apportable* preferences pane as shown in Figure 13-3. At the time of this writing, there was only one option: *Enable MTP for transfers to Android devices*. You may need to uncheck this check box if you're having trouble transferring successfully built apps onto the device. More on this later.

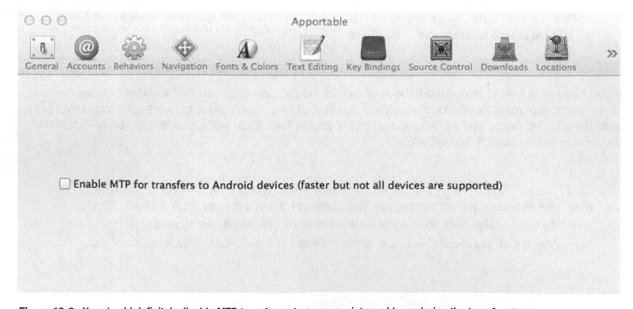

Figure 13-3. You should definitely disable MTP transfers when you run into problems during the transfer stage

For the moment, you may want to uncheck the *Enable MTP* check box to avoid possible transfer problems. Once you've confirmed that the test project is working fine on your Android device, you can try to re-enable it to see whether transferring still works.

At least in my tests with a Samsung Galaxy S4 device, MTP transfers weren't that much faster to begin with. That's the few times it worked. With MTP enabled, I frequently received error messages, mainly stating that "transfer quit unexpectedly" but also mentioning connection loss and timeouts. The Apportable developers confirmed that they found Samsung devices to be notoriously problematic with MTP transfers.

Android Development Prerequisites

If you've never done any Android development before, here's what you need to know.

Installing Android SDK Is Optional

First of all, with SpriteBuilder Android support you do **not** have to install the Android SDK. All that's needed is included in the SpriteBuilder Android plugins. And before you ask: the Eclipse code editor isn't needed either. Not even if you want to write additional Java code for your app. You can do that from within Xcode.

You may still want to install the Android SDK just to have access to the Android SDK offline documentation. It can't hurt, and it won't affect the SpriteBuilder Android plugins.

An Android Device Is Mandatory

Next, you'll need an Android device. There's no way around this. At the time of this writing and the foreseeable future, Android emulators are not supported by the SpriteBuilder Android plugins.

Android emulators also can't really be compared to the iOS Simulator in terms of reliability and accuracy. Perhaps the difference is best explained by how *emulation* differs from *simulation*.

An *emulator* outwardly mimics device behavior but does not run the same code paths, frameworks, and libraries as the device. A *simulator*, on the other hand, implements and uses as much of the device's software as possible, including the same frameworks and software libraries. Where emulation layers are necessary, they are written to mimic the internal behavior of the code as a whole.

If you have the option to choose a device, I recommend that you stick with popular models. That means the Samsung Galaxy and Google Nexus series mainly, but the LG G3, HTC One, and Sony Experia are also popular contenders. Try to get a phone, as they are far more widely used than tablets, unless you want to develop specifically for tablets—in that case, get a tablet.

Be sure to get a device that can be upgraded to the latest Android OS. The Google devices generally receive the most OS updates for the longest time period, with little to no delays.

Connecting an Android Device via USB

Once you have an Android device, connect it to your Mac. Be sure to plug it straight into a USB port on your Mac. Avoid using USB hubs and extension cords, as they can prevent the device from being recognized by the operating system. They may also slow down transfer rates or make transfers unreliable.

The same goes for third-party cables. If at all possible, use the USB cable that came with the device.

> **Note**   Like on iOS, transferring apps and debugging them is not possible via WiFi or Bluetooth connections. A wired USB connection is mandatory for development.

Enabling Developer Options

First, make sure you've installed all available updates for your Android device. The device should be running at least Android 4.2—and 4.4 is even better, as versions 4.2 and 4.3 may cause the app to freeze/hang when debugging due to an Android bug.

Locate the *Settings* app and open it. On the *More* tab, scroll down and tap the *About device* item at the very bottom. (See Figure 13-4).

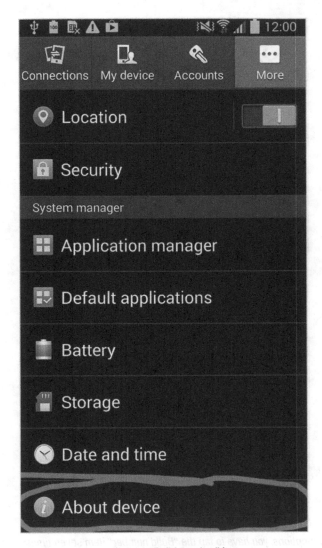

Figure 13-4. Tap on "About device" at the bottom to find the "Build number" item

To enable the developer options, you have to scroll down and locate the *Build number* item. (See Figure 13-5.) Even though *Build number* is grayed out, you can use it by tapping it at least seven times.

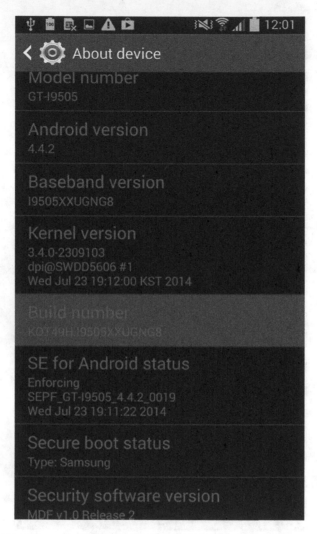

Figure 13-5. To enable developer options, you have to tap the "Build number" item seven times

After a couple taps, you'll see a small popup view telling you that you are only a few taps away from enabling developer options. Keep tapping on *Build number* until the message goes away. Then return to the previous screen, where you'll find a new menu item labeled *Developer options* just above *About device*. (See Figure 13-6).

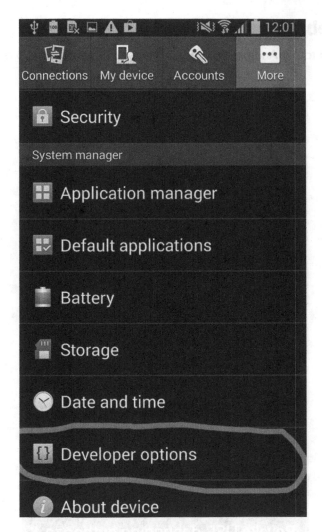

Figure 13-6. *Developer options are now accessible*

Tap on *Developer options*. You may get a warning that developer settings are intended for development use only, which is exactly what you intend.

While there is a possibility that the developer options can cause errors, errors are no more or less likely than when enabling development mode on an iOS device.

Caution   Android has a plethora of debugging features that aren't available on iOS, and they do increase the likelihood of interfering with apps. Some settings can greatly reduce performance and battery lifetime. Some settings can even prevent you from successfully transferring or launching the app. So, until you've completed the chapter, I highly recommend you set the developer options exactly as described here, leaving all other options as they are for now.

Enabling USB Debugging

In order to transfer apps to the Android device, you have to enable the USB debugging setting. (See Figure 13-7).

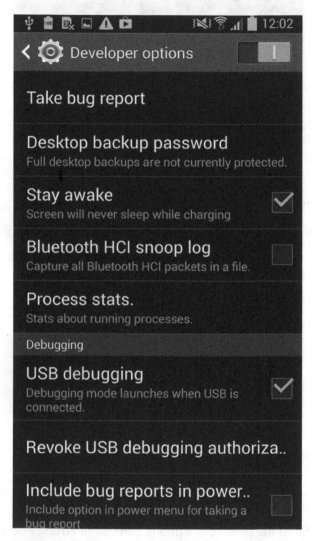

Figure 13-7. Enable "USB debugging" and, to avoid lock-screen issues, enable "Stay awake" mode, too

This puts the device in debugging mode while it is connected to a USB port. This state poses a potential security risk, which Android will warn you about when enabling this option. After all, it allows any computer to write to and read from the device without any security verification whatsoever.

Tip   If you are concerned about the security and privacy of your device and its data, you should consider using a separate Android device just for testing. The option to back up your device and then reset it to factory defaults is considered safe, too. However, it's not something you'll want to do every morning and then restore from backup every evening. It's easier to simply turn the *Developer options* on/off slider at the very top (shown in Figure 13-7) to off when you are done debugging. You can also remove the *Developer options* entry altogether, but this requires clearing the *Settings* data, which means you'll lose all settings in the *Settings* app.

Enabling Stay Awake

Alongside USB debugging, you should enable *Stay awake* mode. This prevents the device from sleeping or going to the lock screen while connected to a USB port. Yet, even with this mode enabled, the screen will dim and go to sleep when you unplug it from the USB cable.

I had to enable *Stay awake* because transferred apps failed to launch after transfer whenever the device was sleeping and showing the lock screen. Either the screen went black with no response from the app or the screen just showed the lock screen. When I swiped the lock screen, the app would just quit or shut down with an error.

Your mileage may vary, and perhaps the actions I observed were pure coincidence. So you may want to test deployment with *Stay awake* mode disabled, but only do so after you confirm that you can build and run apps on your Android device.

Caution   Keeping the device in *Stay awake* mode for many hours poses the risk of screen burn-ins. A *burn-in* is a ghost image caused by displaying the same, static screen for very long time. LCD pixels that stay lit for a long time lose their ability to relax to an unlit state. It's rare for this to happen, but it's a possibility.

Enabling OpenGL Stack Trace

Another option I recommend turning on for now is *OpenGL traces*.

Tap the *Turn on OpenGL traces* item, which is shown in Figure 13-8. A popup will ask you what type of trace you'd like. Pick the *Call stack on glGetError* option.

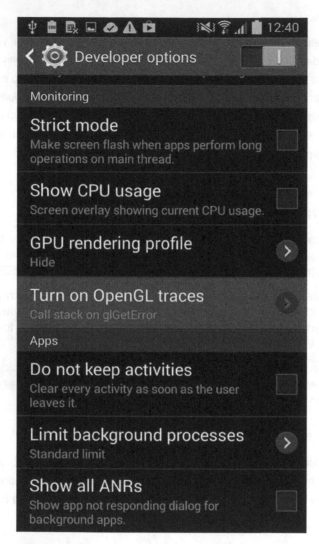

Figure 13-8. Tap "Turn on OpenGL traces" to post the glGetError call stack to the debug log

For some reason, without *OpenGL traces* turned on, my device often failed to launch the app, aborting with a GL_INVALID_OPERATION error. The error appeared long before any of the project's own code ran, even before Cocos2D itself (and thus its OpenGL view) began initializing.

For reference, here's what I saw in my log when the launch failed:

```
D/OpenGLRenderer(11473): GL error from OpenGLRenderer: 0x502
E/OpenGLRenderer(11473):   GL_INVALID_OPERATION
```

Following that: nothing. The app just stopped launching.

Turning on *OpenGL traces* fixed that problem for me; when I turned it off, the app failed to launch again. If you get the same freeze with the same error message, check if enabling OpenGL traces fixes that problem for you too. Since it doesn't hurt to have this option enabled, you can just leave it turned on.

Confirming Deployment to Android

When you create a new SpriteBuilder project with SpriteBuilder v1.3 or later, it will automatically have support for Android built-in.

Over the course of the book, you've already created a decently complex project, and maybe you know this adage: "Complex systems tend to have complex problems." Therefore, it's best to rule out as many additional problems first by trying Android support with a new SpriteBuilder project. You can either follow the descriptions here or open the *14 - HelloSpriteBuilder Android* project.

Creating a New SpriteBuilder Project

Open SpriteBuilder, and select *File ➤ New ➤ Project* to create a new project. Name it **HelloSpriteBuilder**, and save it wherever you like. (Your *Documents* folder would be a good choice.) The new project contains a *MainScene.ccb* with a color node and the SpriteBuilder logo.

Have a quick look at the *File ➤ Project Settings* dialog. You'll see both iOS and Android platforms selected, as shown in Figure 13-9. This means SpriteBuilder will publish two sets of resources, one for iOS and one for Android. You can deselect the *phone*, *phonehd*, *tablet*, and *tablethd* resources for each platform individually. For now, leave them all selected.

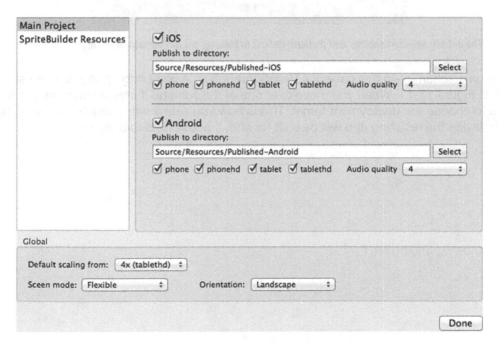

Figure 13-9. The "Project settings" dialog shows both iOS and Android platforms selected

> **Note** If the *Project settings* dialog doesn't show the Android settings, it means the SpriteBuilder Android plugins haven't been installed or failed to function correctly. You may want to try re-installing the SpriteBuilder Android plugins and check the "Troubleshooting" section at `http://android.spritebuilder.com`.

Close the settings dialog and then publish the project (*File ➤ Publish*). Wait for publishing to finish. It shouldn't take more than a couple seconds.

Next, you'll want to quit Xcode (*Xcode ➤ Quit Xcode*) if it's still running. This is just in case SpriteBuilder has installed or updated the Android plugins for Xcode. You want to be sure Xcode has recognized the plugins and loaded the latest versions, which it will only do upon launch.

Using Finder, locate the *HelloAndroid.spritebuilder* folder and open it. There's a *HelloAndroid.xcodeproj* inside, which you should double-click to open the HelloAndroid project in Xcode.

Selecting Scheme and Target Platform

Before you can build and run the project, you'll have to select a scheme and platform. New SpriteBuilder projects typically default to build the iOS scheme with an iOS device as the deployment target, as seen in Figure 13-10.

Figure 13-10. The initially selected scheme and platform default to building the iOS version of the app

By clicking on a scheme—in this case, it's *HelloSpriteBuilder*—you bring up the scheme selection list shown in Figure 13-11. When you move over one of the scheme items, a submenu pops up that allows you to choose the deployment target. This is how you select what targets will be compiled and which device the resulting app will be built for and, if possible, deployed to.

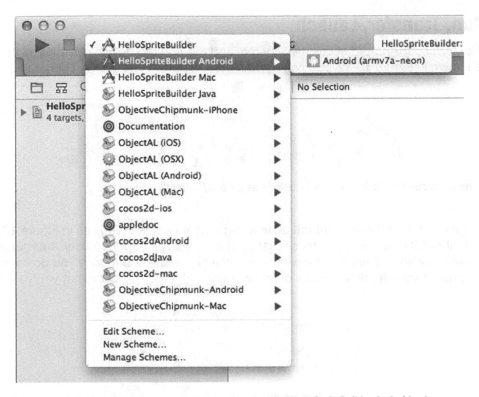

Figure 13-11. Scheme and platform selection menu; you should select the HelloSpriteBuilder Android scheme

You should highlight the *HelloSpriteBuilder Android* scheme, and in the submenu select the Android device as shown in Figure 13-11. The device will have the Android icon next to it.

> **Tip**   If there's no Android device listed, make sure the Android device is connected directly to one of your Mac's USB ports using the USB cable that came with the device. Using USB hubs, the USB ports on your keyboard (also a hub) or third-party USB cables may prevent the device from being recognized. You should also try using a different USB port. The device must also have USB debugging enabled as explained earlier. It does **not** need to have a SIM or SD card installed, you **don't** have to be signed in to a Google or other account on the device, and you do **not** need to install additional drivers. Sometimes resolving connectivity issues is as simple as unplugging the device and plugging it back in. If that doesn't help, try rebooting your Mac and turn the device off and on again. Note that you will have to restart Xcode for it to recognize new devices.

The long list of schemes and platforms can be confusing. Note that if you want to build the project for a different platform, you have to select the corresponding app scheme. App schemes have an icon with a pencil and paintbrush drawn over a ruler, forming the letter *A*. The other schemes are libraries and scripts needed by the project which, when selected and run, will most likely compile but won't produce runnable or deployable output.

Build, Run, Transfer, Launch

With *HelloSpriteBuilder Android* set as the scheme, and the Android device selected as the target platform as shown in Figure 13-12, you can now hit the run button (*Product ➤ Run*).

Figure 13-12. HelloSpriteBuilder Android scheme is selected as the build target

The project will build, and it may point out quite a large number of warnings as in Figure 13-13. You needn't worry about them, except for those that appear under *HelloSpriteBuilder Android* and the *HelloSpriteBuilder* project. Even those are harmless in a new project, but once you do have custom code in your project you should take care of any warnings triggered by code that you've written.

Figure 13-13. Lots of warnings, but nothing to worry about. Carry on

> **Tip**   Some developers like to enable the *Build Settings* flag *Treat all Warnings as Errors* to help discipline themselves so that they are forced to learn, understand, and fix whatever warning pops up in their own code. This is certainly a step in the right direction toward writing warning-free code. It does get in the way when you want to do things quickly, but if you keep doing things quickly, ignoring all warnings, this is a slippery slope to doing things sloppy. Warnings are there for a reason—don't just ignore them if you don't understand their meaning.

If all goes according to plan, after successfully compiling the code (albeit with warnings) the transfer process will start. After a couple seconds, the Xcode Console (*View* ➤ *Debug Area* ➤ *Activate Console*) will log success:

```
Preparing to run org.cocos2d.HelloSpriteBuilder on device cd25acab
4516 KB/s (17771319 bytes in 3.842s)
    pkg: /data/local/tmp/HelloSpriteBuilderAndroid-debug.apk
Success
```

> **Tip**   If you get aborted transfers or a dialog saying that "transfer quit unexpectedly," you should open *Xcode Preferences* and switch to the *Apportable* tab to uncheck the *Enable MTP transfers* check box. If you receive a message indicating "no provisioned Android devices connected," know that the error is misleading. It's trying to tell you that there's simply no Android device with USB debugging enabled connected and that Xcode couldn't find one. There's no provisioning necessary for Android development. If restarting Xcode doesn't fix it, follow the connectivity troubleshooting tips just before Figure 13-11.

If transfer was successful, the app will begin launching. You'll see a lot of things logged to the console. You can safely ignore everything in the log up until the point where Cocos2D begins to initialize. This will be indicated by the line that prints the Cocos2D project name and version number, such as:

```
D/HelloSpriteBuilder(28956): cocos2d: Cocos2D-Swift version 3.3.0-develop
```

Following that will be some system and OpenGL specifications. From this point onward, the log will contain almost exactly the same text as you'll see when you launch the app on an iOS device or the iOS Simulator. There's only one line I like to point out that's Android specific:

```
I/Choreographer(28956): Skipped 159 frames!
                    The application may be doing too much work on its main thread.
```

It's quite normal for an app to skip one or two hundred frames or so when launching. Though it's the same as on iOS: if an app takes too long to launch, it may be terminated by the OS. On iOS "too long" is defined as 10 seconds. And 180 frames equals 3 seconds.

> **Tip**   If, while developing, you notice that the number of skipped frames continues to go up and over
> 300 frames, you should consider launching with an empty scene before you transition from that initial
> scene to the previous launch scene. You should design that empty scene as your loading scene or splash
> screen, where you preload any assets—specifically textures (take relatively long to load) and preferably
> asynchronously (so as to not block the main thread).

At this point, you should see the Android device's screen turn black at first, until it begins to show the *MainScene.ccb* contents. Want proof that this really works? Take a look at Figure 13-14.

Figure 13-14.   Whoa! SpriteBuilder app written in Objective-C running on an Android device—just like that!

Troubleshooting

If you encounter any issues regarding this simple test, the setup of your Android device, getting the device connected, getting Xcode to list the device, having transfers work, and so on, you should search your issue and, if necessary, ask about it in the "Android" section of the SpriteBuilder forum: `http://forum.spritebuilder.com/category/android`.

Before you do so, consider doing the following:

- Be patient. Transferring and launching an Android app may seem to hang with no updates posted to the log for quite a while. The full Bouncy Beast project takes about 90 seconds to transfer, most of it without any log activity. When it launches, it can take another 10 to 30 seconds of inactivity. This is normal and happens every time—there aren't any incremental transfers that speed up consecutive transfers as there are on iOS.

- Ensure you've followed the Android device setup and connection steps described earlier in this chapter. Verify that you didn't enable or disable any development settings not mentioned explicitly.

- Ensure that the HelloSpriteBuilder iOS project runs fine on an iOS device or Simulator so that you know the problem is specific to building for Android.

- Try issuing a *Product ➤ Clean Build Folder* (by holding the Option key pressed) in Xcode. At the same time, delete (uninstall) any previously deployed version of the app from the device. And restart Xcode. Then try running again. Sometimes this can fix the "really weird" kinds of issues.

- Be sure to have read the SpriteBuilder Android documentation, specifically the "Troubleshooting" and "Known Issues" sections: `http://android.spritebuilder.com`.

If you can't resolve the issue, ask about it in the SpriteBuilder forum. When you do, describe in detail what you attempted and observed, what device you are testing with (model, Android version), and what SpriteBuilder and Xcode versions you are using.

> **Note**   I successfully tested Android deployment with both Xcode 5.1 and Xcode 6.0. I tested on OS X 10.9 Mavericks. If you're still using Xcode 5.0 or earlier and you do encounter issues, you should consider upgrading Xcode. The OS X version shouldn't matter though.
>
> If you're using a beta version of Xcode, iOS, or OS X you should consider the possibility that certain issues may occur exactly because you're using beta software. Beta software may introduce compatibility issues with third-party software like Cocos2D, SpriteBuilder, or Apportable's BridgeKit.

Anatomy of a SpriteBuilder App

If you examine the files in the HelloSpriteBuilder Xcode project, you'll notice a few curious additions, especially if you used to work with projects created with SpriteBuilder v1.2 or earlier. Figure 13-15 shows the source tree with some Android-specific files.

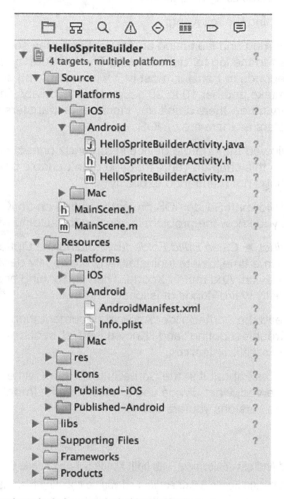

Figure 13-15. SpriteBuilder v1.3 projects include some Android-specific files

First of all, there is a *Platforms* group, which contains iOS, Android, and Mac groups with files specific to each platform. The *Source/Platforms/Android* group contains the *HelloSpriteBuilderActivity.java* file. The contents of the file are reprinted in Listing 13-1.

Listing 13-1. The HelloSpriteBuilderActivity.java file

```
package org.cocos2d.HelloSpriteBuilder;

import org.cocos2d.CCActivity;

public class HelloSpriteBuilderActivity extends CCActivity {

}
```

HelloSpriteBuilderActivity.java simply creates a new class extending the CCActivity class provided by Cocos2D. This goes in line with the *HelloSpriteBuilderActivity* Objective-C class of the same name, whose interface is shown in Listing 13-2.

Listing 13-2. HelloSpriteBuilderActivity.h

```
#import "CCActivity.h"

BRIDGE_CLASS("org.cocos2d.HelloSpriteBuilder.HelloSpriteBuilderActivity")
@interface HelloSpriteBuilderActivity : CCActivity

@end
```

The special macro BRIDGE_CLASS refers to the aforementioned *HelloSpriteBuilderActivity* Java class, essentially connecting the two. There's also an analog for Java interfaces/Objective-C protocols named BRIDGE_INTERFACE. You only need to Bridge a Java to Objective-C if you intend to use functionality not available in BridgeKit. Otherwise, prefer to use the already exposed functionality of BridgeKit, since you can interface with it purely using Objective-C code.

The HelloSpriteBuilderActivity implementation does only two things: launch the first scene and respond to the Back key, telling the app to finish. The code is reprinted in Listing 13-3.

Listing 13-3. HelloSpriteBuilderActivity.m

```
#import "HelloSpriteBuilderActivity.h"

@implementation HelloSpriteBuilderActivity

-(CCScene*)startScene
{
    return [CCBReader loadAsScene:@"MainScene"];
}

-(BOOL)onKeyUp:(int32_t)keyCode keyEvent:(AndroidKeyEvent*)event
{
    if (keyCode == AndroidKeyEventKeycodeBack)
    {
        [self finish];
    }
    return NO;
}

@end
```

The key point to take away here is that Android apps completely ignore the `AppDelegate` class. If you change the launch scene in *AppDelegate*'s `startScene` method, you'll also have to change the `startScene` method in the `Activity` class. Furthermore, any custom code you write in the *AppDelegate* file will not be included in Android builds. Likewise, any code in the `Activity` class will not run in iOS builds.

> **Tip**   You should generally create a class that contains common code and data that needs to be used by both *AppDelegate* and the `Activity` class. The simplest example is to declare a `static NSString*` `FirstSceneToLaunch = @"MainScene";` initialized to the name of the first scene to launch. You can then import that header in both *AppDelegate* and the `Activity` class and use the `FirstSceneToLaunch` identifier in both files. That way, you need to edit in only one place, instead of risking that *AppDelegate* and `Activity` do completely different things.

In the *Resources/Platforms/Android* group, you'll find the *AndroidManifest.xml*. It contains various build parameters as well as settings similar to the *Info.plist* on iOS. You may need to edit this file to use certain Android-specific features, such as Leaderboards and In-App purchases. Refer to the documentation of the Android SDK API in question, which will point out any requirements for the *AndroidManifest.xml*.

The Android version of the *Info.plist* contains just basic information about your app, mainly its name, default localization, and bundle identifier. You'll also find two folder references, Published-iOS and Published-Android, containing the iOS and Android versions of the resource files managed by SpriteBuilder. Of course, only the iOS resource files are included in iOS builds, while only the Android resource files are included in Android builds.

> **Tip**   The two *Published* folders do about double the size of the project, which may be a concern for users of source-control software. You should exclude these two folders from source control. A new user obtaining a copy of the repository would simply have to open the SpriteBuilder project and publish once to create local copies of the published files. That way, you'll avoid storing dozens, if not hundreds, of megabytes of published resource files under source control.

Converting Bouncy Beast

With the simple test project confirmed working, you can take part in the tour de force: converting the Bouncy Beast project. This shall serve as an example of what you may encounter and how to fix or work around issues. Obviously, I cannot present the solution to every conceivable issue.

The Bouncy Beast project was designed with an Android port in mind, though really the only thing I did was avoid relying on Apple and specifically third-party frameworks. Specifically, third-party frameworks can be a problem. You should ask in the SpriteBuilder forum first whether a given framework is compatible with the Android plugins. If no one knows, you should incorporate it into a simple test app like the one you just created. Get the framework's fundamental features to work, such as logging in successfully. Then try to build it for Android and note any errors.

Apple frameworks are generally widely supported, but some may not be available for Android at all—others may be missing a feature or two. The more hardware-specific a framework is, the less likely it is to be portable.

The starting point for the conversion can be found in the *15 - Prior to making Android-specific fixes* folder. It contains a project that was updated to the SpriteBuilder v1.3 format required to publish projects to Android.

Fixing Compiler Errors

Assuming you've originally created the LearnSpriteBuilder project with SpriteBuilder v1.3 or later, you can open the *LearnSpriteBuilder.spritebuilder* project now. If you're not sure which SpriteBuilder version you used to create the project, you can also use the *14 - Prior to making Android-specific fixes* project, which is the same project as *13 - Animations and Effects* before, except that the project has been upgraded to the v1.3 format.

Now go to *File ➤ Project Settings* and verify that the Android platform is included as the publishing target. Otherwise, the Android target would be missing all resource files. Then, just to be sure, use *File ➤ Clean Cache* and then *File ➤ Publish* to republish all files. This may take a minute or two.

When publishing is complete, open the *LearnSpriteBuilder.xcodeproj* project. Select the LearnSpriteBuilder iOS scheme (shown in Figure 13-11) and any iOS device. Build and run. This is just to verify the project is indeed working on iOS. There's no point in trying the Android build if the iOS build is already failing.

Once the iOS build runs successfully, select the *LearnSpriteBuilder Android* scheme and an Android device. Again, refer to Figure 13-11. Try to run the project. If you used one of the projects provided with the book instead of creating your own project, the build may fail a bit earlier. The abbreviated error message will be:

```
Prefix.pch:12:9: 'UIKit/UIKit.h' file not found
```

The UIKit framework is not available on Android since Android uses a completely different user interface framework. However, I can't remember making any reference to UIKit classes anywhere. It turns out that the UIKit reference is included by Xcode projects created by earlier versions of SpriteBuilder. In the latest SpriteBuilder v1.3 beta, there is no reference to UIKit anymore.

Alas, if you need to fix this or similar issues with iOS framework headers, you will have to use a platform-specific macro to prevent the iOS framework header from being imported on any platform except iOS. Update the *Prefix.pch* file, which is in the *Supporting Files* group so that it looks like the one in Listing 13-4 (changes highlighted).

Listing 13-4. Avoid importing the UIKit header when the build target isn't iOS

```
#import <Availability.h>

#ifdef __OBJC__
#if __CC_PLATFORM_IOS
#import <UIKit/UIKit.h>
#endif
#import <Foundation/Foundation.h>
#import "cocos2d.h"
#import "cocos2d-ui.h"
#endif
```

There are three macros provided by Cocos2d that allow you to include or exclude code from building, depending on the target platform:

```
__CC_PLATFORM_IOS
__CC_PLATFORM_MAC
__CC_PLATFORM_ANDROID
```

Only one macro holds the value 1 (is `true`) when building for a specific platform. The others will evaluate to `false`. A typical switch between iOS and Android-specific code would look like that shown in Listing 13-5.

Listing 13-5. Conditional code compilation based on target platform

```
#if __CC_PLATFORM_IOS
// iOS specific code here
#elif __CC_PLATFORM_ANDROID
// Android specific code here
#endif
```

Try to build again. You'll get a nondescript error:

```
GameMenuLayer.m:49:38: Expected a type
```

The problematic line in *GameMenuLayer.m* is the method signature of the method in Listing 13-6.

Listing 13-6. What unexpected type?

```
-(void) applicationWillResignActive:(UIApplication *)application
{
    [self shouldPauseGame];
}
```

If you look closely, you'll notice that Xcode underlined in red the beginning of the `UIApplication` keyword. That's where the error is. So apparently `UIApplication` is also not available on Android. This makes sense because Android uses a different launch mechanism. Since this method isn't crucial (it pauses the game when the app enters background), just exclude the entire method from Android builds for now by adding the highlighted lines in Listing 13-7.

Listing 13-7. Just ignore this on Android

```
#if __CC_PLATFORM_IOS
-(void) applicationWillResignActive:(UIApplication *)application
{
    [self shouldPauseGame];
}
#endif
```

At a later point, you'll want to implement the corresponding equivalent of the applicationWillResignActive: method in the LearnSpriteBuilderActivity class. The equivalent method is the onPause method. For now, it's more important to get the app running on the device. After this fix, compilation problems should be cleared and the app should be transferred to the device.

Fixing Launch Problems

When you get the project to compile and transfer, you're getting close. Now might be a good time to start fearing the worst launch issue of all: a black screen, app freezes, no indication in the log.

If that were to happen to you, the best way to narrow down the cause is to add NSLog statements. Start with the startScene method in *LearnSpriteBuilderActivity.m* as shown in Listing 13-8.

Listing 13-8. Logging the launch of the first scene is a good idea

```
- (CCScene *)startScene
{
    NSLog(@"startScene");
    return [CCBReader loadAsScene:@"MainScene"];
}
```

If that doesn't log anything, you know the problem is related to the initialization of the app. In that case, you should post the full log on the SpriteBuilder forum to request help. This type of problem should be rare. As I found out, such issues can be related to the *Developer options*—in my case, I had to enable *OpenGL* traces and *Stay awake* mode to work around launch issues.

In this case, the project should launch fine until it raises a Java exception, which is printed to the log including a (in this particular case, hardly useful) call stack. The error is reprinted here:

```
W/System.err(17501): java.io.FileNotFoundException: Audio/menu-music.m4a
W/System.err(17501):     at android.content.res.AssetManager.openAssetFd(Native Method)
W/System.err(17501):     at android.content.res.AssetManager.openFd(AssetManager.java:332)
W/System.err(17501):     at dalvik.system.NativeStart.run(Native Method)
```

The message is pretty clear: this is a file not found exception. It can't find the *Audio/menu-music. m4a* file. A quick check in the *Published-Android* folder in the *Resources* group in Xcode reveals that the audio files for Android have been converted to *ogg*, not *m4a*.

Audio resources will automatically resolve to the correct file extension for each platform if you use the same extension as the original resource file that was added to SpriteBuilder. In this case, it would be *menu-music.wav*, and for all other audio files you need to use the *.wav* extension as well, since all audio files were added to SpriteBuilder as .wav files.

The Java exception doesn't indicate what file and line of code the error occurred on. That can create a little problem finding the source of an exception, but in this case it allows you to search the project for the *menu-music* string: press Cmd+Shift+F to search for a string in all project files.

You'll find the music is referenced in *MainScene.m*, in the `didLoadFromCCB` method. Change the audio file's extension to .wav, as shown in Listing 13-9.

Listing 13-9. Playing the correct audio file based on the platform requires using the audio file's original extension

```
OALSimpleAudio* audio = [OALSimpleAudio sharedInstance];
 [audio playBg:@"Audio/menu-music.wav" loop:YES];
```

The alternative is to just comment out the line for now. Playing music or effects isn't crucial for the app to work. When this is your first attempt to port your app to Android, you should make notes of such minor issues, comment out the code, and keep looking for truly problematic issues. Many tasks, like audio playback, should be fixed at a later time, after you've fixed worse problems (if there are any). The same goes for not bringing up the pause menu when the app is paused—again, the app will function fine without it for now.

> **Note**   There are other uses of the ObjectAL `playBg` and `playEffect` commands—for example, in the `presentGameSceneWithMusic` method in the `SceneManager` class. They may cause exceptions as well—for instance, when loading a level. I'm confident that you now know how to handle it. Just apply the original .wav extension as in Listing 13-9.

With that fix implemented (or the `playBg` line commented out), the app should build, transfer, launch, and present you the game's menu screen, including all the effects you've added to the menu earlier. See for yourself in Figure 13-16.

Figure 13-16. *Bouncy Beast launched successfully on an Android device, presenting the menu screen*

Fixing Layout Issues

When you run an app on Android for the first time, things may not always look as neat as they did on the iOS devices. Specifically, the varying screen resolutions can cause unexpected issues.

Representative of issues of this kind is what happens when you tap the play button on the main menu. The level selection scroll view is offset as seen in Figure 13-17.

Figure 13-17. The level selection scroll view is offset on a 1920x1080 pixel resolution device

If you open *MainScene.ccb* and select the *CCScrollView* node, you'll notice that on the *Item Properties* pane the scroll view's *Content size* is set to a fixed size in points: 440x290 (880x580 in pixels).

The Android device I'm testing on has a resolution of 1920x1080 pixels, while an iPhone 5 has a resolution of 1136x640 pixels. Hence, the content size of the scroll view takes up a much smaller portion of the screen on the Android device, which ends up causing a position offset.

The fix is tremendously simple: with the *CCScrollView* selected, change its *Content size types* to % and leave the values unmodified. The values will change to 77.5% and 90.6%. Publish and run the project, and the scroll view will be fine again on this and other devices with larger-than-iPhone screens.

When you find a node at a position different than it was on iOS, it's always a good idea to check whether % position or % content size will fix the problem. However, be sure to verify such changes on iOS, just in case the change merely shifted the problem from one platform to the other.

Isolating Issues

Now I could tell you a bit more about several other problems I've encountered—such as a freeze that occurred when adding a pointer to the `Trigger` class' `NSPointerArray`—but they aren't really representative. After all, I was using beta versions of SpriteBuilder, Cocos2D, and the Android plugins. The `NSPointerArray` bug, for instance, has since been fixed.

But there is always a chance that you run into a bug that you suspect may not be your fault.

In that case, it's best to verify the problem in isolation. This means creating a new SpriteBuilder project as you did earlier, and then trying to see if the same setup of nodes causes the same issue. If it does, you can zip up that project and submit it on the forum or in a github issue report. This will be tremendously helpful for the SpriteBuilder and Cocos2D developers in their efforts to provide you with a fix or workaround.

On the other hand, if you can't reproduce the issue in isolation, it's more likely that the problem is specific to your app, its code, settings, and resources. You should take another approach in that case: Make a copy of your project. (Close SpriteBuilder and Xcode before you do so.) Then edit the project by removing any unrelated parts, CCBs, and code.

You either get to a relatively minimal app that produces the problem, which you can submit as a testable example, or you'll find the problem goes away after removing or disabling a specific part of the project. That would be a clear indicator that the problem is within that area, the piece of code, or the CCB file that you last removed. You should then add that part back into your project to see if the problem surfaces again. You can now focus on a specific aspect of your project and narrow down your search by repeating the process of removing/disabling parts of the project.

In any case, help is just one SpriteBuilder forum post away.

When to Port to Android

The best times to port a project to Android is either right from the beginning or after your app is published to the iOS App Store and becomes successful enough to warrant the effort to create an Android port. It makes little sense to change course midway through a project.

Porting After Publishing on iOS

This approach is what I recommend to anyone new to Android development because it increases your chances of successfully publishing the project on one platform—a challenging task in itself. So many interesting games don't get published at all because developers lose interest or run into a blocking issue and give up. Having to worry about a second platform while tackling your first few projects has to be considered harmful. It increases your workload and deters you from the goal of publishing an app in the first place.

And what point is there in porting an app to Android if it hasn't been proven to be successful on the iOS platform? My thoughts exactly. As an experienced developer, at least you can extrapolate the next app's likelihood of success from your earlier app's successes and failures and build on your previous experiences.

The downside of porting after an iOS release is that once you do have a complete app that's never been tested to run on Android, it will likely be more difficult to get it initially working on Android. Which I understand is increasingly more difficult in particular for beginning developers.

Every cross-platform decision you didn't have to make thus far will come to haunt you all at once. The only advice I can give for such cases is to push through. Tackle one problem at a time, as tiny as it may seem. Every fix gets you closer to the goal.

But even if that should fail, or simply proves to be too much work, I have an alternative proposition to make. Imagine you do have a successful iOS app and you continue to earn some extra cash. You can now do one of two things with relative ease and comfort:

- Hire and pay another developer to (help you) port your SpriteBuilder project to Android.

- Begin working on the improved successor of your game, or simply your next app idea. Start from scratch, but this time build it as a cross-platform app from the start. Spend that extra cash on Android devices for testing.

The common misconception held by beginning developers that I continue to warn about is this: building an app for multiple platforms from the start **does not** increase your chances of success.

It does increase your financial success **if** you have a successful app in the first place. But an app that fails on iOS because it simply isn't a good quality app or users have no real use for it is going to fail on any platform. Yet building a quality app that has the same level of quality on multiple platforms takes more time and resources. So even if the overall revenue is higher for both platforms together, the "revenue for time spent" ratio may actually be less than if you had published for one platform only.

Plus, you now have to do everything post-release twice: releasing updates, answering customer support questions, and so on—even the amount of marketing increases.

To put you in the right mindset: unless you have a few published titles under your belt (on any platform), I recommend you focus on publishing your app for iOS exclusively. Once an app does become successful, thanks to the SpriteBuilder Android plugins, you can port after the iOS release with relative ease. Otherwise, just make another iOS app.

Cross-Platform from the Start

If you do have experience creating and publishing apps for iOS, Android, and/or other platforms, you should definitely start a new project with both platforms in mind. This includes designing the game such that it handles multiple device resolutions well. Plan to have different code paths and resources for slower devices, or plan ahead and exclude certain devices that you expect to be running your app too slowly.

Your day-to-day work with SpriteBuilder and Android will be such that each new feature is added and tested on one platform. Typically, initial development will be done on iOS simply because it's generally quicker and more reliable to deploy and run apps on iOS devices. When it's confirmed to be working, you immediately test the new code and resources on an Android device. If there are any unresolvable platform-specific issues, you can continue working on other iOS features while waiting for an answer to a question you posted.

Note that the overhead of compiling, deploying, and running each feature on two platforms alone means the time it takes to develop for both platforms increases. Like I said, there's no such thing as free ports.

Adding to that: even on iOS it's not a good idea to only ever test your app on one particular device, and doing the same on Android is almost wantonly negligent. Most developers making a living off of selling mobile apps juggle several different testing devices to cover the most widely used screen sizes and performance specs.

You should have at least one device that represents the minimal specifications your app will run on. This enables you to tell with near certainty that your app meets the performance requirements even on the slowest supported devices.

Doing cross-platform development from the start and frequently testing your app on both platforms will lead to better cross-platform apps. You'll also learn to understand the differences in OS design and behavior for both platforms along the way. One problem with apps that have been ported late is that they often feel foreign to users of the other platform. Foreign in terms of terminology, how the app responds to user input, how it integrates system menus, how the user interface is designed, and so on.

Summary

I hope you're as excited about the astounding possibility of being able to write Objective-C code and bringing that to Android devices with relative ease. Personally, I'm delighted that I don't have to use a C++ or Java game engine and framework to do so.

You'll find the Android-compatible version of Bouncy Beast in the *16 - Bouncy Beast for Android* folder. Finally, I made a couple final tweaks and added eight more levels using two additional graphic sets. You can find this final project in the *17 - Final Project with Graphics and Levels for all Worlds* folder.

Chapter 14

Debugging & Best Practices

Debugging is the art of understanding the root causes of a programming or specification issue so that you can either fix the issue, work around it, or alter your program specifications and requirements.

Why mention this at all in a book about SpriteBuilder?

Because you'll inevitably run into problems that you can easily solve on your own with just basic knowledge of debugging tools and techniques. These problems are logging, asserting, adding breakpoints, stepping through code, and inspecting variable values. The latter two are performed while your app is running, which allows you to see exactly which paths your code is taking.

In this chapter, I give many code examples you don't need to add to your Xcode project. The code provided here serves as debugging examples, but it doesn't add anything of significance to the Bouncy Beast project itself.

> **Tip**   You'll find a lot more detailed explanations about debugging apps with Xcode in the Apple developer library: `https://developer.apple.com/library/mac/documentation/ToolsLanguages/Conceptual/Xcode_Overview/DebugYourApp/DebugYourApp.html`.

Logging Messages and Variables

Logging means printing a text string to the Xcode debug console. Logging can be effective in printing out values of variables, especially if these values change over time. It is often used together with marking the flow of program execution, meaning when specific code runs in time relative to other code.

You have used `NSLog` before—for instance, in *MainMenuLevelSelect.m*, to log whenever the `CCScrollView` delegate methods fire. Listing 14-1 shows one use of `NSLog`.

Listing 14-1. NSLog used to log when Scroll View delegate methods run

```
-(void) scrollViewDidEndDragging:(CCScrollView *)scrollView
               willDecelerate:(BOOL)decelerate
{
    NSLog(@"%@%@", NSStringFromSelector(_cmd), decelerate ? @"YES" : @"NO");
}
```

Together with the other delegate method's logging, NSLog will print a series of strings to the Xcode debug console, as seen in Figure 14-1, when you interact with the *Scroll View*.

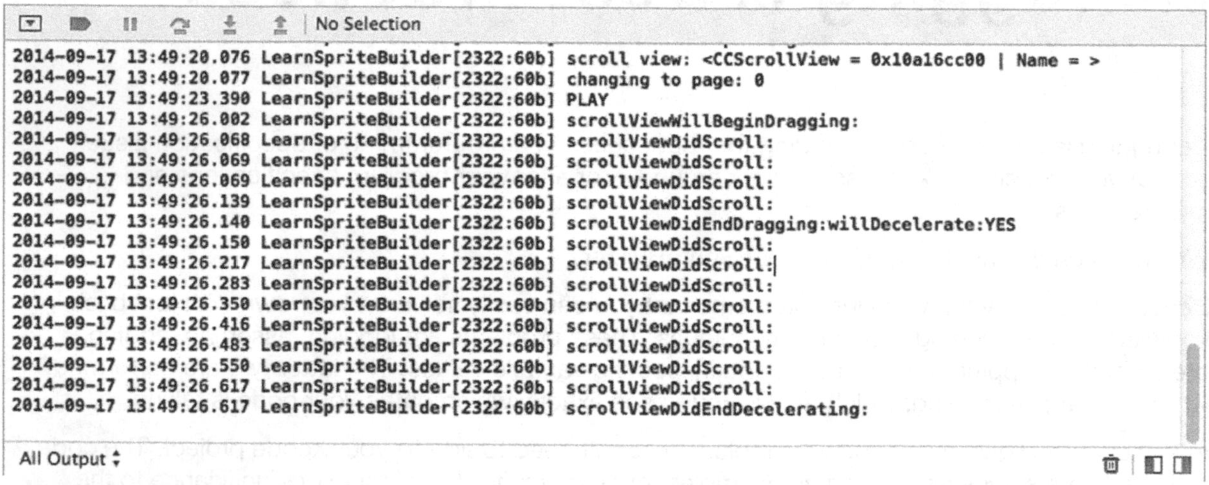

Figure 14-1. NSLog output in Xcode's debug console after interacting with the level-selection Scroll View

This series of log statements instantly visualizes the flow of execution. You can clearly see that scrollViewWillBeginDragging: is the first delegate method called, while scrollViewDidEndDragging with decelerate enabled causes the *Scroll View* to continue scrolling past the point where the user stopped dragging. The *Scroll View* does so to move the nearest page to its designated position. Once the page has been moved to its position, the scrolling ends with scrollViewDidEndDecelerating.

Logging is particularly useful if you need to monitor the change of values over time—for instance, logging the position of a node and its distance to another node in the update method.

> **Caution**   Printing a log line to the console takes time, and printing a long string with many format specifiers and variables will take longer than a short string. If you call NSLog once every frame, it may already be enough to show a noticeable slowdown. So don't forget to remove or comment the NSLog statements after they've done their job.

The NSLog function takes the same format strings as NSString. This allows you to print out any variable along with the message. Listing 14-2 shows how you can log a variety of basic data types.

Listing 14-2. Logging basic data types with format strings

```
int intValue = 123;
NSUInteger unsignedIntegerValue = 456789;
CGFloat floatValue = 0.123456789;
NSLog(@"intValue=%i integerValue=%lu floatValue=%f floatValue.2=%.2f",
    intValue, unsignedIntegerValue, floatValue, floatValue);
```

The resulting log string looks like this:

```
intValue=123 integerValue=456789 floatValue=0.123457 floatValue.2=0.12
```

The most commonly used format identifiers are %i and %u for int and unsigned int values, %f and %.1f for floating-point values. The latter specifies that only the first three digits following the decimal separator should be printed. This helps readability because logging positions as 237.352349x288.927534 is a lot less readable than 237.4x288.9—especially, if representing the exact floating-point value is of little significance.

Sometimes you may see %d being used, which is simply an alias for %i. And if you want to log NSInteger or NSUInteger, you have to use the format specifiers for long integers %li and %lu, as well as cast the NSInteger/NSUInteger value to (long) and (unsigned long), respectively.

> **Caution**   If you get a compiler warning on an NSLog line that indicates you are not using the correct format specifier or that the value will be truncated, you should fix that problem. Otherwise, the logged value may be different from the actual value, which is going to be a source of confusion.

Listing 14-3 shows you how to log Objective-C class instances, also known as *objects*.

Listing 14-3. Logging objects (Objective-C class instances)

```
NSString* helloLog = @"Hello Log";
NSLog(@"string=%@ self=%@ cmd=%@", helloLog, self, NSStringFromSelector(_cmd));
```

The %@ format specifier can be used for any pointer to an Objective-C class instance. The %@ format specifier actually sends the description message to the object, which then returns a description string you can customize by implementing the description method. An example is shown in Listing 14-4.

Listing 14-4. A custom description method

```
-(NSString*) description
{
    return [NSString stringWithFormat:
            @"%@ selfPointer=%p selfClass=%@",
            [super description], self, NSStringFromClass([self class])];
}
```

So instead of formatting the same information repeatedly for multiple NSLog statements, it's preferable to override the description method to return a custom description string that contains all necessary information about the object. In this case, it also prints out the pointer value (the memory address of the object) with the %p specifier and the name of the class, in addition to calling [super description], which returns the super class' description string.

The resulting output string of Listing 14-3 might look like this:

```
string=Hello Log self=<GameScene = 0x10a52bb00 | Name = >
 selfPointer=0x10a52bb00 selfClass=GameScene cmd=didLoadFromCCB
```

Last, there are struct types like CGPoint, CGSize, and CGRect. You can log them by printing each struct field individually, or for the aforementioned structs you can use the conversion methods NSStringFromCGPoint, NSStringFromCGSize, and NSStringFromCGRect. Listing 14-5 shows an example use.

Listing 14-5. There are two ways of printing a point

```
CGPoint point = CGPointMake(1024, 768);
NSLog(@"point=%.0fx%.0f point=%@", point.x, point.y, NSStringFromCGPoint(point));
```

The output of NSStringFromCGPoint is formatted in the same format required by the inverse conversion function CGPointFromString, which takes a string like {1024, 768} and returns a CGPoint. Here's the output of Listing 14-5:

```
point=1024x768 point={1024, 768}
```

> **Tip** You'll need the format specifiers frequently for NSLog, NSAssert, and NSString. The full list with descriptions is available at https://developer.apple.com/library/mac/documentation/Cocoa/Conceptual/Strings/Articles/formatSpecifiers.html.

One last thing: it's not unusual to leave commented-out NSLog statements in your code. Eventually, you may need them again, so this will save you time. If you haven't used a commented-out NSLog statement in weeks, and it doesn't look like you're ever going to need it again, feel free to remove it.

Adding an Exception Breakpoint (Xcode 5)

Before moving on to assertions, there's one crucial item you should always add to your project if you are using Xcode 5: the exception breakpoint. I find it so important that I've added instructions to add the exception breakpoint early in the book. Here I'd like to show you how to add it and what difference it makes.

> **Tip** Xcode 6 users will appreciate that adding an exception breakpoint is no longer necessary to have Xcode point to the offending line of code.

Figure 14-2 shows you what you normally see when the program aborts. Xcode 5 opens *main.m* and points to the `UIApplicationMain` line as the culprit. That's not useful information—it just tells you that the app crashed, but it does not tell you where exactly the exception occurred.

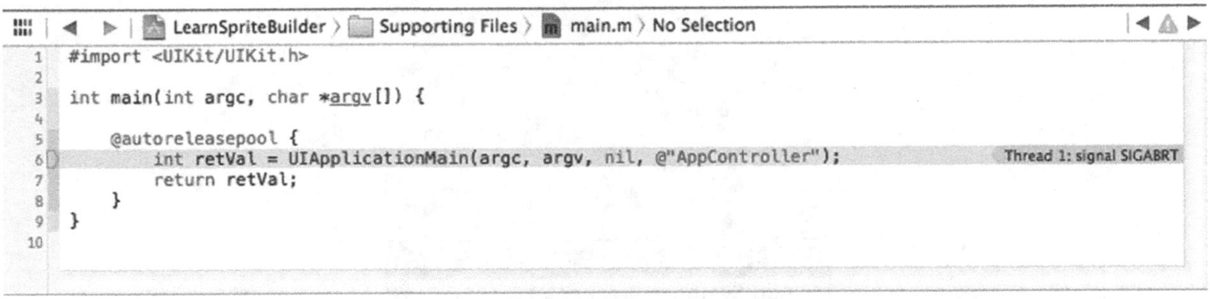
LearnSpriteBuilder
Supporting Files
main.m
No Selection
#import <UIKit/UIKit.h>
int main(int argc, char *argv[]) {
@autoreleasepool {
int retVal = UIApplicationMain(argc, argv, nil, @"AppController");
return retVal;
}
}
Thread 1: signal SIGABRT

***Figure 14-2.** An assertion raised an exception that halted the program. Without an exception breakpoint, Xcode 5 will show you the main function*

To fix that, you'll have to add an exception breakpoint in Xcode 5. Xcode 6 users can still do so. The most noticeable difference the exception breakpoint will have in Xcode 6 is that the app will halt before the exception (assertion) message and call stack have been printed to the log.

To add an exception breakpoint in Xcode, select the *Breakpoint Navigator* tab (which is shown in Figure 14-3), click the + button in the lower left corner, and then select *Add Exception Breakpoint*.

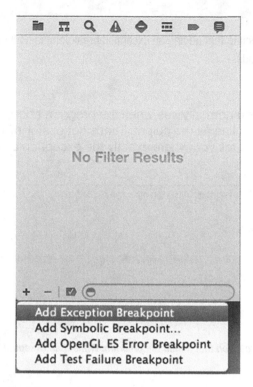

Figure 14-3. Adding an exception breakpoint

Once the exception breakpoint has been added, right-click it and select *Edit Breakpoint* to bring up the popover menu shown in Figure 14-4. Change the *Exception* type to Objective-C. This prevents C++ exceptions from being caught, which you probably don't want. Though normally there won't be any C++ code in your app, the OpenAL framework and possibly others may sometimes raise C++ exceptions you don't need to deal with.

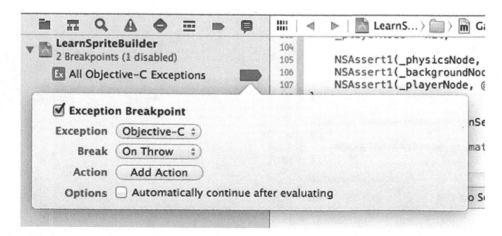

Figure 14-4. Editing the exception breakpoint to catch only Objective-C exceptions

When you run the app and it crashes due to an exception, instead of showing the main() function, Xcode 5 will point to the offending line in your code as shown in Figure 14-5. If the exception is raised in an Apple or other framework for which there is no source code available, Xcode will show the line in your code that makes the call.

> **Note** If the crash wasn't due to an exception, Xcode might still point out the main() function as the culprit, as shown in Figure 14-2. In that case, you have run into a more low-level problem, perhaps a divide-by-zero or buffer-overflow problem or you're addressing an object that has been released from memory.

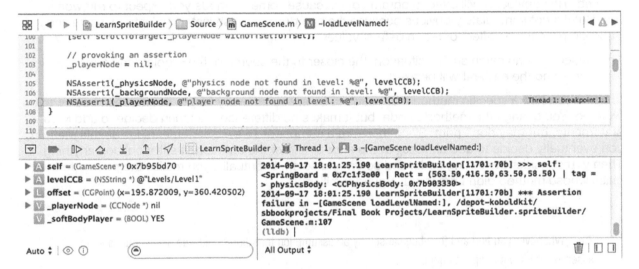

Figure 14-5. With an exception breakpoint added, Xcode 5 shows the line closest to the error for which there is source code available. Xcode 6 behaves like this by default

> **Note** With an exception breakpoint enabled, the program execution is halted before the exception message and call stack are printed to the debug console in Xcode. You can see in Figure 14-5 that the NSAssert message hasn't been printed to the console. If you need that information, just click the *Continue program execution* button once to see the message and call stack in the console. On the horizontal toolbar in the center, it's the third icon from the left—the one that looks like a combined pause and play icon.

Asserting Assumptions

Bugs are unavoidable. They come in many shapes and forms. Code that detects when current conditions prevent the code from functioning correctly is essential to avoiding bugs.

Naturally, your code makes assumptions about the state of the program. Assertions are used to verify such assumptions which, if not true, would cause the app to malfunction.

The NSAssert macro and its variants NSAssert1 through NSAssert5 allow you to write a test within your code that asserts that the given condition must be true. Otherwise, an exception will be raised.

How is this helpful?

Imagine you have an ivar that you expect to be non-nil. This is an assumption. Should the assumption be wrong for whatever reason, and the ivar is nil, all messages to that object will be ignored. This obviously will affect program flow because some methods you expect to run won't run. But it's not immediately obvious because the app doesn't crash instantly; instead, some lines of code simply have no effect or return default values.

The earlier you can catch such a situation, the closer to the source of the problem the error is reported—and the easier it will be fixed.

Imagine you had a specific method that needs to be executed every frame, but it doesn't seem to be working. You change the method's code, but it makes no difference. You then decide to add NSLog statements, but they don't print. Since there are a number of if/else statements inside this method, you eventually decide to add an NSLog at the start or end of the function. It still won't log anything. Then you consider the calling code, and so on and so on. Eventually, you realize the pointer to the class whose method didn't run is nil. Sound familiar?

> **Tip** Whenever you find and fix a bug caused by an assumption that didn't hold true, you should add an assertion in case it happens again.

To avoid such situations, double-check such assignments with an assertion—especially, if one of the failure points includes human error, such as making a typo. For instance, in *GameScene.m*, several ivars are declared (as shown in Listing 14-6), which are supposed to be assigned by editing the node's *doc root var* setting in SpriteBuilder. Some are obtained by a call to getChildByName:, which assumes there's a node matching that name, and maybe even assuming there is only one node with that name.

Listing 14-6. These ivars are partially assigned by SpriteBuilder, by using getChildByName or by other means

```
@implementation GameScene
{
    __weak CCNode* _levelNode;
    __weak CCPhysicsNode* _physicsNode;
    __weak CCNode* _playerNode;
    __weak CCNode* _backgroundNode;
```

```
    __weak GameMenuLayer* _gameMenuLayer;
    __weak GameMenuLayer* _popoverMenuLayer;

    // Other ivars omitted for brevity...
}
```

A lot can go wrong here, and it's quite common to forget to assign the *doc root var* in SpriteBuilder or to make a typo in the node's name. Or you might assign the *doc root var* to the wrong node or in the wrong CCB file, or you might edit a node's name in the Timeline rather than its name property. It is good style to verify the assumption that these variables have to be non-nil after a given point during the initialization of the class.

For instance, the end of the `loadLevelNamed:` method in Listing 14-7 would be a good place to assert that crucial ivars are non-nil.

Listing 14-7. Asserting that specific ivars are non-nil after the level was loaded

```
-(void) loadLevelNamed:(NSString*)levelCCB
{
    // Existing code omitted for brevity...

    NSAssert1(_physicsNode, @"physics node not found in level: %@", levelCCB);
    NSAssert1(_backgroundNode, @"bg node not found in level: %@", levelCCB);
    NSAssert1(_playerNode, @"player node not found in level: %@", levelCCB);
}
```

To test a pointer variable for being non-nil, it suffices to just write the ivar's name. In a condition or assertion, writing *_playerNode* is equal to writing *_playerNode != nil*.

You can also use the same format strings as in NSLog; however, with NSAssert being a macro and not an actual C function, you have to use NSAssert1 through NSAssert5 to match the number of format-string parameters. In the preceding example, there's one format-string parameter, `levelCCB`, so NSAssert1 needed to be used.

An assertion is said to have failed when its condition evaluates to false (NO). The NSAssert macro then raises an exception, which causes Xcode to halt program execution to show you the offending line of code—much like in Figure 14-5.

Assertions are evaluated only in debug builds. Still you ought to limit the use of assertions in code that runs every frame because this can slow down your app in debug builds. You can switch between Debug and Release build configurations by choosing *Product* ➤ *Scheme* ➤ *Edit Scheme* in Xcode. Then select the *Run* profile, where you'll find the *Build Configuration* setting on the *Info* tab.

> **Caution**   Since assertions are evaluated only in debug builds, it is crucial to avoid running any code or calling any method in the assertion's condition that alters the program state. Otherwise, the program will behave differently in debug and release builds.

Adding Breakpoints

Breakpoints enable you to halt (pause) program execution at a specific line of code. Optionally, you can edit conditions that need to be met for the breakpoint to trigger.

You can easily add and enable or disable a breakpoint by clicking on the gray vertical area to the left of the source-code editing window. If you have line numbers enabled in Xcode (*Xcode ➤ Preferences ➤ Text Editing ➤ Line numbers*), that's where the line numbers are shown. In Figure 14-6, a breakpoint was added in line 103. The app ran until the line of code with the breakpoint was reached, and then it halted. The line that will be executed next is highlighted with a green tint—that's the execution pointer.

Figure 14-6. A breakpoint halted program execution

Below the source code window, you'll find the *Variables View*, where you can inspect the values of variables. By default, Xcode will show you the self-reference if the app halted anywhere within an Objective-C instance method, plus any local variables and those being used by the surrounding code. You can change this behavior by clicking on the *Auto* drop-down menu in the lower left corner of Figure 14-6. Also, note that the *Console* view is hidden. You can change the visibility of *Variables* and *Console* views with the two icons in the lower right corner.

So, despite this being a pretty obvious problem, let's try and debug why _playerNode might be *nil*. The breakpoint was set, and the app ran up until this point. You can clearly see in the *Variables View* that the _playerNode variable points to a valid object. You can unfold the object to see more of its properties and ivars, but that's not really the point. What I like to show is how you can run through your code line by line, which allows you to see how variables change after each line and what conditional path is taken and why.

Figure 14-7 highlights the debug toolbar that's also in Figure 14-6.

Figure 14-7. The debug toolbar

From left to right, the first button hides the debug area, and the second shows you whether breakpoints are globally enabled or not. If it's not highlighted in blue, no breakpoints will trigger. The third button pauses and resumes program execution. You normally use it to continue running the app to the next breakpoint (if any) after a breakpoint was triggered.

The fourth button (Step Over), fifth button (Step Into), and sixth button (Step Out) highlighted in Figure 14-8 are what I'm after.

Figure 14-8. The Step Over, Step Into, and Step Out command icons

While the application execution is halted, you can use the Step Over command to advance to the next line in the same function. This essentially executes the highlighted line of code and halts again when it's done. The Step Into command works just like the Step Over command, except if the execution pointer is on a line that calls a method (sends a message), the Step Into command will continue execution inside that method. Sometimes, this will merely bring you to an @property statement or to a method you don't really want to look at, such as a singleton's sharedInstance class method. In that case, the Step Out command runs the remainder of the current method until execution returns to the calling method.

In the preceding example, clicking the Step Over command icon once leads to Figure 14-9.

Figure 14-9. After stepping over the line highlighted in Figure 14-6, you can see that _playerNode became nil

Obviously, in this example it's very clear that assigning nil to _playerNode will have it take on that value. You can see this is reflected by the *Variables View* in Figure 14-9. You don't need to log nor guess—you can actually see when, where, and why the value changed.

Setting breakpoints and stepping over code are as fundamental to debugging as NSLog statements are. The two go hand in hand, with NSLog being most suitable in cases where breakpoints would otherwise trigger so often or interfere with user input that a given issue can't be reproduced. Breakpoints and single-stepping through your code are extremely instructive, as you can literally see what paths your code is taking and, through the Variables View, you can also see why.

The question for you then becomes one of figuring out why a given value doesn't have the value it's supposed to have. But you can quickly arrive at that point by using breakpoints, rather than making changes to your code based on guesses and then trying again, hoping it might work the next time.

Analyzing Your Code

A lesser known feature of Xcode are the so-called *analyze* builds. You can run an analyze build via *Product ➤ Analyze*. This runs the Clang Static Analyzer tool that ships with Xcode.

The analysis tries to find common, known, and potential sources of bugs. This includes memory management and logic errors. However, not all issues reported by the analyzer need to be actual problems. For one, any issue found in code not written by you, such as the Cocos2D and Chipmunk sources, need to be disregarded. Assume that if they are actual problems the developers will eventually fix them.

Figure 14-10 shows the output of an Analyze build. The 12 issues found in the Cocos2d target can be ignored. There's only one issue in the LearnSpriteBuilder project, and a suggestion is made to fix it.

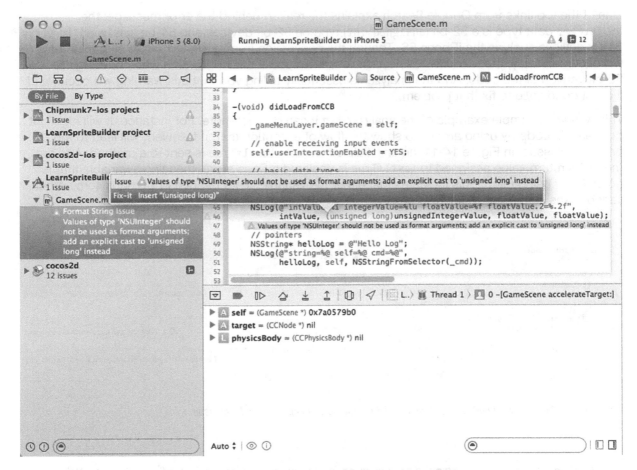

Figure 14-10. The analyze build finds potential issues and makes suggestions on how to fix them

As you may notice from the figure, there seems to be some kind of problem. But the information shown in the figure doesn't tell you why the analyzer deems this a problem. So far the logging has worked fine. What could be the problem here, and should you fix it?

Possibly the best tip I can give regarding compiler errors is so obvious I'm afraid to mention it: Google the exact error message. You don't even have to type it back into Google's search field — every piece of text displayed by Xcode can be copied to the clipboard as text. Where the regular Cmd+C (Copy) command won't work, there's usually a right-click context menu with a *Copy* item.

> **Tip**   When you copy strings from Xcode, they may contain specific references to your project, such as path, file name, line numbers, class, and variable names. If the search results are unsatisfactory or nothing was found, make sure you remove those project-specific references and Google only for the raw error message, stripped of any variable, function, or class names that may exist only in your own project.

One of the top links from Google Search explains the reason behind the error message: the `NSUInteger` data type is a 32-bit (`unsigned int`) type on 32-bit devices and 64-bit (`unsigned long`) on 64-bit devices such as the iPhone 5S. Though the conversion from unsigned `int` to unsigned `long` will occur implicitly, the compiler will nevertheless warn about this conversion when building the 32-bit version of the code. And the analyzer is essentially telling you that this warning will occur, and it's just good style to fix that problem.

This was just a simple example of the analyzer, but it can do a lot more. For instance, it will highlight problems in code by using arrows to show the flow of execution that, if followed, will lead to the proclaimed issue. In Figure 14-11, an uninitialized variable `testIfTrue` is sent to a method. And the method's return value assigned to `testIfTrue` is declared a *Dead store*, meaning a variable that is not actually being used. This indicates that either the variable is not needed or perhaps some other variable was incorrectly used in its place.

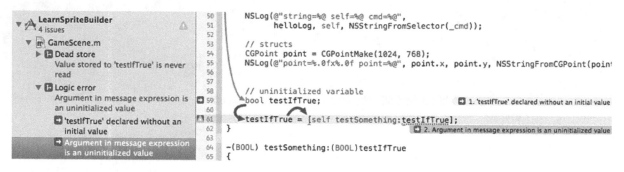

Figure 14-11. The analyze build uses arrows to point out the flow of logic leading to an issue

> **Caution**   The analyze build may sometimes report false positives. Code that it deems flawed but isn't. Not every problem reported by the analyzer needs to be fixed, but you ought to understand the reason for the report well enough to be confident that the issue can be disregarded. It's the same as with compiler warnings.

Cocos2D Framerate Stats

In addition to doing debug drawing for physics, Cocos2D can also draw profiling counters, most notably the framerate display. To enable these profiling labels, you only need to add the line in Listing 14-8 anywhere in your code—for instance, in the startScene method in *AppDelegate.m*.

Listing 14-8. Enabling profiling labels

```
[CCDirector sharedDirector].displayStats = YES;
```

Cocos2D will then draw three numbers in the lower left corner, as shown in Figure 14-12.

Figure 14-12. The game runs with profiling labels enabled

From top to bottom, these numbers are:

- **Draw Calls (here: 12):**   A draw call basically occurs every time OpenGL needs to draw from a different texture, but there are other reasons too. Each draw call incurs a penalty, so the goal is to have as few as possible. The way to achieve that is by using Sprite Sheets to combine multiple images in the same texture, and to use as few Sprite Sheets as possible. The draw call of 12 in this example is reasonably low. You will most likely see performance degradation if the number of draw calls is close to or even above 100.

- *Seconds per Frame* (here: 0.057):   This refers to the average time it took to complete the update cycle for a frame, which includes processing game logic, physics, and rendering. To achieve 60 frames per second (fps), the seconds per frame must be 0.0166 or less. You have twice as long if your framerate target is 30 fps. The main use of the seconds-per-frame counter is to see how much room you have to add more game logic before the framerate drops again.

- *Frames per second* (here: 15.0):   That's the framerate, and before you wonder: it's only 15 frames per second because the screenshot was taken in the iOS Simulator. The Simulator uses a software renderer that is quite slow. The game runs with 60 fps on most devices. Also, note that this value is an average of the most recent frames, so a value of 45 actually means that half of the frames were rendered within 0.0166 seconds (60 fps) and the other half took more than that (30 fps).

It is worth noting that iOS devices have vertical synchronization (vsync) always enabled. The framerate counter gives you an average number of frames over multiple frames. In reality, you can only have a constant framerate of 60, 30, 20, 15, 12, 10, and 6 fps. All of these values are factors of 60. Due to vsync being enabled, if a frame did not complete its update-and-render cycle within 0.0166 seconds, it will be displayed at the earliest in another 0.0166 seconds, not as soon as it's done. So once the game starts taking more than 0.0166 seconds to complete every frame, the framerate falls back to 30 fps.

For some games where the framerate fluctuates heavily between 30 to 60 fps, it can make sense to lock the framerate at a constant 30 fps. This may feel smoother than a constantly fluctuating framerate that skips a couple frames, and thus drops to 30 fps and then renders a few more frames at 60 fps. To change the maximum framerate, you can add the lines in Listing 14-9 to the startScene method in *AppDelegate.m*.

Listing 14-9. Restricting framerate to 30 fps

```
CGFloat framesPerSecond = 30;
[CCDirector sharedDirector].animationInterval = 1.0 / framesPerSecond;
```

The division by framesPerSecond is necessary because the animationInterval is expressed as seconds per frame.

Walking the Scene Graph

Another useful debugging feature of Cocos2D is a function that prints out the nodes and their children recursively, given a specific starting node. (See Listing 14-10.) You may want to add that line to the didLoadFromCCB method in the MainScene or GameScene class, or both.

Listing 14-10. Logging the scene graph

```
[self.scene walkSceneGraph:0];
```

This prints out the scene or node graph recursively, beginning with self.scene. You can use any other node as the starting point. The parameter ought to be 0 because it's used only internally to properly indent child nodes. You can see an example output in Listing 14-11.

Listing 14-11. Output of walkSceneGraph

```
walk tree: -> <CCScene = 0x10a620550 | Name = (null)> 0x10a620550
walk tree: ---> <CCNode = 0x10a36a130 | Name = > 0x10a36a130
walk tree: ----> <CCNode = 0x10a36cad0 | Name = background> 0x10a36cad0
walk tree: -----> <CCNodeGradient = 0x10a36d710 | Name = > 0x10a36d710
walk tree: -----> <CCSprite = 0x10a36e850 | Rect = (0.00,0.00,593.50,406.00) |
                   tag = > 0x10a36e850
walk tree: -----> <CCNode = 0x10a36fe00 | Name = > 0x10a36fe00
walk tree: ------> <CCNodeColor = 0x10a370690 | Name = > 0x10a370690
walk tree: ------> <CCSprite = 0x10a371780 | Rect = (916.5,0.5,102.0,42.0) |
                   tag = > 0x10a371780
walk tree: ------> <CCSprite = 0x10a374a80 | Rect = (916.5,0.5,102.0,42.0) |
                   tag = > 0x10a374a80
```

This can be helpful in determining whether a given node is in the place in the hierarchy that you expect it to be. If it isn't, this tells you where it is or whether it's not there at all. In this case, the CCScene has a single CCNode child node, which in turn has a child CCNode whose name is *background*.

Tip   The formatting and logged properties may not suit all purposes. You may want to make a copy of the walkSceneGraph method found in the *CCNode+Debug.m* file and modify it to generate the output you find more helpful.

Debugging Advice

It is my sincerest wish that you take an analytical approach to debugging. Ask yourself "Why?" constantly. As a programmer, you have the rare fortune to work with a deterministic system where the same conditions always lead to the exact same outcome. Given logs, assertions, breakpoints, and stepping through code, you have all the tools needed to analyze where your code is going wrong.

But don't forget the compiler has a say in this, too—which is to say: don't ignore compiler warnings. They, too, inform you of potential, and sometimes actual, issues. Ignoring them should be done only if you understand the reason for the warning and the implications of not fixing it.

The worst thing you can do when you encounter a problem is to become angry. I know that's easier said than done. Especially, when you're already stressed out, there's a delivery date to meet, and you're working on code that you just don't feel comfortable with.

But being angry and eventually frustrated seriously impacts your ability to approach a problem analytically, which will increase the time it takes you to locate and fix the bug, possibly tenfold. So the best advice I can give when it comes to debugging is to keep...your...calm. Whether you meditate, take a stroll, get a cup of coffee, go shopping, play a game, anything that lets you get away from a really annoying problem is frequently a very good way to solve the problem more easily at a later time.

Where you depend on other code—for instance, when using Cocos2D classes and calling their methods, and they behave unexpectedly—you need to use different tools. The other tools you can use are the class or API references. Class references contain short descriptions of classes and their methods. A good class reference will tell you whether your assumptions about a given class or method and its parameters are indeed correct, and under which conditions the method returns what values. More often than not, you'll find your assumptions about how the class or method works were wrong to begin with.

> **Tip**   The Cocos2D class reference can be found here: `http://www.cocos2d-swift.org/docs/api/index.html`. The Apple class references are easily Googled by using the name of the class followed by class reference—for instance "NSArray class reference".

Nevertheless, if you find that a Cocos2D method is at fault—say, it returns `nil` where you expect it to return an object reference—you can use the Step Into command to wade through the code in Cocos2D. You may be surprised how much you can learn from stepping through Cocos2D code and what assumptions it makes. You might not understand all of it, but you may still be able to get a good grasp of what it does and where exactly it goes wrong if you use the Step Over, Into, and Out commands to follow the program execution to see which path it takes through the Cocos2D sources.

For instance, maybe Cocos2D is simply not able to find the file you're trying to load, and you can see that because it will not step into the `if` block with the `fileExistsAtPath:` condition. And since there's an `NSString` variable in scope, you'll see in the *Variables View* what the actual path is, in case it has been modified by Cocos2D.

Given time and experience, you'll learn to assess such situations intuitively and hunt down the most likely cause more quickly. It's a good idea to set a breakpoint and inspect variables as soon as you run into an unexpected problem. Visually, seeing what the state of variables is and what your code does when you run it line by line will make the majority of issues rather obvious.

Sometimes, even with the debugging tools at hand, you may fail to find a particular problem for hours, or maybe even for days. If you can't find the cause within an hour and think you have tried everything within your power to understand the problem, don't hesitate to ask. Go to the SpriteBuilder (`http://forum.spritebuilder.com`) and Cocos2D (`http://forum.cocos2d-swift.org`) forums to ask any questions related to them. Or go to `http://stackoverflow.com` to ask your programming-centric questions. Of course, you should first narrow down the problem as much as possible and search for all aspects of the problem you're experiencing. There's a good chance someone else already had a similar problem, if not the same problem.

I've even heard from programmers that they were trying to fix a particular bug in their own code for up to a week. That's just madness. You may want to make a copy of your project and then start removing or altering possibly offending sections of code one by one and try again until you can no longer reproduce the issue. The problem must then be related to the code you removed last. Since that is likely going to be more than one line of code, you can use the same approach on that particular class or method until you find out what line may be the problem. When you get close but still can't figure out the issue, that's a good time to post that code fragment and everything you know so far on the SpriteBuilder or Cocos2D forum.

It's also a good idea not to focus too long on fixing a particular bug. Do something else for a while so that you can later look at the problem with a fresh set of eyes, so to speak. Sleeping overnight on a bug and working on it the next day can do wonders. If it's a crash or other showstopper bug, you may be able to work around it temporarily if you want to continue doing something else within your project.

The last point before I let it go of this topic is to consider debugging as a programming task, just like writing code. It's not a hindrance to your work but an essential, fundamental aspect of programming. Both writing and debugging code can be learned through exercise. To write code, you need to learn the programming language, and to write better code you need to learn about code design and architecture. The same goes for debugging, where you need to learn the tools used to debug an application. Eventually, you'll learn about strategies for avoiding issues and catching them early, as well as classifying bugs and picking the right tools for analyzing them.

This advice is just scratching the surface of measures you can try, and it's rather generalized. But I do hope it puts you in the right state of mind: bugs are challenging you to overcome them. And every time you succeed, you become a better programmer, and you'll continue to succeed more often and more quickly because of it. Plus, it can be a very uplifting feeling to fix that pesky bastard of a bug that's been bothering you on and off.

Frequently Encountered Issues

While writing the book, I myself came across many issues that can be attributed to human error or misunderstandings about the SpriteBuilder interface. Some issues surfaced rather frequently, so I would like to summarize them here.

Nil References

A common problem is realizing that an ivar or property is nil. This condition is easy to find out with a breakpoint or NSLog. But why is it nil?

If you assign the variable via SpriteBuilder's *Item Code Connections* tab, check the following:

- Whether the variable type is set to "doc root var."

- Whether there is a misunderstanding, such as the doc root var is assigned to the CCB root node's Custom class, rather than the Custom class of the node.

- Whether the CCB's root node has its Custom class field set to the correct class.

- Whether the custom class in question has declared a corresponding ivar or property of the same name.

If you assign the variable by its name—for instance, by using getChildByName:, you should verify the following:

- Check that the name of the node is the same as the name of the node in SpriteBuilder.

- Check that there is no other node with the exact same name.

- Check that the name of the node in the Timeline and its *Name* property are two different things. Only the *Name* property counts; the node's name in the Timeline is purely informational and not used by Cocos2D.

- Test whether [self.scene getChildByName:@"theNameOfTheNode" recursively:YES] finds the node. If it doesn't, the node in question simply isn't in the current scene. Note that self.scene is nil during a node's init and didLoadFromCCB methods, so be sure to perform that test in onEnter or at a later time.

- Check that the name of a CCB root node will not be used if it is referenced in another CCB file via a *Sub File* (CCBFile) node. In that case, the name needs to be set on the *Sub File* node, not the CCB's root node that the *Sub File* node references.

Animation Playback Issues

If an animation played programmatically through the self.animationManager won't play, check the following items:

- The name of the animation in code matches the name of the animation in SpriteBuilder. Note that the case must match, too.

- Each CCB has its own animation manager instance. If self.animationManager is used by the root node's custom class of the CCB that contains the Timeline, you are using the correct instance. Otherwise, double-check that you are using self.animationManager in a node's custom class that is a child node of the CCB containing the Timeline and isn't a CCBFile (Sub File) reference.

- The Timeline is chained to itself. If it isn't, it won't loop. This means if the Timeline is initially off-screen or otherwise not visible, it may have already played its animation once and then stopped.

If an animation is playing once but isn't looping, try doing the following:

- Check that the Timeline is chained to itself. Perhaps it's not chained or it's chained to the wrong Timeline.

If an animation does not play its sound effect or does not run its *Callbacks* selector, do the following:

- Verify that the root node of the CCB containing the Timeline is not removed from the scene (removeFromParent). As soon as you remove the root node, it will stop playing its Timelines as well as the Timelines of its child nodes. If the Timeline doesn't animate anything, keep in mind that Timelines need an active node to run on.

Audio Playback Issues

If you play back audio programmatically, sometimes the audio won't play. Here are a few things you should check:

- Verify that the path and file name are identical, including the use of uppercase and lowercase. It's easy to forget that you have to specify the folder as well—for instance, @"Audio/effect.m4a".

- Consider that the audio file extension may change during publishing. For example, if the input files have the *.wav* extension, the actual extension will be *.caf* or *.m4a*, depending on whether the audio format was set to CAF or MP4.

- Audio that you didn't create may be corrupt, it might not adhere to the specifications of the format, or it might contain unusual metadata. Audio players are much less picky than OpenAL and AVAudioPlayer, so the sound may play fine on the desktop. To test this problem, open the affected audio file with Audacity and re-export it to the same format or a different (.wav) format.

Subclassing CCSprite for Sprite CCB Classes

This particular error message may occur when launching the app or loading a scene:

```
reason: '[<NameOfClass 0x7a043520> setValue:forUndefinedKey:]: this class is not key value coding-compliant for the key spriteFrame.'
```

It indicates that you created a CCB of type *sprite* and assigned a custom class to it. However, the custom class does not subclass CCSprite but some other class, most likely CCNode. Changing the custom class' superclass to CCSprite will fix this error.

Can't Edit the Custom Class Field

You have a *Sub File* (CCBFile) node selected. In that case, the *Custom class* field is grayed out and can't be edited. The custom class needs to be edited in the referenced CCB file.

Can't Add Custom Properties to a Node

In order for a node to have custom properties, it has to have the *Custom Class* field assigned on the *Item Code Connections* tab. That custom class needs to have properties or ivars matching the custom properties' names.

Physics Collisions Are Not Working as Expected

If two nodes are colliding but shouldn't be or they don't collide but should, here are a few things to check:

- The categories and masks of the two bodies involved must match. If both should collide, the category of one should be in the mask of the other, and vice versa.

- Keep in mind that empty category and mask fields means "match all categories/ masks, which is the exact opposite of what you would expect from an empty field.

- Static bodies do not collide with other static bodies. Two *Gear1.ccb* instances could not be made to collide, for instance.

- Both bodies must have the same *CCPhysicsNode* as their parent (or grandparent or great grandparent, etc.).

- Although you can have multiple CCPhysicsNode instances in a scene, they represent completely separate physics worlds. There is absolutely no interaction between two CCPhysicsNode instances possible.

- Enable physics debug drawing to confirm that the collision shapes, in fact, do overlap. The collision shapes can be very different from the images the node draws. Merely looking at the sprites is sometimes not enough to assess the situation.

- Verify that the shapes are correctly set up without self-intersecting lines. Select the node, switch to the *Item Physics* tab, and look for any lines highlighted in red.

- Bodies connected with at least one joint will default to not collide with each other, unless the corresponding *Collide bodies* flag is checked on the joint.

A Node Is Not Deallocating

Sometimes you determine that a node or the entire scene doesn't deallocate when you expect it to. You can verify this by using Instruments (an Xcode tool for runtime analysis and profiling) and looking at the live objects, or quite simply by implementing the -(void) dealloc method and testing with an NSLog or breakpoint whether the method runs or not. If it doesn't, the object is still in memory.

The reason for this is often quite simple, yet it can be difficult to track down because it all depends on where pointers to that object have been stored or where they have been assigned to. Here are a few things to consider:

- Any object assigned to an ivar or property defaults to being kept in memory (retained) as long as the reference is not set to nil. This is said to be a *strong reference*. Most ivars in the book project are declared as __weak to allow them to be deallocated when they are removed from the node graph.

- As long as a node is part of the node graph (i.e., it is active in the current scene), the node is retained by its parent's children array.

- Quite common are *retain cycles*, where you have at a minimum two classes, A and B. Class instance A has a strong reference to the instance of class B, and the instance of class B has a strong reference to the instance of class A. Both instances will not deallocate as long as they strongly reference each other. You can break the cycle with __weak references or by setting at least one reference to nil at a certain point.

Basically, the question to ask when a given object doesn't allocate is: who is (still) holding a reference to this object? That makes it somewhat easier to debug because you can concentrate on checking every assignment of the object to another property, ivar, or collection (NSArray, NSDictionary, etc.) and whether that reference is still non-nil at the time you expect the node to deallocate.

Summary

You now know how to debug and fix any problem within seconds. Okay, not quite. But I do hope this chapter served to introduce you to the various means of debugging and analyzing an application, as well as common problems and best practices when working with SpriteBuilder and Cocos2D.

If you have any questions or suggestions about the book, SpriteBuilder, or Cocos2D, please stop by on the SpriteBuilder and Cocos2D forums.

You will find me most active at stackoverflow.com. If you include the *spritebuilder* or *Cocos2d-iPhone* tags in your question, there's a good chance I'll have an answer or suggestion for you.

I should also note that this book ends here. I hope you enjoyed reading it and, preferably, learned something from it. You'll definitely learn a lot by making your own games and, above all else, I hope you'll enjoy making them.

Index

S

Get the eBook for only $10!

Now you can take the weightless companion with you anywhere, anytime. Your purchase of this book entitles you to 3 electronic versions for only $10.

This Apress title will prove so indispensible that you'll want to carry it with you everywhere, which is why we are offering the eBook in **3 formats** for only $10 if you have already purchased the print book.

Convenient and fully searchable, the PDF version enables you to easily find and copy code—or perform examples by quickly toggling between instructions and applications. The MOBI format is ideal for your Kindle, while the ePUB can be utilized on a variety of mobile devices.

Go to www.apress.com/promo/tendollars to purchase your companion eBook.